MORE ADVANCE PRAISE FOR *A SOUL ON TRIAL*

"This is an incredible story and wonderfully presented. Robin R. Cutler invites us into a complex tale of an investigation into the internal values and practices of the military, replete with accusations of murder, cover-ups, and undue institutional privileges. In the midst of the Progressive Era, we have a mystery worthy of Hollywood. Cutler's book is better than fiction!"

—**Jonathan Lurie**, professor of history and adjunct professor of law, Rutgers University, and author of *Military Justice in America*

"Cutler provides a panoramic overview of American life in the decade before World War I. Rosa Sutton embarked on an unflinching quest to uncover the truth about the death of her son, a quest that raised troubling questions about the role of the professional military in a democracy as well as the power of the popular press in shaping the national agenda. Sutton's ordeal also illumines from a new perspective the vast gulf that separated, and still separates, the ways men and women experience the world."

—**Michael P. Parker**, professor of English, United States Naval Academy, and author of *Presidents Hill: Building an Annapolis Neighborhood, 1664–2005*

"In this excellent historical narrative, Cutler sheds light on many aspects of the social, cultural, military, and legal history of the Progressive Era. We see in the Corps' handling of the media scrutiny regarding Jimmie Sutton's death that everything old is new again. A super story about military justice and the way military culture and civil society relate to one another."

—**Thomas C. Mackey**, professor of history, University of Louisville, and author of *Pursuing Johns: Criminal Law Reform, Defending Character and New York City's Committee of Fourteen, 1920–1930*

"Robin R. Cutler's *A Soul on Trial* is a gripping mystery story as well as an outstanding example of current social history at its best. This wonderfully fresh and lucid book offers much to the general reader as well as the specialist, since it is a truly insightful fusion of social history, the study of religion and spiritism, the history of military justice, and 'history and memory' inquiries into truth-telling and myth-making. I recommend this book enthusiastically!"

—**Donald J. Mrozek**, coauthor of *A Guide to the Sources of United States Military History* and author of *Sport in American Mentality, 1880–1910*

A SOUL ON TRIAL

A Marine Corps Mystery at the Turn of the Twentieth Century

ROBIN R. CUTLER

ROWMAN & LITTLEFIELD PUBLISHERS, INC.
Lanham • Boulder • New York • Toronto • Plymouth, UK

ROWMAN & LITTLEFIELD PUBLISHERS, INC.

Published in the United States of America
by Rowman & Littlefield Publishers, Inc.
A wholly owned subsidary of The Rowman & Littlefield Publishing Group, Inc.
4501 Forbes Boulevard, Suite 200, Lanham, Maryland 20706
www.rowmanlittlefield.com

Estover Road
Plymouth PL6 7PY
United Kingdom

Distributed by National Book Network

British Library Cataloging in Publication Information Available

Library of Congress Cataloging-in-Publication Data

Cutler, Robin R., 1944–
    A soul on trial : a Marine Corps mystery at the turn of the twentieth century /
Robin R. Cutler.
        p. cm.
    Includes bibliographical references and index.
    ISBN-13: 978-0-7425-4849-7 (hardback : alk. paper)
    ISBN-10: 0-7425-4849-X (hardback : alk. paper)
    1. Sutton, James N., 1885–1907. 2. Courts-martial and courts of inquiry—
United States—History. 3. Courts-martial and courts of inquiry—United
States—Social aspects. 4. United States. Marine Corps—Officers—History.
5. Journalism—United States—History—20th century. 6. Parapsychology.
I. Title.
KF7654.5.S88C88 2007
973.911—dc22
[B]   2007012071

Printed in the United States of America

♾™ The paper used in this publication meets the minimum requirements of
American National Standard for Information Sciences—Permanence of Paper for
Printed Library Materials, ANSI/NISO Z39.48-1992.

For Liz and Carlyn,
my inspiration

Are you good men and true?

—William Shakespeare
Much Ado About Nothing
Act III, Scene 3, Line 1

Governmental actions should be neither secret nor unjust. . . . If we cannot get justice through the courts every newspaper in the United States shall have the facts as we have them and then see what the opinion of the world will be.

—Rosa Brant Sutton

The influence of a gaping and curious public can have no effect on the conduct of the Judge Advocate in this matter. . . . The hallowed grave of a dead son is no more sacred than the grave of a military reputation and there are a great many military reputations at stake in this hearing.

—Major Harry Leonard

Here is an amazing case in which spiritism charges murder though the verdict of the courts is suicide. . . . I am enabled here to give to the world for the first time the details of the part which spiritism has played in the affair from the beginning to the present time; a part so utterly astonishing that it is without a parallel in history.

—Edward Marshall
New York Times

We need absolute honesty in public life; and we should not get it until we remember that truth telling must go hand-in-hand with it, and that it is quite as important not to tell an untruth about a decent man as it is to tell the truth about one who is not decent.

—Theodore Roosevelt
Outlook, May 12, 1900

CONTENTS

Part III

PROLOGUE

May there not after all be a possible ambiguity in truth?

—William James

On a cloudy October afternoon in 1907, a telegram arrived in Portland, Oregon, from the United States Marine Corps: DEATH BY SUICIDE OF LIEUTENANT JAMES N. SUTTON REPORTED FROM ANNAPOLIS. INQUEST ORDERED. NO FURTHER PARTICULARS RECEIVED. Within thirty-six hours a swift and efficient naval inquest confirmed that the young officer had committed suicide. Newspapers on both coasts proclaimed that "Jimmie" Sutton shot a bullet through his brain, though a few reports hinted that mysterious circumstances surrounded his death.

But then something astonishing happened. The dead lieutenant's mother saw a "vision" of her son who denied the charge and asked her to clear his name. As a Catholic, Rosa Brant Sutton believed suicide was a mortal sin; if the navy was correct, Jimmie would spend eternity in hell with no chance of being reunited with his loved ones. Fueled by her faith and her son's apparent postmortem appearances, Rosa embarked on a pilgrimage to save his soul. Her spiritual journey soon became a political one that took her from Portland, through the corridors of power in Washington, D.C., to a naval courtroom in Annapolis, Maryland, and finally, face-to-face with Jimmie's corpse in Arlington National Cemetery. By 1909, this Oregon family's tragedy had become a cause célèbre in the headlines of big-city papers across the United States. America's aggressive press corps did not just report on the bizarre circumstances of the case. Newspapers brought their own often disparate standards and objectives to a search for verifiable truth in the face of daunting (and haunting) odds.

This book is the true story of an attempt to sort fiction from fact that preoccupied millions of Americans a century ago. A murder mystery, ghost story, and courtroom drama, it explores the conflict between democratic values and military justice in the era when the mass media was born. Was Lieutenant James N. Sutton murdered by a fellow marine? Did his spirit really appear to Rosa Sutton in the weeks after he died to explain what happened? Members of Congress, military officials, attorneys, doctors, and journalists all struggled with such questions and their broader implications. Ultimately, Rosa would turn for help to two men who approached the afterlife from entirely different perspectives: James Cardinal Gibbons, the highest official in the American Catholic Church, and James Hervey Hyslop, America's foremost psychical researcher.

A NEW ERA

In 1907, novelist Jack London wrote, "'never in the history of the world was society in such terrific flux as it is right now.'" Americans of the Progressive Era—better educated than ever before—demanded that their government work toward the common good. In a nation permeated by the rhetoric of civic and social reform, men and women fought vigorously to solve social, economic, and political problems. As new technologies and machines relieved them from household chores, more and more women were free to enter public life. In the last two decades of the nineteenth century, while Rosa Sutton raised a family of five children, the inspiring words of activists spurred many (but by no means all) middle-class women to begin the long battle for suffrage. Their first successes would be in states west of the Mississippi, in Wyoming, Utah, Colorado, and Idaho. In October 1902, a few days before she died, Elizabeth Cady Stanton received a letter from fellow suffragist Susan B. Anthony about the enormous gains that women had made in the previous half century. One of these was "the fully admitted right to speak in public." Such conditions helped to inspire and transform Rosa's crusade for justice and the nation's emotional reaction to it.

During the two years after her son died, Rosa's shock and depression turned into anger and ultimately to "righteous indignation," a phrase coined by one of her contemporaries, investigative journalist Ida M. Tarbell. As Rosa learned more about what had happened to Jimmie, her goals expanded, and she demanded government accountability. Rosa's assertion that "no official conduct should fear publicity" echoed the sentiments in muckraking magazines such as *McClure's* and those in city papers across the country. Hoping to rally "the great American people," she wrote to an ally in the Marine Corps: "If we cannot get justice through the courts every newspaper in the United States shall have the facts as we have them and then see what the opinion of the world will be." By the spring of 1909, this feisty forty-seven-year-old mother was the driving force behind what the *Baltimore Sun* described as "one of the most remarkable inquiries of its kind ever conducted in the Navy."

A NEW JOURNALISM

"There is nothing which will make the eagle shriek louder than the shadow of a muzzle for the press," John L. Given declared in 1907 in *Making a Newspaper.* At the end of the nineteenth century, the nation had become a neighborhood, and its newspapers proliferated. New modes of transportation and communication led to the exploding population of America's cities. "Public opinion" was no longer confined to the educated middle classes—a vast urban and immigrant population now turned to morning, afternoon, and evening papers for information and entertainment. For reporters, the story of a heartbroken mother confronting a military bureaucracy proved irresistible; the paranormal aspects of the Sutton story only added to its potential to fascinate.

In an age of mediums, bestsellers about the supernatural, and parlor games such as Ouija boards, table tipping, and fortune telling, the fact that Sutton's ghost had appeared to claim his innocence made absorbing copy. Rosa Sutton's story would compete for attention on the new wire services with the Wright brothers' daring flights, urban calamities, or any one of several grisly criminal trials. All the major New York papers, including respectable ones such as the staid *Evening Post* and the *New York Times*, followed her campaign. The case also stimulated the decade-old circulation war between Joseph Pulitzer's *New York World* and William Randolph Hearst's *New York Evening Journal.* In Boston, Philadelphia, Washington, D.C., Atlanta, New Orleans, St. Louis, Cincinnati, Chicago, Denver, Portland, Los Angeles, and San Francisco (to name a few cities), Americans also read daily accounts of Rosa's efforts on Jimmie's behalf, usually on their papers' front pages with large headlines above the fold.

When the navy agreed to a second investigation, men and women from all walks of life acquired a stake in its outcome. Their newspapers gave them a forum for concerns about naval justice, conditions in their service academies, and at the end of Rosa's crusade, about life after death. But it was the possibility of a government cover-up that for months drew the attention of journalists from a wide spectrum of newspapers. As the *New York Times* observed, the case was not just about the death of one young officer; Rosa stood for all citizens for whom justice was "belated, reluctant and coerced." This last word was clear and self-congratulatory on the part of the editor. It was the threat of disclosure that had caused the administration to reopen the case—at least that seemed to be the situation. The navy, after all, depended on the support of the American people and their representatives in Congress.

MILITARY JUSTICE

This account follows a mother on her tumultuous journey; it is also the story of a proud and honorable Marine Corps plunged into the center of public discourse. With a culture steeped in tradition and the motto *Semper Fidelis*, the marines' hallowed rituals were just as sacred to them as Rosa Sutton's mission was to her. The unprecedented investigation of Sutton's death forced the government's representatives to deliberately cultivate favorable public opinion within a military forum. Americans became fascinated by three second lieutenants in their twenties whose family histories, complex personalities, and military training shaped the way they responded to Jimmie Sutton and to each other. Among the men in charge of these student officers, no one was more concerned with the good of the service and with his own reputation than the commander of the Marine Corps Application School, Charles Doyen. No marine was more conscientious in handling the 1909 investigation than the Corps' brilliant judge advocate. Already a war hero at thirty-three, Harry Leonard would prove a formidable match for a determined mother and her distinguished attorneys and for America's relentless reporters.

The Sutton Inquiry highlighted the distinctions between civilian and military justice a century ago. Naval justice—spelled out in the Articles for the Government of the Navy ("Rocks and Shoals")—was unfamiliar to most Americans, a fact that added to the mystery and the appeal of the case. Before the World War I, Courts of Inquiry and courts-martial had only rarely attracted national attention. Their concerns were specific to the military, with men accused of assaulting a superior officer, of desertion, neglect of duty, drunkenness, or mutinous conduct—all examples of "conduct unbecoming an officer and a gentleman." Navy courts focused not on an individual's rights but on reinforcing command authority, the strong discipline essential for an effective fighting force and the good of the service. In the mid-nineteenth century, when a naval investigation centered on a sensational story such as the 1842 court martial of Alexander Mackenzie for hanging three young seamen on the brig-of-war *Somers*, the reach of America's press corps was still limited. But in 1909, the presence of a psychic mother in front of a naval court put its procedures under a national spotlight. Mrs. Sutton may, in fact, have been the first woman to become an official complainant in a naval court proceeding in the United States.

Once the formal inquiry began in the summer of 1909, Major Leonard and the Suttons' attorney, Henry Davis, engaged in a battle of wits as they debated legal and procedural issues with eloquence and zeal. The questions asked of civilians, and of officers and enlisted men, by the judge advocate and by Davis, a stranger "to the usages of the law" in this military court, were often as revealing as their answers. Leonard was forced to explain and defend naval justice to citizens and journalists who were already skeptical about Mrs. Sutton's chances of a fair hearing from three judges who were Naval Academy alumni. And the spiritual component of the case gave Harry Leonard an even more complex public relations challenge. Christian values were still a fundamental part of the education of most American school children; Catholicism was by then the largest religious denomination in the country. The Marine Corps, it appeared, was responsible for both the death and the afterlife of Lieutenant James N. Sutton. What was more important for the good of the service, six officers' honor or one officer's soul? If the three-man court did not find a way to free the late Lieutenant Sutton from the stigma of suicide, his irrepressible mother counted on nationwide publicity to ensure that her Church and its clergy would judge his guilt or innocence for themselves.

The alleged appearances of Lieutenant Sutton's ghost were less of a problem for the judge advocate than was the fate of Sutton's soul. Major Leonard found a way to use Rosa's visions to attack her credibility in the courtroom, in the newspapers, and before members of Congress. Leonard and Arthur Birney, the attorney for the Marine Corps officers who had been made defendants, would argue that Rosa's charges were based solely on "hallucination, fancy and dreams." And millions of Americans would weigh the Navy Department's arguments as they followed the day-to-day testimony in the only media available at the time.

Between 1907 and 1910, Lieutenant Sutton's death took on a much greater significance for the world at large than his life. One reason is that the key protagonists in this story, Rosa Sutton and Harry Leonard, were such intriguing adversaries. Smart, edgy, and opinionated individuals with strong moral fiber, each defended something sacred to a large number of Americans. Their views had been shaped by hierarchical institutions with larger-than-life missions. Both America's Catholic Church and her Marine Corps had cultural expectations for their members; they demanded total loyalty and a commitment to absolute truths, which in the normal scheme of things would not be incompatible. But in this case they were. An alien in the naval courtroom because of her gender and her goals, Rosa's frontier roots, bold, spontaneous temperament, and unfashionable clothes did not play well in the more refined and formal social circles of Annapolis. And the journalism of the era was not without its own biases—correspondents took full advantage of the sympathy most civilian readers had for Mrs. Sutton's predicament.

MEMORY AND TRUTH-TELLING

Extraordinary primary sources exist to reconstruct the Sutton case; these include Marine Corps and naval officer application and examining board files, government correspondence, legal analyses, autopsy reports, and more than a thousand newspaper articles. The most important source is the record of the 1909 investigation. With close to 1,500 pages of testimony plus exhibits, it provides a unique window into naval justice, society, and the power of the press in the decade before World War I. But these plentiful sources are not infallible. The officers and civilians who testified about Jimmie Sutton's death at the inquiry, and the men and women in Oregon whose signed statements verified Rosa's accounts of his ghostly appearances, were asked to remember events that had occurred two or three years previous. Their recollections reveal the dichotomy between reality and memory that became a critical factor in weighing the evidence about this case. This book explores the values and attitudes of several of these witnesses and of those who tried to solve the case—each of whom experienced the tragedy differently, defining the truth through the lens of his or her own belief system.

Sutton's death had seemed simple at first. According to his death certificate, he had been in

> an altercation with fellow student-officers at the U.S. Marine Corps
> School of Application after which Mr. Sutton attempted to shoot several of his fellow students, inflicting slight wounds on two of them. He

was thrown to the ground in an attempt to wrest the revolver from him, but before this could be done, and while lying on the ground, he turned the pistol against himself and fired the shot into his brain.

These statements, signed by a doctor not present at the scene, were based on "eyewitness" testimony from men who could be implicated in his death. Officers who had not been under oath in 1907 swore to tell the truth in 1909. But a few of the men changed their stories or fell back on a failure of memory—its elusive qualities had begun to fascinate scholars just before the turn of the last century. The Suttons' attorney had no doubt that some of the witnesses were lying; his opponent's defense would be to remind the court that "men do not recall things in the same way" and "memory plays strange tricks." And what of the late Lieutenant Sutton, accused of self-murder in 1907, who had reportedly denied his guilt since then? Is the testimony of a spirit any more reliable than that of a living man? The question—absurd to the uniformed men in the courtroom— was taken seriously by a number of intelligent people. This book begins with no assumptions about the validity of specific marines' testimony, the credibility of Rosa Sutton's apparitions, or even the accuracy of reporters' recollections but instead considers the fragility of memory and eyewitness accounts, no matter whose they are.

Most memories are not distorted, but they can be transformed over time. The first scientific work on remembering and forgetting was published in the year Jimmie Sutton was born. In 1885, German experimental psychologist Hermann Ebbinghaus demonstrated by controlled experiments using his own memory how and why certain memories are harder to recall as time passes. He also underscored the "endless number of differences" in individual memories. Since then, scholars have analyzed many factors that influence our ability to retrieve accurate information about our prior experiences. If a person has been preoccupied with an event (or a vision) and has rehashed it again and again, retention and retrieval might be more reliable than it might be for others who have tried to forget what happened. In a courtroom, when a witness is asked certain types of questions, information within the question itself may have a direct and lasting effect on how a person recalls an incident. Reporters may also ask leading questions that influence the content of the answers they receive. Personal biases and codes of behavior can shape our memories, as can cultural stereotypes, expectations, and a person's age. Witnesses may become increasingly confident about what they are saying the more they rehearse their testimony. Moreover, for accurate retrieval, a witness must have been in a position to pay attention to what is going on around him or her. If a situation was not well illuminated or if events happened quickly and violence or fear was involved, witnesses' memories could be less reliable. Most people think that a traumatic event is easier to recall than a non-violent event, but research has shown that is not always the case. Was the witness under extreme stress? If there was a gun or weapon involved, a witness might focus intently on it rather than on the surrounding details or even the identity of the person with the weapon. All of these variables make it hard to determine the credibility of a witness with a faulty memory.

One thing is clear from the huge paper trail left by this case. A century ago, American culture prized the concept of truth, even as philosophers debated its meanings and criteria. Americans still do—the debate continues in countless books, articles, and multiple forms of media. This story was and is not just about individuals but rather about timeless questions that defy easy answers. The men and women who tackled the murky circumstances of Jimmie Sutton's death and his thwarted afterlife saw and heard things differently. So it is up to the twenty-first-century reader to make sense of the journey of these military men and the Oregon woman who confronted them and to appreciate how complex it was to decipher the intentions, the instances of self-delusion, the lies, and the selective amnesia of the key participants on both sides of this case.

A question that preoccupied many people then—especially psychical researcher James Hyslop—was "do the so-called dead communicate with the living?" For those interested in history, they certainly do through the documents and artifacts they have left behind. With these imperfect remnants of the past we can construct a story that is at best an earnest effort to be faithful to the truth. The real facts about Lieutenant Sutton's death may be sought by corroborating as much evidence as possible, while keeping in mind historian William Cronon's observation that "memory and history have their different truths; neither of which can be evaded if we wish to know ourselves, each other and the world around us."

1

"YOU MUST CLEAR MY NAME"

Halligan Hall still dominates the nearby landscape in Annapolis, Maryland, just as it did a century ago. An elegant sand-colored brick building, it stretches across the top of a gentle slope about a half mile from a tributary of the Severn River known as College Creek. Its four-story-high central pavilion is framed by twin corner towers and flanked by lower connecting wings. More than three dozen arches cover the facade, creating a graceful and friendly appearance, one less formidable than the massive grey granite structures at the nearby Naval Academy. In 1907, the land surrounding Halligan provided a rustic setting for what was then the Marine Corps Barracks and officer training school. Framed by stubble and high grass on its southern edge, the parade ground descended into a marsh with two small ponds. East of the barracks, thirteen tents—each home to a student officer—formed two rows divided by a company street. These tents all faced the Naval Academy hospital high on a hill above them; toward the creek, a cemetery filled with monuments to distinguished naval heroes served as a favorite spot for the "ardent swain and his lady love" who sought privacy on warm evenings.

At about 1:30 in the morning on October 13, a Marine Corps sentry on guard duty at the hospital noticed the voices of several angry men. As flashes of light pierced the darkness on the parade ground below him, he then heard several shots "from a very good-sized gun." Moments later, Colonel Charles Doyen woke up to the sound of someone pounding on his door and calling his name. He hastened downstairs to find Lieutenant Harold Utley, the senior officer in the student camp. Utley reported that Jimmie Sutton had shot two fellow students, "Lieutenant Roelker in the body and Lieutenant Adams in the hand, and then had shot himself in the head." Colonel Doyen dressed quickly and stumbled out into the cool October night. The parade

1

The former Marine Corps Barracks, now Halligan Hall. Courtesy of Special Collections and Archives Division, Nimitz Library, United States Naval Academy.

ground was barely lit by the sliver of a new moon, and only a few lights glimmered in the windows of the barracks. The two men headed south about four hundred feet on the path that led from Doyen's house toward College Creek Bridge. They found Lieutenant Sutton lying face down on the parade ground. Doyen could not see the body clearly, and to test Sutton's pulse, he "felt along his arm and picked up his wrist." The officer's hand was sticky with blood, and although his pulse beat faintly, he was unconscious. An orderly who held up his head said he had been shot in the forehead. But the colonel discovered "a gunshot wound in the right side of his head about an inch and a half above and a little back of the line of the right ear."

Dr. George Pickrell, who was on duty that night, also heard the gunfire. His telephone rang, and he learned that several men had been hurt in a brawl; immediately he contacted his hospital corps. As he made his way toward the parade ground in the black hours of that Sunday morning, Pickrell came upon Charles Doyen pacing up and down the walkway. Doyen directed him to Sutton's limp body, and the doctor turned him over, but "there was apparently no respiration." It was so dark that Dr. Pickrell used matches to locate the wound "near the top" of the officer's head. He noticed a little extrusion of brain matter mixed with unburned powder but hardly any blood. Sutton had a bruise on his lip, on his cheek, and on his forehead on the right side. The scratches on his nose had gravel in them, and, Pickrell figured, they must have come from the fact that his face was in the ground. His four helpers approached with lanterns, lifted Lieutenant Sutton onto a stretcher, and hurried toward the hospital. But the twenty-two-year-old officer died before they made it up the hill. And so, Pickrell later recalled, James N. Sutton's remains were placed "in the dead house to await future action by the authorities."

Captain Charles Johnson Badger, the fifty-four-year-old superintendent of the United States Naval Academy, had only been on the job for three months when he learned of the tragedy at daybreak from Colonel Doyen and Dr. Pickrell. He had little to do with the daily operations of the Marine Corps Application School, but the competence of its administrators and the welfare of its students was his responsibility. No doubt appalled by the news, he was relieved to discover that only one marine had died; Robert Adams had just a trifling wound on a finger, and Edward Roelker turned out to be dazed but fine. Captain Badger wasted no time in asking John Adrian Hoogewerff, head of his department of ordnance and gunnery, to assemble with two other men "for the purpose of investigating and reporting upon the circumstances attending the death of Lieutenant J. N. Sutton." He also sent a wire to George Elliott, commandant of the Corps at the Marine Barracks in Washington, D.C.

REGRET TO REPORT DEATH BY SUICIDE AT 1:30 LAST NIGHT OF SECOND LIEUTENANT J. N. SUTTON U.S.M.C. AT MARINE BARRACKS, ANNAPOLIS. BOARD OF INQUEST HAS BEEN ORDERED. FULL PARTICULARS WILL BE REPORTED AS SOON AS POSSIBLE. REQUEST YOU WILL INFORM NEAREST OF KIN DIRECT FROM HEADQUARTERS AND INSTRUCT ME AS TO DISPOSITION OF REMAINS. ADDRESS NOT KNOWN HERE. BADGER.

By ten o'clock Sunday morning, John Hoogewerff had joined the two members of his fact-finding board at the hospital. Dr. Frank Cook directed the department of physical training, physiology, and hygiene at the Academy, and Major Benjamin Fuller was second in command of the Marine Application School. Also present was the board's recorder, Lieutenant Edward Shippen Willing. The four men first went to inspect the location where Sutton had been found; they then viewed his body, which was lying on a table in the hospital basement covered by a sheet. Dr. Cook stayed in the morgue to perform the obligatory autopsy, while the other three men proceeded upstairs to a room allocated for the inquest.

Frank Cook had been at the Naval Academy since 1906, where he taught midshipmen rather than performing surgery, but he was familiar with the hospital—he had recently been a patient for complications related to appendicitis. (Doctors never had found his appendix.) By his own admission, Cook had no experience with people who had been severely beaten and not much experience treating anyone hit by a .38 caliber bullet. He located the entrance point of the bullet and tracked it downward; it was lodged "just under the membranous covering of that portion near the base [of the brain] known as the cerebellum." Cook decided that was the fatal wound. He found contusions and bruises on Sutton's face but no fractured bones and decided not to proceed any further. After bandaging the lieutenant's head, he went upstairs to the room where the investigation was about to start.

It was close to eleven when Commander Hoogewerff read aloud Captain Badger's convening order; he would ask each of ten witnesses to tell "all you know about the death of Second Lieutenant James N. Sutton," and to answer a few questions. Hoogewerff began by interrogating the board's recorder, Shippen Willing, who happened to be the senior officer at the barracks when Sutton died. After a break for Sunday dinner between 12:30 and 3:00 p.m., the board examined four other marines before adjourning at 6:30 that evening. Three more officers and surgeons Pickrell and Cook would testify the following day. None of the men was under oath, but the commander would caution them all not to speak about Sutton's death with anyone.

In the meantime, Dr. Pickrell had summoned undertaker Harry Raymond Taylor to take charge of Lieutenant Sutton's remains. The lieutenant's arms were tied on his chest with a piece of gauze when Taylor first saw the corpse; he would leave the arms that way so they would look suitable when the body went into its casket. He did notice a small bruise on Sutton's left cheek, and by Tuesday he would find a discolored spot on his forehead. Dr. Pickrell had no idea when any of the officer's family members would arrive, and Taylor was eager to have the body embalmed as soon as possible. His firm occasionally employed James N. Weidefeld, an orderly at the Emergency Hospital in Annapolis, for just that purpose.

As soon as he entered the makeshift morgue, Weidefeld knew his most demanding task was to replace the back part of Sutton's skull which Dr. Cook had removed along with his brain. He used plaster of paris to keep the fluid in and close the dead man's arteries and veins; then he "put the skull back again and sewed the scalp over it." He did not like the looks of the bruise coming out on Sutton's left cheek so he tried to bleach it out by using absorbent cotton saturated with embalming fluid. Finally, he injected this fluid into Sutton's carotid artery; it was a new type that made the body unusually rigid. James Weidefeld ignored the rest of the officer's lean, muscular body—everything but his face would be covered or clothed when he was prepared for burial.

At one o'clock on that same Sunday afternoon, as rumors of a scandal began to break in the usually tranquil seaport town, the assistant adjutant and inspector, Major Albert Sydney McLemore, had wired Jimmie Sutton's family in Portland, Oregon, from the Marine Corps headquarters in Washington, D.C.

2364 NW Hoyt Street is near the top of a hill in a comfortable residential section of Portland. Designed by one of the city's leading architects, Jacob Jacobberger, and completed in 1906, it is a handsome cream-colored house that once aspired toward elegance, though it was built with a budget that could not afford much of it. It stands on a terraced block, and the lawn around it is raised above street level, a characteristic of many of Portland's more spacious homes. Two and a half stories high, with clapboard siding, a hip roof, and overhanging eaves, the house has prominent dormers that let light into the extra half story. Five columns set in piers of brick hold up the roof of the inviting full-length front porch. The porch no longer wraps around the northwest side of the house, but the original brick chimney still stands. The house has not fared as well as Halligan Hall. It is now a multiple-family dwelling showing signs of disrepair, and it looks much smaller than it did before automobiles and utility poles cluttered the street in front of it. But a century ago there was ample space for a large family, with five bedrooms on the top two floors and a generous living room on the ground level; the kitchen at the back of the house had its own dining nook and a small service porch for deliveries of ice and food.

Fifty-year-old James Nuttle Sutton, foreman of West Side Freight Sheds for the Southern Pacific Railroad, had gone into considerable debt to build this home. He was a big, handsome fellow whose thick swirls of curly dark brown hair had lightened and grayed at the temples. A well-trimmed walrus mustache replaced the abundant wiry beard that once covered the lower part of his face. Jim Sutton would never be wealthy, but his family was well connected. His favorite sister, Margaret, married George Jennings Ainsworth, a good-hearted man whose father, Captain J. C. Ainsworth, was president of the Oregon Steam Navigation Company and founder of the Ainsworth National Bank. George Ainsworth would be instrumental in shaping Jim's career before he died in debt in 1895; by 1906 Jim was on the way to earning a eulogy as "one of the most successful railroad men in Portland."

The Sutton family home on Hoyt Street, Portland, Oregon, ca. 1907. Rosa and her youngest child, Louise, can be seen on the porch. Sutton Family Papers.

He was used to strong-willed women, and he had found one in his wife of twenty-six years. Sturdy and attractive, with inquisitive dark brown eyes set wide apart in a round, pale face, Rosa Sutton's flawless skin showed few signs of age. But almost all her chestnut hair had turned silver grey. In public she would wear it piled on top of her head, partially hidden under hats that reflected her self-confidence and impertinence. Jim enjoyed her irreverent sense of humor but not her stubborn, impatient streak. Two fiery temperaments in one family could get out of hand. So he had resigned himself to cooperating with his German-Irish wife on matters that were intensely important to her. Although Jim was Presbyterian, their children were all raised as Catholics. And when Rosa's dreams and premonitions upset her, he tried to be supportive, still amazed that twice before his wife's "visions," as she called them, had saved the lives of one or more of their children. Jim had also gone along with Rosa in building a house that was larger than he thought they needed—three of their children were now grown and usually not living at home. So it was with mixed feelings that he moved his family to Hoyt Street at the end of 1906 from more sensible quarters less than ten blocks down a hill in a more congested area of the city.

Rosa loved their new home, and, especially on holidays, she longed to show it to Jimmie. The Sutton's oldest son had been in the East for almost

James Nuttle Sutton. Sutton Family Papers

twenty-two months studying to be a naval engineer. His parents supported his goals, and the whole family looked forward to Jimmie's frequent letters. A military commission carried great distinction and opportunities for their sons that most parents could not otherwise afford. Rosa's oldest brother had graduated from West Point, and Oregon senator Jonathan Bourne had already sponsored the Suttons' seventeen-year-old son, Don, for the United States Military Academy. But Rosa probably tried not to think about the likelihood of Don leaving, too. In the fall of 1907, four of her children were with her, and 784 Hoyt Street (as the number was then) did not seem too grand at all.

At about nine o'clock one ordinary Saturday evening after supper, the family expected guests when Rosa suddenly exclaimed, "Mercy, what was that?" She developed a sharp pain in her heart and felt as if she had been struck on the head. "Something has happened to Jimmie. Oh God, save him," she cried out. Then she fled upstairs to her bedroom; her younger son, Don, and daughter Louise tried to calm their mother by reading to her

Rosa Brant Sutton. Sutton Family Papers.

out loud. But the book "included the story of a murder," and Rosa lay awake for most of the night.

The following day, October 13, was overcast, with rain threatening and westerly winds, when Rosa went to Mass at six o'clock in the morning. She soon became too agitated to remain in church and returned to the warmth of her family. At close to 1:30 Pacific time, as late afternoon shadows fell on the Naval Academy hospital a continent away and a naval Board of Inquest questioned its third witness, Jim Sutton received a telephone call. Fourteen-year-old Louise noticed that her father "seemed greatly excited" as he left the house to pick up a telegram. About an hour later, she was in her mother's bedroom when her father returned. Unaware of how nervous Louise would be, Rosa insisted that Jimmie had arrived too. For Louise the moment was unforgettable:

> Mother said, "Jimmie is here in the house, perhaps he has gone upstairs to put on his uniform (as he had said that the next time we saw him he would be in uniform), go upstairs and see if he is there." I went and found my father with my sister, they were both very pale; feeling something was wrong I went down stairs and told mother I didn't care to stay home for dinner but would go to my aunt's. So I was not at home when my father told mother of Jimmie's death.

Jim was devastated by the telegram and approached his wife tentatively. Hardly knowing what to say, he asked if she could handle some bad news. "Anything," Rosa responded, wondering if Jimmie had been hurt. But the news was worse, and Rosa was stunned, especially when her husband mentioned suicide. Almost instantly Rosa felt their son's presence.

> "*Mama I never did,*" and reaching out his hands to me, he said: "*My hands are as free from crime as they were when I was five years old. Oh, Mother, don't believe them. . . . I fell on my knees and they beat me worse than a dog in the street. Mamma dear, if you could only see my forehead you would know what they did to me. Don't give way, for you must clear my name. God will give you the men to bring those men to justice.*" I turned to my husband and daughters [Rose, twenty-seven, and Daysie, twenty-five] and said: "Do any of you see Jimmie or hear what he is saying?" They looked at one another and thought I have lost my mind.

As Rosa struggled to make sense of this apparition, a reporter came to the front door and announced with great confidence (and incorrectly) that their son had blown the whole top of his head off after a Naval Academy dance. Jimmie's father told the *Oregonian*, "from other information in my possession I can say that it was not a case of suicide, but an accident. The details will be given out just as soon as we receive them complete."

In the days immediately following his death, Rosa had other postmortem visits from Jimmie. He told her the men who beat him up smashed his [pocket] watch with a kick as he lay on the ground and jumped on him with their feet. One ghostly appearance apparently occurred on Wednesday morning, October 16. Rosa later recalled telling her family and friends that Jimmie said, "'*They put a bandage around my forehead and around to the back of my neck to try to hide what they had done. My face was all beaten up and discolored and my forehead broken and a lump under my left jaw. They put my body in a basement and left it there.*' He said, '*Utley managed and directed the whole affair.*'" Jimmie's ghost began to search the floor. Rosa asked what he was looking for, and he answered, "'*It's my shoulder knot that I can't find.*'"

The Suttons' children were used to hearing about their mother's dreams and apparitions, and they often became impatient with her. Paranormal phenomena made them uncomfortable, but they were also puzzled. They knew that prior messages Rosa received from dead relatives had proven accurate—even life-saving. Years earlier, while Jim held his first job as a telegraph operator, Rosa's brother, Albert, died suddenly in Vancouver at age eighteen. Late that same night, Rosa heard his spirit call out to her until she and her husband woke up just in time to escape from their burning house with their two tiny daughters. On another occasion, her father's ghost had warned her in time to rescue Jimmie (then a toddler) from drowning in a barrel of water on their porch. When Rosa's mother, Louisa, died in Vancouver in 1890, the Suttons were living in Los Angeles; Louisa's spirit told Rosa the news before she heard it from the rest of the family. More than one witness would attest to these unusual experiences.

Jim Sutton knew that Rosa felt especially close to their oldest son. When she claimed to hear from Jimmie, at first he thought his wife "was gone, that her mind was overthrown." Yet Rosa described specific details about Jimmie's fate long before the family had any official news; her husband was not the only person baffled by this information.

While naval authorities took care of the matter efficiently in Annapolis, friends and relatives flocked to Hoyt Street to pay their respects. Rosa spoke about her visions incessantly—never actually using the word "ghost." ("Vision" may have had religious implications for her.) Her descriptions of Jimmie's appearances made an indelible impression on a number of people who had known the family for many years. Some details would vary from person to person, but Rosa told them all that Jimmie had been in a brawl with several men and had been struck on the head. Rosa's youngest sister, Eliza Brant Bruin, who helped her husband run Bruin Detective Agency, was a pragmatic woman who usually paid little attention to her sister's psychical experiences. But this time she was less skeptical. She was positive Rosa knew soon after he died "how badly [Jimmie's] face and head had been cut and bruised and [that Rosa] said there was a big lump under his left jaw." Eliza also distinctly remembered hearing that Jimmie's watch had been broken. Another of Rosa's sisters who lived nearby, Mary Hodgson, learned about Rosa's initial vision when she visited the family the evening Jimmie died. So did her husband, Nephi.

For nine years, Mr. and Mrs. John Hincks had been the Suttons' neighbors when they lived at 187 North Fifteenth Street. One of their daughters had gone to school with Jimmie, and they had all been very fond of him. Mrs. Hincks went to visit Rosa with two of her daughters on Tuesday, October 15. Again Rosa recounted what Jimmie had told her and mentioned "the epaulette was torn from his shoulder." Chrissie Hincks, who stopped by a few days later, recalled that "Jimmie came to [Rosa] and said there was a white bandage around his head," and he said, "'*There's a hole under the bandage in my forehead. They came up back of me and forced me to the ground, and Mamma how could I do anything when they were all down on top of me at the time—oh, Mamma, they got me at last.'*"

Rosa's apparitions would have been frowned on by her Church, which linked the use of mediums to communicate with the dead and Satanism. But Rosa had never needed an intermediary—departed family members apparently reached out to her. And messages from beyond were not the only factor that shaped her response to the loss of her son. The values and the belief system that she acquired as a child would soon prove to be an unexpected challenge for the Department of the Navy.

Rosetta Agnes Brant was born on January 27, 1860, into a pioneer family already overflowing with the laughter and tears of young children. Ten years earlier, Rosa's German father, Joseph, and his Irish wife, Louisa Burgett Brant, had made their way on a journey of close to two thousand miles from Dayton, Ohio, to Clark County, Washington, following the Oregon Trail. Joseph had taken out a donation land claim on the Lewis River, but as his family expanded, he moved his wife and children to the town of Vancouver, on the north bank of the Columbia River. (Vancouver incorporated as a city in 1857.) A wagon and carriage maker by trade, Joseph also owned a livery stable and built and operated a hotel on Main Street with a dance hall and a theater; for several years he served as Justice of the Peace. But suddenly, on

New Year's Eve 1872, Joseph died, leaving his forty-four-year-old wife with twelve children—six were still under thirteen.

Louisa Brant continued to manage her husband's hotel, and her family responsibilities were surely made easier by the Sisters of Charity of Providence. Mother Joseph of the Sacred Heart (Esther Pariseau) had come to Vancouver from Montreal with four other sisters in 1856; for much of the next half century she would have a decisive impact on the Pacific Northwest, raising funds to construct twenty-nine schools, missions, and hospitals. The sisters committed their lives to helping the elderly, the orphaned, the sick, and the poor, but they survived financially by teaching the children of pioneer families. Even before Joseph Brant died, the nuns provided a strong support system for his daughters. Rosa was a student at Providence Academy when the flagship school moved into an impressive new three-story building in Vancouver in 1873.

Between the ages of seven and fourteen, Rosa Brant studied with these dedicated women dressed in long black habits with blue aprons, their faces framed by white garnitures. She learned reading, mathematics, and domestic skills such as sewing under a strict regimen that emphasized cleanliness and self-discipline. The Brant girls also had piano and singing lessons, and Rosa acquired a lifelong love of music among the nuns. But above all, she drew comfort in a precarious world from the spiritual images and icons all around her. Rosa and her sisters learned much more than traditional school subjects. They spent their days reading Bible stories in surroundings filled with visual reminders of the power of the Blessed Virgin Mary and the lives of the saints. Catholicism represented a "web" of relationships between heaven and earth, and Catholics with German ancestry—one-fifth to one-quarter of the American Catholic community—were known for their devotional piety. At its foundation was the presence of God in Communion wafers and in other media such as relics, statues, holy cards, prayer beads, and rosaries. Devotion to the Mother of God distinguished Catholics sharply from members of other religions; her presence was as central to their daily lives as their family members.

By 1900, America's twelve million Catholics formed the largest religious denomination in the United States, and one that was growing rapidly. But in the second half of the nineteenth and the early twentieth century, waves of anti-Catholic sentiment broke out in various parts of the country, underscoring the feeling among many Catholics that they were second-class citizens in a Protestant nation. This provided all the more reason for a church grounded in centuries of history, liturgical texts, and elaborate rituals to demand total commitment from her faithful from an early age.

When Rosa Brant was sixteen, Bishop James Gibbons explicitly addressed misrepresentations of his Church "by the most powerful vehicles of information" in a book that would influence millions of Catholics for generations to come. By embracing the Church, Gibbons wrote, expressing a sentiment that undoubtedly shaped Rosa Sutton's world view, "Your knowledge of the truth is not only complete and harmonious, but it becomes fixed and steady. You exchange opinion for certainty." And Catholics could "enjoy that profound peace which springs from the conscious possession of the truth." At the core of this truth, Gibbons stated, was the belief that "nothing is so essential as the salvation of your immortal soul, 'for what does it profit a man, if he have the whole world, and lose his own soul? Or what shall a man give in exchange for his soul?'"

The future Archbishop of Baltimore and Cardinal, who would play a decisive role in Rosa's effort to save her son's soul, outlined the basic tenets of Catholicism clearly: "The Church has authority from God to teach regarding faith and morals, and in her teaching she is preserved from error by the special guidance of the Holy Ghost." Through daily instruction among the sisters, Rosa absorbed the meaning of the Church's infallibility, of the Holy Sacrifice of the Mass, the moral and religious teachings in the catechism, and the significance of the sacraments. The distinction between the laity and the clergy was fundamental to the daily rituals of the Church. The clergy were part of a sacred hierarchy established by divine law. "Not only does Jesus empower His ministers to preach in His name, but he commands their hearers to listen and obey." The Catholic priest is a king who reigns "over the hearts and affections of his people," wrote Gibbons. "He is a shepherd, because he leads his flock into the delicious pastures of the Sacraments and shelters them from the wolves who wait for their souls." As a member of this flock, Rosa learned that she was "confided to the care of shepherds" who were instructed in the Word of God; these shepherds held the key to eternal life when they consecrated a communicant's grave.

When Rosa studied the Ten Commandments she understood that disobeying them was a grievous offense against God. And by memorizing the questions and answers in her catechism, she learned specific instructions about how to achieve immortality. A century ago, suicide was among the most grievous of mortal sins—the type of offense against God that would send a soul straight to eternal death in hell. Even worse, the prospect of being reunited with one's family and loved ones would be gone forever. Rosa's children had also memorized the Fifth Commandment, and they knew, as she did, what to think on the afternoon of October 13, 1907. God forbade Catholics "to do any injury to ourselves or to our neighbor, in body or soul." According to Catholic doctrine and Canon Law, should the navy's findings confirm what the telegram said, Jimmie Sutton would be denied a Christian burial. But Jimmie also knew that suicide would lead to a "place of eternal torments" rather than one of "everlasting rest," so how could he have killed himself? That question plagued Rosa as much as her visions as she tried to make sense of her son's untimely death.

In October 1907, the Department of the Navy knew nothing about the spiritual agony of an Oregon housewife, but the men in charge in Annapolis could not afford to let the matter of Lieutenant Sutton's death get out of hand. Word of the naval inquest leaked out quickly, and reporters in Maryland and Washington began forecasting its findings. Because outsiders were not privy to the testimony held behind closed doors on October 13 and 14, the press sought information from anyone who would talk. The *Washington Post* ran a long story, "OFFICER A SUICIDE," on October 14 as the last witnesses gave their accounts to Commander Hoogewerff, Major Benjamin Fuller, and Dr. Cook, while Shippen Willing did his best to take down the testimony. The *Post* reporter had help from Colonel Charles Doyen, who had not been an eyewitness, but—despite instructions not to do so—"freely discussed the facts as he had procured them from participants." Doyen's facts, learned primarily from Harold Utley, were that Jimmie and three other men returned to camp from an evening out in Annapolis; when their hired automobile crossed the bridge over College Creek, Sutton "drew a pistol and threatened to shoot himself." The *Post* article, which would prove to have several errors, stated that two lieutenants, Robert Adams and Edward Roelker, took a .32 caliber revolver away from Sutton and received minor wounds. But Sutton apparently had a second gun, and after being thrown to the ground, he shot himself. The reporter concluded that a "decided mystery surrounds the question of where he obtained the revolver and what he could have been doing with two weapons."

Reporters who spoke with marines and navy men commented on Sutton's personality, surely encouraging their readers to shake their heads in dismay at what appeared to be a pathetic young man who had gone astray. According to the *Post*, "There seems to be little doubt Sutton was not in his right mind and that he was not accountable for taking his own life or attempting that of his brother officers, if such was the case. He was of a morose disposition, did not make close friends among his brother officers, and was much to himself." He was "sensitive and inclined to take umbrage about matters most persons would pass over." But, the paper acknowledged, he was also "friendly to enlisted men at times and had been known frequently to extend special favors to them." An Annapolis reporter for the *Evening Capital* had also heard some disparaging remarks about Lieutenant Sutton from the marines, who emphasized that he was a loner who "did not associate with his fellow officers to any great extent."

The *Washington Post* would give the navy the benefit of the doubt. The Inquest Board had conducted a careful investigation, "summoning every person who was present or who had any information on the subject before them." But soon a crack in the definitive conclusions of those in power began to show. It was actually quite difficult to know exactly what had happened to Lieutenant Sutton. The *Post* acknowledged that "[r]umors of the wildest kind were in circulation this morning about the affair. It was first said that Lieutenant Sutton had killed two brother officers and then himself. Officers who were not present were connected with the affair by rumor and the incident was given the most sensational details." The *Evening Capital* projected that the naval court would come up with a suicide finding but also observed that "wild rumors of all sorts" had spread through town and the Naval Academy. One of these concerned "some feeling between Sutton and Adams because of a girl to whom both had been paying attention." Perhaps, an anonymous source suggested, there had been a duel between the officers, but "there were no witnesses except those concerned." On the other hand, the Annapolis reporter wrote, some officers of the law questioned the suicide theory because a man who shoots himself "rarely goes to the trouble of holding the pistol behind his head in an awkward position such as must have been done in this case."

The men in charge seemed to have no trouble turning opinions into certainty, even before the inquest ended. Secretary of the Navy Victor Metcalf learned about the tragedy on Monday, October 14, in a letter from Marine Corps Commandant George Elliott; using unequivocal language, Elliott stated, "Second Lieutenant James N. Sutton, U. S. M. C., committed suicide"—and a board has "been ordered to investigate the case." So the secretary may have expected the findings he received from Charles Badger the following day:

> The board having examined all the testimony bearing on the case that it thinks it is possible to procure, having thoroughly examined the two revolvers, the cartridges and the empty shells found in them, the bullet taken from the head of the deceased and from the coat of Lieutenant Roelker, and gone carefully over the testimony finds as follows: . . . from a view of the body, a thorough investigation, and from the evidence before it, which it believes is all the evidence procurable and is perfectly reliable, [the board] is unanimously and thoroughly convinced that Second

> Lieutenant James N. Sutton, U.S. Marine Corps, committed suicide by
> shooting himself in the head with a revolver at about 1:20 o'clock a.m.
> in the vicinity of the officers quarters, marine barracks, Annapolis, Mary-
> land, October 13th, 1907.

The inquest transcript makes no mention of this examination of the revolvers, cartridges, and empty shells. But the board was also positive that no
one else was responsible for Sutton's death or armed at the time.

When he presented these conclusions to the secretary of the navy,
Captain Badger emphasized how exhaustive the work of the board had
been in "providing findings of so definite and well established a character."
The board, in fact, after examining everyone who had any knowledge of
the tragedy, had "left no stone unturned to arrive at a correct verdict." In
the Wednesday edition of its paper, the *Evening Capital* described the officers' version of the fight and their contention that Sutton shot himself because he was afraid that he had accidentally killed another officer, Lieutenant Edward Roelker. By Thursday, October 17, a local Annapolis
weekly, *The Advertiser*, repeated these findings and the interview with Captain Badger.

Now all that was left for the navy was the disposition of the body. On
Monday, October 14, Commandant George Elliott had wired Jim Sutton
to ask if he would pay for his son's embalming and for a steel casket. Sutton agreed. But as a suicide, Jimmie could not be buried in a Catholic
cemetery. While his parents worked on a plan for their son's remains, the
vast distance between Oregon and Maryland only made their anxiety worse.
As it happened, Jimmie Sutton was now being cared for quite well. Undertaker Harry Taylor considered it his job to look out for the officer until
instructions arrived from Oregon. And so every night, after supper, Taylor
checked on the corpse that still lay unclothed in the basement of the Academy hospital. He too had no idea how complicated the future would be for
Jimmie Sutton's body and his soul.

The members of the Sutton Board of Inquest, who accepted the marines'
account that the officer committed suicide, were in a tough position. Less
than two years earlier, its president had led the funeral cortege of a Naval
Academy midshipman, James Branch (Class of 1907), who died after a boxing match with a younger man, Minor Meriwether Jr. The catastrophe created a media sensation and an exhaustive investigation of conditions at the
Naval Academy by Congress. For John Hoogewerff, the experience was
surely sobering and unforgettable. A suicide at the Marine Corps Barracks

was also tragic but would reflect less poorly on his institution than murder; besides, the student officers seemed so positive about what had happened.

As a Naval Academy faculty member, John Hoogewerff may have remembered that before Lieutenant Sutton became a marine, he had been a plebe in Meriwether's class (1908) for a year. His closest friend, Edward Roelker, had been in the same class. And Lieutenant Harold Utley had spent almost four years at the Academy in James Branch's class (1907). Had these future marines' experiences as midshipmen had any bearing on the events of October 13, 1907? The officers' feelings toward each other had not seemed worth pursuing during the Sutton inquest. It would be close to eighteen months before Americans would want more answers about Jimmie Sutton's death—ones that lay in the culture of military education and in the backgrounds and temperaments of a handful of men whose lives converged at the United States Naval Academy and in the much smaller, younger Marine Corps School of Application.

2

"FULL OF ANIMAL LIFE AND SPIRIT"

To President Theodore Roosevelt, the United States Military Academy and the Naval Academy were "the most absolutely democratic in the proper sense of the word" of all the institutions in this country. Their students represented America "in a higher and more peculiar sense than can possibly be true of any other institution in the land." And he went further, declaring in 1902 that a boy's birthplace, creed, and social standing did not matter at West Point and Annapolis. For in the service academies, "we care nothing save for his worth as he is able to show it." It was this kind of sentiment from a former assistant secretary of the navy that encouraged so many young men to feel pride when they made it into the academies. And yet Roosevelt knew full well that a young man's family connections were critical to the application process.

When Jimmie Sutton set his heart on becoming an engineer, the Naval Academy seemed an ideal choice. Not only would he be paid to attend, but also it had an excellent program with instruction in "four branches of engineering science and practice," although broader training was "sacrificed to the immediate needs of the service." To help their son make it into the Academy, Rosa and Jim Sutton turned to a popular, colorful Republican senator, John H. Mitchell. Fortunately, the three-time senator, who would be indicted in 1905 for perjury and bribery, still had enough influence in 1903 to be a successful sponsor.

His candidate was a limber, athletic five foot, seven and a quarter inches, of medium build, with a ruddy complexion, and dark brown eyes set off by unusually thick reddish-brown hair. The Suttons' former neighbors, who had known Jimmie well, found him "obedient, good and industrious, and a perfect little gentleman," devoted to his mother. As a young boy he loved to experiment with electricity and had a small dynamo in the

18

United States Naval Academy. Detail showing the Academic Building in the center, with its clock tower, and the Marine Corps Barracks across the creek in the background. Courtesy of the Special Collections and Archives Division, Nimitz Library, United States Naval Academy.

basement of his family's home. One of his schoolmates, Dorothy Hincks, thought "his pleasant ways and quiet habits and close attention to what he was doing" would make him a distinguished man; her father assured her that "Jimmie would make an Admiral." Jimmie's prior education had included a Catholic school in Los Angeles when the Suttons lived there for seven years; the Couch School; Portland High School; and while he waited for word from the Naval Academy, one year at a fledgling university and prep school for boys that showed great promise. Located on a bluff overlooking Portland, on property purchased in 1901 by the visionary Archbishop Alexander Christie, it was known initially as Columbia University. (Since the 1930s it has been the University of Portland.) The archbishop hoped that some day his school would parallel Indiana's Notre Dame—both institutions sought to produce Christian humanists and to prepare young men for professional life. In February 1903, during Jimmie's second and last semester at Columbia, the school paper printed a small but telling news item in the "Gossip of the Town" column: "James Sutton is fast recovering from melancholia and is also regaining his dimples. When seen yesterday, Mr. Sutton smiled and said in his own sweet way: 'Force will make me Sunny Jim.'"

Mitchell's nomination probably came through that summer, and Jimmie left home for Annapolis where he would study for the Naval Academy's entrance exams at a preparatory school founded by an alumnus, Robert L. Werntz. The classes worked—at least initially. On April 19, 1904, Jimmie

James N. Sutton Jr. as a midshipman, ca. 1904. Sent to the New York American *newspaper by the Sutton family. Courtesy of the Harry Ransom Humanities Research Center, University of Texas at Austin.*

reported to the Civil Service Commission in Washington for three days of successful testing. He entered the Academy on May 10, having agreed to serve in the navy for eight years. But even with Werntz's help, the Academy's austere environment would prove difficult for Sutton as it was for dozens of sixteen- to eighteen-year-olds in the Class of 1908.

Enrollment at Annapolis tripled between 1903 and 1906, reaching close to 900 (823 attended during 1904–1905). The plebes may have been enthralled by the mystique of the navy when they applied, but many were not prepared for the hot, humid Annapolis climate, their exacting schedule, or the size of the school. Days filled with recitation, drills, and studying began at 6:00 a.m. and ran until 9:55 at night. The emphasis was on discipline, duty, and loyalty to the service, with barely two hours free time in a day and just about no contact with the outside world. Many of the boys did well, but there was one aspect of life at the Academy that some found hard to take.

Prearranged fist fights or boxing matches had long been used to settle disputes among midshipmen and as a method of humiliating the plebes. Contemporary ideas about manliness remained inseparable from a martial ethic, promoted with exuberance by America's own president. Magazine articles—some written by Theodore Roosevelt himself—exulted in masculine values such as those exemplified by America's armed forces. Real men fought in the face of insults and bullying of any sort. But when fighting resulted in lethal injuries, it became a source of great concern among the men responsible for the Academy's funding. In 1903, congressmen declared the Academy must make rules to prevent this and other forms of hazing and expel anyone found guilty of ignoring them. Their reservations were reinforced after the tragic death of midshipman James Branch in November 1905. For the next two years the Academy would be watched closely by the legislators and the media—a situation that put a great deal of pressure on the men in charge when Jimmie Sutton died.

After the death of Branch, a subcommittee of the House Committee on Naval Affairs investigated conditions at the Naval Academy and put together a comprehensive report of its findings. Subcommittee members were disturbed not just by physical hazing (such as forced fights) but also by the demeaning tasks that fourth-class men were required to perform for older midshipmen. When they questioned officers and students between December 1905 and June 1906, committee members found inherent flaws in the system that would be a challenge to correct. The most serious of these was the failure of officers, surgeons, and especially midshipmen to report abuse, and with midshipmen's determination to follow "what are termed the traditions of the academy." Acknowledging that many midshipmen were just boys "full of animal life and spirit," the congressmen suggested that the faculty play a stronger role in upholding discipline.

At the root of many of the problems outlined by the congressional subcommittee in 1906 was the issue of loyalty and its boundaries. You did not break rank—therefore, no matter what an oversight committee might suggest, the men were often reluctant to report abuses. Steadfast allegiance to your comrades (or your unit) and your superiors all the way up to the nation's commander in chief was expected in all circumstances. The boys and young men at the Academy had their own rituals that had been in place for decades and shaped their particular faith and morals. The traditions midshipmen were exposed to transformed them from civilian boys into navy and Marine Corps men who would take their place in a military hierarchy. Most of the men in charge had themselves been trained at the Academy to look out for each other above all else—in the face of calamity at home as well as during conflicts overseas.

Jimmie Sutton's first exposure to military values, and to a large school filled with young men from the East and Midwest, came during 1904 and 1905. Soon after he entered the Naval Academy, "an ordinary enough everyday young stripling," he surprised some of his classmates who "had not noticed his well-knit body by standing second in the strength test for the whole class." A reporter for the *Evening Capital* observed, "The only man who bested him was Archie Douglas, afterward one of the greatest football players and general athletes in the East." Jimmie took classes in boxing, wrestling, and jujitsu, excelling at the latter and "quickly picking up all the tricks that the wily Japanese instructor offered." He became known as an excellent fighter, but he had a temper that flared up: There was a rumor that he drew a knife on a fellow midshipman. He also refused to go along with hazing. His fellow plebes were an elite group from comfortable families, often members of the Protestant Establishment who expected to become part of a naval aristocracy. Not very tall, Catholic, and coming from so far away, Jimmie wanted to impress his peers. He showed off with his Mexican holster and his pistol and soon earned the nickname "Tracy," after Harry Tracy, an outlaw who had escaped from the Oregon State Penitentiary in Salem in 1902. (Tracy killed several people before he was betrayed by his partner and shot himself.) To some midshipmen at Annapolis, Tracy, and by association Jimmie, probably personified their image of a man from the Wild West.

Like his mother, Jimmie could be both melodramatic and stubborn, but "if you knew him well you liked him though and his nerve wasn't doubted"; this same former classmate recalled, "He sometimes had a fight in the afternoon and employed the evening in writing verses." His sensitive and reflective side came out in one of the poems that he sent home. It began, "Thought is my hobby, past time and pleasure / In moments of rest, recreation and leisure," and ended with the words, "For if deception I practice no matter what form / 'Tis bound to return and in the end be a thorn." A righteous streak appears in this poem that could have put him in conflict with the established codes of behavior among his fellow midshipmen. And when he promised his mother he would not get into fights, it would be tough to keep his word at the Academy.

One practice that was rough, even for an experienced boxer, was that plebes often had to fight upperclassmen until they lost. Jimmie would fight furiously when forced into it, and often he won. But in the spring of 1905, after being defeated in a match with a tough young man from the Rocky Mountains where "the reach grows long and the punch hard," he spent time in the infirmary. He fell behind in his studies, failed the final exam in Spanish, and despite the help from Werntz's Naval Academy Preparatory School, performed poorly in math. Jimmie was given a chance to remain at the Academy but decided to leave—partly because of the hazing. He resigned on his twentieth birthday, June 3, joining the eighty-two other young men in his class who would not graduate. He had not, however, given up on a naval career. The Marine Corps provided an option for some of the men who left the Naval Academy—but for prospective marines, there were just as many hurdles to cross.

For much of the late nineteenth and early twentieth centuries the appropriate mission of the Marine Corps within the navy was not clearly defined. Marines had been indispensable in the four-month war with Spain in 1898, and by 1905, as more and more steel battleships that needed manpower were built, the Corps played a critical role in naval operations around the world. When Theodore Roosevelt became president in 1901, close to 6,000 enlisted men and 211 officers served as marines. In his 1905 report, the secretary of the navy asked for "an increase of some 1200 officers and men in the personnel of the Marine Corps." This expansion was judged "absolutely necessary for the efficient discharge of its duties." By 1908, after Congress approved the House Naval Affairs Committee's recommendation for another increase of 55 officers and 750 enlisted men, the authorized strength of the Corps had risen to 332 officers and 9,521 enlisted men. During this same era, as industrialization and technological improvements revolutionized warfare, a movement took place to upgrade the professional training of men in all of the armed forces, including those in the marines.

Largely through the efforts of Commandant Colonel Charles Heywood and Captain Daniel Pratt Mannix, the Marine Corps School of Application became a reality on September 1, 1891, when seven recent graduates of the Naval Academy reported to the Marine Barracks in Washington, D.C. Over the next two decades, the size of the school and the entrance requirements for the young men who hoped to take the one-year course varied considerably; at times, the existence of the school itself seemed uncertain (although it is the forerunner of today's well-established Marine Corps Basic School at Quantico). By 1905, candidates no longer expected to be graduates of the Naval Academy, and in fact, many came from civilian life.

Obtaining a Marine Corps commission was no less arduous than securing a spot at Annapolis or West Point. Passing the physical and mental examinations for the Corps was a challenge but one with specific guidelines that had been spelled out in writing; a candidate could prepare for these requirements. Qualifying to take these exams was a different matter—a much more unpredictable process dependent on the whims of particular men in power who owed their own positions to their political connections and their ability to work the system. There was no set system of nomination by a senator or representative. Those who aspired to be officers had to have families with connections, and it could help to have mothers who understood patronage. These women appeared to take a backseat in the public arena to their husbands, but they could play a critical role in the future of their sons.

Letters from influential men were the most important way to prove to the Navy Department that you were an officer candidate with the right qualifications. Mothers often pushed hard for these letters as they advocated on their sons' behalf. Some women monitored their sons' military careers with an intensity that was both hard for men in power to ignore and no doubt easy for them to understand as sons themselves. In cities and towns across the United States, women lobbied men whom their husbands, fathers, or brothers knew through their professions, their churches, their alumni networks, their local governments, or their volunteer service on boards and committees. Occasionally, mothers wrote directly to the Navy Department themselves.

Between the fall of 1905 and the beginning of 1907, three women from Oregon, Washington, D.C., and Illinois—each of whom had a son who had not completed his course at the Naval Academy—decided to make sure their sons had a chance at the Marine Corps Application School. These persistent mothers had no way of knowing the young men's experiences and training as midshipmen would carry over into their lives as marines, with unintended consequences for their families and for the Corps.

When Jimmie Sutton applied to the Corps, once again, the Suttons had good contacts. Remembering how Senator Mitchell had sponsored Jimmie for the Naval Academy, Rosa and her husband asked their friends to send endorsements to another of Oregon's Republican senators, Charles Fulton, rather than directly to the Department of the Navy. Charlie Fulton was a trial attorney from Astoria, a veteran of the state senate, a savvy political ally of John Mitchell, and not above corruption himself. The senator would be the Suttons' primary contact with the Department throughout the application process, and he enthusiastically used his influence on their behalf. On August 14, 1905, he wrote Navy Secretary Charles Bonaparte to explain that Sutton had failed to pass the Naval Academy examinations "by a very slight percentage" because of "the condition of his health." Sutton was, however, eager to enter the service and, Fulton continued, "comes of an excellent family and many testimonials to his worth and high character have been furnished me, coming from the best citizens of Portland, Oregon."

Secretary Bonaparte acknowledged Senator Fulton's letter on August 21. A few days later, on August 26, William Loeb, secretary to President Roosevelt, sent a note from Oyster Bay, New York, on White House stationery to Bonaparte: "The President directs that Mr. James N. Sutton be put down for the examination following the coming one, for appointment as second lieutenant in the Marine Corps. Would you please advise Senator Fulton accordingly?" Two days later, Bonaparte placed his large, bold signature on a note informing the senator that "in accordance with the direction of the President," he had ordered that James Sutton be permitted to take the examination early the following year.

Although a White House endorsement was hard to match, Rosa Sutton also saw to it that Archbishop Christie wrote for Jimmie—after all, he had been among the first young men to attend the archbishop's school. In a handwritten letter, on stationery from his official residence in Portland, Archbishop Christie informed the secretary of the navy that so far as he knew, James Nuttle Sutton Jr. "is a young man of excellent reputation, and I hope he will prove himself qualified for the position that he is seeking at your hands." His letter was enclosed with the application Jimmie sent to the Marine Corps in December.

As fate would have it, Jimmie did not take the exam for more than a year. He had just turned twenty, and Bonaparte told Senator Fulton he was not eligible before the age of twenty-one. His age was not the only cause for delay. The requirements may have been quite discouraging. He certainly could prove he was "mentally sound," pass a "rigid physical examination," and demonstrate through letters of endorsement that he was a man of "good moral character" and not "addicted to the use of intoxicating liquors." But after his experience at the Naval Academy, he would still need help with academic subjects—especially mathematics. He would be grilled in arithmetic, algebra, geometry, plane trigonometry, the use of logarithms, and the elements of surveying. The list went on, adding English grammar, history, geography, and familiarity with the Constitution of the United States and its government. Once he saw these instructions, Jimmie agreed to take no chances. He would spend all of 1906 studying in a preparatory course in Washington, D.C., finally taking the exam on January 15, 1907.

Throughout 1906, Jimmie (known as Jim among his peers) shared an apartment with John Layne who, three years later, recalled his former roommate in glowing terms to a reporter from the *Philadelphia Inquirer*. According to Layne, by then the personal assistant to William Lorimer, a junior senator from Illinois, Sutton "studied hard" and had "fully mastered mathematics and engineering by late in 1906, but still had some trouble with languages." Layne told the paper that Sutton's "whole life seemed wrapped up in working out the brilliant future which he believed awaited him, and devoting himself to his mother and sister of whom he had talked to me often." He hoped to make his family proud, never said "an unkind word to anyone and I never heard anyone quarrel with him." Always philosophical, "his spirit of never give up helped him at all times." As for being a loner, Layne went out of his way to contradict that impression. Lieutenant Sutton "was invited out almost continually" by "serious minded sober men with a purpose in life." He "had all the friends any man could want." Among these friends were men he had known at the Naval Academy; he saw them at night when he frequented Washington drinking establishments such as the Garrick Club.

Edward Roelker was undoubtedly one of the men Jimmie fraternized with in the nation's capital. He had joined the Naval Academy Class of 1907 two months after Jimmie did, and they became close friends. Only slightly taller than Jimmie at five feet, eight and half inches, twenty pounds lighter, and just three months younger, Roelker sported a fair complexion, brown eyes, and hair redder than that of his fellow plebe from Oregon, so much so that he was always called "Red" or "Reddy" by his peers. A Washington insider, for at least part of his childhood his family lived in Georgetown at 1434 Q Street; records indicate they attended St. John's Episcopal Church. His German father was a mechanical and construction engineer for the United States Navy. Rear Admiral Charles R. Roelker decided early on to have his uninhibited and feisty son succeed him at the Academy. For much of Edward's adolescence, Admiral Roelker and his loyal wife, Parthenia Porter Roelker, worked hard to achieve that goal.

When Edward was not yet sixteen, they sent him to one of the oldest military schools in the United States, Pennsylvania Military Academy, in Mrs. Roelker's home town of Chester. In October of 1902, on the recommendation of an alumnus of the school, they transferred him to the Virginia Military Institute (VMI). Over the next two years, Roelker's parents wrote frequently to the superintendent, General Scott Shipp. Mrs. Roelker assured him she would "spare no effort" to see that Edward qualified for the Naval Academy. Roelker was doing well in the spring of 1903, and, she informed Superintendent Shipp, she fully intended to take a journey (of close to two hundred miles) to Lexington, Virginia, to provide moral support during his exams. But Roelker's record at VMI was not consistent, and he soon acquired a large number of demerits. Ultimately, his father's navy connections made a difference, and he pulled his son out of VMI in May 1904, to bone up for the Naval Academy exams. Roelker entered the Academy on July 7, 1904, to the great relief of his parents.

Roelker made it through the first year but still found it hard to follow rules; he accumulated 272 demerits for a range of offenses including smoking, playing cards, and disobedience to orders. Jimmie Sutton had left Annapolis in July 1905, and Roelker did not do well during the first semester of his second (third class) year. He performed poorly on his exams in languages and mechanical drawing. But (like Jimmie) he was not asked to leave. Instead, on March 6, 1906, he decided to resign.

Edward Roelker had not given up on the navy nor would his mother have let him. Parthenia had already written the president with good results; on the day after her son left Annapolis, Roosevelt's secretary, William Loeb, instructed Charles Bonaparte that Roelker should be designated to take the next set of examinations for the Marine Corps. The navy sent Mrs. Roelker a circular with a long list of requirements; the academic ones may have been intimidating as they were for Jimmie Sutton. Besides, her son would not be twenty-one until the end of September, so it made sense to have him study in Washington for the rest of the year. He would take the exams right after the holidays on the same day as his former Annapolis classmate. And his mother would follow his progress diligently every step of the way.

Roelker's family navy connections may have been the reason he had not needed outside references to support his candidacy for a Marine Corps commission, but for most applicants that was not the case. In a tiny town eighteen miles from Springfield, Illinois, Emma Hickox Utley began her own personal campaign in the summer of 1906 to see that her son became a marine officer. She was in a tough position. He was her only child (an infant daughter had died in 1884), and her doctor husband, Joseph, suffered from a terminal illness.

Harold Utley's departure from Annapolis had been devastating for him and for his mother. He had not needed a preparatory course to get in; he had performed exceptionally well before graduating as a cadet sergeant from

St. John's Military Academy in Delafield, Wisconsin, in the spring of 1902. He followed the rules, studied hard, and unlike Sutton and Roelker, he was an excellent student in mathematics and in Spanish (all qualities Admiral Roelker hoped Edward would have as a young man). And that fall, as Roelker entered VMI and Jimmie Sutton studied at Portland's new Columbia University, Harold Utley came east from Illinois to start his plebe year at the Naval Academy at the age of sixteen years and five months.

But he had been trying hard to please his parents in a military school with stringent rules at least since the age of fourteen. Once he reached Maryland, he seemed burned out. Most of his classmates were at least a year or two older, and Utley earned one of the lowest scores in efficiency and conduct in the class. He had to repeat his plebe year—a setback that still put him in the Class of 1907, one year ahead of Sutton and Roelker, even though he was a few months younger than they were. It was rough to see his classmates go on ahead; a less determined young man might have resigned. But when the new plebes arrived in the fall of 1903, he could teach them the ropes and even have a slight advantage. By the late spring of 1904, when Sutton and Roelker came in as plebes, Utley had been toughened up by two years of hazing and drills; he was obviously self-assured and arrogant enough to earn the nickname "Highcock" from his peers. His looks helped. Just under six feet tall, trim, with blue eyes, light brown hair, and an extremely handsome face, he had the appearance of a born leader, of a young man with great potential for courage but not necessarily kindness. As a third-class man he relished the opportunity to put the plebes below him in their places by forcing them to do menial chores or engage in fights. He had even reported Roelker for minor infractions. And he had taken an intense dislike to Jimmie Sutton.

Harold Utley was still at the Academy in November of 1905, finally a second-class man, when James Branch died, and his classmates felt bad enough to assure the congressmen that hazing would stop immediately. In the spring of 1907, their senior year, these young men would admit in their yearbook, *Lucky Bag*, that they felt "heavy and heart-sick" about the tragedy and would pass a unanimous but idealistic resolution "to abolish at the United States Naval Academy, absolutely and without reservation, hazing, class fighting, running, fagging, and all similar practices." And then, reminiscing about the old days when they had been third-class men, they reflected on the media sensation created by Branch's tragic fight with Meriwether: "The whole nation was aroused by several incidents of hazing, and was inflamed by the thousand and one yellow journal reports which erred far from the truth. It was like a revolution. Attack followed attack, and to say it mildly we were riddled." But by that time, Utley was no longer a midshipman. Unlike Sutton and Roelker who had resigned, he was dismissed in 1906 after failing two exams. His worried mother would try to explain her son's failure to the Navy Department while doing everything she could to ensure his future. Her correspondence with the Department of the Navy reveals the enormous personal stake she had in Harold's career, as well as a protective streak that may have encouraged his egotistical self-image.

Her family had superb connections, and Emma Utley did not hesitate to use them. In July, this forty-nine-year-old housewife began writing her friends and relatives. As soon as Harold completed his application for the Corps, the Honorable Shelby Moore Cullom, who had been governor of Illinois and one of the nation's most distinguished senators since 1883, wrote directly to "Navy Secretary Charles Bonapart [*sic*]" stating how anxious he was that Utley be given an opportunity to take the exams. Senator Cullom reminded the secretary that he had met Mrs. Utley in person, and he appealed to Bonaparte's empathy. "His mother, whom you remember as visiting your office with me, is a very excellent lady, and is wholly depending upon her son for future support and care." Within two days the secretary had turned the letter over to Truman Newberry, the assistant secretary, "charged with the duty of making up this list of designations from the large number of applications received"; and the following day, August 1, writing from Watch Hill, Rhode Island, Newberry assured the senator that Harold Utley would be permitted to take the examination. But Emma Utley did not know that yet, and she and her friends wanted to be positive the Department knew what a splendid young man Harold was.

Harold Utley's application had already gone in with references from three naval officers, including Commander Frank Bartlett; two more would write before he took his exams. Then, during the first two weeks of August, Senator Cullom's son-in-law, William B. Ridgely, president of the Ridgely National Bank in Springfield; Joseph Cannon, Speaker of the House; and Senator Albert J. Hopkins, chairman of the Committee on Fisheries, added their endorsements. (Hopkins' letter was quite perfunctory.) Ridgely had known the Utley family for decades. "They are excellent people, and have all occupied responsible and prominent positions in this community." Other men would agree with his statement that Harold Utley had "good habits and high character." What is clear from all the support he garnered is that Utley was intelligent and had the potential to be an effective officer in the Marine Corps. According to the president of St. John's Military Academy, who also wrote on Utley's behalf, he was "a gentleman born."

Despite all these endorsements, at the beginning of August 1906, Emma Utley still held out hope that her son might have a chance to return to the Academy. On August 3, she wrote a lengthy explanation to Truman Newberry about her family's predicament. Apparently, she blamed herself for failing to tell the Academy's Academic Board that on May 8, before he took his final exams, "while stationed 150 feet above deck," Utley had "been hurled 20 feet higher by the haste or ignorance of a Fourth Classman [sic] and while suffering no physical injury, did sustain a severe nervous shock, and has been troubled with nervous headaches frequently due to this shock." As a consequence, she explained to Newberry, her already slender son lost eighteen pounds. But he never complained and was not worried about the exams. On the day of his physics exam he was plagued by another "blinding headache" and took the exam anyway. "He needed so little to be safe," Mrs. Utley pleaded. Instead, he learned he had failed physics just as he was about to take the mechanics exam. Emma Utley thought it only just that her son have another chance, and, she said, "it is hard to give up a career he is so well fitted for by nature." Her son was despondent and "suspense was hard for him to bear" in his present state of unhappiness; if he lost any more weight brooding about his future, she was afraid he would fail the Marine Corps physical exam. Please, she entreated, might the secretary give her some good news soon.

Harold Utley was still living in Annapolis on November 24 when he finally heard from Brigadier General Commandant George Elliott that the next examinations for the Marine Corps would take place on January 15. When he arrived at the Washington Headquarters at Eighth and I, he may have recognized at least two other men in the room—Jimmie Sutton and Red Roelker. Out of a group of about fifty candidates who had made it this far, only eleven men would pass both the mental and physical exams that winter. It would take eight weeks for them to be notified. On March 21, 1907, Jimmie Sutton, Edward Roelker, and Harold Utley were among the small group who executed their oaths of office as second lieutenants in the United States Marine Corps. Their commissions would officially be registered by the adjutant and inspector's office on March 23; their mothers could now at long last breathe sighs of relief.

Colonel Charles Doyen was in charge of the newly minted second lieutenants who arrived at the Marine Corps Barracks and Application School that April. A dedicated career officer, the forty-eight-year-old New Hampshire native was in his element. He had been in the Corps for twenty-four years, graduating from the Naval Academy in 1881 and serving in the Spanish-American War and in the Philippines. And he was already familiar with many of his students, at least by reputation. On the day of their exams, he was president of the Marine Examining Board. But Colonel Doyen's tenure at the school had an unexpectedly rough beginning. He had long been troubled by health problems—some of them self-induced. Between 1889 and 1899 his medical records indicate he frequently sought help on board ship for excesses in eating and drinking, "errors in diet," and debility attributed to "debauch." Plagued by alcoholism that ultimately damaged his liver, he assured the Marine Examining Board in March 1900 he would not drink again. And he proved to be a good officer; by 1898 he had become a captain and by 1905 a lieutenant colonel.

Doyen's health deteriorated again just as he took over the Application School in 1907. He spent a discouraging thirty-seven days (May 18 to June 24) at the Naval Academy Hospital, while his wife, Claude Fay Doyen, and two children settled into their new quarters—one of three spacious residences east of the barracks allocated for senior officers. Doyen did not see much of the students during their first two months in Annapolis and turned his duties over temporarily to a skilled officer, Major Benjamin Fuller. Ever vigilant about his own reputation and that of his men, he did have some guidance for Major Fuller.

To supplement the official course of instruction, Doyen created his own fifty-one "Regulations for Student Officers" that covered every detail of daily life. Upon first reporting for duty, the lieutenants had five days to call upon the superintendent of the Naval Academy—in this case Charles Badger. Because of the rivalry among students at the Academy and the Marine Corps school, one rule stated that no midshipmen were allowed within the limits of the camp, nor were marine student officers permitted to join the Naval Academy Club. Tobacco was permitted in most circumstances, and understandably, given his own history, Doyen insisted, "no wines or liquors of any kind" were allowed in student quarters. The rooms (or tents) were spartan, with no pictures or decorations allowed; swords hung at the foot of the men's beds, and their rifles were slung from the right side with butts toward the head. A surprising number of rules focused on "attention to the little points of etiquette"—even at meals in the general mess, the new officers were expected to observe "the ordinary rules for polite society." And, Doyen emphasized, the "senior officer present in quarters will be held strictly accountable for any undue noise or disturbance in camp or quarters." It remained to be seen how many of these regulations would be taken to heart by the young lieutenants in the summer and fall of 1907.

Major Fuller had the task of seeing that Doyen's rules were followed; with his commanding officer in the hospital, he would be in full charge of the Marine Corps Barracks and the school until June 23. The son of a federal circuit court judge from Big Rapids, Michigan, Fuller had been a mere fifteen-year-old boy when he entered the Naval Academy in 1885; he graduated in 1889, and over the next half century he would devote his life to the navy and the Marine Corps. He took the first course offered at the School of Application, which was then at the Marine Barracks at Eighth and I Streets in Washington, D.C. By May 1907, at the age of thirty-seven, he was a major and an instructor.

Lieutenants Sutton, Roelker, and Utley had come on board while Fuller was at the helm. They now found themselves in a pastoral setting, thankfully away from the construction of new buildings across College Creek that had long disrupted life at the Naval Academy. Five days a week the men studied field engineering, infantry, gunnery, military law, minor tactics, hygiene and sanitation (including first-aid to the wounded), and signaling. Saturday mornings were allocated to drills and exercises. The course was rigorous, filled with recitations and frequent exams, but during the summer months there would be breaks from the routine, and the atmosphere was quite relaxed. The men had more time to enjoy the historic town not far from their quarters and spent many evenings at Carvel Hall. This grand hotel had been the center of social life in Annapolis for tourists as well as for Naval Academy men and their families since 1903. At various points during the summer, trips of several days each to Norfolk and Camp Admiral Harrington in Williamsburg, Virginia, for target practice, and to Camp Perry in Ohio for the National Rifle Matches, would give the student officers a change of scene, though not much relief from the heat that the cooler scenic views from the docks in Annapolis provided.

During the first two months of the school session, Benjamin Fuller had a chance to size up the eleven officers who had arrived in April—and they got to know each other. It was not a group that could easily form a cohesive unit. The men came from nine states, Massachusetts, New York, New Jersey, Pennsylvania, Maryland, Arkansas, Ohio, Illinois, and Oregon, and, with Edward Roelker, the District of Columbia. No one except Lieutenant Sutton had lived west of Chicago. And there was quite a discrepancy in their ages. The officers were all born between 1880 and 1885, but most were two to five years older than the lieutenants who had been at the Naval Academy together. Several had spent time in universities such as Harvard, Penn, the Massachusetts Institute of Technology, Ohio Northern University, and the University of Maryland. Defying precedent, one of the men, twenty-seven-year-old Howard Judson, was married. Height was so important to them that the men recorded it on their application forms to an eighth of an inch; that spring Jimmie Sutton was definitely the shortest man in the class.

For Benjamin Fuller (and Charles Doyen when he returned from the hospital), what mattered most was these men's performance. In May and June, Major Fuller would fill out their "fitness reports," evaluations that would stay in their files for their entire careers and could determine their chances for promotion. Harold Utley made a good impression right away, and Fuller gave him excellent marks for the period between April 19 and June 23. He had the right attitude, conduct, and bearing. After four years at the Naval Academy, Utley knew how to survive both socially and academically—and this time he would not let his mother down. His evaluation only dropped slightly to "very good" when the men were at Camp Admiral Harrington during the first two weeks of July.

Lieutenant Sutton's fellow students were more sophisticated and more seasoned than he was. He appeared insecure and vulnerable at the start of the term. At first Major Fuller found his conduct and bearing only "tolerable" and explained, "This officer while intelligent and capable is inattentive and not industrious, does not profit by instruction and appears to be of the opinion that having received his commission, no other effort is necessary." On May 5, Sutton missed roll call and was confined to the barracks for six days. His one serious infraction occurred on May 20 when his cowboy instincts got the better of him again; he was slightly intoxicated, fired some shots in the air, then threatened to make two other officers dance with what was by then an unloaded gun—one of these men was Harold Utley. Fuller suspended Sutton for ten days "for being under the influence of liquor and making a disturbance in camp about 11 P.M." He apparently had learned his lesson and apologized the next day. He had shown "no inclination towards serious misbehavior" before then, nor did he afterward, according to Fuller. But the incident got him off to a bad start, and the immaturity and bravado he had shown would come back to haunt him—even after he died.

When Colonel Doyen returned to command the barracks and the school at the end of June, the young men under his charge were well into their course—with the exception of two men from Pennsylvania who arrived in July; both had passed their mental exams in January but had "physical defects" that needed to be corrected before they could become marines. Twenty-six-year-old Edwin McClellan came in with superb references from the University of Pennsylvania and with strong support from Senator

P. C. Knox, chairman of the committee on coast defenses. Despite the senator's best efforts, and the written statements from two Philadelphia doctors, the Marine Corps would not accept McClellan until he had surgery for hemorrhoids. Once he did join the school, he apparently learned quickly that "nobody else around the camp" was on good terms with Sutton and that if he became friends with Sutton he would not be popular with them. He had barely settled into the routine when another Pennsylvanian that he had known at the university, Robert Adams, finally arrived to bring the number of students at the school to thirteen. He would have the most to lose after the death of James N. Sutton.

According to the pastor of his church, Robert Adams had "dreamed all his life of a naval career." Like that of Harold Utley, Adams' candidacy had been sponsored by some of the most prominent citizens in the capitol of his state, in this case Harrisburg, Pennsylvania. And both of the new officers had faced their share of tragedy at home. By the time Robert was born, his father, Civil War veteran William J. Adams, had a successful furniture business in Harrisburg and had become active in city government. But when Robert was not yet three years old, William's wife, Emma Welker Adams, died (possibly in childbirth), leaving him with an infant and five other children. A year later he married Harriet (Hattie) Mann who would raise Emma's children and her own two daughters by William as well. Robert Adams was at a vulnerable age when he lost his mother, and tragedy struck his family again in the middle of the winter of 1897: His father died of a heart attack.

William's children, now orphaned, were totally dependent on the good graces of their stepmother and the bond they shared with each other. From then on, the male head of the family was Robert's brother George, fourteen years his senior and a partner in his father's business since 1891. Robert's first inquiry letter to the Marine Corps, on October 24, 1905, went in on George Adams' letterhead, "Dealer in Fine Furniture, Carpets and Bedding." After learning about all the requirements, Robert finally filled in his application the following May 26. One of his many endorsements came from J. C. Delaney, the chief inspector of factories for the state. Adams, he said, is the "true type of young American manhood" that should be in our army and navy. "He is finely educated, splendid physique, temperate, moral and of real good family."

Adams described himself as five feet, eleven inches tall, with brown hair and gray eyes. A stocky man with broad shoulders and a moon-shaped face, Adams had been at the University of Pennsylvania between September 1902 and May 1904 studying chemistry and playing football. Only a credible student, he was a superb athlete who had made the varsity swimming team, the track team, and the baseball team; he had won a fifty-yard novice race and second place in the hammer throw at the freshman-sophomore track meet. But after his sophomore year he left the university.

Adams and his family knew the competition for a Marine Corps commission was fierce even for a member of one of Harrisburg's oldest families. His recommendations reveal the breadth of his widowed stepmother's connections almost ten years after the death of her husband and those of the rest of his relatives as well. His primary sponsor appears to have been Congressman Marlin E. Olmstead, chairman of the House Committee on Elections; a letter sure to attract notice was a short note endorsing Robert Adams over the huge signature of Governor Samuel Pennypacker. Adams not only qualified, but also he had scored third on the Marine Corps mental exams in January, according to Congressman Olmstead. However, despite his "splendid physique," Adams' physical exam was both disappointing and a bit embarrassing. The surgeon suggested he have an operation for a slight varicocele (an enlarged vein in the scrotum) that could cause pain and infertility. The recovery took longer than expected, putting the robust young athlete in an awkward and frustrating position.

Finally, on July 19, 1907, Adams reported for instruction at the Marine Barracks in Annapolis. Coming in three months after the session started left him behind in the class work and at a considerable social disadvantage. He was painstaking by nature and unsure exactly how he would fit in among the other marines. Jimmie Sutton was one of the first men to reach out to Adams, trying to be helpful. They even "made a call on a girl together." But their camaraderie would not last long. Within a matter of days, Adams would be warned by his University of Pennsylvania friend, Edwin McClellan, to stay away from Sutton if he wanted to make it in this particular group of men.

Over the course of the summer, Jimmie Sutton's one close friend at the Marine Corps Application School appears to have been Edward Roelker. His attempts at befriending Adams and McClellan failed, and his relationship with a few of the other men apparently had gone from bad to worse by September. Earlier that summer he had written home, according to his mother, that he had conquered himself and nothing ever upset him now. But he also told her he "never had to mix with such cads as were in his class and they call themselves gentlemen. You try to think they are and in the next moment they spoil it with some cadish trick but I don't say anything

I keep my opinion to myself." Nevertheless, Jimmie stayed the course, earned a "very good" rating on his fitness report and won a medal for sharp-shooting. His younger brother, Don, who had recently completed his junior year at Portland High School, was waiting to hear whether or not he had made it into West Point, and Jimmie took his role as a mentor seriously. On July 27, he wrote his brother one of two surviving letters that shed light on his own personality and family life.

> My Dear Don,
>
> I am mighty glad to hear you are out in the open and doing something in line of a vacation. It will do you more good than anything. Don't get homesick now and go chasing back to Portland before you have made a start. Put in a couple or three months at it. It will do you a lot of good, boy. You will want to save up enough money to carry you through school next year and buy yourself some good clothes etc. Say you work two months and then go home and get straightened out a bit, and then before school starts you ought to take a little trip somewhere. Not much, you know but just get on the train and go. You are old enough to take care of yourself now and ugly enough as well. Do you smoke or drink any? Well, if you do, don't let it get away with you.
>
> Let kid nonsense and childishness go. Don't expect people to take care of you and help you out and you won't be disappointed; and above all, when you give your word of honor to any one, why, walk across hell on a rotten rail to keep it if necessary. Don't you tell a lie for the best man or woman going, Don. If you do, by God you lose me. Now that you are getting older, I am looking on you as a pal and not as a kid brother. When we get together we ought to be able to make a team that will show them a bit or two.
>
> Your loving brother, JIM

On September 3, Jimmie told his family, "'I have taken out insurance ($3500) in the Navy mutual aid. It is cheap and sure. It is run by the Navy department and the funds are in the U.S. Treasury. Only Naval and Marine officers can join. It is made out to you and dad. I'll send you the certificate later.'" The next day, he and two other officers, Rex Ludlow and Robert Adams, were confined to their post for one week for being absent from a setting-up exercise. Right after the confinement, Jimmie requested duty in the Philippines. By September 30, he had written his father that some of the men "were out to get him," but reassured him, "I will give them a good tussle and show them that I am right there." His prospects changed a few days later; Jimmie was thrilled to learn that his orders were not just to go to the Philippines but on the highly publicized cruise of what would be known as Theodore Roosevelt's Great White Fleet—"the dream of his life" had finally come true.

The first decade of the twentieth century was an era of intense patriotism, inspired in part by the president himself. Following the Spanish-American War, America's navy and Marine Corps were key to the security of her new possessions in the Philippines, Guam, Cuba, and Puerto Rico. By 1907, Roosevelt had launched a plan to ensure that the United States was not left behind in the naval arms race among Great Britain, Germany, and Japan for control of the seas. On December 16, sixteen steel battleships would leave from Hampton Roads, Virginia, for a voyage around Cape Horn to San Francisco. (The Panama Canal would not be completed until 1914.) *Western Life* described these "heavy-weight sea warriors" as "not only the most formidable Fleet ever assembled under the stars and stripes, but probably it surpasses in magnitude any naval fleet ever dispatched by any foreign power upon a cruise of like length." Initially publicized as a voyage to the west coast, the fleet would actually travel on a world cruise. From California it would cross the Pacific to Australia and New Zealand, then head for the Philippines and Yokohama. Japan had stunned the world with her victories in the Russo-Japanese War in 1905 and was now a force to be reckoned with. After the Japanese witnessed the magnitude of American sea power first hand, the fleet would then turn south, winding its way through the China Sea, the Indian Ocean, the Red Sea, the Suez Canal, and the Mediterranean before turning home. For much of 1907, newspapers forecast the plans for this voyage, and reporters would follow it at every port.

On Thursday evening, October 10, Jimmie Sutton wrote to his mother to tell her his exciting news. "My dear Mum," he began, already assuming the mind set of a sailor, "Well, here is good luck to yez, and hoping you are all shipshape." His eight handwritten pages were characteristically thoughtful; clearly aware the letter would be shared, he mentioned each member of his family. He thanked Rosa for sending a photograph, which had appeared in the *Oregonian*, of his oldest sister, Rose, saying, "She looked right pretty in the picture the paper had." He sent a message to Daysie, referring to her as "a foin girl." Jimmie's paycheck helped the family pay for Louise's Catholic school, and he apologized because he would be late in sending the money home. And he asked whether or not Don had been accepted at West Point because "it's getting late in the game." Jimmie also promised to write his father soon with pictures from the local newspapers. At the end of the letter, he commented on Portland's politics and asked for an introduction to Oregon senator Jonathan Bourne who had sponsored Don for the Military Academy. But most of the letter was "the new dope" about his trip:

> I'll be detached from here (along with others) about the first of December and be sent to a battleship for the cruise around the Horn. If that is the case I shall not have the unbounded pleasure of seeing you all until next year sometime. I suppose you want lots of pretty things from South America etc. Well, I'll be able (better) to purchase more this time and bring the junk home. Shawls, skins, and such wonderful jewels that old Sinbad the Sailor would feel like a piker if he could see them. Sounds like the "wild dream of a rarebit fiend" doesn't it?

"I am feeling fine and frisky these days, mum," he said in the final paragraph. "Am going to sit for a picture next Saturday, and will send probably a week later. . . . Hoping that this finds you all well and happy, I remain, with love to all, your loving son, Jim." He mailed this letter on Friday morning, October 11, and looked ahead to spending time with new friends over the weekend. But within thirty-six hours Jimmie Sutton would be dead.

3

"SISTER COMING FOR REMAINS"

In August of 1907, *Western Life* described itself as a brand new "High-Class Monthly Magazine, devoted to the Interests of the West and the Western Home." Portland, Oregon, the "New York of the Pacific," would be the subject of one of its first features. Portland's location at the confluence of two rivers, one the "magnificent Columbia, draining more territory than any other river in the United States excepting the Mississippi," made the area an ideal place to work and live. Surrounded by hills and a continental mountain range dominated by Mount Hood, the city also hugged the west bank of the Willamette. E. C. Giltner, the enthusiastic secretary of the Chamber of Commerce, assured would-be settlers who read the magazine that snow-capped peaks provided a "never failing supply of pure water for drinking . . . and will furnish power sufficient to run the machinery of every factory that will be erected for many years," and, he added, enough power to "light all our cities." Giltner also boasted that Portland's waterways made her "the only freshwater harbor of any consequence on the Pacific Coast." Ships from across the globe unloaded cargo at the city docks, while northwest products such as wheat and lumber went from Portland to places as far away as Asia and South America." The city's population would almost double between 1905 and 1909, reaching more than 207,000 people.

Portland residents enjoyed their cosmopolitan city—quite refined despite acrid smells, heavy dust, and the grating sounds of construction, clanging trolley cars, horse-drawn fire engines that raced over cobblestone streets, and steam engines chugging into the Union Depot. Bicycles were still by far the quietest form of transportation, and automobiles were not yet a threat to cyclists or to carriages and horses. In all of Oregon there were only 218 automobiles in 1905 (40 in Portland); the number would increase to 552 by 1909. Another contemporary, journalist Ray Stannard Baker, compared the city to parts of Manhattan: "a square with the post office in the center, tree shaded streets, comfortable homes, and plenty of churches and clubs, the signs of conservatism and solid respectability. And yet no decay." Baker praised the city's financial institutions, its "fine clubs and hotels, its good schools and libraries." Her mild climate would also make Portland the "Rose City," unrivaled for her rich-scented flowers in various sizes and colors that lined the sidewalks and filled gardens everywhere, "all the well known desirable varieties being grown." The year 1907 would be remembered as the year of Portland's first Rose Festival—promoters claimed it would soon eclipse other festivals with the "bewildering profusion and magnificence" of its flowers.

But there was a seamier side to the vibrant river port. Known as a wide-open city filled with licensed gambling and prostitution, Portland "'had become a popular headquarters for all the vicious characters in the Pacific Northwest.'" After many years under the control of the Republican Party machine, the victory of a Democrat in the race for mayor, environmentalist Harry Lane, seemed to many residents to signal a new beginning.

Panorama of Portland, Oregon, ca. 1908. Courtesy of the Oregon Historical Society, #OrHi67370.

Lane took office in June 1905, with the opening of the Lewis and Clark Centennial Exposition; it was a time when Portland "caught the attention of the world." "Westward the Course of Empire Takes Its Way," declared the motto over the entrance to the fair. "Before the Exposition was a month old, Portlanders were certain that it marked [the] beginning of a new, hopeful era when the big things seemed to go right." The "Great Extravaganza" drew three million people to the city, one reason the population began to grow so fast. The summer of 1905 had been an exuberant and magical time—especially for Rosa Sutton; after almost two years in Annapolis, her oldest son had returned home for the remainder of the year.

During July and August, Jimmie's family explored the exhibits from across the world. Along Lewis and Clark Boulevard, a European Exhibits Building highlighted the accomplishments of the industrial age and complemented an elaborate million-dollar exhibition from Japan. Nearby, huge whitewashed buildings were devoted to manufactures and liberal arts, or agriculture and horticulture. With thousands of other Oregonians, the Suttons could marvel at sunken gardens, wide walkways lit by electric globes, elaborate fireworks, and carnival attractions. Several exhibits had been planned to instill pride in the citizens of the Pacific Northwest. An enormous Forestry Building, constructed of giant logs with the bark left on, sparkled with light bulbs that were especially enchanting at night. Displays of all kinds of lumber as well as mounted elk, bear, varieties of birds, and a panther killing a five-point deer amazed Portland natives and tourists. Elsewhere along "The Trail," tourists might buy nougat candy, relax at a French café, sample a roast beef sandwich, try their hand at a shooting gallery, or wander through a maze of mirrors, a haunted castle, or the "streets of Cairo." Baby incubators, live fish, slot machines, diving elks, a temple of mirth, balloon rides, and an Indian village astonished curious children and their harried parents. The exposition remained open until mid-October, providing many attractions for the Suttons and their extended family and friends; they could celebrate when a portrait of Jimmie's sister Rose won first prize in a photography exhibit. No one could have imagined that the summer and fall of 1905 was the last time they would all be together. That December, Jimmie had left for Washington to prepare for his Marine Corps exams.

For more than two weeks after he died, Rosa and Jim Sutton heard few official details about the fate of their son. And the family's other information came from two questionable sources: Rosa's inexplicable visions and accounts that appeared in local newspapers. On Monday, October 14, while the last witnesses testified at the naval inquest, the Suttons woke up to this headline in the *Oregonian*: "NAVAL OFFICER SHOOTS HIMSELF." The story came by dispatch "from the best obtainable information" and appeared next to a column about the impending world cruise of Theodore Roosevelt's battleship fleet, a big topic in the national press that week. Jimmie's family had not yet learned what a sad coincidence it was that their late son's high school photo appeared in the center of the fleet's itinerary.

By Monday evening, *Oregon Daily Journal* readers may have been less certain about the events surrounding Lieutenant Sutton's death. "BULLET IN HIS BRAIN" ran the headline followed by the statement that Lieutenant Sutton had been shot "under mysterious circumstances at Annapolis." And the portrait of Jimmie that emerged in the Oregon press was quite different from that in eastern papers. "Young Sutton," said the *Oregonian*, "was of a cheerful lighthearted disposition and was extremely popular at the Naval Academy." These sentiments were echoed in the *Portland Evening Telegram*. A reporter had spoken with Mrs. Sutton, who assured him that Jimmie was "always of a cheerful, happy, optimistic disposition" and "always frank with us about all his personal affairs. We expect to hear that his death was due to some accident." It was clear that a family member needed to travel East, and the Suttons' oldest daughter volunteered to help. Jim Sutton sent a return telegram to the Marine Corps that arrived in Washington at close to 10:00 p.m. Eastern time on October 13: "PLEASE WIRE PARTICULARS SUTTON S DEATH PREPARE BODY AND HOLD. SISTER COMING FOR REMAINS."

Twenty-seven-year-old Rose Beatrice Sutton Parker was a petite and slender brunette with unusually large dark brown eyes framed by a porcelain complexion. Married for six years to Army First Lieutenant Hugh Almer Parker, she often became restless with military life and was grateful to her husband for indulging her interest in travel, study, and writing. Hugh Parker was stationed in Guantanamo Bay in 1907, but Rose could not stand the oppressive Cuban climate. At the beginning of August, she had returned to her family's new home in Portland for a visit that would last several months. When her brother died, she was in the middle of a lawsuit for fifty thousand dollars against the Hicks-Chatten Engraving Company, which advertised itself in *Western Life* as "the largest engraving plant in the west." A story in the *Oregonian* on October 1 said, "because of her beauty," the company had used a prize-winning photograph of Rose from Portland's 1905 Exposition in advertisements. "'This publicity, that has been thrust upon me,'" Rose allegedly told the reporter, "'is something that any woman who wants only a quiet home life and her circle of friends would naturally avoid at

Rose Sutton Parker. Sutton Family Papers.

almost any cost.'" Rose and her family were apparently insulted by the use of her image to make money, but a "quiet home life," would elude her for much of the next two years.

On Sunday afternoon Rose sent her own wire to Annapolis to ask for details about her brother's death. "Coming immediately," she informed a Marine Corps captain. She received a response from Captain Badger that her brother "shot himself, dying immediately. . . . Investigation in progress, full particulars not yet known." He agreed to delay the interment and asked to know her wishes for the disposition of her brother's body. She notified Badger on Monday afternoon that she would depart that night; the Navy Department should "hold body until I arrive."

For those who could afford a Pullman sleeping car or parlor car, a trip across North America would take six days on Union Pacific trains. Rose probably took the "Portland–Chicago special" which claimed to have "no superior among transcontinental fliers." The first part of the trip, eighty-eight miles between Portland and The Dalles, gave her a spectacular view of forests, mountains, and streams as well as the Columbia River from her window. At Huntington, "without change of car," she could make a direct connection to the Oregon Short Line Railroad, which would take her through Salt Lake City, Denver, Omaha, Kansas City, and on to Chicago in just under seventy hours. On this leg of the journey, Rose had a puzzling dream: Jimmie appeared in a white shirt and told her he had been struck unconscious in the back of the head before he woke up in eternity. Not at all accustomed to the premonitions and dreams that plagued her mother, Rose wrote her parents to tell them about it. While she took a second sleeper from Chicago to the nation's capital, residents of Washington and Annapolis had begun to mull over the newly published findings of the navy's inquest board.

In 1907, suggestions that mysterious circumstances surrounded the lieutenant's death did not cause a scandal; few people questioned the navy. A bank panic in New York, diplomatic crises between the United States and Japan, Roosevelt's plans for his Fleet, and his exploits bear hunting in Louisiana (during the week Sutton died) preoccupied reporters. By the time Rose Parker's train reached Washington, the case, it seemed, had been put to rest. The *Evening Capital* mentioned (in error) that she was expected to carry her brother's body back to his former home.

Rose telephoned Colonel Doyen as soon as she arrived in Washington on Saturday, October 19. She would journey to Annapolis by train to meet him the following day. During her eight days in the East, Rose became familiar with the places and the men who had been part of her brother's life;

Main Street, looking West from Market Place,
Annapolis, Md.

View of Annapolis, ca. 1908. Main Street from Market Space toward Church Circle. Courtesy of the Maryland State Archives Special Collections (Mame Warren Collection), unknown photographer. MSA SC 985-1-116.

she formed her first impressions of a town known in the eighteenth century as the "Athens of America," and to her contemporaries as the "Venice of the Chesapeake." Coming from a bustling city and international port, she now found herself in a charming, slower-paced seaport with fewer than ten thousand people, whose residents had greeted Mark Twain earlier that year with their customary "placid dignity." Yet the area had grown considerably in its past quarter century. By 1896, eight bridges linked the Annapolis peninsula to the surrounding countryside. A reporter noted with pride that the new Annapolis was no longer a "sleepy town," and a "colonial fossil of decay and dilapidation." At the turn of the last century, it had "a uniformed police, electric light and gas, extensive waterworks, water which analysis shows to be second only in purity among the cities of the country, telegraph and telephone, and railroad communications maintained by twelve trains daily," all signs of great progress. Automobiles, referred to as "machines," still frightened country folk and horses; and, as in Portland, bicycling remained extremely popular for men and women.

Captain Arthur Marix was very familiar with the Sutton case when he met Rose Parker at the Annapolis station on Sunday, October 20. Third in command at the Marine Corps Application School, he had been one of Jimmie's instructors; Marix and Harold Utley had served as a "Board of Inventory" that sorted through her brother's possessions. As he escorted Rose to his home, Rose may well have wanted to see where her brother died. If so, they would drive through part of the Naval Academy across College Creek en route to the senior officers' quarter to pass the very spot where Jimmie Sutton took a bullet in his brain. Marix's quarters would likely have been near those of Charles Doyen, in one of the three homes with gracious verandas east of the barracks, architecturally not unlike 784 Hoyt Street, though quite a bit grander.

Charles Doyen was close to her mother's age, and he greeted Mrs. Parker warmly and with respect. But she had come close to three thousand miles to see Jimmie, and her heart sank when both men advised her not to view his body. Colonel Doyen described the condition of his bandaged forehead, the lump under his jaw, his swollen lips, and the bruised and discolored condition of his face. Even his "nose seemed to be a little bit to one side." Doyen said he thought "it would be very much nicer" for Rose "not to remember Jimmie as he then looked." Arthur Marix added that Lieutenant Sutton was "a very stern looking fellow." When Rose told him she was not afraid to see Jimmie looking stern, he said "worse than stern." And so, reluctantly, she took their warnings to heart.

After their meeting, Captain Marix escorted Rose off the Naval Academy grounds into the town that had been the capital of Maryland since 1695. Over the course of the next several days, Rose would be surrounded by large shade trees, prosperous looking shops, and the mix of colonial and Victorian architecture that lined the cobblestone streets. From almost everywhere, she could see the dome of the State House that towered over the ubiquitous row-house chimneys with the same authoritative bearing the Washington monument held over its city thirty-four miles away. The spires of close to a dozen churches and chapels also punctuated the skyline; one of the most graceful was that of the Victorian gothic Church of St. Mary's, on Duke of Gloucester Street, about a twenty-minute walk from the massive Naval Academy chapel with its landmark dome that was still under construction in 1907. Built on the property of Charles Carroll of Carrollton, the only Catholic signer of the Declaration of Independence, St. Mary's was undoubtedly where Jimmie had gone to church and a place that Rose would visit.

Perhaps no structure in Annapolis symbolized the merging of old and new as much as Carvel Hall where Rose stayed, a place so familiar to her brother and his friends. The hotel had two entrances—one on Prince George Street—the red brick mansion built in 1765 for former Maryland governor William Paca. The second entrance—barely five years old—faced King George Street; it led to the central area of the massive new building now attached to the Paca house. Wings for two hundred rooms stretched outward on either side toward the Academy. Carvel Hall's large assembly room was furnished with divans and chairs set up in cozy seating arrangements. Rose had been assigned a combination bedroom and sitting room on the Prince George Street side of the hotel, "to the right of the office as you go in." It was a small room furnished with enameled white wicker, a place where she might focus on the funeral arrangements for Jimmie. She had already wired a friend in New York with enough influence to help her obtain a grave site at Arlington Cemetery. She knew that a priest would not bury a man who had committed suicide, and she did not want her family to "suffer the indignity" of having him refused a place in the family plot in Portland.

That Sunday afternoon, Rose reportedly went to the Marine Corps Barracks where the casket of her brother was "lying in state." When she entered the dimly lit room she almost tripped over "a little girl" who was kneeling down and praying earnestly near the head of the casket. She had a rosary in her hands as she murmured prayers for the dead. Rose's unexpected arrival caused the young Japanese woman to jump in surprise. Rose learned from Mrs. Doyen that Ulsin had been brought from Asia by the colonel and his wife to be educated. They had given her "the practical duties of governess of their two children." To Rose, so the story goes, Ulsin appeared to be "the one person who manifested real grief because of my brother's death." Jimmie had apparently befriended Ulsin after running into her on his way to the barracks from the student officers' camp. When Ulsin's own mother died, Jimmie taught her to say her prayers and helped her "become a convert to the Catholic Church." Colonel Doyen had told Ulsin she could not attend the funeral for fear she would create a scene. But she had picked the wild flowers that were on his casket.

On learning of Mrs. Parker's imminent arrival, undertaker Raymond Taylor had finished his job that weekend. With an assistant, he had dressed Sutton's body for burial in clothing picked out by Arthur Marix and Harold Utley: socks, a suit of underclothes, Sutton's undress blue uniform, a set of collar devices, a pair of cuffs, and two shirt buttons. By then the officer's limbs were "exceedingly rigid," and Taylor had to split his jacket in the back in order to get it on over his arms. On Monday morning, while Navy Chaplain Henry H. Clark conducted a brief service, Rose was truly alone. A few moments after she sat down, she noticed that the last person to arrive was a young officer in full dress blues wearing his saber. He took a spot at the end of a bench, and, Rose recalled, "he never took his eyes off of me the whole time. He kept staring at me and we sat looking at each other across the coffin . . . and I knew perfectly well there was some reason for it." Rose did not know his name, but she was sure he could tell her something about her brother's death.

After the brief service, noncommissioned Marine Corps officers escorted Jimmie's body to the Annapolis station. Major Fuller commanded the funeral cortege, a small procession that included two companies of marines and the Naval Academy band; the marines fired a volley from their rifles, and readers of the *Evening Capital* would learn that the young officer "who committed suicide last Sunday morning by shooting himself . . . was escorted to the station with military honors." Rose then traveled with the coffin to Washington where, "shortly after two o'clock," body bearers from the Marine Corps Barracks and a detachment of field artillery men from Fort Myers moved her brother to a hillside at Arlington Cemetery; there were no other graves nearby in the "Southern division, officers' section."

On this chilly October afternoon, Rose Sutton Parker was the only family member to hear trumpeter Sam Nolan play the mournful sound of taps at Jimmie's grave. A *Washington Post* reporter observed, "No salute was fired and no service was read" at Arlington. The unadorned government-issued marker of white granite held no dates—only the inscription "Lot 2102 Jas. N Sutton Lieut. U.S.M.C." Rose made sure that roses, chrysanthemums, and daisies covered the lonesome grave. Dwarfing the headstone behind it, a wreath stood propped against a stand encircling the word "DAD." Below it, on the mound of fresh earth, was a rectangle of large white flowers with the word "MOTHER" at the center. The lower part of the grave was buried under bouquets of assorted flowers. But the site had not been blessed by a priest; eight days after his death, the future of Jimmie Sutton's soul remained very much in doubt.

Rose Parker was after specific information that might exonerate Jimmie from the stigma of suicide. Up to this point, she only knew what she had read in the newspapers or perhaps in the leading chronicle of military affairs at the time, the *Army and Navy Journal*, which summarized the tragedy that weekend. If she saw the article, possibly in the assembly room of Carvel Hall, she read that "according to the evidence upon which the board's findings were based, Lt. Sutton has shown a disposition recently which raised doubts as to his sanity. He quarreled frequently with brother officers and had made threats about shooting somebody." The article also described Jimmie's fate with what would prove to be incorrect informa-

Grave site of James N. Sutton, Arlington National Cemetery, October 1907. New York American *photograph. Courtesy of the Harry Ransom Humanities Research Center, University of Texas at Austin.*

tion. But Rose still did not know much, and she developed a plan to learn more.

On Tuesday, October 22, she returned to the Marine Corps Barracks with Colonel Doyen to claim Jimmie's possessions. On the way to the quartermaster's storeroom, they ran into the officer who had caught her attention at the funeral. Doyen introduced Rose to Lieutenant Robert Adams, and, she later recalled, he "seemed very ill at ease and embarrassed," and "something about his attitude made quite an impression" on her. But she was soon distracted by the task at hand; Lieutenant Harold Utley waited for her with Captain Marix. Rose was startled to learn the two men had already been through Jimmie's tent and compiled an inventory without a family member present. They even made a note that her brother's bank account was overdrawn at the Farmer's National Bank by $7.91. Rose was especially moved when she opened Jimmie's suitcase. While Colonel Doyen, Captain Marix, and Lieutenant Utley watched, she examined the clothes her brother had on when he died: his jacket with its shoulder knot missing on the left side, his muddy shoes, and his full dress trousers with a scarlet stripe on the outer seam of each leg. The sight of them almost broke Rose's heart; they had red mud on the knees, and "the suspenders still fastened to them, and they were just as they had taken them off of him, and his socks were just as they had pulled them off his feet, in little rolls." She also received a gold pocket watch, fob and locket, gold cuff buttons, and a rusty steel blue pistol with a holster and cartridge belt.

One item listed on the inventory was missing—Rose never received Jimmie's shoulder knot. As the wife of an army officer, she no doubt realized that each ornament on a uniform was designed to precise specifications related to the man's rank, as valuable as a prized pin or a ring might be for a woman. Perhaps, she might have thought, it had been stolen. Rose informed the Marine Corps officers that she would take her brother's trunks and suitcase back to Portland, and she had them delivered to Carvel Hall. Convinced that there was more to the story than the official findings, she then asked Colonel Doyen if she could meet the men who had last seen Jimmie alive. He could not order them to come, Doyen replied, but he would suggest that they speak with her. She made a special point of requesting a private interview with Robert Adams.

The following afternoon, several lieutenants converged on Carvel Hall to comply with Rose Parker's request. They came to her quarters two or three at a time. Rose would later admit that she had little confidence in Harold Utley—an impression that was reinforced when he apparently told her, "Mrs. Parker, personally I hated your brother." Her talk with Lieutenant Edward Osterman was more encouraging, even though he had not been present when the final shot was fired. He said he did not dislike her brother and had not intended to get in a fight with him shortly before the fatal brawl. The fight had been "thrust upon him," and he was "very sorry that he had ever had any part in it." At one point, while the lieutenant remained standing at the door for a few minutes by himself, he admitted to Rose that he had not understood why her brother had been so unpopular but said that "there were some officers that did not like him and did not intend to let him be popular." At least that is the way Rose recalled their conversation.

At about four o'clock, Lieutenant Robert Adams arrived unexpectedly, and sent his card to her room. Rose had a feeling that Adams knew more than the others about Jimmie's fate, and she thought if they met privately he would speak more openly. "Naturally," she had assumed, "after having been with a man who had such a tragic death, he probably would tell that man's sister more of it when there were no people around than he would tell before other people." Zeroing in on the task at hand, she put any consideration of her own reputation out of her mind. Rose did not seem to care whether people frowned on an officer spending several hours alone with her in her private quarters.

Lieutenant Adams had been warned by Colonel Doyen that Mrs. Parker was "a shrewd-looking woman," and he was on edge because she had asked to see him alone. As he put down his cape, Rose asked the lieutenant not to spare her feelings. She had not yet seen the inquest testimony, and she had little to go on as she questioned Adams. He reported that Jimmie Sutton was kind to him and even loaned him linens and other articles when he first arrived in Annapolis. Actually, he liked her brother for a few weeks after they met, but "some of the officers had come to him and told him that if he was going to be friends with Sutton he could not be friends with them, that they did not like him." Then, he said, Sutton humiliated him in front of his friends by swearing at him during an artillery drill; the other men had told him "he was a fool" to take it from Sutton; after all, he was not an enlisted man and "ought to knock Sutton's block off." Adams admitted that he had exchanged heated words with him, and though her brother resisted a fight, both he and Osterman had beaten him. Robert Adams also confirmed that Lieutenant Utley had hated Sutton for years. According to Rose, Adams said Harold Utley told him that "Sutton was cocky and had an idea he could lick anybody, and that somebody ought to take it out of him."

Rose took notes when Adams spoke and later recalled that he said he was not sorry he beat up her brother "because I knew that night that if your brother lived my life would not be worth anything." Then, he allegedly told Rose, Jimmie had threatened to kill him; so she warned Adams a jury would not hold him guiltless after these remarks. "Yes," Adams reportedly answered, "But I am not saying it to a jury. I know that if your brother had lived he would have gotten me." He also said, in "a moment of excitement," that "everyone in Annapolis thinks I murdered your brother." Rose tried appealing to Robert Adams' sympathy because she hoped to enlist his help in proving "her brother had been accidentally killed, or anything other than suicide"; she told Adams why—Jimmie was Catholic and as a suicide he would be lost.

Lieutenant Adams would never actually deny making these self-incriminatory statements to Mrs. Parker. But he later claimed to have forgotten much of their conversation. He did admit to telling her Jimmie had a bottle of whiskey, and he thought he'd had several drinks. She asked him what became of the bottle. Adams replied that Captain Marix had taken the whiskey, and a couple of nights after Sutton died, he asked a few of the young officers "to have a drink on Sutton." Adams had appeared at her door just as Rose was about to leave to meet a chemistry and physics professor from St. John's College, B. Vernon Cecil, and an Annapolis doctor, J. J. Murphy, who had waited for her for several hours. So she invited the lieutenant to join her party for dinner. He accepted. Before the evening ended (and after Adams returned to the barracks), Professor Cecil told Rose that he had not heard that Adams murdered her brother, but he had heard that Jimmie "did not commit suicide, and that he was brutally beaten."

Toward the end of her stay in Annapolis, Colonel Doyen lent Rose a copy of the inquest transcript. The large role played by Harold Utley in orchestrating the events that took place before, during, and after her brother's death was immediately apparent as she read it. And Rose was no doubt shocked by the marines' testimony describing the beating Jimmie received from Robert Adams (regardless of who provoked it). It was obvious that the witnesses did not agree about what happened at the moment the final shot was fired. By the time she began her return journey to Portland on Tuesday, October 29, Rose Parker—as she later admitted with a restraint that belied her fury—"was not at all satisfied with the suicide verdict."

Although it was mentioned in the *New York Times*, the death of Lieutenant James N. Sutton attracted interest primarily in Portland, Annapolis, and Washington, D.C. Newspapers had alluded to a mystery surrounding Sutton's death, but most reporters appear to have been appeased by the naval investigation and took little notice of Rose. Few wondered if there were any repercussions to the tragedy within the Corps itself. And once Rose left the area, the lieutenants in Sutton's Marine Corps Application School class probably did not expect to hear from his family again.

In Oregon, Rose's parents and siblings struggled with their heartache, eager for the news she would bring home. Four days after he died, Jimmie's mother received his joyful letter from Annapolis about his upcoming voyage on the Great White Fleet; it was almost more than she could bear. Soon afterward, the Suttons' copy of the October 19 *Army and Navy Journal* arrived in the mail with its harsh evaluation of Jimmie, adding insult to injury. Rose reached Portland in early November with news that seemed to confirm what Jimmie's ghost had told her mother. Rosa was stunned when she began sorting through her son's clothing, books, and papers. She noticed a shoulder knot missing from his jacket, and when Rose handed her Jimmie's watch case, she opened it to find "the crystal was shattered into a hundred pieces." "Jimmie is here, listen to his watch ticking," Rosa re-counted.

> My daughter said, "You are crazy." I said, "Listen," the watch ticked for three minutes (it had stopped at 1.15). Jimmie says, "*that's how long I suf-fered.*" My daughter shook me by the shoulders saying, "Mamma, you have lost your mind." I said, "Listen it's ticking again." It ran two min-utes and stopped at 1.20. Jimmie said, "*That's how much longer I lived.*" The watch was taken to a jeweler and he had difficulty in getting it to run. Afterwards my other son carried it and every night it stopped at 1.20 for a year; at last it was made to run by a New York firm.

Three years later, Jim Sutton recalled, the incident about the watch ticking "when Mrs. Parker returned to Portland with Jimmie's clothing and belongings in his chest," was the most "singular thing of all" to him as he tried to fathom whether his wife's postmortem visits from their son could really have happened.

As Rosa spoke further with her daughter, her confusion and sorrow changed into the clarity and resolve of a mother now enraged. She knew that Rose had to return to her husband, but she had made up her own mind to seek redemption for Jimmie. In the coming weeks, Rosa began a cru-sade that continued throughout the world cruise of Roosevelt's fleet—one that had more significance for the Marine Corps and for the nation than the salvation of Jimmie Sutton's soul.

4

"WE ARE NOT SLEEPING"

When her oldest son died, forty-seven-year-old Rosa Sutton had long since given up the rugged life of her childhood near Fort Vancouver. She had become an urban woman, raising her five children in Portland and Los Angeles, where the family lived between 1890 and 1897. And she visited San Francisco often—not just because it was the center of cultural life in California at the time but also because it was her husband's birthplace. Inspired by her daughter's journey to Annapolis, Rosa spent much of the following year collecting information that would help make a case for a second investigation of Jimmie's death. Over time, she framed her struggle in broader terms, demanding high standards of justice (as she saw it) from the government. Rosa's understanding of her own rights stemmed from American legal culture; the legitimacy of her claims was rooted in the Constitution and the Bill of Rights and in Americans' inborn suspicion of concentrated power. In most respects a traditional Catholic homemaker, she would never be a reformer or a suffragette. But Rosa was an inquisitive and engaged citizen, an avid reader of the news, and conscious of the enormous social and political changes that swirled around her.

Although Rosa Sutton probably never finished high school, during her lifetime American women's sense of their own potential changed dramatically. By the first decade of the twentieth century, middle-class women were better educated and more powerful economically than at any time in history. These quite privileged women, who did not have to work outside their homes, formed clubs and book groups, attended classes, and became involved in civic causes as never before. Across the continent, popular magazines and big-city papers celebrated women's accomplishments and explored topics that would appeal to them. Both married and single women pushed for political and social reforms, including suffrage, and sought changes in public policy. The rapid growth of women's organizations was one indication that educated motherhood was now a public force to be reckoned with. In March 1908, the National Congress of Mothers convened its First International Congress on the Welfare of the Child in the nation's capital. Its delegates' active lives and political agenda did not escape the attention of President Roosevelt, who was a master at captivating an audience. He told the women assembled at the White House, "It is the mother, and the mother only, who is a better citizen even than the soldier who fights for his country. . . . The mother is the one supreme asset of the National life; she is more important by far than the successful statesman or businessman or artist or scientist."

Living almost three thousand miles from the center of power, Rosa began her crusade with the only weapons she had—pen and paper. She sent dozens of letters to men who might know something about Jimmie's death in her bold, forceful scrawl. She wrote fast and furiously, with minimal punctuation, often filling as many as ten pages of black-bordered mourning stationery. She did not contact the officers Rose interviewed at Carvel Hall, but she did write to others, including Charles Doyen, and to civilians who, she now knew, had been with Jimmie on his last day alive. Just before Thanksgiving, she heard from one of these men, Gilbert Coleman, a Naval Academy English and law instructor who, together with a young woman they both admired, spent the afternoon and evening with Jimmie on Saturday, October 12. Coleman wrote from Carvel Hall on November 17 and apologized for taking so long to respond—he had been on sick leave. (He suffered from chronic insomnia.) He explained to Rosa that he had only met Jimmie two weeks before he died. He offered the young marine a ride to the train station as they were both headed for Philadelphia. Coleman wrote,

> On his return to Annapolis early the next week we renewed our friendship, and from then until the last I saw him every day. The young lady you speak of was a Miss Stewart of Pittsburgh who has a brother here preparing to enter the academy. Jimmie and I were introduced to her at the same time, and that evening we had supper together here at Carvel Hall (where I live, and where Miss Stewart was then staying). We also played cards together and, I believe, dined together two or three times more.

On October 12, Gilbert Coleman and Mary Elizabeth Stewart went to the Navy-Vanderbilt football game with Jimmie, "making quite a jolly party." After the game, they stopped at the Marine Barracks, "as he wished to get his cape from his tent, the air having become quite chilly."

Coleman then provided Rosa with the only detailed description of her son's final hours. "That evening we did not go to the hop, but accompanied Miss Stewart to the house of a friend near by in order to hear Miss Stewart sing, she being quite an accomplished vocalist. On our return to the hotel, we sat and chatted in the assembly room until nearly twelve o'clock. I remember distinctly laughing and joking with your son as I bade him good night." He assured Rosa that they were all in a happy mood and found each other congenial companions; they made plans to go for a drive the following day. Jimmie showed them a letter that Rosa had written in her distinctive penmanship and asked them whether it had come from a man or a woman. (They guessed correctly.) Coleman observed, "I did not notice anything at all unusual with Jimmie on that night. On the contrary, he seemed very cheerful, and, to me, lovable. It was this last quality that attached me to him especially. During the time I knew him, he was invariably courteous, jolly and absolutely without a sign of excitement or displeasure." Coleman had tried to learn more by contacting Captain Marix, but said he "could ascertain nothing beyond what has been published. A statement kept appearing in the press to the effect that Jimmie had attended the hop, and there involved himself in a quarrel, etc. This was wholly false, and, on reading it, I at once saw the Superintendent of the Academy and told him the truth." And he closed the letter by volunteering to help Rosa in any way possible. "I sympathize with you sincerely, for I know what a true, brave spirit has gone before us. But it seems that God calls upon them first always."

Gilbert Coleman's letter only increased Rosa's resolve to continue learning more. Why, she might have wondered, had the inquest board not considered what he told Arthur Marix and Charles Badger? Her husband, meanwhile, had asked Senator Charles Fulton to appeal to the Department of the Navy and request that the case be reopened. When the request was denied, Rosa blamed Senator Fulton, whose reaction would be printed in the *Oregonian*. "Of course it is seldom if ever possible to satisfy a mother that her son was in the wrong," he wrote, insisting that he had made an earnest effort on the Suttons' behalf and that Jim Sutton had thanked him for it. Fulton agreed that Rosa had collected some impressive evidence but not enough to overturn the testimony of the "apparently entirely disinterested" witnesses at the inquest. The senator assured the reporter that Assistant Secretary of the Navy Truman Newberry was "one of the most sympathetic, kindly men I have ever known." But most important of all to Rosa, Newberry had given Senator Fulton the record of the case and said he had withheld it only out of "'consideration for the parents of the dead boy.'" At the end of 1907, neither of Jimmie's parents had seen a copy of the inquest testimony. Charlie Fulton's office apparently sent one to Jim Sutton in January 1908.

His wife read the transcript over and over again but not without several preconceived notions about the witnesses acquired from Rose, from her own correspondence, and from her postmortem visits from Jimmie. Now, with the text in front of her, Rosa could see for herself how Lieutenant Utley's account of her son's fight with his fellow officers had shaped the publicity surrounding the event. Gradually, she pieced together the marines' at-times-confusing explanation with what she had already learned about the circumstances preceding Jimmie's death.

While Jimmie sat chatting with Gil Coleman and Mary Elizabeth Stewart in the assembly room of Carvel Hall, he noticed six Marine Corps officers who had been at a Naval Academy dance come into the hotel. They all knew Jimmie—five of them were his fellow students. The men went downstairs to a private room near the bar and billiard table; they ordered beer and some sandwiches. Shortly after midnight (once his guests had retired), Jimmie came into the room where the men had gathered and offered them whiskey (from a bottle he had picked up at the bar). He also suggested they share his ride back to the camp. The lieutenants turned down the offer of whiskey, but Robert Adams, Harold Utley, and Edward Osterman joined Jimmie in one of the automobiles for hire that waited outside the King George Street entrance of the hotel just for this purpose. (The other three men went on ahead in a second automobile.)

Lieutenants Adams and Osterman had both testified that Jimmie initiated the trouble with his abusive language toward Adams during the car ride from the Carvel Hall Hotel back to the student officers' camp. But Lieutenant Utley recalled at the inquest that Adams and Sutton each used provocative language toward the other. Concerned that they might be coming in past their curfew, the marines were at odds over whether or not they should ask driver William Owens to stop his noisy automobile before they reached the camp, to avoid waking up the men in charge. Jimmie, they said, wanted to drive on ahead to camp (and brave the consequences). After they crossed the creek that separated the Naval Academy from the Marine Corps Barracks, Owens was told to stop the "machine" and all the officers got out. Adams took off his hat, cape, collar, and jacket to prepare for a fight. Lieutenants Utley and Osterman persuaded the two men not to go at it, but they both testified that it was Adams—not Sutton—who wanted to fight. Then Jimmie, supposedly resenting Osterman's interference, struck him, precipitating an unavoidable punching match in which Jimmie lost out. Now furious, he ran back to the camp, threatening to get his gun and kill them all before sunrise.

Rosa knew her son well—he did have a short fuse. The marines' story of what happened initially was not implausible. But their accounts must have been more upsetting the more Rosa read. No matter how bad his behavior, Rosa soon realized Jimmie had been far outnumbered by men who should have been his comrades. Her daughter had told her about her conversations with the marines in Annapolis, and she may even have described some of them to her mother—Adams was a tall, stocky officer. When she read about the beating Jimmie received from Robert Adams later that night, she was more convinced than ever that his ghost had told the truth.

Rosa kept on reading the testimony. Three men said that her son was found face down on the ground; he wore only his evening mess trousers and a white shirt—"a stiff bosom shirt." Rosa realized that none of the officers who had been near or on top of her son when the bullet went into his brain (Adams, Utley, William Bevan, Edward Willing, and James De Hart) told exactly the same story about how that occurred. One of the officers said specifically that he supposed Jimmie had "shot himself in the forehead" and that the hospital steward "felt the wound in the front part of the head." Rosa would remember this too, and she decided that Jimmie's forehead had been crushed. Many gaps and inconsistencies came out in the testimony, but still Rosa assumed all the witnesses were under oath to tell the "sacred truth." Poring over the transcript convinced her that Jimmie had been beaten senseless before he was shot.

In February 1908, Rosa received a letter from Colonel Charles Doyen who had been on examining board duty. He apologized for taking two weeks to reply to her questions and repeated much of what he had said at the inquest. Jimmie's "forehead appeared smooth and clear," Doyen wrote, perhaps in answer to a direct question from Rosa. But, he continued, "the nose had been bleeding and one side of his jaw was swollen. I saw no blood about his head front or back except at the nose and at the side of the head near the opening of the wound." He assured Rosa he had made a "most searching investigation," and

> had there been a vestige of suspicion of any foul play the suspected ones
> would have been held to account strictly and prosecuted fully; but there

was absolutely none; had it not been for the testimony of Lieuts. Willing and Bevan the officers on duty and entirely disinterested, both steady and reliable young men and eye witnesses, I would have held everybody else connected with the affair under suspicion until an investigation released them from suspicion; but there is no shadow of doubt in my mind that it was just as I indicated in my last letter.

Doyen expressed his sympathy but also said he was sure Jimmie's mental capacities "were not in balance" and that he had been drinking. It was fortunate, he told Rosa, that Jimmie had not killed Edward Roelker, "his intimate friend" who "was engaged in trying to save him from trouble and future disgrace."

The navy's findings had greater implications for Rosa than Charles Doyen realized. No one at the inquest had represented her son, and Rosa would never believe that Jimmie was mentally unstable. Besides, if he had been drinking to excess, he would have been even more helpless. And she was curious to know why so little blood had come from his head wound. Perhaps she would show the colonel's letter to some local doctors. By the late winter, waves of depression intensified by the enormous distance between Portland and Washington left Rosa Sutton feeling desperate. She slept with Jimmie's sword by her bed. She appeared especially high strung and vulnerable in March when she began writing to a man who assured her he was one of Jimmie's friends.

Harry Swartz, a Marine Corps private, worked in the Mills Building in Washington, D.C., as a clerk in the paymaster's office. Rosa found a receipt from Swartz among Jimmie's papers, and she wrote on March 13 to ask whether she might correspond with him "as a true friend to my dear boy." She explained that she was upset because many of the men in his class at the Application School have "said such mean things about him." She wanted to write Swartz in confidence but said "I don't feel I can do so until I hear from you and if you were not Jimmie's friend I will admire you more for you to say so than not to be and make believe you were. Those brutes that killed him are alive and seemingly doing well while my poor boy is dead five-month today. . . . Oh God," Rosa lamented, "how could those men be such brutes. Tell me can I trust you as one that knew and liked Jimmie and I will write you. When I tell you how dear Jimmie was beaten up you wont [sic] wonder my heart is broken. Did you believe he killed himself[?] He was dead or nearly so when shot and that I believe was done to hide it."

Swartz answered to her satisfaction on March 31, and Rosa immediately wrote back, revealing her most personal thoughts to her new confidant. Using the transcript, notes from her daughter's trip East, letters she had received from Annapolis, and what she thought she had learned from her paranormal experiences and those of her family, Rosa would gradually spell out her theories about what happened on October 13. Feeling isolated from the scene of her son's death, and even more so from his grave, she pleaded with Swartz to help her find out the truth about Jimmie. Their activities would be their secret; she wrote to him in the strictest confidence—a situation he accepted. Her fury at specific individuals becomes clear in these letters, and some of her accusations would prove more plausible than others.

In a letter dated April 10, Rosa asked Swartz what right Captain Marix and Lieutenant Utley had to go through her son's trunks, and "everything he owned," when they knew his sister was on the way from Annapolis. She pointed out that Utley was with Adams and Osterman when Jimmie was killed and that she believed "he engineered that fight that was planned when they went to Carvel Hall." She noted that Lieutenant Osterman sat down with Jimmie, Miss Stewart, and Professor Coleman in the assembly room "and asked Jimmie to have a drink with him"; after about twenty minutes, Adams "came to the door and beckoned him to come out. My Jimmie's back was to the door and he did not see Adams. Osterman got up and went out and Ms. Stewart asked Jimmie what kind of a man Osterman was and Jimmie said quite a nice fellow but very weak can be led into anything good or bad." Rosa continued, explaining to Swartz that when Ms. Stewart and Professor Coleman said goodnight to Jimmie at midnight, "he was so happy and talked about his expected trip on the fleet and said he was going right to camp."

Rosa described what had happened to her son, some parts of which would prove more accurate than others. She had clearly been talking to anyone who would listen in Portland, including doctors, and wrote,

> His forehead was crushed nose broken lip cut open teeth knocked out big lump under his jaw from a blow or kick and an incision on the back of his head 1 1/2 inches long. How do you suppose all that happened. His clothes showed no struggle. When he was shot the bullet ranged down and not a drop of blood from the shot[.] Now the doctors here say as my common sense tells me if Jimmie had not been dead or nearly so he would have bled freely.

She looked to Swartz to share her outrage almost as if he was a substitute for her son and railed against these "wild beasts" who were still alive while her son lay in his grave, "stamped a suicide." Her impressions may have been derived in part from Rose's interviews with Lieutenant Adams and Utley. Others clearly came from the inquest transcript or from Jimmie's personal papers. She also told Harry Swartz why she was sure, initially, that her son's beating had been premeditated. She had been outraged by the stories in the paper that branded her son a coward and a man with a "morose disposition." And she was positive that Edward Roelker had nothing to do with Jimmie's death and, in fact, that he might know something about it—even if they had quarreled just before Jimmie died. Rosa refused to believe that Jimmie had his own guns that night and implored Swartz to find out if the officers "beat him to death and then shot him to hide their crime." She acknowledged that her son "was headstrong and as wild as most young men but a more tender affectionate heart [a] man never had as he always said mamma my greatest happiness is when I am making others happy." And then she lamented, "I used to scold him for being so generous and that was always his answer and when Adams went to Annapolis it was Jimmie that loaned him his bed linens and it was Adams that sent him to his grave."

It was here, for the first time in writing, that Rosa accused Lieutenant Robert Adams of murder. But Rosa was sure no one else would see these rambling, frantic letters, which occasionally lapsed into self-pity. She was so grateful for Swartz's support, she began to worry about his welfare and said, "I promise your name will never be mentioned in connection with anything you might find out and tell me. . . . Jimmies friends are our friends and welcome at anytime for my dear boy's sake."

Rosa heard back from Harry Swartz, and on May 3 she wrote another letter to him at the "Pay Department U.S. Marine Corps." Still assuming that the men had been under oath, she said the officers who testified in 1907 could be convicted on their own sworn testimony. She was sharply critical of Sergeant James De Hart, a man who claimed not to recognize which officer handed him Jimmie's gun: "Now he knows he is lying," Rosa decided. And she promised to loan Swartz a copy of the inquest testimony. Harry Swartz's letters to her have not survived, but Rosa did make one suggestive comment that indicates his attitude. "Do you mean to say if we prove what we know those men cannot be punished simply because they belong to the Navy[?]" Rosa asked. Perhaps Harry Swartz tried to discourage her from pursuing her goal. Rosa thought of little else. She had read "in the papers" of an army first lieutenant who committed suicide in San Francisco. "The facts were stated publicly and then the matter ended." Yet in her son's case, she said, the matter had far more publicity. "These men know why they are so secret about the affair, but we are not sleeping and I think the United States will be compelled to sit up and take notice of what kind of men run the navy and shield a pack of low brutes."

By the time she wrote this letter, Rosa was livid about the damage done to her son's reputation and what she now assumed was a cover-up by the Department of the Navy. Her own sense of entitlement as a citizen with rights of redress began to come out in her venting to Swartz. No topic was off limits, as Rosa let the Marine Corps clerk in on what her son's ghost had told her; occasionally, she filled in gaps in her knowledge by imagining what Jimmie had gone through. Harold Utley, she decided, grabbed Jimmie by the shoulder to pull him out of the auto and tore his shoulder knot off; someone had "kicked him in the side and smashed his watch," and "after I had located this young lady and professor Coleman of the Naval Academy I proved the rest and after repeatedly demanding the evidence [the transcript] after 4 months I got it." "Nothing could separate Jimmie from me," she wrote, "not even death and Adams Utley Potts and Osterman will never know a moments rest on this earth why should they." Rosa would seek another investigation, "and when this trial comes I'll be there to ask a few questions myself for trial we will have. My dead boy calls for justice and he shall have it at any cost." And then, in the most important statement she made to Harry Swartz, Rosa declared, "I cannot understand why everyone cannot see how they are trying to hide the real crime and protect those men. If we cannot get justice through the courts every newspaper in the United States shall have the facts as we have them and then see what the opinion of the world will be."

Most Americans were not Catholic, but they were Christian and could still identify with her dream of being reunited with her son in heaven. And Rosa knew that all citizens could understand a moral crusade against governmental actions that appeared covert and unjust. She informed Swartz that she intended to come east herself; she appreciated his friendship and urged him to be careful so that neither of them would be found out.

In April, a man from New York heard about the case and apparently decided to help the Sutton family. He did not know the family and had never met Jimmie, but according to Rosa, he believed the tragedy "one of the worse [sic] crimes ever committed in the United States." This mysterious benefactor tracked down William Owens, the driver who had taken Jimmie and his fellow marines back to camp on October 13. Owens wrote to Rosa the day that she mailed her third letter to Harry Swartz. His letter, sent from Annapolis, confirmed her worst suspicions. He assured Rosa he was "never out of the city" in the days after Jimmie died. He said he wondered why no one contacted him to ask him about the events of that night. According to Owens, when the four officers got in his car at one in the morning, they were all apparently having a good time. Jimmie did not use vile language, and he "seemed in good humor and did not want any trouble." He also observed, "Your son was drinking but he was not in a stupid state, he seemed to be in a lively mood. . . . I did not know the other three men's names," he wrote, "but I did know your son because I always had him in my car. . . . The officer that sat in front [Adams] ordered me to stop." Owens said the officers told him to pull over at the ash pile because "they said my car made too much noise, but they had that for an excuse." Adams got out of the car and "took off his coat and hat and walked up to your son, then some of the crowd ordered me to leave, but I would not leave at first, then they called Central."

Toward the end of his letter, Owens wrote, "I thought it very strange the affair was not investigated, I fully expected to be summoned but it was all hushed in a short time. It should have been investigated. Your son did not take his own life, satisfy yourself to that." He continued, "Your son seemed to be a friend to everybody, he was liked by all and why he was murdered is a mystery. If it had been left to Annapolis authorities it would have been properly investigated, but it was the navy's affair."

William Owens' account of the car ride from Carvel Hall to the barracks contradicted the officers who testified that Jimmie started the trouble. Rosa had several copies of the letter made, and she sent one to Harry Swartz when she next wrote him. "Mind what I tell you Mr. Swartz I'll have Jimmie avenged this year unless I die I cannot see why we could not convict those men on the evidence." Clearly frustrated, once again, she would be fortified by a visit from Jimmie's ghost.

Throughout the spring and summer of 1908, reporters who had long since forgotten the Sutton case wrote daily accounts of the world cruise of America's fleet of battleships. Rosa could read about every port where the fleet stopped to refuel and imagine her son having the adventure of his lifetime as the ships rounded South America. By the beginning of May he would have visited Trinidad, Brazil, Chile, Peru, and Mexico. The exploits of Jimmie's peers on the Great White Fleet became even more compelling when the battleships reached San Francisco on May 6. The fleet would stay on the Pacific Coast for two months before leaving for Honolulu and then for Asia. Rosa had her own unique recollections of the day when "several vessels came to Portland," and "immediately after their arrival, I heard some one run up the steps of our house and I went to the door and saw Jimmie in full uniform, a blaze of glory and full of happiness. In a few seconds he disappeared." That summer, Rosa would take a journey of her own. In August of 1908, she firmed up her plans to travel to Washington to confront the Department of the Navy herself.

5

"THAT NO INJUSTICE
MAY BE DONE"

After four years of construction, Washington's magnificent white granite Union Station north of the Capitol had officially opened on October 27, 1907. The terminal had been designed by architect and urban
planner Daniel Burnham, already renowned as the creative force behind the
1893 World Columbian Exposition in Chicago. Built by Italian labor gangs
to impress and accommodate huge crowds, every facade reflected Burnham's devotion to Classicism. Its triumphal arches at the main entrance reminded sophisticated travelers of Imperial Rome. On top of six columns
stood twenty-five-ton statues sculpted by Louis Saint-Gaudens: Prometheus
and Thales (fire and electricity), Ceres and Archimedes (agriculture and
mechanics), and Freedom and Imagination. The barrel-vaulted ceiling,
with a concourse reportedly large enough to hold the Washington monument on its side, amazed visitors. Like so much other Washington architecture, Union Station symbolized an era when wealthy businessmen put large
chunks of their fortunes into monumental homes, luxurious hotels, and
sumptuous apartment buildings.

On September 14, 1908, six days after departing from Portland's own
Union Depot, Rosa Sutton arrived in Washington for a stay of undeter-
mined length that would stretch into almost two years. On this particular afternoon, she was more focused on finding help with her luggage and on locating Harry Swartz than on appreciating the Beaux-Arts architecture
surrounding her. Swartz met her as he had promised he would, and on that
same day he accompanied her on a sacred journey—to visit Jimmie's grave.
As they crossed the Potomac on the way to Arlington, Rosa may have
thought of her daughter's lonely vigil almost a year earlier. The size of the
cemetery was sobering, but her son's remains lay just off McKinley Drive on
the edge of a hill with a few young trees in the distance. Jimmie's austere

government-issued marker had no dates, and Rosa would try to raise funds for a better one. Perhaps the solitary grave reminded her that her son felt like an outsider among some of his fellow officers. For now she could find solace in the company of a man who had become her friend—a marine who seemed to take his loyalty to Jimmie and to her quite seriously.

A century ago, long-term visitors to Washington were often shocked at the high cost of housing. In a city of close to 338,000 people, few could afford to buy or even rent single-family homes, no matter what their government positions. Boarding houses and residential hotels proliferated, especially near Thomas Circle. There politicians and other distinguished visitors lived in residences such as the wedge-shaped Portland Flats, which still overlooks a corner at Fourteenth Street and Vermont Avenue. One block west, between L Street and Thomas Circle, the fashionable but larger and more reasonably priced Burlington Apartments appealed to Rosa. With 380 rooms, a homelike atmosphere and café service to satisfy "the most discriminating tastes," it would serve as her home for her stay in Washington.

Edmund Van Dyke had law offices at the ornate Bond Building on Fourteenth Street and New York Avenue, not far from Rosa's apartment. It is not clear how Rosa found Van Dyke, but during her first four months in Washington, he became an important advocate for her cause. Van Dyke, who would turn forty in November, was a lifelong Washingtonian who had put his career first for many years—only at thirty-eight did he finally marry a young woman from Michigan. His professional credentials would serve him well as he developed a plan to help his unusual new client. He had served as secretary to the chairman of the House Committee on Military Affairs, had studied under two distinguished attorneys to supplement his law degree, and had been Justice of the Peace for the District of Columbia. Between 1901 and 1905, Van Dyke headed the legal department of the rapidly expanding Chesapeake and Potomac Telephone Company. When Rosa Sutton arrived at his office, he was engaged in the general practice of law with his brother Harry.

Once he had reviewed the transcript of the 1907 naval inquest, Van Dyke clearly thought the Sutton family had a case to be made. In the fall and winter of 1908–1909, he created extensive "Notes on the Evidence" that examined whether or not Jimmie Sutton's suicide had been established "beyond a reasonable doubt" by the information presented to the inquest board. According to the *Baltimore Sun*, in late November 1908, through U.S. District Attorney John C. Rose, Rosa (surely with Van Dyke's help) had already submitted a statement to the Federal Grand Jury in Baltimore, which had criminal jurisdiction in the case. The hearing was apparently held on November 27. With Rosa was William Owens, Raymond Taylor, the undertaker for the Naval Academy Hospital with his assistant, and navy surgeon Frank Cook. No finding was reported, and the records were destroyed in a fire.

Rosa's disappointment in Baltimore made Van Dyke's efforts in the nation's capital all the more critical. His analysis would be crucial to her effort as she sought allies among Washington's politicians. Van Dyke's strategy was to focus on the discrepancies in the marines' testimony and provide alternative scenarios to suicide, a finding that placed a criminal stigma on Lieutenant Sutton who "could have been shot accidentally" or who could have accidentally "shot himself while not engaged in an attempt to shoot anyone," or he could "have been shot deliberately by one of the other participants." Using his wits and logic as much as his knowledge of the law, Van Dyke constructed an argument as long as the inquest transcript to demonstrate that "suicide was the least probable conclusion of all." For one thing, the three witnesses who had been in the auto with Jimmie [Lieutenants Robert Adams, Harold Utley, and Edward Osterman] would want to put their own conduct "in as favorable a light as possible" and blame Sutton who was dead "while they were still alive, with courts martial staring them in the face."

In their accounts about Sutton's last few moments alive, Van Dyke found that "Lieutenants Utley, Adams, Roelker and Sergeant De Hart . . . [were] so widely variant in detail that it is impossible to reconcile any two of the versions." Starting with Lieutenant Edward Willing's testimony, and moving to the words of Lieutenants William Bevan, Adams, and Utley, Van Dyke reviewed the inconsistencies in the statements of the officers who were present when the alleged suicidal shot was fired, underscoring points of special significance. How is it, Van Dyke asked, that

> not one of these witnesses claims actually to have seen by whom that [fatal] shot was fired. They all cite *circumstances* which may have led to the conclusion that Lieutenant Sutton fired it himself—indeed one or two of them say they are positive he did—but not one testified that he saw him. Under the conditions described by them, in such a state of confusion and excitement as must have existed, and dark as it appears to have been, is it at all likely that they could have seen exactly what did happen, or that their opinions were based on anything more than mere conjecture?

The attorney also found flaws in the circumstantial evidence that he assumed led the board to say that Sutton fired the last shot. For example, the men's testimony did not agree on whether or not Sutton had been drinking, or on the location of Sutton's guns for several hours after he died. Finally, Van Dyke argued, the wound (as described by Dr. Cook) was evidence that suicide was improbable—especially with two men on Sutton's back (Lieutenants Utley and James De Hart) and a third (Lieutenant William Bevan) at his shoulders. It made no sense to suggest that Sutton, given the position he was in with his face in the ground, shot himself above his right ear, rather than, for example, in his heart or his temple. Besides, neither of the two naval surgeons, who testified for less than ten minutes, was asked if Sutton could have fired the fatal shot *under the circumstances* in which he found himself. Their answers to the questions posed by the inquest board were, in fact, both general and noncommittal.

Van Dyke proposed that the three-man Board of Inquest, from a legal standpoint, had based its conclusions on immaterial, irrelevant, and incompetent evidence. In fact, the board had failed to bring out material facts apparently within the knowledge of the witnesses. And so, at the end of his analysis, Rosa's attorney proposed another theory about what happened to Lieutenant Sutton, specifically stating, "it is not the intention . . . to accuse any participant in the affray . . . of murder or of any criminal complicity in Lieutenant Sutton's death." But because there was more than one possible cause of Sutton's death—suicide, accident, or death by someone else's hand (criminally or otherwise)—Van Dyke hoped to persuade the Department of the Navy that another more thorough investigation was justified. He laid out his proposition carefully and took great pains to draw his information only from the actual testimony that had been heard by Commander John Hood, Major Benjamin Fuller, and Dr. Cook. There was another officer, he suggested, Lieutenant Robert Adams, who had been enraged enough to have pulled the trigger. But Van Dyke was careful not to accuse Adams of a crime; instead, he used Adams' obvious rage at Sutton to demonstrate that suicide could not be proven beyond a reasonable doubt.

Edmund Van Dyke closed his "Notes" by going outside the inquest testimony to present evidence from two civilians: Gilbert Coleman's letter to Rosa and driver William Owens' account—now in the form of an affidavit—about the trip back to the barracks. Owens swore that, contrary to what the marines had said, Lieutenant Adams ordered him to stop the car at an ash pile a short distance from the student camp and that "there was no quarrel or unpleasantness of any description" in the automobile before that time. Lieutenant Sutton, in fact, "was in a cheerful mood and did not enter into a dispute with Lieutenant Adams on any subject, or tell him to go to hell, or call him vile names, or say anything to him whatsoever." After Sutton paid for the trip, "'Lieutenant Adams then walked toward Lieutenant Sutton,'" and Owens

> "heard Lieutenant Sutton say, 'Go on away; I don't want to scrap,' or something to that effect; . . . Lieutenant Adams stopped for a moment, and the other two grabbed Lieutenant Sutton by the arms and said something to him, which the affiant did not hear, but that he heard Lieutenant Sutton reply, 'All right; if he wants to fight, I'll fight him,' or something like that."

Isn't it significant, Van Dyke asked, that the testimony of the witnesses given just a few hours after the tragedy "differs only as to the incriminating details?" There was, in fact, nothing in the testimony to indicate that Sutton did not fire on Lieutenant Adams in self-defense. And so, Van Dyke observed, the events of that black October night could be interpreted in more than one way.

His client would certainly agree. Van Dyke had been able to put her at times emotional and disorganized presumptions into a methodical series of arguments, and by January 1909, she was more than eager to present her family's case to the U.S. government. But Roosevelt's second term was about to end; his successor would be inaugurated in March, and there were many more pressing issues on Roosevelt's agenda and that of the men in charge of the Navy Department than the loss of a reportedly unpopular young marine. So now, the question was, would Edmund Van Dyke's analysis of what had seemed to be a routine naval inquest lead to a reconsideration of the case?

The State, War, and Navy Building, an enormous Second Empire–style structure reminiscent of the French Renaissance and distinguished by a facade filled with columns and windows, had been completed in 1888. When he became Roosevelt's sixth and last secretary of the navy, on December 1, 1908, forty-four-year-old Truman Newberry moved into an expansive new office in the east wing of the building, one suitable for royalty, with marquetry floors and elaborate ceiling and wall stenciling. It was in this grand setting that on or about the first of February he received the transcript of the 1907 Sutton inquest along with Van Dyke's commentary from Oregon senator Jonathan Bourne. Bourne had taken just enough time with the material to question the suicide finding himself. Would the secretary order a review of the matter so "that no injustice may be done" to his constituent and her family?

Newberry had only been in his position for eight weeks when he received Bourne's request, but he was a veteran in the Department, and as the

The State War and Navy Department Building with the cow of William H. Taft. Courtesy of the Historical Society of Washington, D.C.

assistant secretary of the navy (1905–1908), he had selected the applicants who ultimately made it into Jimmie Sutton's class at the Marine Corps Application School. On February 3, without much enthusiasm, he sent the papers over to the judge advocate general, Edward H. Campbell. Newberry observed in his cover letter that

> no question was raised [by Van Dyke] as to the competency of the Board of Inquest as constituted, nor of the regularity of the proceedings. It is also, undoubtedly, true that the evidence adduced at the time of the Inquest, which was held immediately following the affray, is more reliable than any that might be secured at this time, even if it were considered advisable to reopen the case.

Campbell, a native of South Bend, Indiana, and a Naval Academy graduate, was also very familiar with the Sutton case. He had been new at his job in 1907 and may have had a say in the original suicide finding. But, faced with Van Dyke's rigorous "Notes," he informed Newberry on February 9 that "the Board of Inquest did not follow each clue to its finish as would have been done by skillful attorneys in a trial at bar and should have been done to have made its findings absolutely uncontrovertible" [*sic*]. As for the affidavit of driver William Owens, which Van Dyke included, Campbell said it "throws no light on the facts attending the actual shooting." The fact that it contradicted the marines' testimony on how the quarrel started was beside the point. The thirty-seven-year-old judge advocate general continued, "There is a sufficient lack of clear evidence regarding the actual shooting to warrant the existence of a doubt as to the correctness of the finding, from a mere reading of the testimony." But it was obvious that reopening the case would be a logistical nightmare, and, Campbell observed by including a list of them, the witnesses to the shooting are "widely scattered" all over the globe. Moreover, there are no other witnesses who could testify "to the circumstances of the shooting." The conflicting testimony is not unnatural, he argued (putting a different spin on the same conditions Van Dyke had noticed), "inasmuch as the various incidents occurred in rapid succession, on a dark night, and with all the participants in a state of great excitement and some of them probably befuddled with liquor." Campbell did not think a Court of Inquiry would come up with a different finding; therefore, he was "firmly of the opinion . . . no good purpose would be achieved by reopening the case at this late date." Besides, the inquest board said it had made a thorough investigation.

Just before he received Campbell's memo, the secretary of the navy found a letter from Rosa Sutton on his desk—Edmund Van Dyke had helped her draft it. She had written on behalf of her husband and herself to explain her case further to the secretary because Senator Bourne's letter had been so brief. Mr. and Mrs. Sutton sought a second investigation—"a fuller examination of the witnesses who testified before, but of much other and very material evidence which I am led to believe can be procured, both in the Navy and from outside sources." And if a re-examination proved other than suicide, or left any doubt about it, Rosa hoped the stigma attached to her son's name would be removed and "probable responsibility for his death fixed." Finally, she hoped that further action could be taken against anyone thought to be responsible for Jimmie's death.

In the final paragraph, Rosa's growing confidence about what she had accomplished over the previous year is evident:

> My own investigations have convinced me that my son did not commit suicide but was killed by one of the officers who were with him at the time of his death, but many attorneys who have read the testimony given before the former Board of Inquest tell me that important and material facts were not brought out at that hearing which would have thrown much light upon the question whether my son killed himself or was killed by one of those officers, and that the record as it stands is far more indicative, if not conclusive, of the fact that he was killed than that he committed suicide.

Secretary Newberry replied cordially to Rosa the following day; he told her his Department would be glad to examine her affidavits and offer any assistance "the facts may warrant" to establish that her son did not commit suicide. However, "the Department," at least his judge advocate general (JAG), had already decided to turn her down. So when Newberry sent his final response to Senator Bourne, he reiterated Edward Campbell's opinion that no good purpose would be served by a new investigation. He added that "if the relatives of Lieutenant Sutton should desire to charge any person with the murder of the deceased the matter would be one for action by the civil authorities as a naval court martial would not have any jurisdiction of the offense." According to a later report in the *Baltimore Sun*, the secretary also told Rosa "the case is closed forever, and you, as the boy's mother, should thank God for it."

During the frigid winter weeks that followed, headlines would be dominated by the return of the "magnificent and impressive" battleship fleet from its fourteen-month cruise. On February 22, the ships pulled into Norfolk, Virginia, in the misting rain to be welcomed by thousands of spectators. "It was the apotheosis of Roosevelt, the one supreme magnificent moment in the career of a man who more than any other made possible this review of the biggest aggregation of splendid warship tonnage that was ever gathered under one flag." Roosevelt was there in person on the presidential yacht, *Mayflower,* to see the ships "brilliant with flags and vivid with the flash of guns." The *New York Times* found it to be "the most impressive pageant that ever made the American heart beat fast or the American breast swell with pride in his country and his flag." When the fleet came to its "brilliant end," Rosa and Jim Sutton were three thousand miles apart. They both surely thought about Jimmie, who had planned to return on one of these ships with exciting stories to tell and arms full of presents for his family.

Rosa Sutton coped with the despair she felt by remaining fixated on her mission, and fortunately, Jonathan Bourne continued to pursue the case. A resident of Portland, five years older than Rosa, the senator knew of the Sutton family—he had nominated Don Sutton to West Point. Like many Oregon politicians of his generation, Jonathan Bourne was not a westerner by birth. He came from wealthy New England stock—his father had owned a large fleet of whaling ships in New Bedford, Massachusetts. The younger Bourne was an adventure-loving soul and a nonconformist who left Harvard in his senior year to go to sea. After he was shipwrecked near Formosa, he decided to settle in Oregon where he made a success of several commercial enterprises including farming, cotton mills, and mining. By the time he was thirty, Bourne had made it into the Oregon House of Representatives. He had been a member of the Republican National Committee and was among the first men to become a U.S. senator by popular vote rather than by appointment. Bourne was at the peak of his career when he served in the senate from March 4, 1907, until March 3, 1913.

Bourne had been active in William Howard Taft's campaign, and when Taft became president-elect on November 3, 1908, he had carried Oregon and twenty-eight other states. Taft and Bourne would not always see eye to eye, but in 1908 and 1909 they shared an interest that gave them ample time together. On July 30, 1908, they had met at the Homestead resort in Hot Springs, Virginia, where the two walked the four-mile golf course for the first of many times. Bourne also played golf with Taft at Augusta. Once Taft was in the White House, the press would report that Bourne became "the constant companion of the big man on the links," often joining him to play at the Chevy Chase Club. The two men would be seen together so frequently that the *Oregon Daily Journal* reporter, and others, suggested Senator Bourne join Taft's cabinet as "Secretary of Golf."

U.S. Senator Jonathan Bourne of Oregon. Courtesy of the Oregon Historical Society, #OrHi11274.

On March 17, less than two weeks after Taft's inauguration, Senator Bourne wrote Edward Campbell, who had survived the change in administrations, to remind him that Mrs. Sutton was coming to meet him "on March 20th at 3 o'clock at your office in the Navy Department." He hoped to accompany her, and added, "I would personally greatly appreciate your giving the most careful consideration to Mrs. Sutton in this matter, as her case excites my warmest sympathies." The judge advocate general may have been weary of the case, but he now served a different secretary of the navy.

George Von Lengerke Meyer had moved into the elegant office space on March 6. A sportsman, businessman, diplomat, and Republican activist, Meyer was close to both Roosevelt and Taft and probably knew Senator Bourne; he had been postmaster general between 1907 and 1909 when the senator worked on the Committee on Post Offices and Post Roads. The new navy secretary needed a reason to reverse his predecessor's decision on the Sutton case, and he found one that mirrored Bourne's argument. On April 5, two weeks after Rosa met with his judge advocate general, he agreed to reopen the case—to see that no injustice was done. But his focus was on justice for "the officer accused by Mrs. Sutton of being the cause of her son's death." Meyer hoped that a second investigation would come to "a definite and incontrovertible finding." He asked the senator to inform Mrs. Sutton that it would take at least three months before a Court of Inquiry could be assembled. She would be notified if she kept the Department informed of her address, and he added, "She will have the right to be present, or be represented by attorneys."

Nothing could have kept Rosa from this proceeding, nor would she quibble with Meyer's reasoning. It did seem curious that he referred to her charges against a specific officer. Van Dyke had proposed that Robert Adams was certainly angry enough to have killed her son, but in April 1909, no one had accused Adams of murder—at least not in any official document. A year had gone by since she had shared her intimate thoughts with Harry Swartz and revealed her plan to prove that Robert Adams murdered Jimmie. But that had been private correspondence, written in the distant past, and after an eighteenth-month struggle, she now looked eagerly to the future. Three months did not seem too long to wait.

With the Navy Department's decision, Rosa Sutton would enter a forum—in fact, a separate subculture—that was as unfamiliar to her as it was to most civilians. Then, as now, Americans lived in "a democratic society committed to civilian control of the military." The Constitution had ensured that Congress and the executive branch of the government had power over the armed forces. But military society remained distinct from civilian society in several respects that had a direct bearing on her case. Marine Corps justice was and is governed by the United States Navy. And naval law, with its roots in the law of Imperial Rome, had one fundamental goal—to maintain military discipline, thereby protecting the good of the service, not an individual citizen or society in general. Many rights taken for granted by civilians, including that of complete freedom of expression, were given up by those who joined the military. As the *Army and Navy Journal* put it in 1907, "Military exigencies require not individual liberty, but subordination, obedience. The very rules which are found to protect the individual rights of the people would destroy discipline." The article raised an issue that was central to the Sutton case. Those in charge of administering military justice had been accused of avoiding courts-martial that might bring "disgrace and reproach" on their service. The writer refutes this charge and insists that it is foreign to officers "to shield from justice one of their own body who has committed acts unbecoming an officer and a gentleman."

In 1909, the procedures in place to answer Mrs. Sutton's accusations were spelled out in the Articles for the Government of the Navy—a document enacted by Congress in 1800 (and recompiled and amended in 1862) that had its origins in seventeenth- and eighteenth-century Britain. The president and the secretary of the navy (or commanders and others representing them) had the authority to appoint the men who served on boards of inquiry and general courts-martial. On this point, the *Army and Navy Journal* observed, many criteria that may be appropriate in selecting a jury "are wholly absent in the military service." Military courts are drawn from "a body of educated gentlemen versed in military law, sworn to administer justice, with no interests but to maintain discipline and the honor of the Army" (or the navy). And, most significant, there was no formal appellate procedure in the military court system for an Oregon housewife who objected to a navy finding on behalf of her late officer son.

Certain assumptions shaped the way the military justice system operated—commanders made all key decisions that affected the fate of an accused man. They selected the members of a court from among their own community; naval justice of necessity was expected to be swift and efficient. Courts of inquiry and courts-martial were "simply instrumentalities of the executive power provided by Congress for the president as commander in chief" or his authorized representative. Military courts were, in fact, adjuncts of command; they were the "right hand of the commanding officer to aid him in the maintenance of discipline." Rosa Sutton, who had come to Washington seeking impartial justice, was not prepared to come before a

court that was in many respects "above the law" and not necessarily governed by the law. At the same time, the officers who served as members of
a naval court were assumed to be acting on their honor as they administered
justice that was fair according to the institutional values they had learned—
at the Naval Academy, in the Marine Corps Application School, and just as
frequently on the job.

The Sutton Court of Inquiry would be much more formal than the
1907 inquest; it had the power to subpoena witnesses, all of whom would
be sworn in before testifying. Individuals with a direct interest in the subject could be designated parties with certain rights, if that seemed necessary. In 1907, there had been no parties to the investigation, no one to present Lieutenant Sutton's side of the story or to object when the board
accused him of a crime against himself. And the inquest had been closed to
the public, a practice not supported by military tradition. In most cases, an
inquiry or court-martial permitted members of the public, including newspaper reporters, to view the proceedings (although an inquiry could be
closed at the discretion of the court at any point). But the new Board of
Inquiry was an administrative fact-finding body, not a court-martial or even
an adversarial proceeding—at least it started out that way. No one had been
charged with any crime. Nevertheless, by the end of July, Rosa Sutton
would find herself in a position at the inquiry that may have been unprecedented in the annals of naval justice.

For the United States, reopening the case was an expensive job filled with
paperwork and logistical headaches—witnesses were scattered as far away as
China. On April 5, 1909, Secretary Meyer sent a memorandum to Commandant George Elliott instructing him to take the necessary steps to ensure the appropriate marines would be available as witnesses. Almost all the
men in Meyer's initial request had testified before the 1907 inquest board;
however, one name was not on the list—Lieutenant Edward Roelker was
no longer in the Marine Corps. Rosa Sutton was certain Roelker could
shed light on Jimmie's death, but within five weeks of the tragedy, he had
been accused of being "under the influence of intoxicants and unfit for the
proper performance of his duty," while in a signaling class. Roelker had
twice before been disciplined for overindulgence; this time he came before
a general court-martial at the Marine Barracks in Annapolis. His troubles
began on the evening of November 19, 1907. A fellow student officer,
Allen Sumner, ran into him in the assembly room of the Carvel Hall Hotel at about 5:30 p.m. The two went downstairs to the bar and had several
drinks; Lieutenant Sumner estimated that Roelker had not more than four

or five gin fizzes. Neither man expected there would be a signaling class that evening because their camp had been broken up for the winter. It turned out they were wrong. When they got to the old camp site at close to eight o'clock, Sumner was so drunk the instructor sent him back to the barracks. But Edward Roelker thought he was sober enough to handle the drill—the Ardois system of night signals; he would use a keyboard to activate red and white electric lights to transmit the Morse code visually at various signal stations. Lieutenant Epaminondas L. Bigler, the drill instructor that night, had not seen a problem when Roelker first arrived, but he would be the one to bring charges against him.

When the court-martial convened at 10:30 in the morning on December 4, Edward Roelker's future was at stake. He had enough confidence in the process to serve as his own defense and plead not guilty. Lieutenant Sumner testified briefly about where the men had been that night, and then Lieutenant Bigler took the stand. Roelker, he said, became "so much intoxicated that he was unable to perform his duty." The liquor began to show about fifteen or twenty minutes after drill started. At one point Roelker fell down—the drinks began to "work on him." When he tried to get up, Bigler said, he did not recover himself readily "as a man in a normal condition would have done." Edward Roelker asked Lieutenant Bigler why he had allowed him to remain while sending Sumner back to his quarters. "Your condition was not as pronounced as Sumner's when I came there and each minute of the time while I was there I noticed that your condition became worse," came the response. Besides, Bigler continued, it was raining, and he knew they were going to quit the drill any minute.

Roelker's defense of himself was to point out why he had fallen; unprotected foot-deep ditches covered the practice site (every tent had been surrounded by a ditch, and the tents were now gone). It had been dark, he did not see the ditches, and the bright lights made him so dizzy he fell into one. Three of Roelker's classmates testified, and none thought he was as drunk as Bigler portrayed him. Lieutenant John Potts agreed that he was intoxicated but not "to a very pronounced degree." The signals had been poorly sent that night, but Potts acknowledged that Roelker was not quite up to par in reading them. Howard Judson recalled that Roelker had been drinking but said he fell into a ditch not because he was so inebriated but because he had been playing with a dog. Judson explained that although he was "not in full possession of his faculties," Roelker had enough self-control "to walk straight, to talk coherently when he tried, to assist me to get another officer [Sumner] to his quarters," and "even to make up the latter's bunk for him." For the most part, Roelker read the signals correctly, according to Judson. Roelker had also persuaded Robert Adams to testify briefly on his behalf. Lieutenant Adams had been on duty in the squad room and seen Roelker making up Sumner's bed. He assured the court that he had not noticed anything unusual about Roelker's condition or behavior.

Despite the conflicting testimony as to the extent of his intoxication, Edward Roelker's defense did not work. On December 9, barely eight weeks after the death of his friend, Captain Campbell submitted the record of the proceedings against Roelker to the secretary of the navy and President Theodore Roosevelt. Both men agreed with the court's recommendation that he be dismissed from the Marine Corps.

Eighteen months later, as witnesses were summoned from across the globe for the Sutton inquiry, Parthenia Roelker accepted a subpoena for her son at the family's home in Georgetown. But he would not be easy to find. A moving and suggestive tribute to Edward had appeared in the 1908 *Lucky Bag*. Even though he had resigned after two years, his Naval Academy classmates included him in their yearbook, selecting a quotation from Wordsworth to describe Roelker. They placed the quotation under his familiar name, "Red," in their class list: "A youth, to whom was given / So much of earth, so much of heaven."

By the beginning of July, most of the government witnesses except Roelker were within easy traveling distance of Annapolis, and the Navy Department focused on selecting the members of the Sutton court. A forty-nine-year-old "grizzled haired and mustached" navy captain, John Hood, from Florence, Alabama, was appointed president. Hood had been on the *Maine* when she was blown up in Havana Harbor, and he served in the Russo-Japanese war between 1903 and 1905. In June of 1909, he assumed command of the *Severn* in charge of ships at the Naval Academy. He would speak and act for the court as its "representative and mouthpiece"; he had no separate authority. With him was Major Wendell C. Neville, a thin-faced marine with close-cropped light brown hair who served on Roelker's court-martial. Thirty-nine when the court convened, he had seen action in many parts of the world. (Neville would become commandant of the Corps before he died in 1930.) A navy lieutenant, Henry Norman Jensen was the youngest member of the court at thirty-three; the recipient of two medals for action at Santiago in 1898, Jensen had just returned a few months earlier with the Great White Fleet—he had been an ordnance officer. These three men, all Naval Academy alumni, had orders to gather in Annapolis on July 19 to "inquire into the circumstances attending the death of the late Second Lieutenant James N. Sutton, and to fix the responsibility therefor." The court was expected to give the Department "a full statement of all the facts which it may deem to be established by the evidence adduced, together with its opinion as to what further proceedings, if any, should be had in the matter." The men would act as a unit and "behave with decency and calmness," not assuming "a controversial attitude" at any time during the proceeding.

While the final decision about the cause of Sutton's death would be in the hands of this court, three other men would find themselves in the limelight throughout the dramatic proceedings. For the navy, the key figure was the judge advocate—there had not been one at the inquest. A note in pencil attached to Lieutenant Sutton's Marine Corps application file makes that clear: "Get a detail for Court of Inquiry to meet at Annapolis on July 19th to investigate the Sutton case. Be sure and get a good judge advocate for there will be a need fr [sic] one in this business." The author of the note is unknown, but the navy's choice for its prosecutor (who was actually neither a judge nor an advocate) was indeed a good one, thirty-three-year-old Henry ("Harry") Leonard. Although he said in 1909 that he had "little legal experience," Major Leonard was a man with a stellar reputation. A Washington native with two law degrees, he joined the Marine Corps in 1898 just in time to serve in the Spanish-American War. Tall, thin, handsome, and slightly balding Leonard was a distinguished soldier and an experienced equestrian. He hoped to be judge advocate general of the navy and, in 1907, had come close to securing the position. But he lost out to Edward Campbell and instead became the commanding officer at the Naval Prison in Portsmouth, New Hampshire. He liked the job and the climate, and his fitness reports indicate that he was good at it—"able, energetic and enthusiastic in all that pertains to his profession," constantly staying up to date with practice and instruction.

Harry Leonard wore the unmistakable mark of a veteran with great dignity; he had been severely wounded in 1900 during the Boxer Rebellion as the marines tried to defend the foreign settlers inside Tientsin. His left sleeve was empty; his arm had been amputated at the shoulder.

In spite of the injury, he remained a model member of the Corps for another decade. In May 1907, the Chinese government had awarded him the Order of the Double Dragon for his work as a foreign attaché, but that did not make up for the pain he still fought on a daily basis. He put himself on a strict regimen: no cigarettes, alcohol, or caffeine; "going to bed early, taking regular exercise"; and living the "most regular life" to avoid nervousness and stifle the sensation of burning and pulsating at the site of his missing arm. Leonard would not begin to practice law until he left the Marines in 1911 because of his injury, but by 1909 he had been part of several boards of inquiry and Marine Corps examining boards.

Throughout the Sutton proceeding, Leonard would report directly to the judge advocate general, Campbell. He would be the first to question each witness and go to considerable lengths to make sure every piece of evidence was considered. But as the judge advocate, Leonard was not subject to challenge; ideally, he had no personal interest in the result of the inquiry or animosity toward the accused, if there should be one. His primary role, other than that of prosecutor, was as legal adviser to the court and as its recorder (though he would have professional help in that capacity); he would not be present when the court made its final decision behind closed doors.

On June 30, Edward Campbell sent a letter to Leonard in Portsmouth with all the papers from the JAG office related to the Sutton case so that he could become familiar with the details. He explained, "the mother of the deceased dissents from the finding of the board of Inquest." Leonard began work immediately, making sure the court had a stenographer and reviewing all the papers from Campbell. He undoubtedly had a copy of the arguments made by Edmund Van Dyke on Rosa's behalf. On July 6, he wrote to Commandant George Elliott for permission to come to Washington ahead of time to study the case. More than any other individual, Harry Leonard would shape the tone and the course of the inquiry, and he wanted to be prepared—it was critical the navy not be accused of a cover-up this time around.

The Sutton inquiry also gave two distinguished civilian attorneys their first opportunity to argue in a military courtroom. Although no person had been accused of murder when the inquiry started, Robert Adams had the right to be present, to cross-examine witnesses, and to offer evidence; he would automatically have a military counsel. But his navy attorney, Captain Thomas Brown, would not speak up during the coming weeks. Instead, with the Department's blessing, Adams' family engaged an experienced prosecutor to represent him. Of Irish and Dutch descent, Arthur Alexis Birney came from a long line of intellectuals and political figures; his grandfather had been a leading abolitionist. Birney had gone into partnership with his eminent father in Washington, D.C. He played a key role in the reorganization of the Howard University Law Department, and in 1893, President Harrison appointed him U.S. Attorney for the District of Columbia, a position he held until 1897. *The Washington Law Reporter* described Arthur Birney as "a man of lovable qualities, a lawyer of signal

Arthur Alexis Birney. Courtesy of the Historical Society of Washington, D.C.

ability and sterling integrity," and he earned the respect of his colleagues throughout his career.

The Suttons' right to bring an attorney to the proceeding was a courtesy of the Department of the Navy. Edmund Van Dyke had been notified by Major Leonard on July 5 that he could be present in court, could cross-examine witnesses, and could offer "such competent evidence, pertinent to the issue as you may desire." Although he would attend the inquiry, and his "Notes" would be a valuable guideline to the arguments in favor of the Sutton case, Van Dyke probably suggested to Rosa that she retain a seasoned trial attorney. He may even have known the man who agreed to help. Henry Edgar Davis was considered by his contemporaries to be one of the "most highly honored" and "best beloved" members of the D.C. Bar as well as a gifted orator and "brilliant lawyer," who radiated "kindliness, friendliness and good humor." One colleague said that his "appearance in court was like the coming in of a sunbeam." Three years younger than Arthur Birney, fifty-four-year-old Davis graduated from Princeton with highest honors, and like Edmund Van Dyke and Harry Leonard, studied law at Columbia University (now George Washington University). He too served as U.S. Attorney for the District, and Davis had been admitted to the Bar of the Supreme Court of the United States in 1882. A short, balding man, and a bit stout by 1909, photographs reveal that Davis' physical appearance reflected that of his client, much as Birney's tall stature mirrored that of Robert Adams. Henry Davis and Arthur Birney both would have their sunny dispositions challenged in the naval courtroom in Annapolis. During the coming weeks, Davis found himself at odds with Birney, and especially with the much younger judge advocate over matters of procedure and issues such as what evidence was admissible.

Henry Davis enjoyed challenging cases, those that might be "test cases in both the civil and criminal branches of the law," but he had given himself a more difficult task than he realized when he took on the defense of Rosa Sutton. And though he would enter the courtroom in good faith, Annapolis was a refined and insular world for such an outspoken woman. The navy had its own legal and ethical standards, and its own cultural expectations that shaped those rules. Davis needed to be sure everyone had their signals straight. On July 17, from his office in the Jennifer Building at Seventh and D street, he wrote the acting secretary of the navy, Judge Beekman Winthrop, to ask for a copy of the daily testimony once the inquiry began. It would, he hoped, enable him to be of assistance, "which I sincerely wish to render the court in reaching a satisfactory and just conclusion." He would pay for the copy, he said. But the letter was also a vehicle for Davis to confirm his understanding of what was to happen in the coming weeks.

"As you probably have learned from the press if not more directly," he began, "I am of counsel to Mrs. Sutton." He understood that

> the inquiry is to be for the information of the Department and that, as
> in strictness there is no party defendant, there is, accordingly, no party

Henry Edgar Davis. Courtesy of the Historical Society of Washington, D.C.

in a position to assert or ask anything as of right; and further that even though the proceedings . . . are expected to be open, that fact will not of itself operate a change in the rule or practice of regarding the proceedings as in effect confidential [in its final deliberations] within the Department.

However, Davis wrote, because Mrs. Sutton had a copy of the transcript of the first inquiry, and the matter had "attracted such wide publicity," confidentiality would be difficult to achieve in this case. Davis appears to have genuinely wanted to help and saw the investigation as a collaborative effort: "It is my purpose to co-operate with the Judge Advocate and the court in the effort to elicit the truth of the sad occurrence and not, primarily, to seek to place the blame for Lieutenant Sutton's death upon anyone in particular." But Rosa's attorney did hope to take the blame off of Lieutenant Sutton who could not defend himself (though his ghost was apparently trying). Within the week, he would be in a situation that would test his patience as much as his skill.

Henry Davis received a quick response to his letter from Edward Campbell who agreed that he could have a copy of the testimony but made no comment on Davis' characterization of the upcoming investigation. Like others about to spend the summer in Annapolis, Davis was keenly aware of the unusual circumstances that he faced. Would information come out to support or to disprove the "spirit testimony" Rosa Sutton had heard? Through their newspapers, millions of Americans would follow this "remarkable" drama as it unfolded in the coming weeks.

6

"A WIDER FORUM"

Amerca's newspapers began to carry the Sutton story during the first week of July, usually on their front pages above the fold. Often several articles related to the case appeared on the same day. Rosa was, after all, a grieving mother confronting an impersonal bureaucracy in an era when motherhood was revered. Reporters used that hook to appeal to their growing audience of women readers; "MOTHER WINS FIGHT" proclaimed the *Washington Post* on July 7. A "mother heart had been wounded," and in response, a Board of Inquiry had just been appointed in Annapolis to investigate the death of a young marine "shot in a lonely part of the Naval Academy." According to the *Post*, a precedent had now been established by the Navy Department because the inquiry was the "fruition of the tireless labors of a bereaved mother," who hoped to "prove to the world that moral cowardice was not responsible for her son's death." As members of the press picked up the story through the wire services, several papers, including the *Baltimore Sun*, played up the mystery surrounding Jimmie's death, one that would confound a far larger audience than it had in 1907. Rosa's crusade held huge appeal for Hearst's and Pulitzer's sensationalist editors, reporters, and photographers who reveled in stories of the underdog. But papers targeting a refined readership, those that could rightly claim to be more objective and reliable, recognized the enduring significance of a patriotic citizen (and a mother, no less) taking on the United States in a military forum. In the summer of 1909, thousands of inches of column space would be given to the search for the truth about the matter.

Following the Civil War, the impact of the press corps on Americans' lives expanded in small towns, and especially in the increasing number of big cities across the nation. The typesetting machine, more efficient presses, and improvements in manufacturing cheaper paper all made the news more affordable; with each passing decade literacy increased, and more and more citizens read the news as intelligent, informed, and critical consumers. (The number of high schools in America jumped from close to one hundred in 1860, the year Rosa Sutton was born, to six thousand by 1900.) No longer primarily organs for political parties, newspapers became independent and more professional; their staffs had gained respectability after 1880, when Rosa Sutton began her life as a young mother. By the end of the nineteenth century, many reporters were college educated and took more active roles in shaping their own stories. Journalism was now a field for study in its own right, and authenticity remained the goal for most papers, if at times an elusive one. As John Given explained, "Usually reporters strive to get the exact facts. Persons who find fault with the newspapers for their errors would have less to say if they spend a single day gathering news." Sorting out the conflicting opinions that existed about every aspect of the Sutton case would be a complex task, one that would be attacked with vigor in the era of "new journalism."

By 1900, the options available to readers had grown enormously as well, thanks in part to leased wire services and the New York–based Associated Press, by then a powerful monopoly with 800 member papers that could reach close to twenty-five million readers each day. Americans could choose between 1,967 general-circulation English-language dailies compared to 489 thirty years earlier; during that same period the number of urban residents had tripled. Newspaper readership climbed from thirty-six to fifty-seven million people between 1890 and 1905, and big-city papers with subscribers in surrounding towns reached more than one hundred thousand people each. (After 1897 free rural delivery was supplied by the federal postal service.) The figure would soon climb to two to six times that amount in New York City, the center of American journalism. Urban papers often had two or more editions, giving their readers ample opportunity to keep up with the news as it happened. In the nation's capital, newspapers set up offices not far from Capitol Hill; Teddy Roosevelt, who described newspapermen as "'public servants,'" and used them constantly to his own advantage, was the first president to make space for a select group of reporters at the White House. President Taft held weekly meetings with members of the press but admitted that they "'properly complained that I did not help them to help me.'"

Reporters' influence was no longer confined to specific regions, states, cities, or towns. America was now a nation of newspaper readers—"only in the present day" has the power of the press "to create public opinion" been "developed to its fullest limit," James Edward Rogers wrote in 1909, after studying some fifteen thousand papers, most of which he found to be too sensational and commercial. In America's largest cities, like New York, Chicago, New Orleans, and San Francisco—each of which represented a region of the United States—"the newspapers reflected the desires and hopes of the country." People wished to be amused and entertained, and for a mere penny or two the newspapers by and large gave them what they wanted. Rogers argued that newspapers mirrored their communities, and he deplored the taste of the average reader.

Military court proceedings rarely involved as many elements that would hook exactly this type of reader as Rosa Sutton's confrontation with the government. Now that citizens could "participate in the news" on a large scale, the case provided a unique dilemma for the navy. Perhaps for the first time within a naval courtroom, the judge advocate would speak deliberately and frequently to the nation at large. By July 1909, a national audience had a stake in the Navy Department's findings because reporters, feeling Mrs. Sutton's cause was just, kept it before the public. As John Given observed, they might "gain adherents" for a cause "by referring to it as if its merits were everywhere acknowledged." Suicide was widespread at the turn of the last century, and Given found that reporters would "squeeze a suicide into the semblance of a murder or try to make the suicide into a mystery." Such techniques would not be necessary with the Sutton story— here was a genuine melodrama that also raised serious issues. The media's natural antagonism toward any hint of a cover-up put Rosa's crusade in parlors, saloons, clubs, hotels, and libraries across America—several papers plastered their pages with large headlines, photographs, diagrams, and even drawings about how Jimmie Sutton might have died. At the same time, the press corps, on the whole, did a conscientious job of presenting the government side of the case.

America's service academies were held in high esteem, and New York's financial and literary elite who read the *Evening Post* or the *New York Times* could follow the story on a daily basis. In 1909, under the path-breaking leadership of Adolph S. Ochs, the *Times*—whose readers, according to the editor, Elmer Davis, represented "a far wider range of political opinion than the ordinary newspaper constituency"—was on its way to becoming one of the great newspapers of the world. Promising impartial coverage of all the news that's fit to print, the *Times* ran more than fifty-seven articles and six editorials about the events surrounding Jimmie Sutton's death. This relentless spotlight would touch everyone who suffered through the heat wave of 1909 at the inquiry in Annapolis. The press coverage would have a decisive impact on witnesses' testimony, the actions of the judge advocate, and the arguments of the attorneys whose closing rhetoric left no doubt as to the power of the new journalism. Intimations of this power were evident when newspapers set the scene for the inquiry before it opened.

On July 7, the *Washington Post* paired its account of the Annapolis inquiry with another Sutton story in an adjacent front page column. In an ironic twist of fate, Rosa's other son, nineteen-year-old Don, who was now at West Point, was in the hospital following a hazing incident that had been kept under wraps for almost three weeks. This new calamity would generate even more publicity, propelling the family to the center of a national conversation about conditions in America's military training schools. For two weeks after Don Sutton's injury, no one outside of West Point seems to have known what happened.

Don testified that on Saturday, June 19, at 11:35 at night, he was on his first tour of duty as a sentinel. As he walked past post number 9, a group of cadets in their pajamas, some covered in ghost-like sheets, came toward him. He ordered the men to halt and asked, "Who is there?" Instead of responding, they started after him. "I immediately called the Corporal of the Guard, grabbed my gun, and advanced down to the end of my post to resist this advancement," Don said. The cadets approached with two long tent poles; one hollered to get the pole between Sutton's legs and make him "ride on the rail." When they did that, Don recalled, "I was hurt and went down on my knees. As soon as I was on my knees all these cadets jumped on me, some on my back and the rest on my gun and tried to take the gun away." Don called the corporal of the guard a second time. He fought the cadets, tackling two of them as they started to run away. Don said he was dragged about ten yards off his post when they broke loose. Although he was in considerable pain, Don stayed on his post until he was relieved at 8:45 the following morning. After he left the post, he was told to get medical help from Captain Oscar Charles; subsequently, three men senior to him warned him "not to do any unnecessary talking about [the incident]; they said if I was asked I would have to tell about it but not to talk unnecessarily about it." Don's injuries to his side and his groin area put him in the hospital for twenty days.

Don did not want Rosa to know he had been hurt, and understandably, no one at West Point did either. But early in July, the incident came out in several local and national newspapers. In fact, Rosa first learned of Don's troubles through reporters. Alarmed by the news that he might have been in a "serious accident," she left Washington for Highland Falls. On July 6, Hearst's *New York American*, which called itself "the twentieth-century newspaper," also ran two front page stories—each emphasized the secrecy maintained by the armed forces in their service academies. For a penny, citizens could read about the "Boy Attacked by Ghosts While on Post," who "fought until overpowered and helpless, if not unconscious." President Roosevelt, the paper noted, had once reinstated eight cadets who had been expelled from West Point, making it more difficult for Superintendent Hugh Scott to maintain discipline. "The American people own West Point," Colonel Scott said in an interview that came out in the *American* on July 8, "and the American people through their representatives at Washington have recorded it as is their will that there shall not be hazing at this Academy." Claiming that "never before in the history of West Point has a hazing tribunal been held under circumstances which brought up the Academy to such tension," the *American* described the mood in Highland Falls with the same dramatic flair that would characterize its blow-by-blow coverage of the Annapolis Sutton case: "Although a hop was scheduled for the evening, and gay young women in summer costumes gathered in ever increasing numbers under the avenues of elms which skirt the great central lawn, the cadets gathered by themselves in little groups talking in such low tones that the nearest passerby could not overhear their words." Into this environment Rosa Sutton arrived from Washington, D.C., "dressed in deep mourning" for her other son and adding a "peculiarly pathetic element." "'They murdered one of my boys' she said in a low but firm voice, 'so that as soon as I heard that the only son I have left had also been in danger I rushed to his side as fast as railroads could carry me.'"

Several papers noticed that Don Sutton was taking the opposite tack from his late brother who had supposedly turned in fellow midshipmen for breaking the rules while at the Naval Academy. "Cadet in Hospital Shields Assailants," proclaimed the July 7 *New York Times*, noting that "Sutton is physically one of the best men in the fourth class" and was a victim of the "old-time ghost trick." The *Washington Post*'s almost identical lead story also told readers that Don Sutton "refuses to make a charge" against those suspected of hazing him. But Superintendent Scott remained silent as numerous cadets were being questioned under oath. In stark contrast to his dead brother, Don, who was also a star basketball player at West Point, acquired the nickname "Hero" among his fellow cadets for not revealing the identity of his assailants.

While Rosa was in New York, curious correspondents flocked to Annapolis to devise the best strategies for covering the main Sutton drama. Early stories focused on the character of Jimmie Sutton; the role of Pittsburgh beauty, Mary Elizabeth Stewart, in precipitating Sutton's death; the disappearance of a key witness Lieutenant Edward Roelker; and the Sutton family's efforts to obtain justice for their son since 1907. Stories and interviews combined facts with speculation and occasionally fantasy, usually a safe practice as the articles were almost never published with a byline. Presenting a balanced view of the Sutton tragedy ahead of time would prove challenging. According to the *New York Times*, "opinion in this quaint little Maryland city is that Lieutenant Sutton was murdered"; in "naval circles the utmost reticence is being observed, and no opinions are expressed" except outrage at the "sensational stories" being sent out from Annapolis.

Colonel Charles Doyen was one officer willing to speak up, just as he had in 1907—his reputation was on the line once more. He told the press that he had learned what happened primarily from Lieutenant Harold Utley, but this time he added some new details. First, he repeated Utley's story that Sutton had been abusive to Lieutenant Robert Adams in the car ride back to the barracks; and then, according to Doyen, Lieutenant Utley specifically said Sutton had told Sergeant James De Hart that he was going to kill Lieutenant Adams and had gone out searching for him. This reference to Sutton singling out Robert Adams had not been mentioned at the inquest; it now came out in several papers. And it was an issue that would be raised in the courtroom with other questionable stories published in the news.

Who was Jimmie Sutton? In 1909, as in 1907, the answer depended on whom you asked. As opening day for the inquiry drew nearer, a *New York Times* reporter noticed: "There are numerous stories afloat around the city as to Sutton's peculiarities. None of them, however, can be substantiated and they may have been set afloat by his enemies to discredit him. The dead lieutenant from all that can be learned, was not popular with his brother officers." Some papers contrasted comments from Sutton's fellow officers in the Marine Corps with those of his friends to "define the issues." A special correspondent to the *Washington Sunday Star* (on weekdays the *Evening Star*) spoke with an anonymous Annapolitan. "It seems very strange . . . that none of us around here ever heard of Sutton's alleged unpopularity until after his death. Until then he seemed quite popular." On July 19, the *Baltimore Sun* and the *San Francisco Chronicle* cited one of Sutton's unnamed comrades: "There is nothing in Lieutenant Sutton's record to be ashamed of. He was a martyr to the hatred and jealousies of his comrades. He did not fire the shot that killed him." But the papers also said a Marine Corps officer claimed Sutton's record would startle those investigating his life and that he "shot himself either intentionally or in trying to kill his comrades."

The *New York Times* and the *Washington Post* quoted A. Wollett Webb, once a classmate of Sutton's at the Naval Academy and "a man of prominence in Baltimore" who worked for the Consolidated Gas and Electric Lighting Company. Webb said Sutton had been very unpopular and "repeatedly hazed and forced into fights" while at the Academy because he turned in several of his classmates when they violated unimportant regulations. Some of the men who disliked Sutton during the year he spent at the Academy had disagreements with him when they were together in the Marine Corps, according to Webb.

The longest interview about Sutton's character appeared on the front page of the July 12 *Philadelphia Inquirer*. John H. Layne "knew him more intimately probably than anyone outside of Lieutenant Sutton's immediate family," observed the reporter. Layne emphasized that Sutton had been devoted to his mother and sister and had not had any love affairs when they were roommates; above all, he focused on his work and was determined to overcome his weakness in languages. Layne took great pains to challenge every negative rumor flying about the town related to his former roommate. And then he stated that Sutton was "not the type of man who would be an aggressor, but if forced to the wall he was the type who would fight." John Layne was sure Sutton had not committed suicide; in fact, he thought "it was practically decided to call the case 'suicide' before the first investigation was made." At the end of the interview, Layne said he hoped the matter would be gone into thoroughly.

Layne would have his wish. The press corps delved into the matter from every angle, including a romantic one. Was Jimmie involved with a popular Pittsburgh society girl, a talented singer whose "sole ambition was to become a prima donna"? And, if so, what could she tell an eager public about his character? Rosa Sutton had learned about Jimmie's recent friendship with Mary Elizabeth Stewart from Gilbert Coleman, and probably also from her daughter Rose. "SUTTON'S DEATH DUE TO HIS SUCCESS IN LOVE AFFAIR" proclaimed a headline in the July 9 *New York American*. A friend of the lieutenant apparently had told the paper that Sutton and Mary Elizabeth Stewart "had fallen in love at first sight and from the first Sutton was most devoted. . . . It is said that she has never recovered from his death." Reporters across the country latched onto the story of Miss Stewart—not always getting her name right but often adding a photograph or drawing of the beautiful blue-eyed blond.

A New York *World* reporter wrote from Pittsburgh that Miss Stewart, who had left the country for health reasons, had been expected home on July 11; she decided to stay in Canada and give up her Pittsburgh apartment "at the fashionable boarding house of Mrs. Sara W. Bryer, No. 6338 Marchand Street." Miss Stewart had become estranged from her father and was not on speaking terms with her stepmother. "'Mary is very headstrong and careless,'" Mrs. Charles Stewart allegedly complained. "'Neither her father nor myself knows anything about what she has done lately. We never knew anything about the Annapolis affair save what we read in the papers. . . . She has gone to Canada with some young lady.'" Her father, a former Pittsburgh city councilman, contradicted his wife and said he was indeed in touch with his daughter. On July 13, the *Philadelphia Inquirer* asserted that everyone Stewart had discussed the case with agreed with the "consensus of opinion in Annapolis" that Lieutenant Sutton had been murdered. Mary was finally found in a cabin in Staney Brae, Ontario, on Lake Joseph, where she had gone to recover from an attack of "nerves." "'She always has suffered from nervous trouble of different kinds, and when the death of Lieutenant Sutton occurred she became ill,'" her father explained. "'I went to Annapolis to be with her, and she talked about the affair, but she said nothing that would shed light on his death.'" Charles Stewart would not allow his daughter to return to Annapolis to testify unless her health improved and it was absolutely necessary. Furthermore, he assured the press that she had not gone to Canada to escape the inquiry. In Pittsburgh, a rumor spread that Lieutenant Adams, another Pennsylvania native, had called on Mary recently, but no one would confirm it.

According to the *Evening Capital* (Annapolis), Miss Stewart had been "prostrated" by the news of Sutton's death and ended up in the "Emergency Hospital" where she was operated on for a type of hysteria. The *Chicago Tribune* also played up the romance, asserting that she was "ardently in love" with Sutton, who told his own comrades he had fallen in love with her at first sight. However, four days later, Mary emphatically denied any romance in a *New York Times* piece, "MISS STEWART SAW NO GLOOM IN SUTTON." When shown a newspaper article from Washington that suggested Lieutenant Adams had been in a fight with Sutton, she said, "Yes, that is what I have read too. . . . I know only the gossip of the affair and the newspaper reports." The *New York Times* reporter who tracked Mary Stewart down at a Canadian boarding house near the village of Staney Brae published her fond memories of Jimmie. Nothing that happened between them led her to think that Jimmie had contemplated suicide. The idea seemed impossible, she told the *Times*. He did not drink and was not subject to fits of temper, as far she knew. Admitting that she had been in a weak nervous state the morning after Jimmie's death and fainted at the news, Mary defensively added, "there is nothing wonderful or significant

about that. Any girl is apt to have a fainting spell at such shocking news."
The reporter continued,

> "Did you believe Sutton unpopular with his comrades in the Marine
> Corps?" Miss Stewart was asked.
>
> "Quite the contrary," she replied. "He seemed well-liked. His first ob-
> ject was study, but that didn't keep him from mixing in the social life. I
> was told of a few occasions when he broke loose on a jamboree, but was
> assured it was not frequent."
>
> "Was there ever a question of jealousy between Adams and any of the
> other officers and Sutton?"
>
> "About me?" Miss Stewart asked laughingly. "Jealous over me? That
> is even more absurd than anything I have yet heard."

Severance Johnson, a female reporter for the *New York American*, also
went to the wilderness of upper Ontario to find Miss Stewart. (She would
be one of three journalists to write about the case with a byline.) Traveling for a full day north from Toronto, she reached Mary only after a thirty-
mile boat trip "stopping at a score or more landings" on the way. Her
emotion-laden interview printed on July 15 reveals why some women reporters were dubbed "the sob sisters" or the "pity patrol." "At the very
mention of the name of Lieutenant Sutton Miss Stewart paled perceptibly.
When at last she regained her composure she said 'it is awful to drag me
into this affair. I had no part in it. It just happened that I was with the
young man on the night before he—' the voice of the speaker sank so low
that the last words of the sentence were inaudible." Mary told Miss Johnson that Jimmie had been "in the happiest of moods," and they were together almost constantly on his last day alive. "He wanted to be with me.
It was such a pleasure." She described how supportive he was of her goal
to become an opera singer, and when they returned to the Carvel Hall Hotel on the fateful night, we "talked of our hopes and ideals and life." Finally,
she said, Jimmie loved the navy.

Rosa told reporters she received at least two letters from Mary; one
spoke of her plans to go to church with Jimmie early on Sunday, October
13, and spend another day with him. At first, Rosa claimed Mary and her
son had been in love with each other. But on July 16, the *New York Times*
reported that Rosa now accepted Miss Stewart's statement that she was not
well acquainted with her son, and there was no attachment between them.
Two days later, a *Times* correspondent spoke again with Mary at her Canadian retreat. She contradicted any stories that suggested she had run away
to escape the inquiry with the words "I know no more about Lieutenant

James Sutton's death than anyone who merely reads the papers." Miss Stewart would not return to Annapolis as a witness in 1909.

Despite Mary Stewart's inaccessible location, it was much easier to find her than Edward Roelker. Throughout July, articles appeared in various papers with possible sightings. In its large magazine spread on the story on July 18, the *Washington Post* noted that Roelker, one of Sutton's friends and one of the most important witnesses, "has mysteriously disappeared." The *St. Louis Post-Dispatch* was more blunt: "The Navy Department is doing nothing" about finding Roelker, and "this indifference" is responsible for the reopening of the case. Although he had spent a few days with his family after being dismissed from the Marine Corps for drinking, "members of his family say they have no knowledge of his whereabouts." Admiral Roelker, who had retired from service in 1908, claimed to have "employed every known means the past year to locate his son." And Parthenia Roelker, who had worked so hard to secure a position for Red in the Marines, told an *American* reporter that Mrs. Sutton had paid her a visit. Mrs. Roelker said she felt sorry for Rosa, but she did not know "anything at all about the unfortunate occurrence; only what I have read in the newspapers. Lieutenant Roelker and Sutton were good friends, I believe."

The *Baltimore Sun* found it peculiar that only Roelker had been court-martialed not long after Sutton's death. However, the paper stated, two days before the inquiry, acting commandant of the Marine Corps Colonel Charles Lauchheimer, Captain Edward Campbell, Major Harry Leonard, and Henry Davis also claimed to have exhausted "every known means" to locate a man who may have been Jimmie's only good friend in the Corps and "the most important witness in the approaching investigation. . . . Official naval channels throughout the world have been employed within the past three months to locate Roelker, but without avail." For all those involved, Roelker's fate would become one of the most puzzling aspects of the Sutton case, and the press would keep looking. The thirty-one-thousand-plus readers of the *Oregon Daily Journal* could ponder a blunt accusation that probably occurred to many people, whether justified or not: "the navy department knows where Roelker is."

Most high officials declined to discuss the case, but the press created drama by juxtaposing interviews with Marine Corps witnesses and plain citizens. Two young men who stood on opposite sides of the fence held a special appeal for reporters: Lieutenant Robert Adams and chauffeur William Owens. The *New York American* located Adams in Sea Girt, New Jersey, awaiting the inquiry. He had been recalled from China along with

Edward Osterman. Interest in his side of the story increased after it became clear that the Navy Department had given him the privilege of being represented by counsel. Adams insisted the charges had been trumped up against him, and referring to Sutton's ghost, said he did not recognize "'the spirit that seeks to gain a hallowed grave for a man long dead by trying to trump up a case of murder'" against innocent marines. Sutton had started the fight, used abusive language, and called him a vile name. The *Chicago Tribune* headlined its similar piece "ADAMS SEES RELIGIOUS PLOT."

William Owens had a "remarkable story" that contradicted that of Lieutenant Adams, all the more intriguing because he was a civilian. The chauffeur reportedly had been visited at his home by no fewer than thirteen officers who cautioned him against saying anything until the new court met. Owens must know "much more than is generally supposed," surmised a *New York Times* reporter, who also claimed (and Owens would deny it) that he had been in Washington "in consultation with Mrs. Sutton." Owens, who was shying away from reporters, did say the naval authorities had made him mad "'when they said I skipped out of town the next day. I was here all the time running the same car all that day.'" He had not been examined by the original board of inquest, and the implication was always that he should have been.

But most headlines focused on the mother and daughter team of Mrs. Sutton and Mrs. Parker. Rose was said to be largely responsible for the inquiry. Reporters seized on the story of how she grilled the Marine Corps officers in Annapolis during the week after her brother's burial. More than one paper would describe her as a modern-day "Portia," the clever and beautiful heroine of Shakespeare's *Merchant of Venice*. "But many years she has devoted to literary work, writing short stories for various periodicals," stated an *American* reporter. "At one time she was stationed in Pekin [*sic*] as a representative of the Associated Press." When she got to Annapolis, this woman of "unusual intellect and experience" decided to probe the crime herself. New Yorkers and Chicagoans were among those who could read stirring accounts of Rose's sleuthing. She acted as a judge and prosecutor, organizing her own "veritable court-martial" to grill the men who had been at the scene when her brother died. Just as fascinating to reporters was the apparition of her brother that Rose saw on her train ride East. "She was not the sort of woman to give much credit to dreams," an *American* reporter decided. But Rose was sure that she had seen Jimmie as she was crossing the Rocky Mountains by train. "WOMAN IS SLEUTH FOLLOWING VISION," began a comparable *Chicago Tribune* story of Lieutenant Sutton's sister who held her own investigation. In Cincinnati, the *Enquirer*, which always began

"I HATED SUTTON," New York American, July 11, 1909. Courtesy of the Harry Ransom Humanities Research Center, University of Texas at Austin.

its feature stories about this case with one-word headlines, chose VISIONS on July 19 to introduce the fact that both Rose and Rosa had seen Jimmie's ghost.

Big-city dailies put the Sutton inquiry on their front pages alongside the insanity trial of Harry Thaw, the latest daring feats of the Wright Brothers, international crises, and local disasters. As the suspense grew, some headlines appeared in red ink. And Rosa Sutton was the leading lady; her photograph often appeared next to one of her son, or in a collage of images of principal actors and locations in the case. Despite reported attempts to get her to drop the investigation, Rosa had talked to the press openly while at the West Point Hotel, insisting she would not give up the fight. Chicago's *Tribune* described her in a headline as an "UNTIRING NEMESIS," while the *World* (New York) reported that she and her husband, "now a broken man," had been ignored by President Roosevelt. *American* reporters, who followed her everywhere, implied that Rosa had a special relationship with their paper. Rosa had promised she would "give out a statement covering the entire matter," as soon as she returned to Washington from West Point and saw her lawyer. Very much in line with the spirit of the era, Rose supposedly declared, "I decline to be silent for I realize that if such newspapers as *The American* do not delve into matters of this kind they will be hushed quickly by those in authority." While she was at West Point, the paper asserted, Rosa was "besieged by powerful influences to withdraw from the proceedings which promised a national sensation." The *Evening Journal* (New York) took this idea even further with a headline "LIEUT. SUTTON'S MOTHER IS THREATENED" by "mysterious forces" and by "persons who begged her to let the sensation rest."

Rosa's attorneys warned her not to talk to the press when she returned to the capital from the New York Highlands on Wednesday, July 13. But she recognized an *American* reporter in the lobby of the Burlington Apartments and said what he (or she) would want to print the next morning:

> I want to thank *The American* for its generous and hearty support. Your paper has treated me most kindly, and I want you to know that I appreciate it. I am very sorry that I can say nothing tonight but you see that I am in the hands of my counsel and they forbid all further statements for the present. If I had anything further to say you may be sure *The American* should have it. As a matter of fact there is nothing new to be said in regard to the case. Everything that could be said has been printed.

Old friends of the Suttons in California followed the case through the *Los Angeles Times*. Like papers on the East Coast, the *Times* gave it lengthy coverage on the weekend before the inquiry and quoted Rosa Sutton in connection with the "now famous case."

> The whole world will know that my boy did not take his own life but that he was the victim of a brutal murder. My son was neither an angel nor a saint . . . but there was not one drop of a coward's blood in his veins. Determined to clear his name of the stigma which was placed on it by the Board of Investigation which convened in Annapolis a few hours after his death, I have been working single-handedly for nearly two years to have the Navy Department reopen the case.

Thanks to the comprehensive coverage in their papers, Americans could also consider the navy side of the story. There was no question that the second time around the investigation would be transparent, and witnesses would be under oath. Acting Secretary of the Navy Beekman Winthrop explained that a public inquiry would ensure that the correct version of the testimony would be circulated. As for the criticism that civilian witnesses were not called by the first inquest, the Department, according to the *Philadelphia Inquirer*, answered that the navy had been "without authority to compel the attendance of civilian witnesses" in Courts of Inquiry or courts-martial—that is, until 1909. Other than Senator Charles Fulton's remarks in the *Oregonian* in response to Rosa's accusations, there was no answer as to whether the Department tried to secure volunteer testimony from civilians such as William Owens.

The navy had agreed to the inquiry because of discrepancies in the 1907 testimony (pointed out to the Department by Oregon senator Jonathan Bourne). After an "exhaustive study" of the records, Navy Secretary George Meyer admitted he had decided another hearing was necessary. Meyer assured the *New York Times* that there would be no whitewashing; he would interfere if he saw "the slightest inclination on the part of anyone to strive to gloss the affair over." Commander John Hood and Lieutenant Henry Norman Jensen, the two navy representatives on the court, were glad the hearing would be public so that the navy and Marine Corps would prove the matter had not been hushed up. "Officers, particularly those of the Marine Corps, feel that their service is now on trial before the American people," said the *Times*. Because no one was punished in 1907, "now is the time to clear the service of hiding anything in the first investigation and to see that those who were in the mess are punished." The affair had attracted so much publicity, those in charge were of the "unanimous opinion" that there must be a definitive resolution of the case.

But while the press expected that a genuine effort to find "all the facts" would be made, the *Atlanta Constitution* brought up the "reluctance on the part of the Naval Academy people to get very far away from the suicide theory." Projected outcomes of the inquiry were frequent. An unnamed "officer of high rank" said his theory was that Sutton was shooting at a man who was at the back of his neck holding his head to the ground, and he did not kill himself intentionally. A number of officers were said to predict the verdict would be changed to death by accident, which would be "more charitable to Sutton and his family."

On July 18, a prominent feature in the *Washington Post Sunday Magazine* made sure that readers in the nation's capital stayed with the story: "THE VEILS OF MYSTERY TO BE DRAWN IN SUTTON TRAGEDY." Photographs of Rose and Jimmie appeared in the center bracketed by larger photos of Rosa Sutton and Henry Leonard. Will there be a startling truth revealed by this new hearing? asked the *Post*. The *Evening Journal* began publishing an illustrated serial for its New York readers about the mysterious fate of the young lieutenant. In Portland, Rosa's husband and two other daughters, Louise and Daysie, could read a similar feature in the *Oregon Sunday Journal* with a photograph of Rosa in her pearls. Correspondent John E. Lathrop, who had traveled all the way to Annapolis, was enthralled by both the plot and the setting of the drama before him. "Victor Hugo could of this material weave a romance as good as he ever penned," he wrote, providing his readers with an engaging description of the historic town and his adventures as a reporter there. Lathrop had gone undercover—he decided to stay at the Carvel Hall Hotel and pretend he was a country tourist "from Podunk or somewhere." He chatted with waiters and clerks who acted like aristocrats toward him because he did not have the "social distinction attaching to this naval establishment." Rosa and her daughter would be treated the same way—a point foreshadowed by Lathrop's comment that "the Chinese wall is a band of flimsy ribbon compared with the wall of social exclusiveness erected around the Naval Academy to keep out marine corps men"—and by implication their family members, too, who had the gall to challenge the system.

Between July 19 and August 18, when the "WRAITH of Lieutenant Sutton" went "on trial," journalists and photographers would present blow-by-blow accounts of Rosa's activities, those of the men who took up her cause, the reactions of military personnel, and above all the daily testimony in Annapolis. As the press set the stage, the principal players settled into their Annapolis quarters for a long, often sultry, month. On Sunday, July 18, at noon, Rose Parker, who had come east "against her doctor's orders," arrived at Union Station from St. Paul, Minnesota. She spent the afternoon in her mother's apartment. At about five that afternoon, the two women likely took the new Washington, Baltimore, and Annapolis Electric Railway to Annapolis. Harry Swartz accompanied them to the station and wished them well. They reached Annapolis just in time to dine with attorney Edmund Van Dyke, who would observe the proceedings now that Henry Davis was their chief counsel.

The only patrons left in the Carvel Hall dining room when Mrs. Sutton and Mrs. Parker arrived were Lieutenants Adams and Osterman who had rooms in a boarding house across from the hotel. Rose spoke to them courteously, but the lieutenants were not in uniform, and she did not mention who they were to her mother until after dinner. A reporter quoted Osterman: "If Owens has any friends they had best warn him to be careful how he talks, otherwise he may lay himself open to charges of perjury." For

"A Mystery That Stirs the Navy," New York Evening Journal, July 19, 1909.

the lieutenants, the new inquiry was "almost like a class reunion." When they learned Edward Shippen Willing was staying at the Carvel Hall Hotel, they went off to try to find him before court convened the next morning "TO WIPE OUT THE MYSTERY" of Jimmie Sutton.

That night, when Monday's *New York Times* came off the presses, an editorial appeared titled "SCANDALS WILL COME TO THE SURFACE." It would be the first of several *Times* editorials about Lieutenant Sutton's death. For the *Times*, the story was about integrity—evidence of the "danger or the folly of attempting to conceal the facts in a case that involves the commission of a crime or other serious wrong." The editor laid out a challenge for Commander John Hood and Major Henry Leonard: "The original mistake was in showing a tenderer regard for the repute of the navy and the Marine Corps than for their character." And then, alluding to the Dreyfus Case, still a point of reference for matters pertaining to military justice, the editor wrote,

> It is one thing . . . to hush up a private scandal, affecting only a family or a little group of friends. And quite another to do the same thing when public interests are deeply involved. France had a dreadful lesson as to what may come from confounding the "honor of the army" with a reputation of a few of its officers. Whatever the facts in the SUTTON case may have been, nothing would have hastened them toward a safe oblivion as much as a prompt clearing up of the whole mystery. The credit that would have come from that will now be lost, as it always is when justice is belated, reluctant, and coerced.

7

A SERIOUS AND GRAVE AFFAIR

On Monday, July 19, a reporter from the New York *World* described the colorful scene that greeted those who gathered for the Sutton inquiry.

> A fresh wind was blowing from the harbor and carrying the strains of "I Wish I had a Girl" over the parade grounds from the bandstand. Jaunty midshipmen togged in white, grizzled seamen their faces tanned to a leather by the seven seas, dignified officers with varying shades and degrees of shoulder straps, and white frocked women carrying varicolored sunshades which take the place of hats in Annapolis, mingled with an army of industrious photographers and newspaper writers in front of the Administration Building.

Commander John Hood, Major Wendell C. Neville, Lieutenant Henry Jensen, and Harry Leonard, judge advocate, arrived just before ten o'clock in their crisp all-white summer service uniforms decorated with lace and gold braid. Lieutenant Robert Adams, appearing calm, followed the court accompanied by his attorneys, Arthur A. Birney and Captain Thomas Brown. All of the principals would pass through a "lane of clicking cameras" before they crowded into the tiny, stuffy court-martial room.

Rose Parker led the Sutton party with their associate counsel, Messrs. Edmund and Harry Van Dyke. A "striking brunette" with a girlish figure, she wore a black and white checked suit and a patent leather walking hat with a wide brim. As soon as she entered the public spotlight, reporters commented on her eyes—unusually large, piercing, and "as dark as her jet black hair." Her mother, stout but attractive, with "masses of gray hair," would be dressed in black for much of the inquiry. On this first day, Rosa's silk suit and unstylish hat with its short mourning veil proclaimed her "not

The Sutton Court of Inquiry, New York Evening Journal, July 20, 1909. From left to right: Major Henry Leonard, judge advocate, Major Wendell C. Neville, Commander John Hood, and Lieutenant Henry Jensen. Courtesy of the Harry Ransom Humanities Research Center, University of Texas at Austin.

the woman of fashion, yet as being refined and in well-to-do circumstances." Her "comely features scarcely betray the determination of character she has shown" over the past two years, observed the *Washington Post* the next morning. At one point her escort and attorney, Henry Davis, "an active little man with a spacious bald spot," lagged behind, and Rosa Sutton faced the cameras alone. Neither woman seemed depressed as they "greeted the swarm of clicking photographers with smiles." Once inside the cramped room, Rosa "settled herself in the chair allotted to her at the long table of the court without a word."

It was clear at the outset that this room could barely hold the parties to the inquiry, and it would certainly not accommodate the press corps or the public. So the first session of the Sutton court was just long enough to take care of the preliminaries. After Commander Hood gave the customary announcement that "in obedience to orders, it would sit with open doors," Major Leonard read out loud the Navy Department's precept authorizing the proceeding. He then asked all the men and the two women at the table "if they objected to any member present." No one did. Leonard administered the oath to the three members of the court, who swore they

"PRINCIPAL FIGURES IN SUTTON INQUIRY," New York Evening Journal, *August 9, 1909.*

would "examine and inquire, according to the evidence," into the matter now before them "without partiality." Hood, as court president, then swore in Harry Leonard whose official job it was to truly "record the proceedings of this Court and the evidence to be given in the case in hearing." Acknowledging that Henry Davis had requested a copy of the daily transcript, Major Leonard offered one to Arthur Birney; later that day he declined. At 10:25 a.m. the court recessed for two and a half hours so preparations could be made for a larger space only a short distance away.

The Academic Building was one of several Beaux Arts structures designed by architect Ernest Flagg for the new Naval Academy. Now known as Mahan Hall, it stands on the northwest side of the yard across from Bancroft Hall, the immense dormitory that Jimmie Sutton and his classmates had lived in for at least part of their plebe year. The symmetry and size of the rectangular building inspired awe in reporters and visitors unfamiliar with Annapolis. The entrance to Mahan is almost as impressive as the interior—a double reverse turn stairway at the front leads up to huge double-paneled wooden doors, each decorated with metal rosettes and knockers representing Neptune with dolphin's heads. The parties to the Sutton inquiry would spend much of the next month inside an elegant two-story-high auditorium with a balcony facing a stage. At its back and sides, tall arched windows could let in whatever breeze there was on steaming summer days. Less than two hours before Lieutenant Sutton died, several of the Marine Corps lieutenants about to testify had been at

The Academic Building at the United States Naval Academy, now Mahan Hall. Courtesy of the Special Collections and Archives Division, Nimitz Library, United States Naval Academy.

a Naval Academy dance—the first of the 1907 social season—in this same room.

An upright piano, a music stand, and a table that would be used for the civilians' straw boater hats stood just below the stage, now the backdrop for a proceeding that would have many theatrical moments. Parallel to the stage, two tables had been pushed together to form a single long one for the court and the parties to the inquiry, who now assembled around it in leather armchairs with high-tufted backs. John Hood sat at one end of the table with the two members of his court on either side. Harry Leonard would lead the proceedings from the other end. On the first day, he used an empty armchair to his right as the witness stand; his court reporter, Herman Pechin, sat on a straight-backed chair to his left. About a dozen civilians watched from two smaller tables behind the judge advocate, pencils poised to take notes. These were likely some of the members of the press who attended the inquiry. All of the civilian and military witnesses subpoenaed by Leonard had arrived for the first day—but they would wait in the corridors. By day three Major Leonard would insist that they stand at least one hundred feet away from the doors.

The picturesque audience would grow as the inquiry progressed—a fact that pleased the "townsfolk" who hoped to make some extra money. Men, and the women who usually outnumbered them, took their places on high-backed wooden benches reminiscent of church pews. Among the spectators were high-ranking officers, enlisted men, society people from Annapolis, and even excursionists from Baltimore who came down by boat on the steamer *Tolchester*. Wives of navy and marine officers sat alongside "a score of young girls garbed in the latest summer fashion who followed the testimony when not profane and giggled profusely." They were obviously in sympathy with the Marine Corps witnesses, not with Henry Davis in his "immaculate suit of white flannel." On this first day, playwright and novelist Paul Armstrong could be seen in the audience, as could Claude Fay Doyen, whose husband was now relegated to the corridor as a witness.

"The ghost of Lieutenant James Nuttle Sutton of the United States Marine Corps was put on trial here today on the charge of suicide," announced the *New York American* in its summary of the day about to begin. Several officers would be called to testify against this specter, and the first of these was Robert Adams. Wearing his blue-black uniform jacket and sky blue pants, Adams moved quickly from his seat at the table to the armchair next to Harry Leonard, only a few feet from Rose Parker. Reporters noted the heavyset, round-faced young lieutenant stood tall and walked in gracefully, his sword trailing behind him. While his brother, William, watched closely from a bench in the auditorium, Robert Adams solemnly swore that the evidence he would give "shall be the truth, the whole truth, and nothing but the truth," and that he would state everything within his knowledge "in relation to the matter under Inquiry: so help me God." But before Adams could say much, his attorneys halted the proceedings to confirm that no official charges had been brought against him—even though he had been given the right to have counsel. His status as the only witness (in addition to Rose Parker and Rosa Sutton) to be allowed in the courtroom through the entire inquiry made it obvious to reporters that the Sutton family suspected Adams of foul play. For Henry Davis this was a dilemma. Should Adams testify under oath as an accused person, his willingness to answer openly could be compromised.

It was immediately apparent that Robert Adams recalled many more details than he had a few hours after the tragedy, ones that put Jimmie Sutton in a worse light before and during the fatal brawl. He told the court that during the car ride back to the barracks Lieutenant Harold Utley (who was in charge of the camp) suggested they get out and walk before they neared Colonel Charles Doyen's house because the machine was so noisy. Adams agreed, and at that point, Jimmie Sutton allegedly said, "'You are a damned cold-footed coward' or words to that effect, and I turned around and said 'Don't you talk to me that way to me, Sutton.' He said, 'If you don't shut your Goddamn mouth, I will take you out and beat hell out of you.'" Sutton was the one to insist that they stop the machine once they reached the dump, thirty-five or forty yards on the other side of College Creek Bridge. When they stepped out of the machine, Adams said, Sutton did not disrobe for a fight; Utley prevented the fight. But Adams now added, "Mr. Sutton said the threat that he was going to shoot me." Lieutenant Adams next described Sutton's fight with Edward Osterman, lowering his voice on repeating the epithet "Dutch-son-of-a Bitch" (which Sutton called Osterman) as he glanced at Rosa Sutton and her daughter "whose incredulity was reflected in their faces." At this point, several ladies entered the auditorium and "clustered in the pew-like seats within a dozen feet of him. Adams seemed to know them." The lieutenant explained that Sutton got up and ran up a little incline, just where the electric light was, and said, "'I am going to kill you all before sunrise.'"

Lieutenant Adams then mentioned that he and the other lieutenants "had known that Mr. Sutton had shot up the camp before." For Adams, who had arrived in July, the May 20, 1907, incident was hearsay—hardly admissible according to Rosa's attorney. However, Adams explained that was why, after the initial fracas, he felt threatened and went to the barracks with Edward Osterman to try to get revolvers or rifles that were kept under lock and key by the sergeant of the guard. Over and over again during the coming days, Major Leonard would ask each government witness about the May 20 event, assuring the court it was relevant, while Henry Davis protested.

Although Adams and Osterman were not able to get hold of guns, Adams said they ran into Lieutenant Utley who told Adams to "'go down to the place where the fight took place and see if you can find any clothes other than those you have, lying there.' Utley was the senior officer present, and I obeyed his orders. That is all I know," said Adams. These were not orders Adams recalled in 1907; but now, the witness claimed, he ran into Sutton on the way to get these clothes. Sutton said,

> "That is that Goddamned Adams, isn't it?" I said "Yes." He said "Where are you going?" I said, "I am going down here to pick up the clothes." Then he said "You are like hell; I am going to kill you." With that he shot. I kept on walking, just for a moment I stopped, but it was not any perceptible time—I kept on walking during our conversation. Immediately upon his shooting the first time, I rushed at him. He shot again, and just as I got to him he shot a third time, which struck me in the fin-

ger. I had just about touched the muzzle of his revolver, which I am quite positive was a Colt's pistol.

Adams continued his account of the critical moments before Sutton's death: "I grappled with him, and got him by his hand, by his wrist, and got my chest against his back, where he could not use his guns." He threw Sutton to the ground, "on his face, a few feet to the right of the road or concrete path. . . . He fell with his arm under him, the right arm under him, like this [indicating] and his left arm spread out. I was on his back and trying to keep him from using either pistol. I don't know just how long I was on him; but while I was on him somebody jumped on his left hand. Who that was, I don't know."

"That was the one that was extended?" asked Leonard.

"The one that was extended, yes sir."

"Did you see anything in the hand of that arm?"

"Not then. . . . I didn't take any notice. He had two pistols when I first rushed him, but after that I don't know. I haven't any recollection of how I got off of him, at all. The next thing I remember was that I was standing back of him. I can illustrate this better—"

At several points during the inquiry, the men and women in the auditorium would be entertained (or shocked, depending on their perspective), by re-enactments of the moments just before Sutton died. With the court's permission, Robert Adams now engaged the help of a sturdy orderly in a white uniform. Lying on the auditorium floor near Rose Parker's feet, pretending to be her dead brother, he explained: "I was trying to force him to the ground, where he would not be able to see where I was, and then somebody said something about Roelker, and I turned around and there was Roelker on the right side of the road, and two officers or one officer was picking him up. Mr. Roelker was apparently dead. He was at least limp or unconscious, and just as I said that—"

"What did you say?" asked Harry Leonard.

"I said, 'My God has he killed Reddy?' Or 'Has he killed Roelker?' I don't remember whether I said Reddy or Roelker and as I said that Sutton turned his head in this manner (indicating, the witness being down on the floor) and pulled his pistol out something like this, and I saw a flash and it evidently jumped between three and four inches—"

After explaining that he had been on Sutton's right side, Adams stood up, returned to the witness chair, and continued. He assured Major Leonard he had never taken a revolver from Sutton, and over the next few minutes he explained to the court that Sutton had the reputation of being nasty.

Adams now emphasized that Sutton threatened to shoot him, another point that, like his nastiness, had not come out in 1907. And he described the two pistols Sutton had—a smaller one he thought was probably a .32 caliber and the other one, which was a service revolver. As for the fatal fight with Sutton, Adams admitted he shoved Sutton's head "in the ground as hard as I could with my shoulder and hand. I hit him the moment I reached . . . him and that is what caused me to take hold with my left-hand—because I intended to hit him, if I could, with my right. I reached him, but I don't know how much damage I did to him." Sutton "put up a struggle for possibly 20 seconds or more, and then he seemed to weaken," but not, Adams assured the court, because of the blow from him. The lieutenant was hazy about how he got off Sutton, and as for the rest of the incident, he said, "I have forgotten it."

Commander Hood asked why Sutton and Adams were not on speaking terms although they had once been so friendly and even "called on a girl" together. Adams explained that he had been warned by Lieutenant Edwin McClellan (who had arrived at the school about ten days before Adams) not to befriend Sutton or he would get into trouble. But he had other reasons as well. At an infantry drill in August 1907, Adams had been detailed company commander irrespective of rank. But Sutton was actually senior to Adams and "was acting leader of the first section for instruction." And "he simply got in front of the company and told the First Sergeant to dismiss the company." It was "a nasty knock officially at me," Adams said, and then he gave another example. "In the artillery field, he ordered me to stand out beside the muzzle of a three inch field piece. I told him it was not right, and that Capt. Marix would probably call him down for it. He used vile language, and after that I thought it was better not [to] have anything to do with Sutton." Sutton had disrespected him at a time when he needed recognition. Robert Adams surely knew this account would earn the sympathy of all the military men in the room.

A *New York Times* reporter noticed that Rosa Sutton "eyed the witness closely while he testified occasionally shaking her head."

When Harry Leonard finished his initial questioning, Commander Hood announced that following the direct examination by the judge advocate, each witness would be examined by his or her own attorney and then cross-examined by the attorney for the opposing side.

Arthur Birney, who had no doubt prepared Lieutenant Adams for many of the questions that he had been asked, had a few points he wanted his client to clarify for the court.

"I understand you to say that you did not see the two revolvers after you clutched Sutton?" Birney asked.

"After I clutched him I don't know how the revolvers were fixed at all," came the response. "I think in my former testimony I told that it seemed as though he shot [himself] when he pulled the revolver out, and he pulled the small revolver out; but how the change came about I don't know. That is only my impression, that it was the small revolver."

"When you threw Sutton down he fell on his face, as I understand it?"

"Yes sir."

"And you fell across him?"

"I fell right down with him. I had my shoulder right near him."

"Were you resting upon his body?"

"Yes sir: I was momentarily, and trying to block his arm from being withdrawn from under his body."

Adams had apparently tried hard, using his elbow or his knee to keep Sutton from getting his right hand out, but after that point he had no recollection of what happened or how he got up. It was then that he saw Lieutenants William Bevan and Edward Willing, as well as Sergeant James De Hart. But he did not say they were on top of Sutton. He described the position of the other lieutenants after Sutton had been shot, demonstrating again by pantomime. But why had Adams gone back to the scene of the original Sutton-Osterman fight at all? Especially if he felt threatened by Jimmie Sutton. Under further questioning by his own attorney, Adams repeated that Lieutenant Utley's "direction to me was to go down there to get clothes."

Harry Leonard had a good reason for wanting to know more about the officers' clothing when they left Carvel Hall. Some of the men were in dress uniforms—Adams described their dark blue mess jackets with red lining and no pockets (except a little pocket for cards). During the brawl they still had their white vests and white shirts on. Their trousers were "cut very tight" and came up under the jackets. Adams was sure it would have been impossible for any of them to carry a revolver and not have it noticed.

Leonard continued, asking Adams detailed questions about the shots that had been fired that night. Again Adams came up with some new information about the fifth and final shot, saying, "my impression is that the shot he fired with which he killed himself was fired with the small pistol"—Sutton's personal Smith & Wesson.

"But you do not know that?" Leonard asked.

"No sir; I cannot state that positively, but that is my impression."

For the moment, Leonard was through with his questions.

Every day the court would break for lunch at close to noon or at 12:30, with testimony resuming at 2:00 p.m. Henry Davis began his cross-examination after the midday recess.

He returned to Adams' hostility toward Sutton who, despite his much smaller stature, had allegedly told Adams he was going to "beat hell" out of him. Adams insisted that Sutton singled him out and threatened to shoot him that night and that he had only followed Lieutenant Utley's orders when he returned to the parade ground to see if anyone had left clothes there.

Though there was no apparent reason for Utley to have given Adams this order, Adams started down the path "absolutely alone" until he came across "something white" and discovered "this white object" moved and it was Sutton—who "seemed to be stooping over." And then he "straightened up." Sutton then, according to Adams' new version of the incident, again said he was going to kill him and fired at him. Although he was unarmed, Adams went after Sutton from eighteen to thirty paces away, knowing Sutton held two revolvers. The final and fatal shot, Adams repeated once again, came after he had thrown Sutton on the ground and then suddenly noticed Edward Roelker lying on the ground as well. Adams told Henry Davis, "I cannot say positively, but my impression is that it was from the little pistol. It was dark and I cannot say positively. Beside that he had that pistol in his right hand, which he did not have when I first rushed at him. I explained that before in my testimony, that that was only my impression, that I had no way of knowing."

By this time, Adams said he had already gotten up from Sutton, although he had no idea how, and left him lying on the ground.

Davis was not convinced. "Although he had threatened to kill you twice, had fired at you at least three times in an effort to kill you, and although you knew he had two weapons, and you did not know whether either one of them was exhausted or not, after you've got him on the ground and ground his nose into the ground and tried to disable him, still you got up and left him lying there?"

"Yes sir."

"With a revolver in his hand?"

"With a revolver in his hand, under him, yes."

"Do you think he was unconscious?"

"I gave it no thought. I thought assistance had arrived, because I felt somebody jump on his left arm."

Adams fielded questions from Davis in a "quick and straightforward"— even "spirited"—manner, though nervous, defiant, and "momentarily confused at times," according to more than one newspaper. Pausing for frequent drinks of water, he answered frankly, sometimes trembling with excitement. The *Army and Navy Journal* had a loyal following in Congress and among the public. For the duration of the inquiry there would be weekly columns on the Sutton case. The *Journal* attributed Adams' unease to his "concentration rather than apprehension." Regardless of the cause, the press would notice that Rosa and Rose stared at him intently from across the table, their faces reflecting resignation rather than animosity when he described how he ground Jimmie's face in the dirt. An Annapolis reporter's florid prose may have encouraged even more townspeople to come to the auditorium: "These two women sit by the hour looking deep into the eyes of the man talking as though to read his very soul. Then they will chat with each other and with their counsel, sometimes smiling or even laughing." A *New York American* correspondent revealed that Rose Parker took notes in a leather book and frequently made suggestions to Davis. Adams was "visibly affected" by the severe questioning from the judge advocate and from attorney Davis.

Finding ways to attack Robert Adams' credibility was key for Henry Davis; if there was a chance that Adams had pulled the trigger that sent the bullet into Sutton's brain, reasonable doubt about Jimmie Sutton's guilt could be established. This had been a point raised by Edmund Van Dyke who sat right behind him throughout most of the inquiry. Again and again, Henry Davis hammered at the point that Robert Adams was supposed to be defending his life, and yet he got off Sutton (but didn't remember how) and left this man who had just tried to kill him and "still might have arisen and put his threat into execution." Finally somewhat exasperated, Davis asked the lieutenant, "Do you mean to be understood that he shot at himself?" Unintentional death by one's own hand was not strictly suicide.

"I was asked for my opinion, at the former court, as to what he shot at. I have no opinion as to what he shot at. I simply saw him shoot," said the witness.

It was close to 3:30 p.m. when Davis brought up the testimony Robert Adams had given in 1907. Leonard now placed the official transcript of the Board of Inquest into evidence as Exhibit G. And Davis went after the discrepancies in Adams' two accounts.

In 1907, Adams said he—not Utley or Sutton—had been the one to tell William Owens where to stop the automobile. Adams now did not remember how he testified two years earlier, and Davis asked him—as he would others—"Which do you think is more likely to be correct, your recollection then or your recollection now?"

"Well," Adams answered, "my most accurate recollection of that testimony is what I am giving now. It may differ in detail from what I said then. I have tried to forget this thing, and I have never recalled the thing at all and my testimony may vary in detail. That is natural, I think." Adams would be the only witness to suggest that his memory had improved over time. He said that verbal abuse from Sutton in the car began because the men were late getting back to the barracks. It was not the result of long-standing hostility between the two of them. Rather, "The entire subject started over whether we had better take this noisy machine up by the camp." Discrepancies also appeared in what he had said about Lieutenants Utley's role that evening, and what happened when he first met the armed Lieutenant Sutton in the dark.

"I want to direct your attention to this," said Davis,

> that on the former Inquest which was held the very day of this occurrence you testified that you went down this path, and that Mr. Sutton challenged you to halt, that he challenged you twice, and because you did not halt he fired. You now say today that you were on your way hunting for some clothes and he asked you where you were going and you said you were going to get these clothes, and without any challenge, he said "Like hell you are" and that he was going to kill you. Which is right?

From Robert Adams' perspective, if he was accused of murder, it would certainly help to argue a case of self-defense.

"What I said today is exactly as I remember it," said Adams, insisting that the first thing Sutton said to him was, "'Is that that Goddamned Adams?'" and, he now claimed, Sutton had not asked him to halt.

Robert Adams had "no explanation to make" for his change of story, one that now made Jimmie Sutton the aggressor in the fracas. Davis underscored the fact that in 1907 his testimony had been read back to him and approved by him. Moreover, he had said Sutton was apparently unconscious when he made the comment about Roelker—so how could Sutton have shot himself because he thought Roelker was dead?

The news media had set the stage for Davis' next question by reporting on Rose Parker's detective work. "You know Mrs. Parker, Lieutenant Sutton's sister, the lady who is sitting by me?" Adams admitted that he had met Rose Parker at the barracks and seen her at the Carvel Hall Hotel. He had gone to her room at her suggestion. Adams recalled that they spoke mostly of her brother's relationship with other officers. And he did not remember making any statement to Rose about her brother's death. "I think I told Mrs. Parker that she could get the Board of Inquest record and see the statement I had made."

It was almost four o'clock. The bells on the Academic Building's clock tower rang eight times just after Henry Davis began grilling Adams about his meeting with Rose Parker. But Major Leonard kept to a tight schedule as the president of the court had requested. Every afternoon, a reporter observed, he would "look up over his gold-rimmed spectacles" before announcing to the witness of the moment, "This will be the last question." Court adjourned promptly at four o'clock.

The first day of the inquiry came to a close on this balmy Monday evening. There would be fourteen more days of testimony before the attorneys would present closing arguments on August 13. Observers from the press spoke with Rosa, who assured reporters her son "was a dead shot" and would not have missed if he had wanted to kill Lieutenant Adams. As for Adams, he supposedly complained that Sutton's sister was plotting "to have him hanged."

Americans could read lengthy comments on the day's testimony apparently given to the press by Davis on Monday night. He reviewed the glaring discrepancies in Adams' testimony between 1907 and 1909; clearly there was much more specificity in Adams' testimony two years after Sutton's death. "FRESHENED MEMORY REMARKABLE," proclaimed the *Chicago Tribune*. And in New York, the *Evening Journal* enticed its readers with "TRAP ADAMS IN DENIALS."

Across America, the families of the Marine Corps witnesses surely followed the daily accounts of the inquiry. In the coming weeks, the papers would frequently publish several stories on the same day covering various aspects of the case. One mother with a great deal at stake was Emma Utley, recently widowed, and now living in Springfield. She and her many friends, who had lobbied so hard to secure a spot for her only child in the Corps, looked forward at least once a day to learning what was going on half a continent away. The *Illinois State Register* was one of Springfield's oldest papers. In the summer of 1909, it sold for three pennies during the week and five cents on Sunday—but for a mere thirteen cents a week a subscription was available, and Harold Utley's mother may have had one. Less polished than some of its New York counterparts, it ran ten to twenty-four pages, depending on the news of the day. Occasionally, typographical errors showed up in its articles. But, unlike the *Chicago Tribune*, the coverage was not sensational; in fact, the reporting was quite straightforward. The Sutton case dominated its front page during much of July and August. The *Register* published few photographs other than two large head shots of Rose Parker and an arresting picture of Leonard that did not appear in most Eastern papers. Mrs. Parker, according to the *Register* and other papers, was the person most responsible for gathering evidence that led to this second inquiry.

On July 20, following Lieutenant Adams' first day of testimony, Mrs. Utley found herself mentioned in a story accompanying a summary of the testimony, "SPRINGFIELD YOUNG MAN WAS COMPANION IN AUTO RIDE WITH SUTTON NIGHT OF TRAGEDY—FATAL FIGHT FOLLOWED." For the next several weeks, the fate of the "former Springfield boy and a son of the late Dr. Utley and Mrs. E. H. Utley" would be watched closely. Any references to Lieutenant Utley would make it into the news even before he arrived from Europe on the *North Carolina*. But the *Register* did not make editorial comments. It would be up to Mrs. Utley to sort out the conflicting testimony about Harold's role in the case.

When the inquiry reconvened at 10:00 a.m. on Tuesday, July 20, another sunny and mild day, Lieutenant Adams was told the witness chair had been moved. Some members of the press took this to mean that the judge advocate did not want Adams in a position where he could see his notes. Robert Adams now found himself across the table from Rose Parker, who "fixed her eyes upon him and they scarcely left his face for an instant while he continued on the stand." But the onlookers were forced to be patient. Davis did not begin by questioning Adams about his meeting with Mrs. Parker. Instead he went over more of the lieutenant's previous testimony and his supposed conversations with the news media.

"I understood you yesterday to say that the last shot fired by Lieutenant Sutton when he was on the ground killed him. Do you state that as a matter of opinion or as a matter of knowledge, from your observation?"

Adams hesitated. "I think my statement was to the effect that I saw him draw his hand out from under his body, turn his head to the right, and shoot. I think my statement yesterday was to the effect that I did not realize what had happened at that time." For several moments, Davis went over statements Adams made in 1907; Adams insisted that two years earlier he "stated the truth and the whole truth, just as I am doing now, as I remember it."

Again Davis returned to what Adams knew about the fatal shot. The lieutenant repeated that he had no opinions on the subject of Sutton shooting himself, even though he had referred to the gunshot that "he killed himself with." In fact, Adams countered, that remark was unintentional because "you will see I also stated that I was so dazed that I did not realize he had shot himself. I stated that as hearsay and also a matter of my own opinion."

Davis would not let up. "I want you to say whether you saw Lieutenant Sutton kill himself."

"I saw Lieutenant Sutton pull out a revolver, as I have said, from under his body, and turn his head in this direction [Adams demonstrated] and pull the trigger. I saw the flash jump possibly that far [indicating]. That is the extent of my knowledge on it."

"And then you saw him dead?"

"I did not see the bullet."

"Of course you did not—" Davis was exasperated.

"And I did not see him lying there at all, because for some reason or other whether I was sent away or not, I must have left there, because my recollection after that is very vague until I found myself on the parade ground, as I have said, near the electric light somewhere."

"You do not now undertake to say, as a matter within your knowledge, derived from your observation at the time, that Lieutenant Sutton killed himself?"

"I can say it, and I cannot say it, the shot evidently entered his head. I can say that I simply saw him make that maneuver. If I had seen the bullet, which is impossible, I could positively state it; but I simply saw him go through what would appear to have been killing himself."

Now Harry Leonard showed his own impatience. "This is all unnecessary it seems to me." At which point Davis said he was through with that line of questioning.

Davis next focused on the guns. Adams did not remember whether there had been one or two guns at the 1907 inquest. Although he could not identify it absolutely, he still thought Sutton had shot himself with a small revolver he "saw in the courtroom the next day." In fact, he was surprised when he learned that Sutton had a .38 caliber bullet in his head because he thought the small revolver was a .32 caliber revolver.

"And so you must have seen that small revolver in Mr. Sutton's hand as the revolver with which he fired the last shot, or otherwise you could not identify it, could you?" Davis asked.

Finally, annoyed himself, Adams replied. "I have told you a half-dozen times this morning that it was my idea, because the revolver he had with him in his hand at the time did not seem to be as big as a service revolver, I could not see it in a dark place, and then have it shown to me here and absolutely identified it." It was a nickel-plated revolver, but the nickel seemed to be worn off, Adams recollected from the earlier inquest. And, he would learn later, that the small revolver was also a .38 caliber revolver after all.

Turning to a new line of questioning, Davis determined to prove that Adams saw himself as an accused person and that his answers to questions had been shaped by that fact. "On July 7 this month did you have an interview with a reporter of the *New York American* at Sea Girt?"

"I don't remember, there were three or four came down there and one of them put an interview in the paper which I did not give him."

"What paper was that?"

"I think it was the *New York American*."

"I have before me a clipping from the *New York American* of Thursday Jul. 8th [*sic*] purporting to give an interview with you," said Davis who began reading from the newspaper: "'I do not know much about Christianity—'"

Adams jumped in, "I did not say that—"

Davis ignored him and continued reading, "'—but I do not recognize the spirit that seeks to gain a hallowed grave for a man long dead, by trying to trump up a charge of murder against two who are innocent.' Did you say that?" This was the first mention in the testimony of Jimmie Sutton's "spirit."

"I did not say that. I did not say anything about not knowing anything about Christianity." When correcting this testimony, Lieutenant Adams later claimed that he misunderstood the quotation when Davis read it to him— he thought it said he did not believe in Christianity and that is why he had denied making the statement. The actual quote may have been misrepresented by the reporter; it would have made sense for Adams to say he knew nothing about Catholicism.

"Did you say anything about anybody trying to trump up a charge of murder against two who are innocent?"

Major Leonard objected to the question, but Davis replied that "the relevancy of it and pertinency of it must be obvious."

"To my poor mind they are not obvious," countered the judge advocate.

So Davis explained. "If the witness has come here under the impression and under the belief that he is under a charge of murder, that fact goes to his bias and credibility as a witness, and I think, my learned brother the judge advocate will recognize that at once."

But Leonard said he was not convinced of any bias on the part of the witness. "He has heard the precept read, he knows he is not charged with anything, so far as the Department is concerned, that this is not a trial, and that he is not under the onus of disapproving any offense. I cannot see its relevancy." In a startling change of direction, Harry Leonard would come up with a different perspective within the week. For now, it was critical to his navy that this witness's testimony be deemed reliable.

Henry Davis would try one more time to get the court to acknowledge that Adams was more than a witness—after all, he was represented by counsel. "The rule of the law, everybody will recognize, is that when an accused—I do not say that he is an accused, but I am saying this by way of analogy—that when an accused person takes the stand in his own behalf, as the law allows him to do, the jury is invariably warned and cautioned that his interest in the case is to be considered by the jury in weighing and determining the force of his testimony."

Leonard, "who has a rather harsh voice when aroused over anything," took offense.

> Under the procedure of courts of inquiry, the party directly charged with an offense is known as the defendant. The witness has at no point appeared as the defendant in this case, nor do we know of any complaint. There are two parties to the inquiry before the tribunal, and I think the Court ought to be able to determine whether its procedure is error or not. I do not believe that it requires the injunction of counsel to compel it to avoid a course which may be error.

Davis assured Major Leonard that he was not trying to warn this court against error, though in the courts he was familiar with—including the Supreme Court—that has historically been the function of counsel. But he wanted to know once and for all whether or not Lieutenant Adams was speaking "under the spur [of] self protection or whether he is speaking in his own mind and in his own heart as an ordinary witness seeking to enlighten an inquiry." In light of this argument, Leonard withdrew his objection.

But Arthur Birney now spoke up on behalf of Lieutenant Adams. He and his client supported the broadest inquiry into the facts of this case. "We do not recognize for a moment," he said, "that Lieutenant Adams is here as a person accused of an offense." Still, Birney could not see what the court could learn "from the introduction of newspaper rumor or the embellishments which newspaper reporters may have made from time to time of the slender facts which have come to their knowledge."

Leonard then consulted with his colleagues on the court and reiterated the fact that Lieutenant Adams was not in the position of an accused person. So Davis changed his line of questioning, but he was not yet ready to relinquish the subject of reporters.

"I will ask you, Lieutenant Adams, whether before coming to the witness stand, you saw a statement published in several of the newspapers, including the *New York Herald* or the *Baltimore Sun*, of July 13, 1909, purporting to be a statement by Col. Doyen, of the United States Marine Corps with reference to the circumstances of this case?"

"I read a column of Colonel Doyen's statement, which was practically the only thing I read, after I saw this sensational affair come out in the paper."

"You read it all, did you not?"

"I read all of Colonel Doyen but none of the rest of it."

"I will hand you this clipping from the *New York Herald* of Tuesday, July 13, and ask you to turn your eye over and see if that is what you read."

"As near as I can remember that is probably the article. That is the general trend of it."

Davis knew that the article said Colonel Doyen had heard Sutton had threatened to kill Adams.

Without asking another question about the subject, Davis finally turned to a topic that everyone in the auditorium anticipated, Robert Adams' unusual meeting with Rose Parker. In answer to a query by Birney, Davis admitted that he hoped to demonstrate that Adams had made statements to Rose that were not consistent with what he had said in the courtroom.

He asked Lieutenant Adams if Rose Parker told him to tell her the truth about the affair. Adams admitted that she had implied the truth had not yet been told. From then on Adams did not remember much. He insisted he made no statement to Rose Parker related to his role in the affair except to tell her she should refer to the [inquest] record. Davis did not like that answer. He was determined to get Rose Parker's questions, and some indication of Adams' response, into the record. He began to grill Adams on the assumption that he had spoken to Rose about his fight with her brother. Arthur Birney objected to this tactic, and Davis gave an impassioned response.

"If this were not so serious and grave an affair," he said, "I should be tempted to ridicule the position taken by counsel, which amounts to this, that although the witness may have made a statement which I have put to him, and which I am prepared to prove he made, I may not inquire further of him, after he denies making it."

Birney was not placated. "The objection is that the counsel is asking him to assume as he did say something, when the witness says he made no such statement. Your question necessarily requires the witness to assume that such a thing did occur, and the witness denies it occurred."

The attorneys would continue sparring until the judge advocate broke in. Davis agreed to change the form of his questions. He had Rose's notes taken only a few days after her brother died, and he was able to get her statements about what Adams told her in the record. But the witness always answered, "I don't remember"—"with almost parrot-like repetition."

Lieutenant Adams did not recall telling Rose that Sutton was apparently unconscious before the final shot was fired, nor did he recall admitting to her that he had been furious at her brother; that he only stopped beating him when someone kicked him (Adams) in the ribs; or that if Sutton lived, his own life would not be worth anything. He did acknowledge telling Rose that he had been warned not to be Sutton's friend, but he would not repeat his statement that the other marines told him that he ought to "knock Sutton's block off" when Sutton had pulled rank on him.

Major Leonard then took over for a few minutes. He was curious about the logistics of the interview Adams had with a young woman so close to his own age. Adams had no trouble remembering these details at all.

"Where did you have this interview with Mrs. Parker?"

"At the Carvel Hall Hotel."

"Well, the Carvel Hall Hotel is a large hotel," Leonard observed wryly.

"I went there and sent up my card and she sent down word by a boy to come up to her room."

"Was it a bedroom?" Leonard asked, as Rose Parker watched him closely.

"There was a bed in the room, yes. It was on the first floor, just in that little annex, to the left of the office facing the front."

"Did Mrs. Parker indicate her purpose in having you come to her room?"

"I know of no purpose at all. The only thing was I went down there on my guard because she desired to see me alone."

"What were you going to guard against?"

"Colonel Doyen had said she was a very shrewd looking woman, and I agreed with him: when I went down there I went there on my guard." At this comment there was "a burst of merriment on the part of Mrs. Parker, her mother, and counsel."

"Where did you go after you left Carvel Hall?"

"After I was in there about an hour or two, Dr. Murphy and Professor Cecil of the St. John's college came into her room."

"Her bedroom?" Leonard was surprised and amused.

"Yes, sir. They had sent their cards up once or twice before and she had sent back word to wait a few minutes. And finally they came up themselves and rapped on the door. We sat there a few moments, and then somebody suggested that we go to Bonds and get something to eat." Adams had, in fact, gone along with Rose and her two friends for dinner.

Now Arthur Birney had a few more questions. Just in case the court or the correspondents had doubts about his client's selective memory, perhaps he could open up the possibility that Mrs. Parker had one too.

"You said you were on your guard when you called on Mrs. Parker?"

"Yes sir."

"On your guard against what?"

"Against most anything, anything at all; I was looking for anything to happen."

This best be clarified, thought Birney. "You mean by that against misrepresentation of anything you might say?"

"Yes, exactly," said Lieutenant Adams.

And then, at his attorney's request, Adams spelled out in minute detail every place he had been on duty since October 1907, with the dates of his assignments—including those in China and Japan. In answer to a final question by Arthur Birney, Adams told the court that he had no time to think about the details of Lieutenant Sutton's death since then.

Before Adams resumed his own seat at about 11:30 on that Tuesday morning, Commander Hood informed him that he would be asked to read the transcript of his testimony and pronounce it correctly or make changes. By then it was obvious to everyone in the auditorium that, before the inquiry ended, the court would need to consider whether or not Rose Parker or Robert Adams had told the truth.

8

"AN OFFICER SAID IT"

Most of the Marine Corps officers who had testified in 1907 came before the new court during the first week of the inquiry. Given the
gap of close to two years, reporters expected some discrepancies in their
testimony. But in July and August of 1909, Americans also learned fresh information about the events preceding Jimmie Sutton's death—and these
new facts would be scrutinized on a daily basis by newspapers with a vari-
ety of editorial perspectives. The pressure on judge advocate Harry Leonard
was intense; by July 25 the Washington *Evening Star* would conclude, "the
whole Marine Corps is on trial."

Perhaps that was why Harry Leonard emphasized more than once in
the coming days how thorough *this* inquiry really was. Every precaution
would be taken to ensure that the officers were not on the defensive when
they testified; Leonard underscored the fact that the marines had not been
accused of a crime. For him, the testimony that mattered the most was that
of five men (Lieutenants Robert Adams, Harold Utley, William Bevan, Edward Shippen Willing, and Sergeant James De Hart) who were the only
witnesses present when the bullet went into Sutton's head. But he would
also see to it that every Sutton family witness had a chance to speak. The
two women seated on his right had made harsh accusations based on infer-
ence, second hand information, and even more incredulous, the testimony
of a ghost. Major Leonard would soon admit that he had a "carefully
thought out plan" to protect the reputation of his fellow marines. For now,
he kept it to himself.

Much of Lieutenant Adams' account of the auto ride back to the barracks and the moments before Sutton armed himself was corroborated by Edward Osterman. A twenty-five-year-old from Columbus, Ohio, Lieutenant
Osterman had been a cadet while studying at Ohio Northern University,

where he was found to be "a thorough student and a cultured gentleman," known for "his reliability, upright character and amiable disposition." Osterman had served in the army for a number of years and was used to military life when he became a second lieutenant at the Marine Corps training school in March 1907. When he gave his testimony, he was stationed at the naval prison in Portsmouth, New Hampshire—Harry Leonard's home base as well.

Osterman entered the auditorium late Tuesday morning, July 20, in his white service uniform with gold buttons; he appeared to be a husky man, even heavier than Lieutenant Adams, but he was not as tall. His light blond hair was parted in the middle, and his clean-shaven face seemed "obviously frightened at first." He spoke earnestly, though with a "nervous air," when Commander John Hood advised him to give only the facts that were within his own knowledge. Lieutenant Osterman was under no suspicion of foul play because he had not been near Sutton when he died. Under questioning by the judge advocate and Henry Davis, he confirmed Adams' account that Sutton was not popular—especially with the men who had been having a beer that night in Carvel Hall. He too described the incident in May when Sutton shot up the camp. But it would gradually become evident that Osterman did not dislike Lieutenant Sutton. After the Naval Academy dance, when the men first came into the hotel, he stopped to chat with Sutton and Mary Elizabeth Stewart in the assembly room.

A short while later, the men were all sitting around a table on the lower level of the hotel in a small room next to the bar and the billiard room; each of the officers had a sandwich and a bottle of beer. Lieutenant Osterman described "a little stunt we had been doing." They tuned up some bottles and "were blowing on them and somebody said we were making a racket down there and to pipe down." And then Lieutenant Sutton turned up with this bottle of whiskey and offered to share it with the men. But, as the court knew at this point, they turned it down.

Osterman stated that on the way back to the camp Sutton was in the rear seat of the machine in the center, wedged onto his and Utley's knees because it was so crowded. (An awkward, even humiliating position, but Sutton was by far the smallest of the group.) The high-power gear on the automobile chauffeured by William Owens became disarranged, and "we were running under low-power which was making considerable noise." It was past 1:00 a.m., and there was some doubt as to whether the men were still on liberty; Osterman said he thought Utley suggested Owens stop the car so they could get out and walk from the bridge to the camp to avoid waking up Colonel Charles Doyen. When Lieutenant Adams also wanted to

Courtroom scene during Lieutenant Edward Osterman's testimony as published in the New York American, *July 21, 1909. (1) Robert Adams; (3) Rosa Sutton. Courtesy of the Harry Ransom Humanities Research Center, University of Texas at Austin.*

walk, Sutton suggested he had no nerve or something like that—Osterman could not remember the exact language. He did testify, however, that Sutton started the quarrel in the car. After the four men got out, Osterman said he tried to prevent the brawl with Adams and told Sutton he was "acting like a damn fool," at which point Sutton called him a foul name and struck him in the back of the head. Osterman lost his temper and overcame Sutton in the tussle that followed, knocking him down more than once. Lieutenant Osterman's eye was scratched when Sutton got his finger in it.

Osterman confirmed that Sutton then threatened to shoot them all and ran back toward the camp. Lieutenants Adams and Osterman failed to get weapons at the barracks when they went to find the officer of the day. On the way back to their tents, they ran into Lieutenant Utley. Lieutenant Osterman heard something to the effect that Utley and Adams were "to go down and look for clothes." Utley told him to go back to camp, but he stayed nearby to see what was going to happen because "My curiosity got the better of me." He explained to the court that he only saw the brawl from a distance. But after it ended, he accompanied Lieutenant Adams to the hospital.

Between 12:30 and 2:00 p.m. when the court took its customary break for a meal, a St. Louis reporter described a bit of drama in the Carvel Hall dining room (about a ten-minute walk from the auditorium). The head waiter seated Mrs. Sutton, Mrs. Parker, and their attorneys at a table "three feet away" from Lieutenants Adams, Osterman, and Willing, and Adams' navy attorney, Captain Thomas Brown. "The young men were manifestly uncomfortable and did not tarry long over their meal. When a photographer asked Adams to pose, he replied with considerable feeling. 'Go and get these,' indicating Mrs. Sutton and her daughter. 'They like the limelight.'"

When court reconvened, Major Leonard had just a few more questions for his second witness. Osterman insisted he had not gravely or seriously injured Sutton when they had fought and, somewhat unwillingly, admitted that the epithet Sutton had called him was indeed a "Dutch son of a bitch." Arthur Birney had nothing to add, and at about ten minutes after two, Henry Davis began his cross-examination. At the inquest Osterman had said that Sutton ordered the automobile to stop, and now he suggested it was Utley. In contrast to that of Robert Adams, Edward Osterman's explanation was that his former testimony "was a great deal more correct than any I could give now because it was fresh in my mind and I have not given the matter much thought since it occurred, and there are great many details that I have forgotten." But, Davis noted, he too was more specific about some details two years after the fact. Only at this inquiry did Osterman remember that Sutton called Adams a "cold footed coward," in the automobile on the way to the student officers' camp (an insult sure to result in a fight). And only now was there any mention of anyone going back down the walk where the confrontation took place to retrieve clothes. Osterman replied that in 1907 this information "may not have come to my mind." Under repeated cross-examination, he could not recall whose clothing was missing—unless it was Sutton's—nor, Davis observed, could he account for the fact that "here today for the first time," as "Lieutenant Adams did yesterday for the first time," both men talked about a reason for returning to the scene of the fight.

Toward the end of Osterman's testimony, Harry Leonard thought of a clever way to account for the discrepancies in the officer's testimony by asking him if in 1907 he had wanted to be considerate to the family and so left out the "harrowing details." Osterman concurred, but Davis accused the judge advocate of leading the witness; after much debate, the court allowed the question to stand. Moments later, Osterman was excused.

It was close to 3:30 p.m. when Lieutenant William Bevan entered the courtroom and took a seat across from Rosa Sutton and her daughter, who was exactly his age. Bevan was five foot, eleven inches, with curly dark brown hair and gray eyes set off well by his dark blue uniform jacket. A Virginian by birth and "popular in society circles," his connections had been evident in the number of politicians who endorsed him to the Department of the Navy in 1906. A "highly educated and well-balanced gentleman," wrote Senator William Pinckney Whyte in elegant handwriting to Truman Newberry. An ideal man for the marines, "a young gentleman of excellent capabilities, of excellent habits and general character," proclaimed Representative Sydney Mudd. Bevan was, in fact, one of the best educated new officers in the Marine Corps Application School in 1907. Of even greater interest to the Department, his aunt was the wife of Maryland senator Isidor Rayner, a former attorney general of Maryland.

Between midnight and two o'clock on the morning of October 13, 1907, William Bevan had been officer of the guard at the Application School and second in command. When Major Leonard asked him to account for his time, Bevan said that he first encountered Sutton when he heard that a fight was going on and went down from the barracks to the camp. When he reached the Company Street between the two rows of tents, he found Sutton in front of his tent with a revolver in each hand. Lieutenant Roelker stood about three feet in front of him. The revolvers were apparently pointing at Lieutenant Roelker's feet, and, Bevan testified, Roelker was trying to get Sutton to put his guns away; Lieutenant Bevan placed Sutton under arrest and ordered both men back to their tents.

But Sutton yelled "damn the arrest" and ran down the boardwalk, exclaiming he was going to get his mess jacket and collar and "leave the reservation for ever" or "something to that effect." Bevan was the first witness to point out that it was Sutton—no longer in full uniform but in his white shirt—who left the camp not with murderous intent but to get his cape and other clothing left at the site of his fight with Edward Osterman. A few minutes later, Lieutenant Bevan followed him. On the way, he ran into Lieutenant Willing, and they heard "several shots fired. I don't recall how many, but I should say somewhere between four and eight." Lieutenant Bevan was sure that when he entered the crowd he found that "Lieutenant Utley and Sergeant De Hart were sitting on Lieutenant Sutton's body." Bevan continued,

> Lieutenant Utley, I think, was sitting at some point about his knees and Sergeant De Hart about his waist. He was lying face down. Lieutenant Adams was standing on his right side, as I recollect it, making efforts to hit Lieutenant Sutton. I ordered him back, and I think at the same time somebody in the rear pulled him away. I knelt on the left side of Sutton's body and placed a hand on each shoulder, so as to hold him to the ground. The last time I had seen him he had a revolver in each hand, and I felt sure he still had them. My idea was to pin him to the ground so he could not use them. His arms were apparently on his chest under his body. We were in that position a minute or two—less than that; I

suppose thirty seconds—and somebody exclaimed, "My God, he has killed Roelker" and I think "Adams." That, of course, I knew was a mistake. Immediately I felt a slight motion and one of Sutton's arms shot out and there was a flash over the top of his head and immediately his body became limp. There was a dull report. I never heard a report like it from a revolver. Lieutenant Willing reached out and took the revolver from his hand.

Bevan thought it was his right hand. At that point, Bevan, Sergeant De Hart and Lieutenant Utley got off of Sutton and stood back from the body.

William Bevan did not believe that Lieutenant Sutton had been under the influence of liquor that night but was rather very angry. During the course of his testimony he described several instances in which he and Sutton had been quite friendly and had heart-to-heart conversations. At one point, as they shared hot sausage, Sutton reportedly told Bevan that someday he would shoot himself. Bevan said he had often been in Sutton's tent, and "he related to me a number of incidents of his life and hunting trips and experience, I believe, in southwestern Canada and various places, and he would show these revolvers and express his fondness for them." One of them was a smaller revolver and the other his service revolver. Both, Bevan thought, were of the same caliber. He also thought it was the Colt service revolver that Willing took from Sutton's hand after the last shot.

At this point, bells from the clock tower again announced the end of the day's work, and William Bevan would have to wait until Wednesday morning to finish his account.

The number of spectators had grown when Bevan resumed his place in the witness chair at ten o'clock on July 21. All the commotion distracted Commander Hood who was deaf in one ear, especially when, in addition to the "Navy men and women who have attended the proceeding forty or fifty young women from Annapolis wandered in and out" of the auditorium. An *Evening Capital* reporter commented on Hood's "rotund figure and his placid countenance appearing in strong contrast to the nervous witnesses and the thought-wrinkled countenances of the attorneys. But the 'frou-frou' of feminine skirts upset him today, so that he ordered a couple of mild-mannered newspaper photographers out of the courtroom."

John Hood cautioned William Bevan that the oath he had taken the previous day was still binding, and the "high strung" judge advocate—who may well have been troubled by pain at the site of his missing left arm—began his questions. Lieutenant Bevan described the clothing that the "gentlemen" involved in the fight wore, but in contrast to Adams, he thought, given the darkness of the night, any of the marines could have been carrying a revolver without his knowing it. So now Major Leonard raised another leading question that would give the marines a rationale for their actions. Did Lieutenant Bevan know of any incidents when Sutton had threatened other officers? A debate on hearsay evidence occurred once more. But this time Davis turned the question to the Sutton family's advantage. Was the judge advocate suggesting "that there may be evidence tending to show that Mr. Sutton was killed by someone other than himself?"—perhaps someone who believed he was defending his life against Sutton? Major Leonard insisted that he only sought the reason someone might be charged with killing Sutton.

Lieutenant Bevan said he did not think that Sutton would have threatened or injured Edward Roelker that night. In fact, after persistent questioning, he said that Sutton was more defensive than aggressive when confronted by Roelker at his tent. So Leonard moved on to the moment when the last shot was fired and asked how much time had gone by between Adams' remark about Roelker being killed "and the shot which killed Mr. Sutton?"

"It was a lapse of a very few seconds only," Bevan replied. "The shot was fired almost contemporaneously with the exclamation."

"Did the movement of Mr. Sutton's body which you have described commence before or after the exclamation as to Roelker being killed?"

"As I recollect it, the movement of the body and the flash of the revolver in front of his head happened in very rapid sequence." Still, Lieutenant Bevan, who was kneeling on the left side of Lieutenant Sutton, was certain the shot that killed him came from a revolver in his own hand. But, he also acknowledged, Sutton was lying absolutely motionless up to the time preceding the shot and may or may not have been conscious. Bevan again described "a movement of the shoulders. One of his hands went out in front of him; I don't recall which one. The flash followed immediately after that movement." Lieutenant Bevan could not be definite about what Sutton knew, but because he thought Lieutenant Utley and Sergeant De Hart had put him on the ground, he assumed that Sutton knew they were the men sitting on him. As Bevan spoke, young navy wives in the audience nodded "their shapely bonnetless heads approvingly."

Davis began his cross-examination at close to eleven o'clock, and Bevan confirmed much of what he had said earlier. He explained he had come to the scene of the brawl from lighted apartments in the Marine Corps Barracks, making a very dark night seem darker to him. Davis insisted Bevan be precise in describing the last movement of Sutton's arm.

"The direction was in a line parallel to his spinal column I might say; in other words, a motion apparently of that sort, towards the front of his head. I recollect the vigorous movement of one of his arms. I don't recall now which arm it was." Bevan's head was slightly behind that of Sutton when he saw a flash "over the top of his head" and the front of Sutton's head "lit up." Instantly, Lieutenant Willing reached over to grab the revolver from Sutton's hand. In his 1907 testimony, Bevan had said he "supposed he had shot himself in the forehead." (And Rosa had taken that description to heart.) Bevan could not see Sutton's hands "because they were apparently under his body." But Davis asked him to explain why he now claimed Sutton's hand was in front of his head. Then, he asked, "the account you are reported to have given on the former inquiry is, according to your best recollection, inaccurate?" Bevan's explanation was that his "memory may have been treacherous. I know that the statement made at the former trial was true, and the statement I am making now is also true to the best of my recollection."

But William Bevan had not thought Sutton was about to do anything harmful when he left the camp in a hurry, except "to gratify a fondness which he always displayed for fire arms. . . . He always liked fire arms, he was a good shot, and I had no idea on this occasion, he had any intention to inflict any injury." Bevan, in fact, was sure Sutton was just going to blow off steam and decided "it would be better for him to be out of camp rather than in camp."

Following the noon recess, Commander Hood questioned Lieutenant Bevan for about thirty more minutes. By this time, the president of the court had become quite troubled by the obvious chaos among the marines on the night of the tragedy. William Bevan had been one of two men, both senior to Harold Utley, who failed to keep matters under control when, it seemed, both Lieutenants Sutton and Adams had run amok. John Hood now asked Bevan to describe his obligations as officer of the guard—especially "in regard to preserving order within the limits of the Post."

Bevan complied: "His duties are to see that the guard performs its duty. He is immediately under the officer of the day, who is a representative of the commanding officer."

"In the case of any violation of Naval regulations, is it not the specific duty of the officer of the guard, in the absence of the officer of the day and his immediate commanding officer, to suppress it?" Hood asked. The witness agreed, and Hood continued, making sure the navy's regulations made it into the record. Bevan admitted that he should have stopped the fight before things got out of hand during his watch. The reason he gave for not using his own sword against Sutton was that he thought Sutton was just bluffing and partly crazy as he had seemed once before. He simply "had these revolvers out to impress somebody with his bad character. I don't mean to say that he had a bad character, I am not passing an opinion on that, but that he simply wanted to make what is called bluff." And, in his final moments on the stand, Bevan explained he had failed to call out the guard because once he reported the incident to Edward Shippen Willing, he was subject to his orders.

Lieutenant Willing, "the first cousin of Mrs. John Jacob Astor [IV]" had been stationed at the League Island Navy Yard in Pennsylvania when he was summoned to Annapolis. He felt right at home in a state where his family had roots extending back to the eighteenth century. Raised in the historic Philadelphia neighborhood of Chestnut Hill, Edward Willing had gone to private schools in Philadelphia and to St. Paul's in Concord, New Hampshire, but he never attended college. When he applied to the Corps in 1906, he was a bond salesman, still living in Chestnut Hill, and just five days shy of his twenty-sixth birthday. He had been a soldier in the First Troop Philadelphia City Calvary since 1900 and had come into the Corps with glowing references from his troop captain, from Senator Boies Penrose, and from his grandfather, Edward Shippen, who had written President Roosevelt as well as Secretary of the Navy Victor Metcalf on behalf of his grandson.

Lieutenant Willing, whose friends called him "Shippen," was just about to turn twenty-nine when he took the witness stand, and like Lieutenants Adams and Utley, he was close to six feet tall. He had been in the marines for seven months when he marched on guard as officer of the day at 8:30 on the morning of October 12, 1907. Late that night, when the disturbance broke out near the student officers' camp, Shippen Willing was the senior person in charge. His blunt testimony revealed his contempt for Jimmie Sutton; it would not go over well with the court. At first he said he had been asleep on a bunk in his office at the barracks when Harold Utley notified him that Sutton had "gotten a couple of guns and said he was going to kill somebody." When he and Lieutenant Bevan got to the scene of the brawl (Utley had gone on ahead), Willing said there were several people standing around. Adams "had hold of Sutton by the back of the neck and was punching him." He verified that Bevan tried to stop the fight and then said, "I told him [Adams] to go ahead and punch Sutton's head off, but somebody either led Adams away or he obeyed the order of Mr. Bevan to stop."

At these remarks Rose Parker's "black eyes were rapid fire batteries of scornful glances which the good-looking young marine carefully avoided." A reporter claimed to overhear Rose whisper to Davis, "How can they let him sit there and make a joke of my brother's death? I wish I were a man and outside the Court." One can only imagine how her mother felt. Willing's cavalier attitude was not lost on a reporter from the Washington *Evening Star* who described him as "a large slow young man of the 'fine fellow' type. He has a handsome dark face, and smiles as he sits in the witness chair with a smile that becomes him, but suggests that the investigation tends to amuse him. Women spectators in the court admire him and listen closely to his answers." His "somewhat insolent smile" sets him off from the other officers.

Shippen Willing could not remember whether Jimmie Sutton was on his feet or on his knees during the beating or, for that matter, who threw him face down on the ground. He did recall that Lieutenant Bevan was one of the people kneeling beside Sutton or on top of him. And there was "somebody else sitting on his legs, or possibly across his hips," but Willing had no idea who it was. He did say that Sutton's hands were underneath him, his elbows were out, and his hands were under his chest. Major Harry Leonard questioned him repeatedly about this incident, perhaps because the previous night at Carvel Hall, Leonard had a "long and earnest discussion of the case" with Mrs. Sutton and Mrs. Parker. He knew both women believed Jimmie had been beaten unconscious before the bullet entered his brain.

Willing said that when he saw a flash from the corner of his eye, one hand was "just in front of [Sutton's] head a little bit." "Barely a fraction of a second" had passed between the remark Adams made about Roelker and the shot. "I then looked over my shoulder towards Roelker, and I suppose the flash and my looking around were almost coincident." When asked if Sutton had fired the shot which caused the flash, he did not hesitate. "I am absolutely sure in my own mind that he did. There is not the slightest doubt, not the slightest doubt." But Willing did not actually see Sutton shoot himself, nor was he sure on what side of Sutton the flash occurred or where Lieutenant Adams was at the time of the flash. "There was no struggle at all when the shot was fired," Willing said. Instantly, he dropped down, put one hand on the back of Sutton's neck, and removed a .38 caliber Colt service revolver from his right hand. Lieutenant Sutton, Willing said, was absolutely limp all over. And as soon as he touched him, he had a "queer kind of feeling; it was subconscious, probably I knew he was either dead or very near dead."

After joining other men who had gone to the aid of Roelker, Willing returned to the barracks with the service revolver and its shells, and "put them in a large envelope" in the desk of the officer of the day. The next morning, he put the envelope in the post quartermaster's safe before taking it to the Board of Inquest. Willing had heard that Sutton had another revolver and that it had been taken away from him.

"How do you know that?" asked Leonard.

"I don't know it."

"You simply know that someone said that?"

"Yes. Of course I am positive it was so, because an officer said it, and therefore I know it was so."

"It was said at that time, regardless of its truth or falsity?"

"I think so."

From then on, the witness could not recall much of what happened two years previously. He was asked to describe any incidents when Sutton used guns inappropriately and mentioned the evening of May 20 when he shot off his gun in camp. But Willing made light of it. Sutton, he said, "was just making a little display" and immediately gave Major Benjamin Fuller his gun. At the inquest on Sunday, Willing, as recorder, had both of Sutton's revolvers. "I picked the other one up [the smaller Smith & Wesson] on the parade ground about daylight on the morning of the 13 of October," he told Arthur Birney. "It was about 150 yards from where the incident took place in some grass—on the outer edge of the parade ground, that is toward the river, toward college Creek." He again claimed to have seen the gun in Sutton's possession because he carried it around a lot; he recognized it, "as far as anyone can recognize a pistol."

Davis' cross-examination was instantly met by brash answers. "Read my testimony," was Willing's counter to his first question. Davis asked about the moments before Willing got to the scene of the brawl, then zeroed in on Lieutenant Adams punching Lieutenant Sutton. Sutton, he noted, was armed with a gun.

"And you said, 'Let Adams go on and punch Sutton's head off?'"

"Yes" came the smug response. "I thought it would do him a lot of good." Reporters jotted all of these comments down in their notebooks while spectators snickered and Mrs. Sutton and Mrs. Parker sneered, according to a headline in the *Hartford Courant*.

As for who had thrown Sutton to the ground, Willing responded with more than a hint of condescension, "I haven't the faintest idea. I didn't know then and I don't know now." However, perhaps to Davis' surprise, Willing did not think it was Adams, and he agreed Sergeant De Hart and Lieutenant Utley were probably sitting on Sutton but he could not be positive. Then, in striking contrast to Robert Adams' account, Willing said Sutton's nose was "right straight down in the ground," when the shot was fired. By the time court adjourned promptly at four, Henry Davis had decided that Shippen Willing was not a very satisfactory witness.

Thursday, July 22 (day 4), began with a few corrections in the record and with Willing's late arrival—he gave no explanation for his failure to appear on time. Commander Hood warned him that any further repetition of this behavior "will cause your arrest and charges to be preferred against you for contempt of court."

"Very good, sir," came the reply as Davis took over again, focusing now on the inconsistencies between Willing's recent statements and those he made in 1907. Each time, the witness said his earlier testimony had been more reliable. Moreover, when Davis pinned him down, he admitted he had misquoted Harold Utley—who actually had not said Sutton left camp with a couple of guns to shoot somebody. What had Utley really said? Willing could only come up with, "I'll be hanged if I know . . . it was something like that, but there was trouble over there and I had better go over." Lieutenant Willing did not like the specificity required by Rosa's attorney, but Davis kept at him. How had he known where to find the small pistol on the parade ground? Davis asked. De Hart said he threw it away and the next morning De Hart had shown Willing where it was. With that remark, Davis pulled Jimmie Sutton's rusty pistol out of a leather bag at his feet and showed it to Willing who admitted it was the same make and same caliber, though he would not positively identify it.

Willing's testimony came to a close with an examination by the court. Profoundly disturbed by the young lieutenant's callous role in the affair, Commander Hood put on his glasses and read out loud Article 266 of U.S. Naval Regulations. It had clearly been Willing's duty as senior line officer present to suppress the disturbance and "arrest those engaged in it" on the night that Sutton died. However, the lieutenant was unable to tell the court whether he was familiar with these regulations or not. Moments later, he was excused from the witness chair.

A new theory circulated after the first four days of the inquiry—that Sutton shot himself while trying to aim at the men on his back. Although the Sutton women were not impressed, the *Washington Post* suggested it could be a way to remove the stigma of suicide from Jimmie Sutton.

Navy surgeon George Pickrell, who had barely testified for five minutes in 1907, would now be given a chance to elaborate. Describing Sutton's bullet wound, Pickrell said, "It was simply a penetrating wound to the brain; there was a little extrusion of brain matter." Sutton's "hair was seared. The brain that was extruded was intimately mixed with unburned powder," but there was hardly any blood. After this description, Pickrell said he had assumed a thorough official postmortem would be done by a surgeon on the board of investigation. The head wound was "between the top of the ear and the center line of the skull, corresponding to the longitudinal suture." A semicircle drawn over Sutton's head from ear to ear would have passed through the rear end of the bullet hole; Pickrell also said the apparently fatal wound could have been inflicted within "the distance of two feet from his head."

As for other details about the condition of Sutton's body, in Pickrell's opinion he had not shown signs of a severe beating—certainly not one that would have caused his death. But he "had a bruise on his lip, one on his cheek and one on his forehead, all on the right side of the face. His nose was slightly scratched, and perhaps a little bruised, but not much." When asked about Adams' wound on his finger, the doctor described it as "trifling in its nature. I put a simple dressing on it."

All the men were talking at once, explained Dr. Pickrell, but he thought that both Osterman and Adams had told him Sutton shot himself. Dr. Pickrell verified that Roelker had not been hurt. Again Leonard asked a leading question. Was it "the consensus of opinion in that gathering that Sutton had shot himself?" Henry Davis balked at this "extravagant stretching of the rule" and "going off on excursions of this kind all the time"; this time Commander Hood backed him up and disallowed the question.

Davis went straight to the heart of the matter and asked Pickrell, "So that without any invidious distinction your examination may be said to have been rather perfunctory?"

"Yes, my functions ceased when the man was dead." The surgeon knew nothing about the direction of the wound or the caliber of the bullet—everything was to have been obtained in the official postmortem. So Davis went further and asked how he could be so sure, given this rather perfunctory exam, that there was no doubt about the possibility Sutton could have shot himself. To prove the point he pulled out the Smith & Wesson again and handed it to the surgeon; Rosa and her daughter smiled as he broke the revolver to show it was not loaded. Then Pickrell "took the revolver in his right hand, extending his arm above his head, with his elbow bent at an awkward angle, and pointed the muzzle directly at the top of his head toward the middle and rear of the skull. . . . The women spectators in the courtroom seemed to enjoy the exhibition. There was an audible giggling among them." The only way Sutton could have shot himself, Pickrell finally decided, was by using his thumb on the trigger. After a few brief questions from the judge advocate and Arthur Birney, Dr. Pickrell withdrew. Colonel Charles Doyen was called to the witness chair.

Doyen probably had a better idea than most witnesses as to what had been going on in the courtroom—his wife had come for the first day of testimony and likely remained at least until her husband testified. He had not said much before Rosa's attorney raised an objection. When Doyen said that Lieutenant Utley had woken him with the words, "Lieutenant Sutton has killed Lieutenant Roelker and then shot himself," Davis repeated that no civil court would admit this type of statement—he wanted to rule out all hearsay evidence. But Leonard's reply was simply, "I shall get out of the witness what I can." He preferred to have Davis speak up each time he found testimony objectionable so that the court could rule on it.

"We have all the time there is," said Major Leonard.

"You may have," responded Davis. "The United States Marine Corps is eternal, but I am mortal." While Davis argued, Commander Hood broke in to support his judge advocate; he had decided that each time Davis had an objection, it should be entered in the record. Davis tried again to explain how the matter would be handled in a civilian court. But Hood insisted, "This is not a court of trial. It is a court of inquiry." Davis said he would try not to make a nuisance of himself and would continue to object on a case-by-case basis. It would only be a matter of days before the commander would use the word "trial" himself to describe this very proceeding.

Once he was allowed to continue, Colonel Doyen recalled that a hospital apprentice holding Sutton's head said he had been shot "in the forehead." Doyen came up with little other new information, though he described in some detail his own investigation of what happened that night. When he questioned Lieutenant Adams at length, he said he found him sober, excited, and nervous and "got from him a hurried, disconnected tale of the occurrence." Doyen also spoke with Lieutenants Willing and Bevan, and because they had not been directly involved in the altercation, he gave their accounts considerable weight and took no further action.

Doyen said that after the inquest Sutton's Smith & Wesson was "secured with his effects" and eventually turned over to Rose Parker. Major Leonard, who looked for every opportunity to bring up the night in May 1907 when Sutton allegedly shot up the camp, now asked the colonel about it. As had Shippen Willing, the colonel made little of it. Benjamin Fuller, who had been in charge, had found Sutton "swinging [a revolver] around at the feet of two or three officers who were standing close by"; so he "walked up to him and took the revolver out of his hand, and placed him under suspension for ten days." The colonel knew of no occasion when Lieutenant Sutton threatened to take his own life or threatened the life of any officer. But he had noticed Sutton alone a lot and asked the instructors about it. They told him the other students found him "overbearing in his manner, that he affected or put on an air of superiority over the others, and was constantly calling them to account, making fun of them and correcting them." But, Doyen admitted, "I saw nothing of this myself." That October, he said, the young men were not thoroughly familiar with navy regulations. They had only had superficial instruction in the various duties they were to perform—"they knew nothing or very little of the customs of the service." In fact, they needed constant supervision and "during daylight this was always done." But clearly that had not been the case in the middle of the night.

Doyen's opinion was that none of the officers "had been guilty of shooting Lieutenant Sutton." But he had been troubled by Sergeant De Hart's evasiveness when he asked him who gave him Sutton's revolver. "I could get no reply except that he did not know. That worried me." And, he added, it would "always remain a mystery in my mind." De Hart's role would puzzle many people; when his testimony began after the noon recess, it would be a pivotal point in the investigation.

Sergeant James De Hart had come to Annapolis from the Camp of Instruction in Sea Girt, New Jersey, where he had been shooting for the rifle team and made the team twice. The papers would describe him as light haired, slender, tall, and boyishly handsome. On this sunny Thursday afternoon, he would prove a good navy witness by "retracting his own opinions and testimony and confirming that given by his superiors."

James De Hart had no qualms about telling the court he had returned to the barracks after being in Annapolis in a saloon and was "slightly under the influence of liquor" on the night in question. Though he had been "happy," his head was pretty clear, and he was not at all confused about what was going on. But he had no recollection of what had happened in town. He was on his way to his quarters when the corporal of the guard, Archie Todd, told him there was trouble.

As De Hart responded to Leonard's questions, he earned "many a glance of apprehension" from his superior officers. They had nothing to worry about. De Hart said he ran into Lieutenant Sutton and agreed to accompany him to look for some clothes. Sutton, who had two revolvers, went on ahead. Shortly after De Hart heard gunfire, he had the impression that Sutton had been shot but thought it was "just a little scratch." De Hart did not think Sutton was seriously injured and said, "I don't know why I had that impression, but that was the impression I had; because it did not seem to be taken seriously. I don't think that anyone thought he was seriously injured." One of the officers told him to go on back to the barracks, and he thought it was Lieutenant Utley. He went about twenty yards into the grass but could not resist going back to see what was going on among the group of men standing around Sutton.

"Just about that time there was someone handed me a revolver."

"Who handed you that revolver?" Major Leonard "roared."

"I cannot say, sir," responded De Hart also raising his voice.

"To the best of your recollection, who handed you that revolver?" Leonard was determined. This was a key moment in the inquiry—Sutton's Smith & Wesson could have been the murder weapon.

"I have never from that day to this, from the next morning to this time, I have never been able to tell who handed me that revolver. The day after I was handed that revolver I asked Lieutenant Utley—the next morning—who handed it to me. I said 'Do you know who gave me that revolver last night?' And he said that he didn't, or something like that. He didn't tell me."

De Hart did remember that the unidentified person was standing between him and the body of Lieutenant Sutton on the side toward the parade ground. He put the gun in his trouser pocket although he was not sure what kind of revolver it was or, despite lengthy questioning on the subject, exactly how large the revolver seemed in his pocket, which was about seven inches deep. Then, on his way to find the hospital steward, he threw the revolver away on the parade ground. When he got back to the scene of the encounter, he recalled that Colonel Doyen sent him to the stable to get the horse and the wagon. It was only when he went back to the barracks to turn in that he decided he might have made a mistake in getting rid of the gun. He had been foolish—he had thrown it away "because I knew someone had been shot, and I thought it was bad to have a revolver on me."

Later that night, the sergeant said, he went back to the camp and told Lieutenant Utley what happened because he had been the senior student officer present. Harold Utley told him to get the gun the first thing the next morning. De Hart said he never saw the gun again because he could not find it. In fact, Lieutenant Utley informed him that "they had gotten the revolver." Arthur Birney turned down the opportunity to question De Hart, and Davis' cross-examination began. Step by step, Davis made him review his actions, referring often to De Hart's 1907 testimony to help refresh his memory. When they headed off to get Sutton's coat—though he had no recollection of what happened to the coat—Sutton, he said, may have said something like "it has gone too far." The only person he would specifically identify at the scene of the fight was Harold Utley, though he said he did know all the men involved. As he spoke, "Mrs. Parker kept her big, keen and lustrous black eyes to which all kinds of mesmeric influences have been attributed concentrated on the face of the young marine. He did not glance in her direction."

"But you do deny that you sat on Sutton?" Davis asked him twice. "Yes, sir," came the reply. Noting that enlisted men are not allowed "to associate with officers in any way," De Hart said the matter was "strictly an officers' affair, and I had no business there." He said that one of the officers told him to leave. And again, he repeated to Davis that after all the shots had been fired, the men were "just standing around in a group, and I think they were talking and trying to fix up Lieutenant Sutton's head, or doing something like that." Nobody said he had been killed.

"What did the officer say to you who handed you the revolver?"

"'Take this' or words to that effect."

"Did he tell you to keep it?"

"No sir."

"Or take it anywhere?"

"No sir."

"What did you expect to do with it then?"

"My idea was that they were fixing Lieutenant Sutton up, but they were trying to do the wound, or something like that, and the revolver was in the way. They wanted me to hold it while they were fixing his head."

"If that were so, when you started off why did you not give it to someone else?"

"I don't know. I just threw it away on the impulse of the moment, threw it on the parade ground." The only person he spoke to about it was Lieutenant Utley. Davis would not be any happier with De Hart when he completed his testimony the following morning.

Friday, July 23, was a grey, muggy day when rain and drizzle took the sparkle out of the granite walls of the Academic Building. But the temperature was not unbearable; it would remain in the seventies through the afternoon. Civilian men and women, encumbered by black umbrellas, crossed King George Street at a brisker pace than usual until they reached the massive doors of the now-famous building and, once inside, tried not to slip on the marble floors. Henry Davis made one last and unsuccessful effort to jog James De Hart's selective memory when court began that morning, perhaps relieved that he would have a more friendly witness to deal with before the hour ended.

Davis could not understand why De Hart had been curious enough to watch what was happening, even though he had no business doing so, and yet his curiosity did not compel him to notice who the officers in the group were or what officer had given him the revolver. He urged De Hart to think about his testimony carefully one more time. "These officers with whom you had no business were engaged in an affair respecting which they told you [you] were not needed and directed you to go away, and yet, instead of one officer handing this gun to another, he handed it to you, the man out of place. Did that make any impression on you? Did it strike you at all?" De Hart replied it did not.

Rosa's attorney, now exasperated, asked the witness if he was in full possession of his faculties. De Hart testified that, early the next morning when he went to look for the gun out on the parade ground, he discovered that Utley had already found it. De Hart then decided to ask the lieutenant if he knew who had originally handed him the gun. Harold Utley apparently had no answer either. Yet every time Davis tried to get more specific information from De Hart, his recollection failed. Reporters would comment, "Everything that he could deny he did." He was "steadfast in his sensational contradictions." Now he was under oath as he had not been in 1907, and Davis asked De Hart to reassure the court that he was telling the truth. "It is a solemn fact, on your oath and on your soul, did you not sit on the lieutenant's body at any time that night?" Again the sergeant answered that he had not.

James De Hart's testimony turned out to be disappointing for both parties. But *New York American* reporter James Dorrance found De Hart was "in many ways the most illuminating witness who has yet been called. There were various indications that he had been schooled in his testimony, but there are just as many breaks which show the lesson not yet learned." De Hart, Dorrance observed, was an enlisted man who liked Jimmie Sutton "even as much as student officers are said to have hated him." In fact, De Hart confided in "friends in Annapolis" that the student officers with commissions were trying to get him into trouble. Soon after the first four days of testimony, the press had begun to forecast that, regardless of the court's findings, a number of marines would be punished for their discreditable conduct on the night of October 12–13. Surely a court-martial would be held to remedy this condition of affairs.

By late morning, six of the eight marines and one of the two doctors first examined in 1907 had again given their impressions of the night when Lieutenant Sutton lost his life. It would be up to the court and the attorneys to sort out the new and contradictory information they had heard. When the officers claimed to have no memory of critical information, Rosa's attorney was clearly on the spot. Arthur Birney could argue that the violence and confusion before Sutton died and the passage of almost two years made it hard for Robert Adams and his fellow marines to remember details clearly. But if a witness came up with new details—especially self-serving facts—was he telling the truth? Did his story change or his memory falter in part for the good of the service or loyalty to his compatriots? Davis might well be skeptical about any information a witness—especially Robert Adams—had simply forgotten to mention in 1907. The testimony of Sergeant De Hart could have been affected by his drinking, by stress, or by his fear of alienating the line officers. Some of the government "eye" witnesses could have been confused by post-event information gleaned from peers, bystanders, or even from newspaper articles. How would it be possible to determine the truth of the matter? The members of the Court of Inquiry and the Sutton family—ostensibly in Annapolis for a collaborative effort to find facts—had different objectives as they listened to these men and weighed their words.

Rosa's attorney was not alone in eagerly anticipating the arrival of Harold Utley, who, with surgeon Frank Cook, was still en route from Naples, Italy, to Provincetown, Massachusetts. And there was another mystery, the whereabouts of Edward Roelker, a man Rosa Sutton and Rose Parker had much more faith in than Lieutenant Utley. But he was still nowhere to be found.

The *Baltimore Sun* was just one of many papers that hoped to come up with news about Roelker. Describing the young man as "one of the best-liked officers" at the barracks, the *Sun* reviewed his case, including his prior reprimands for drinking too much before he had been dismissed from the Marine Corps. Apparently, once dismissed, Roelker left Annapolis for Baltimore and telephoned to ask for his trunks a few days later but never claimed them, and had not been seen since then. Perhaps he went to Washington to see his family. But on July 20, a businessman from Martin's Ferry, Ohio, with a fantastic story to tell, claimed to have spotted Roelker working under an assumed name for a coal company in Wheeling, West Virginia. Two days later a report said that "former Lieutenant Edward P. Roelker . . . has been located at Kittaning, Pennsylvania. Secret Service men are supposed to have gone there to get him." And Harry Thomas, who had tried but not made it into the Marine Corps, had another bit of information to share with the press. A couple of weeks before Sutton died, he had shown Thomas a letter from Robert Adams challenging him to a duel with pistols because Adams had become interested in "his girl." Sutton also reportedly told Thomas "he had had a notion two or three times to kill himself." Meanwhile, Mary Elizabeth Stewart, who found it unbelievable that Sutton committed suicide less than two hours after they parted company, had emphatically denied that anyone else competed with Jimmie Sutton for her attention.

9

"SUTTON MYSTERY DEEPER"

When Sergeant James De Hart left the auditorium, Rosa Sutton and Rose Parker were no doubt relieved that one of their own witnesses would finally testify. At about eleven o'clock that Friday morning, judge advocate Harry Leonard called on twenty-three-year-old William Owens, a "lanky stripling" whose "well-worn though neat grey business suit without a splash of color" matched the overcast sky. He would be one of thirteen men whom Henry Davis introduced—with the court's approval—on behalf of the Sutton party.

To those in the auditorium without direct ties to the military establishment, William Owens may have been a refreshing change. He was the first man to take the witness chair in civilian clothes, and once he sat down facing the Sutton party, he identified himself. He lived on West Street in Annapolis and had worked for the Adams Express Company for about a year. In October 1907, Owens had just taken a new job "running an automobile for Mr. Chaney." He explained to the court that he lost this job after a month because Chaney decided that he only wanted to run one car. Owens had also been employed by the Annapolis Automobile Company, and he had once driven a carriage for hire around Annapolis. He knew Lieutenant Sutton quite well; unlike the other lieutenants, Sutton had always given him generous tips. He now gave his version of what had happened on the night of the tragedy during and immediately after the automobile ride back toward the student officers' camp (and before Sutton's fight with Edward Osterman). Owens' story coincided with the sworn testimony he provided Edmund Van Dyke, though he now added additional details.

Lieutenant Sutton had wanted to hire his machine to return to camp, but Owens said he suggested they wait for several other officers who might be going so he could earn their fares as well. Owens had been sitting at a table on the lower level of Carvel Hall talking with another driver, Edward Griffith, when the six marines came out of a room opposite the bar. They seemed amicable, and Sutton offered to have three from the group join him in Owens' Cadillac. The two cars started down the driveway to King George Street, but the "high speed broke" on Owens' car, so Edward Griffith took his passengers on ahead.

Owens recalled that an officer in the tonneau (rear seat) "hollered" to him to go into the Naval Academy grounds through the new Oklahoma Gate (gate 4). No one was arguing, said the young driver; the men in the back seat were just "talking and laughing." Owens thought his machine was hardly making any more noise "than the engine of the other car that went to the camp." Once they crossed College Creek Bridge and reached the ash pile or dump area, someone in the back seat ordered him to stop the machine. At that point, Lieutenant Robert Adams jumped out and threw his hat and coat down on the ground. Lieutenant Sutton paid the dollar plus tip for the car (twenty-five cents a person); Owens assured the judge advocate who was doing the questioning that often one person in a group would pay the fare.

As soon as Lieutenant Sutton got out of the car, Owens recalled, in testimony that was surely a surprise to the court, "these other two officers grabbed Mr. Sutton, grabbed his arms, and I saw Lieutenant Adams make a rush toward Mr. Sutton. Mr. Sutton said 'Go away, Adams; I don't want to have any trouble,' just like that." Then one of the officers who was holding Sutton ordered William Owens to leave. Adams, he said, stepped back, but then "rushed Sutton a second time and Sutton said 'If he wants to fight, I will fight him.'" Owens was positive that the noise from his car had not prevented him from hearing some of what was said. When he hesitated to drive away, either Osterman or Harold Utley called out for a sentry. Owens insisted Sutton did not want any trouble because he had said so. On the other hand, he said Adams had remained silent during the auto ride even though he started the fight afterward. Under pressure, Owens acknowledged that he did not actually see anyone strike Sutton. But when he told the sentry what was going on, the man replied, "If they give Sutton a fair fight he will clean up all of them."

Arthur Birney knew William Owens was one of Davis' best witnesses, but try as he might, he failed to prove that the young driver was a close friend to Mrs. Sutton. Owens would only say that he recognized her (she had used his chauffeur service); he could not recall ever having a discussion with her. Birney cross-examined Owens about what happened when the lieutenants got out of his automobile, but the witness became cautious and said he did not want to be "wrong on a question." Finally, he agreed with Birney's suggestion that there could have been a fight in which two officers "were going to hold a third officer while a fourth officer beat him." Owens was the first witness to mention that when Sutton came down to the bar it was already closed; the barkeeper had left a package—a bottle of whiskey— wrapped in newspaper and tied with string. Owens saw Sutton pick it up, and he had certainly not had a chance to drink it before he offered it to his fellow marines.

Owens' testimony would, for the most part, be corroborated by his friend, Edward Griffith, a messenger for the Adams Express Company, who gave his account later that afternoon. Griffith stated the engine of Owens' car was making "a good deal of noise," making it too loud for Griffith to hear what the men were saying. (He was much farther from the scene than Owens.) He had recognized both Lieutenants Utley and Adams and said that once the officers had gotten out of their auto, Lieutenant Utley was eager for the drivers to leave and told both to "get off the ground." When they hesitated, Utley called a sentry. Griffith noticed that one of the officers had hold of Sutton's right arm (he thought it was Utley), but he hadn't seen anybody actually fight; he then left the scene of the altercation ahead of Owens. Griffith had not talked about the incident with anyone, he explained, because he only knew what he had seen in a newspaper report.

Perhaps because he testified directly after the enigmatic sergeant, James De Hart, reporters described William Owens as the first witness "with a memory" and as "decidedly the best witness that has appeared." The driver "impressed everyone with the truthfulness of his statements." Owens' account led some to conclude there had been a "prearranged affair"—a "'frame up'"—to go after Sutton. He had certainly suggested that in his letter to Rosa Sutton. To the *Washington Post*, Owens proved "frank and intelligent, his memory clear and his statements were direct and much more convincing than those of some of the officers of the marine and naval service who preceded him." Owens "bears an excellent reputation in Annapolis," James Dorrance told his *New York American* readers. He presented his story "in an earnest, straightforward manner to the evident distress of the large gallery of naval men and women who had all but applauded the young Sergeant De Hart for his faithfulness to the service even to the extent of losing his memory on the most final points." The officers who had been in the fatal brawl with Sutton may have been less impressed with Owens. Dorrance observed Robert Adams, "resplendent in a white service uniform," reading while the young driver spoke.

At 2:43 p.m. that Friday afternoon, court adjourned early for the weekend, a break that would provide several people the opportunity to reflect on the merits of the government's case. The press coverage of Owens' testimony helped the Suttons gain credibility in the eyes of the public. After the young chauffeurs told their stories, the *Evening Capital* published a commentary by a "leading Annapolis attorney," who, as others had, found the investigation reminiscent of the Dreyfus Case; it "suggests some of the most wonderful features of any case ever heretofore presented to the United States authorities," he wrote. The unnamed attorney then launched into a defense of Sutton's character, noting that the marines, in his view, had contradicted their own characterization of Sutton as unsociable and autocratic. After all, he had "gone to the rooms of his fellow officers on the night in question and carried his private bottle of whiskey" to share with them. Plus "he invited them to ride to the barracks in his automobile." For this attorney, the suicide position was "absolutely untenable."

By the end of the week, Arthur Birney and Henry Davis both seemed pleased with the way things were proceeding; a *Washington Post* reporter caught their reactions. Birney emphasized the flimsy case against Lieutenant Adams, who "has not been connected in the slightest degree by the testimony of the week with anything on which any charge might be based against him." And, he said, "as it is, there is nothing for us to combat, and we are more than satisfied with our situation." Davis, on the other hand, focused on Jimmie Sutton's innocence. "'You can say for me . . . that I came to this inquiry fully prepared in my case. There has not been a single adverse surprise for me, and what surprises there have been have been highly favorable to our contentions.'" Rosa's attorney all but guaranteed *Post* readers that the court and the "'public which is taking so great an interest in the case,'" would learn "'young Sutton did not commit suicide.'" But he would be in for more than one unwelcome surprise in the coming days.

Reporters stayed on the job during the first weekend after the start of the inquiry, stirring up even more interest by emphasizing its adversarial aspects. On Saturday, July 24, the Annapolis *Evening Capital* allegedly spoke with Rosa who said she was "'constantly'" receiving letters "'from families of men in the Navy and Marine Corps who had died suddenly and violently and whose deaths, according to the writers, had never been properly investigated.'" One example "was that of a young marine officer whose body was found in the Philippines with his throat cut from ear to ear. Her mail at Carvel Hall is unusually large and creates some comment."

The *Washington Post* noted the strain the testimony of the marines caused Mrs. Sutton whose "impatience and indignation" at times became manifest. And in a rare comment showing sympathy for Robert Adams, the reporter (not realizing that Adams had been raised by his stepmother), wrote, "There is another mother whose heart is wrung. Lieutenant Adams had to arrange to leave here this evening to go to his home in Harrisburg, [Pennsylvania,] the distress of his mother having become such that he was urged to go to her if it were at all possible." In Springfield, Illinois, a third mother rooted for her son and his brother officers, though possibly with mixed feelings about Rosa inspired by two unusual interviews printed in the *Illinois State Register* on Sunday, July 25. Although Emma Utley's future depended on Harold's success, she may have been moved by the words of former secretary of the navy Truman Newberry, who had helped her secure a place for her son in the Marine Corps three years earlier. Speaking from his home in Detroit, Michigan, Newberry said there was "not a shred of evidence that Sutton was killed by any of his companions." Yet he could understand the need for a second investigation:

> Any mother would do her utmost to remove the stain from her son's memory, and I can understand and appreciate her position. I had an interview with Mrs. Sutton. In fact, the story that I refused to see her and turned her down was an absolute lie. I treated her as I would my own mother, and was very sympathetic; but there was not a shred of evidence, and her attitude is simply the result of natural feelings of a mother, who wants to save her son's name.

If Newberry's words softened any hostility Emma felt for Rosa Sutton, a second interview in the *Register* printed underneath Newberry's calming words probably changed her mind. Rosa Sutton responded to some of the accusations that had come out in the marines' testimony. She insisted that the officers intended to "first beat [Jimmie] unmercifully and then so humiliate him that he would be forced out of the service." And then she allegedly went further, and specifically accused Harold Utley of turning the other officers against Jimmie because her son had "soundly thrashed" him when they were both at the Naval Academy.

That same weekend, newspapers on both coasts began to focus more on the significance of the case. The *Evening Star* observed that the causes of Sutton's death could lie buried in the historic rivalries between the navy and the Marine Corps. At a Washington social function there were reported rumblings from members of Congress—especially those from Oregon and

California—who were shocked by the lack of discipline in the Marine Corps training school. A Portland paper named four senators who were "concerned over the affair": Senators George Earle Chamberlain and Jonathan Bourne of Oregon and Senators Frank Putnam Flint and George C. Perkins of California, where the Suttons lived for many years.

> Although they are very busy with the tariff bill, members of Congress have been watching the Sutton case closely and it is thought that investigation into general conditions in the Marine Corps will be ordered this fall, no matter what the outcome of the present hearing may be. It is charged that since the preparation of Marine Corps officers was turned over to "schools of application" that politics has had overmuch to do with the issuing of commissions.

Two western senators are quoted (without their names) in this same United Press Wire on July 26 to the *Oregon Daily Journal*. Both urged that there be a congressional investigation, and one decried the "'spirit utterly foreign to that which should mark the men who have charge of our sea police. It may be necessary to thoroughly reorganize the system of appointing and training Marine Corps officers.'" A *Baltimore Sun* correspondent spoke with another unnamed senator: "'The idea that the navy or the military is supreme and beyond the plea of justice so far as a civilian is concerned has developed sufficiently far . . . it is time we were learning more about the inner personal affair[s] of the military service. This Sutton affair will probably be an eye opener.'"

The press could still not find the missing witness, Edward Roelker, but reporters did track down Minor Meriwether Jr. whose strong fists had accidentally caused the death of James Branch a few months after Sutton left the Naval Academy. Meriwether was in St. Louis and was said to have been a classmate and friend of Lieutenant Sutton. He said he would not be surprised if Sutton's bones had been broken because in the Naval Academy a man never gave up in a fight until he was unconscious. Meriwether claimed Sutton was popular with his classmates, but he did not volunteer "to break the Naval Academy code of silence" on Sutton's behalf.

On Monday, July 26, readers of the *Baltimore Sun* began the week with the headline "SUTTON MYSTERY DEEPER—NAVY DOES NOT SHOW UP WELL UNDER THIS INVESTIGATION." "Military people who originally thought this new investigation was pointless" have now "joined with the general public to take a much graver view of the whole affair." An increasing number of "bystanders" had taken an interest in the drama, and the *Sun* forecast record crowds when the Sutton women testified. The paper contrasted the careless way the first inquest had been conducted with the conscientious performance of Major Leonard. Even Henry Davis applauded his work.

The weekend press coverage underscored how much was at stake for the Navy Department and for its judge advocate. When court reconvened, Major Leonard announced that he would put Rosa Sutton on the stand as soon as he examined a few additional witnesses. Much of the day was taken up with prior witnesses corroborating or making minor changes in their testimony and with a few additional questions for drivers Owens and Griffith. Little new information came out, but John Anthony, who had been tending bar at Carvel Hall on October 12, 1907, confirmed that Sutton had not been drinking, but he had ordered the quart of whiskey wrapped up; he had seen Lieutenant Sutton sitting in the corner of the assembly room talking with a young lady. And then, at about three o'clock on Monday afternoon, according to a statement that was melodramatic especially for the *New York Times*, a new witness dressed in khakis "dropped into the situation like a bolt from a clear sky."

Marine private Charles Kennedy was the slender, youthful sentry who had spoken with William Owens and who apparently saw part of the brawl when Sutton died. Of medium build, with "keen brown eyes and light hair," Kennedy had been summoned to Annapolis from Norfolk as a Sutton witness, and Henry Davis made sure he told the court he had never met any of the family or their attorneys. Kennedy supported Owens' view that Sutton had not started the initial scuffle with Adams and the other marines. On October 13, 1907, at fifteen minutes to one in the morning, Private Kennedy recalled, the corporal of the guard (Archie Todd) woke him in time to get to his sentry post by 1:00 a.m. On the way to the hospital guard station, he heard loud voices and came upon Lieutenant Adams in his shirt sleeves, and Lieutenant Sutton, who asked him to hold "his cape, his coat and hat, and I did so." Then Sutton turned around and said, "'Adams if you want to fight me, I will fight you, sir'"; they started fighting after calling each other names for a few moments, both striking each other. This was a fight mentioned by both Owens and Kennedy but not by any of the marines. Lieutenant Utley "finally got them separated," Kennedy reported. At first Kennedy said that Sutton "came over to me and asked me would I please tell the man with the automobile to go away, and I told him I didn't have anything to do with the automobile at all." At this point, Davis turned his witness over to the judge advocate.

Kennedy insisted that the initial fight took place directly under an electric light where the road forks down in a hollow at the dump near College

Creek Bridge (others would call it Cemetery Bridge.) For several minutes, Harry Leonard questioned him about each officer and about this supposed fight that took place, according to Kennedy, for about five minutes. "The result of the fight was that Mr. Sutton's face was bleeding in several places. I noticed that Mr. Adams had his face to bleeding." Kennedy was sure that he could identify Adams, Utley, Osterman, and Sutton. When they started fighting a second time, Kennedy continued, "Mr. Sutton hollered and told me to come back." More than once, he said, the men had "started to calling each other names." He could not be specific, but they were "not very pleasant names." He did not return because he was on the way to duty, and (as an enlisted man), "I didn't think it was my place." In the meantime, Kennedy had given the clothes to Utley.

At about half past one, now at his post, Kennedy said he heard gunfire; he was sure about the time because "bells were striking." From the steep hill behind the hospital he could see the men and hear them insulting each other. He saw Adams go up the road "running like he was going to the camp or the barracks." Kennedy recalled seeing flashes, and though he heard the four loud shots from a "pretty good sized gun," he apparently did not hear the muffled sound of a fifth shot. Then Lieutenant Utley ran up to the hospital and told him that "Lieutenant Sutton had killed himself." A short time later, Kennedy saw the men bring Lieutenant Sutton's body to the hospital, and he distinctly remembered Robert Adams telling them "he got his finger shot off."

Private Kennedy's testimony did not help the Corps' image, and Major Leonard tried a new tactic on the enlisted man, one that he had not used on the line officers who testified. (The *Baltimore Sun* would call it bulldozing the witness.) Leonard hoped to discredit Kennedy by pointing out repeatedly that he had been disciplined a number of times while in the service. And he asked whether Kennedy had discussed the events of October 13, 1907, with anyone else. Kennedy insisted that he had not because Harold Utley had come up to him the next morning "and told me to keep quiet, and I did keep quiet." In fact, he assured Lieutenant Utley that he would say nothing because (as an enlisted man) "'it is not my place to say anything.'" But the judge advocate kept coming back to Kennedy's track record as a marine, asking over and over again about his prior offenses, "drinking, breaking liberty, having an argument with an orderly." Knowing his credibility was on the line, Charles Kennedy was careful to point out that there had been no leaves on the trees when Sutton died, and he could see better from his post at the hospital than was possible in July. He emphasized again, when Arthur Birney had a turn at him, that he even heard the "shockingly bad language" the men used as they grappled with each other. And he flatly contradicted Lieutenant Edward Willing's assertion that he had found Sutton's gun. On the morning after Lieutenant Sutton died, Kennedy said, "Mr. Utley walked down in front of the company I was in on the parade ground and walked up to the corner there and picked up a black or blue steel .38 caliber service revolver out of the grass."

The *Philadelphia Inquirer* and the *New York Times* both declared that Private Kennedy "told a frank, straight forward story of some of the incidents prior to the shooting which had not been mentioned by any of the young officers who have already testified." Only on a few occasions did he say he "disremembered" the answer to what he was asked. On July 27, the *Times* was one of several papers (some in much more sensational language than others) to notice how the judge advocate singled out Kennedy to criticize his record; its readers, who had no access to the court transcript for context, could also consider that Kennedy had not said anything about the tragedy because his superiors, Lieutenants Utley and Adams, "had both admonished him on the morning following the shooting to 'keep quiet.'" Kennedy's testimony made the Suttons' story even more plausible and left many in the auditorium curious about what Harold Utley's reaction to it would be. The staff correspondent of New York's *World*, as usual, gave a vivid summary of the day's events. The "thin-flanked," "humble" private delivered his testimony "out of his humorous mouth with a most fascinating brogue." During his ninety-four minutes as a witness, Kennedy not only brought the "white-uniformed and brass-buttoned officers of the Sutton Court . . . up on their toes," but also he "caused Lieutenant Adams to reveal a crimson flush in his round, chug face, and provided some apparently embarrassing questions for Lieut. Harold Utley to answer when he gets home from the Mediterranean."

Tuesday, July 27, had started out to be a clear day, but the weather quickly turned cloudy, humid, and unbearably hot. The president of the court and the judge advocate began by clearing up a number of procedural matters with the opposing attorneys. A six-year-old blueprint of the scene under investigation served to jog witnesses' memories, and Henry Davis urged the three-man court to "visit the scene of this occurrence and traverse the lines indicated by the various witnesses, including the witness Kennedy." On the previous evening, Davis and Edmund Van Dyke, their clients, and reporters had done just that. A *New York American* correspondent reported that they went "over the ground of the Sutton tragedy with a measuring line," to demonstrate "beyond all doubt" that Kennedy could have seen what he described today. Commander John Hood agreed to confirm Kennedy's statements but said his court would do it alone.

By this time it was evident that Lieutenant Harold Utley and surgeon Frank Cook would not reach Annapolis for several days. So the judge advocate would call a recess, but only after he put in place an idea he had come up with well before the investigation began. He presented the court with a letter that would clarify the origin of the inquiry, "fixing the responsibility of it" on Mrs. Sutton. At first, Henry Davis saw no reason to object. The auditorium emptied while Commander Hood, Wendell Neville, and Henry Jensen studied the letter. After a few moments the tall double doors on each side of the auditorium were opened, and Major Leonard, the parties to the inquiry, their counsel, the stenographers, the spectators, and the news gatherers returned to the room.

It was close to eleven that Tuesday morning when Harry Leonard focused his attention on Rosa Sutton. Reporters had noticed that the ladies of Annapolis had been quite unfriendly to Mrs. Parker and Mrs. Sutton. Only recently had a few called on the two Oregon women and nodded to them in court. Rosa was sworn in from her own seat; she did not want to move to the witness chair with its back toward the audience—a "large percentage of which was unsympathetic toward her." Now every expression of her face "could be observed clearly by the many pairs of almost hostile feminine eyes which regarded her."

After she gave her home address, Leonard asked Rosa to identify the letter she sent to the secretary of the navy on February 8, 1909. He then asked that the letter be read out loud. Henry Davis began to feel uneasy, but Leonard knew exactly what he was doing and said so himself. He completely reversed the position he had held since day one of the inquiry.

"If it please the Court," he began, "I desire to move the Court that it [is] now transpiring that Mrs. Sutton is the complainant in this case, that she be so regarded by the Court and a notation of that fact be entered in the record—that Mrs. Sutton is now a complainant instead of simply a party to the inquiry." Leonard continued in his decisive, self-confident tone: "I further move the Court that all officers who were present on this occasion be now regarded as parties defendant to the inquiry and be authorized to present their case, if any they have, to the Court; and to cross-examine witnesses either produced by the Court or the other party to the inquiry."

Davis was astounded—this was a Board of Inquiry and not a Board of Trial. Despite his admitted ignorance of naval regulations, he knew this proceeding should "exclude the idea of a complainant and a defendant."

Major Henry Leonard, New York American, July 18, 1909. Courtesy of the Harry Ransom Humanities Research Center, University of Texas at Austin.

Again he emphasized that he was not present "as counsel accusing any particular person of any particular thing in this inquiry, and I do not wish myself to be personally transformed into such." The huge room was cleared a second time so that the court could consider the matter in private.

The judge advocate's decision took Rosa's attorney completely by surprise. Not only was he not informed of this plan, but in all his years of courtroom experience he had never seen a change of procedure in the middle of an investigation. When the inquiry resumed, he tried to control his anger; he spoke in a somber voice, warning the court that if the action proposed by the judge advocate was taken, it would "disintegrate this Court and render any recommendation by it a nullity." Davis' understanding was that this was purely a Court of Inquiry; Leonard had just created an alignment of parties "outside of the precept, and outside of the scope of the precept as I interpret it." At the outset, the Sutton court had ruled in no uncertain terms that Lieutenant Adams was not to be considered a person accused.

Major Leonard was ready for these objections. "Up to this point in the inquiry," he began,

> I have sedulously avoided having it appear to the Court or to the public, or to any person whatsoever, that any party appeared before this Court

as a party complainant. The convening authority had not so directed; and in order that the fullest, most unbiased, unprejudiced view of the situation might be brought before the Court by the witnesses produced to testify, I have avoided, as I have said, introducing any party complainant and any parties to the inquiry as set forth by the convening authority. . . . This Court of Inquiry is convened for the specific purpose of informing the convening authority; to arrive at facts according to law. In so far as it arrives at facts in the manner prescribed by law, it has attained its only purposes. Now, I cannot see that it affects the inquiry in any way if Mrs. Sutton at this point becomes a complainant rather than a simple party to the inquiry, beyond this, that it sets forth in its true light the nature of this proceeding, the cause or causes by which it was pre induced, and offers to the parties who are now set forth of record as accused, an opportunity to appear and cross-examine witnesses adduced by the complainant, or the new party to the inquiry.

For Leonard, the facts that mattered seemed to be those established by the government witnesses. "But as far as the material effect on the record is concerned," he argued,

it can have no effect, naturally. My method of procedure, in reserving this until the Government was about to rest its case, was in the interest of the most unbiased and coldest blooded attainment of facts, unprejudiced by any feeling on one side or the other; but if there be any doubt still left in the mind of the Court, after having read the letter offered in evidence I shall now proceed forthwith to produce other evidence which will leave that matter in no doubt whatsoever.

"Evidence as to what?" asked Davis, on edge, now that he had been caught off guard.

"As to the relation of Mrs. Sutton to the subject matter being inquired of," Leonard answered. What evidence could he possibly have against his client? Davis wondered. But Rosa's attorney moved on. He would agree that she was the moving party behind the inquiry. "If that constitutes her a complainant, within the regulations, she is a complainant." Davis assured those present at the table that he was not trying to avoid work. He just wanted to know "if this is going to impair this proceeding." And then, Henry Davis said, trying to establish a lighter tone, "I do not want to have to come back here next winter and do this thing over. I like Annapolis in the summer."

Once he had read Rosa Sutton's letter, Commander Hood agreed with his judge advocate. The newly named defendants were Lieutenants

Willing, Bevan, Adams, Utley, and Osterman, Sergeant De Hart, and "the late Lieutenant Roelker, who is not within the jurisdiction of the Court." This was the first and only mention of the missing witness Edward Roelker as deceased. Had John Hood made a mistake? Major Leonard then added that either one of Adams' attorneys could represent Utley after his ship arrived. The officers would be advised of their rights; Rosa Sutton's statement had said she was convinced that her son "was killed by one of the officers who were with him at the time of his death," so now all the marines present when the apparently fatal shot was fired would enjoy the privileges of their new status. "You have a right to be present, to hear testimony, to cross-examine witnesses, to have the assistance of counsel, and to offer any testimony that you may want to offer," declared Commander Hood.

Henry Davis suddenly had a new role—one he did not like. He asked that the court suspend the hearing until he could decide what to do. From the perspective of a veteran criminal attorney, the proceedings were "in grave peril of irregularity, in view of the fact that Lieutenant Utley, who is on his way here in the character of a witness, will find himself when he comes here in the role of the accused." Davis asked that no further testimony be heard until Lieutenant Utley arrived. At that point he would decide whether he would "on my own responsibility as a man and a lawyer, accuse any of these officers of Lieutenant Sutton's death, which I now do not."

Somewhat on the defensive for having caught Davis by surprise, Leonard argued that it was not the court's responsibility to notify Mrs. Sutton's attorney of her "relation to the subject matter of inquiry." But Davis stood firm. The judge advocate should not have waited until this stage of the inquiry "to embarrass both counsel and parties as to their relation to this inquiry." So why had Leonard decided to introduce this change at the moment Rosa Sutton was about to testify?

"The Court is entitled to know," Leonard said, "prior to the witness speaking, that she appears as a party complainant." There had been no oversight on his part but rather "a carefully thought out plan" to change the nature of the proceeding before Rosa testified. Then, looking directly at Davis, he said, "The Judge Advocate conceives his duties in this Court to be of too sacred a nature to make any mistakes other than those that his limited ability compels him to make."

Davis still accused Major Leonard of bad judgment; plus, he felt it was inappropriate to assume that Lieutenant Utley should have the same attorney as Lieutenant Adams. But Arthur Birney assured the court that he and Captain Thomas Brown would be happy to represent all the officers including Harold Utley. It was the Marine Corps lieutenants and Sergeant De

Hart whose reputations had been tarnished. With these matters resolved, court adjourned at five minutes after noon. The eighth day of testimony would be held one week later, as soon as Harold Utley and Dr. Cook arrived in Annapolis.

Reporters made the most of this dramatic turn of events; it was news that could keep their readers' focused on the story throughout the upcoming recess. "TURNED INTO A TRIAL!" a *Baltimore Sun* headline announced on July 28. "LEONARD SPRINGS SURPRISE" proclaimed the Annapolis *Evening Capital*. At first, the *Sun* reporter assumed the inquiry would become a court-martial; for "it is believed . . . in many quarters that the Court of Inquiry has overstepped its authority." The *Sun* observed that Leonard's court "has gone afoul of naval regulations" and that Acting Secretary of the Navy Beekman Winthrop said that, in fact, the court "had no authority to take the action reported." "Leonard got hung up with a crying farce instead of blazing forth with a melodrama," claimed the *Washington Post*. In Cincinnati, readers attracted by a large *Enquirer* headline, "TRICKERY, CRIES ROSA SUTTON," learned about the "carefully planned coup of the Navy Department skillfully engineered by Henry Leonard . . . in a twinkling of an eye the whole status of the inquiry was changed." Henry Davis was "red in the face and ready for fight."

The hostility between Davis and Leonard that would last for the remainder of the inquiry originated on this Tuesday morning. Davis wrote Winthrop a twelve-page letter on July 28 explaining why he believed Leonard had gone beyond the directive given in the precept of the court. Citing the court's own statement that there "is no one accused, and there are no accusers," Davis recounted his understanding of the prescribed instructions and appropriate legal procedure. He then described what Leonard had said in the courtroom and voiced his objection: Leonard, it seemed, had gone beyond the scope of this inquiry; he had created an alignment outside of the precept. Henry Davis saw his own relationship to the case as one of "seeking" information; Lieutenant Harold Utley had suddenly become an accused person who could "stand mute" and refuse to testify "or else have the benefit of full and free conference with the witnesses who have preceded him, and of access to his testimony before the Board of Inquest, a situation which I am constrained to say so strongly smacks of the scandalous as of itself to call for your intervention." How could Mrs. Sutton's letter have been merged into the precept without her counsel knowing it? Davis asked that Leonard's ruling be vacated and the court returned to its original status.

The newspapers followed the progress of his protest, and many used the occasion to explain various aspects of naval justice and Mrs. Sutton's options to their readers. On July 30, the news leaked out that Davis had been overruled. He was informed that he had misconceived the effect of the ruling; the court was still a "Court of Inquiry" seeking after facts; it was not a judicial tribunal with power to try or punish. He was assured that if it was decided that Sutton did not die by his own act, other persons would be brought to trial. The Department desires, Winthrop said, "the fullest and most complete investigation of the entire matter." But Davis' request that Major Leonard's ruling be annulled was declined. This change in the nature of the inquiry had almost caused Davis to leave the case. "'I do not know whether to go on or not,'" he told the *Baltimore Sun*.

During the week-long recess, Harry Leonard returned to the cooler climate of New England to check on the Naval Prison in Portsmouth, and Henry Davis took a much needed break. He told his office staff in no uncertain terms to hold off any inquirers: "'I want to go over and get acquainted again with the girl I married 27 years ago, and I don't want my weekend interrupted by the Sutton case or even by the President of the United States if he should need my help on the tariff.'"

This time off gave the press a chance to reflect further on the case and build up suspense about the remainder of the inquiry. The New York *World* printed an editorial once again comparing the case to the trials of Captain Dreyfus in which the "'honor of the service'" is more important than in arriving at truth. The paper chastised the court for its treatment of Charles Kennedy and the "lack of respect supposed officers and gentlemen behaving badly give enlisted men." "Mrs. Sutton has not posed as a complainant. Presumably, like the rest of the country, she wants to know the facts." The next morning, a *New York Times* editorial applauded Leonard for introducing Mrs. Sutton's letter and formally charging the marine officers as defendants. Still, the *Times* criticized the investigating officers for their treatment of Private Kennedy in blunt language: "At Annapolis the officers make servants of the enlisted man. The caste spirit prevails, with enforced abject servility on the one side and a tendency to tyrannical behavior and the excesses of gentlemanly vices on the other." The paper was inclined to agree with Mrs. Sutton, who had written, "'The record as it stands is more indicative, if not conclusive,'" of the fact that her son was "'killed than that he could have committed suicide.'" "Luckily," the editor concluded, "in this land the investigation into Sutton's death cannot be made a Star Chamber proceeding.

Publicity will force out enough of the truth to humble the overbearing spirit of the service."

In Annapolis a local reporter put together a series of essays entitled "THE CITY OF BROKEN HEARTS." "There is much that is interesting in wondering how Jimmy Sutton died," he began. One answer might lie in the "eternal feud" between marines and naval men. Emphasizing how rugged the curriculum was at the Naval Academy, he suggested that Sutton may have still had his old prejudices against marines just appointed from "cit" [civilian] life when he came to the Marine Application School. Referring to Adams' testimony, the reporter speculated—not without reason—that this was why Sutton acted arrogantly toward Robert Adams, incurring his hatred. By the beginning of August, the *Evening Capital* and the *Baltimore Sun* both forecast there would be a Marine Corps housecleaning before long. "The Marine Corps feels the reflection cast upon its ancient and honorable body, as the Sutton family feels the stigma of suicide upon the name of Lieutenant Sutton." Military personnel and their supporters could find a more reassuring perspective in the *Army and Navy Journal* editorial comment. The *Journal* objected to the sensational and biased way news gatherers—especially those in New York—reported the Sutton case. Some of the newspaper men omitted "the connecting links between the isolated bits of testimony reported," and drew "unjustifiable conclusions from these facts" when they criticized Major Leonard's tactics. The accused officers were young men who should not have been expected to have the seasoned ability and discipline of older officers. Besides, these facts showed that most of the young men present were acting as peace-makers, "but the tempest was too strong for the peace-makers to still."

In this same issue, the *Journal* also ran an excerpt from the *New York Times* about another tempest. During the week-long recess of the Annapolis inquiry, news from West Point about Don Sutton's case preoccupied the press and the public. A board of army officers had just submitted a long report to Colonel Hugh Scott, the superintendent of West Point. Until the War Department acted on its recommendations, the specific activities of the West Point board would not be published. But newspapers kept the topic alive. On July 26, the *Times* predicted, in "HEAVY PUNISHMENT THREATENS CADETS," that a number of the most popular third-class men could be severely disciplined. A cadet who escaped punishment would owe his good luck to plebes (such as Don Sutton) who refused to reveal the names of the men involved. An editorial in the *Times* that same day suggested hazing was a legitimate way for the boys to relieve stress. The editorial ended by applauding Rosa's son: "Hurrah for young Sutton who can foil the meddlers even though he did get hurt a bit while receiving the not least valuable part of his education." But a day later, another *New York Times* editorial took the opposite view; stern punishments should be meted out for hazing because it was so hard to draw the line between horsing around and cruelty.

Discussion generated through the parallel stories of Jimmie and Don Sutton would fascinate Americans through the summer. On August 4, 1909, the *New York Times* printed a letter that zeroed in on why there was so much interest in the case among members of Congress and reporters. It came from a plain citizen known only as "M.E.G.E." and read in part as follows:

> It seems to me that the American public ought to be made to feel that the sin and shame of the Sutton trial is their sin and shame. The appointment of cadets to Annapolis and West Point rests with Congress. Congressmen are elected by the people. Every man whose vote helped to elect such men is responsible. It doesn't matter so much who killed Sutton as the fact (as appeared in the testimony at the trial) that three officers of the Marine Corps should have attacked one man. The testimony before the investigation proved that these men are without power or any notion of fair play.

Despite newspaper reports about his injuries and the fact that he remained hospitalized for almost three weeks, Don had been very effective in convincing his family that he was fine. Rosa Sutton and Rose Parker had not even asked their attorneys to look into the matter. Their focus was now on phase 2 of the Annapolis inquiry and the testimony of Lieutenant Harold Utley, who, it was hoped, would clear up several unsolved questions. Reporters said he could refuse to answer any questions "with any information that might incriminate him," now that the judge advocate had changed the nature of the inquiry. In "THE DILEMMA IN THE SUTTON CASE," *The New York Times* editor emphasized Utley's potential value as a witness and cited Henry Davis' concerns. The editor agreed with the naval court that with the possibility of homicide more and more likely, "the accused men are entitled to the rights and immunities of defendants." Henry Davis had lost this fight. For the remainder of the inquiry any semblance of disinterested fact-finding would give way to rising acrimony between the two parties—a situation that only added to public interest in the case.

10

"TO THE BEST OF
MY RECOLLECTION"

As soon as the USS *North Carolina* reached Boston, Harold Utley headed straight for Annapolis. He arrived by train on Wednesday, August 4, now sunburned and as dashing as ever. The following morning, under welcome cooler skies, all six newly named defendants took their places together in the Naval Academy auditorium for the first time. Only Lieutenant Robert Adams, who stood out in a khaki riding uniform, remained in his customary seat at the inquiry table. Lieutenants Edward Willing, William Bevan, and Edward Osterman sat together in their white duck summer uniforms on a bench behind Adams and "whispered incessantly" to each other while the minutes of the previous session were read. Lieutenant Utley, who had come in early in his service blue uniform, sword dangling at the side, "sat at arms length" from the other three officers. Further down on the bench, Sergeant James De Hart waited in his service blues. Close to two hundred people, "white uniformed officers of court, white frocked women and a sprinkling of cadets and enlisted men" would watch Utley describe "the tragic events that brought him from Europe." Although he was only twenty-three, considerably younger than the other officers involved in the calamity (now that Jimmie Sutton was dead and Edward Roelker had disappeared), an *Evening Star* reporter assumed the tall, handsome lieutenant exerted a "strong personal influence" over Adams and Osterman because of his superior intelligence and character. On the other hand, the man still known as "Highcock" to his former Naval Academy classmates appeared confident, the "darling of the corps and none knows it better than he." Two stenographers were ready to record the proceedings, guaranteed from this point on to be more dramatic if not more complicated.

Harold Utley had taken a room at the same boarding house as Lieutenants Osterman and Adams, and his coolness toward them caused comment. Once he took the witness chair, Commander John Hood told him, "there has been a charge of crime made against a number of officers, in which you are included, which puts you in the position of the defendant before this Court. That being so, you have the right to be present to offer testimony, cross question witnesses, and to be represented by counsel if you so desire." Next, Lieutenant Utley heard the proceedings of the previous session (day 7) read by stenographer Herman Pechin, including the full text of Rosa's letter to the secretary of the navy. At first, Commander Hood advised Utley that "as a party interested in the trial and as a defendant," he could not refuse to give testimony, but he could refuse "to give testimony that will incriminate yourself." Harry Leonard disagreed, and cited Article 1663, Paragraph 1 of the Naval Regulations. The defendant actually could decline to testify, but if he elected to testify on his own behalf, he was not required to answer questions that would incriminate him. Under these circumstances, Utley, who "was counted on to blow aside the fog of conflicting testimony" seemed perfectly willing to oblige. But Henry Davis knew the witness's new status might well shape his answers, or lack of them.

Following his initial narrative, Lieutenant Utley said he was unsure who started the disagreement in the auto ride back toward the student officers' camp, but he explained why he asked William Owens to leave once he thought Lieutenants Adams and Sutton were about to fight: "I considered it bad for any civilian to be present when the officers were fighting and I directed the machine to go on out of there." Utley recalled telling a sentry or member of the guard (at first he was not sure which) to see that both machines went on across the bridge. When Harold Utley informed Adams that this was not the time or the place for a fight, Adams "seemed afraid that Sutton would not fight afterwards." He clearly wanted to have it out with Sutton, and Utley admitted that he too had heard some things "to make me think he [Sutton] would not fight . . . a great deal of it was common report about him, which I had never heard denied or disputed, dating back to the time we were both at the Naval Academy." But Major Leonard did not encourage him to elaborate further on this curious remark.

The judge advocate did ask about Sutton's fight with Edward Osterman, and Utley was the first to say Osterman precipitated it because he "made some remark derogatory to Mr. Sutton," so Sutton struck him, and once a blow had been struck, a fight between the two could not be postponed. Edward Osterman (not surprisingly, given his size) "got the best of the fight from the start to the finish." But once Sutton was down, he "refused to get up and fight and refused to say that he had had enough." Once the two men had been pulled apart, Utley said Sutton told them they were all "sons of bitches" and ran back to camp. So he too went back to camp, changed from his evening clothes to his undress blue uniform, and contacted the officer of the day (Willing) to say he had put Sutton under arrest. Because Utley had been away from camp for several hours and was the senior officer in the camp ("there was no officer in charge of the camp" when he was gone), he then decided to check each tent to see who was present. It was at that point that he saw Sutton about to leave his own tent, pointing a single gun at Edward Roelker, trying to get him out of the way. Sutton then rushed out of the camp, allegedly telling Harold Utley to "fuck the arrest."

Under judge advocate Harry Leonard's astute and thorough grilling, Harold Utley seemed a cooperative witness and answered each question carefully. He said that he followed Sutton, and only when he saw him with Sergeant De Hart did he notice the officer had a gun in each hand; the sergeant was trying to get him to give them up. At one point, Utley, Roelker (who had also come on the scene), and De Hart were "in a sort of semi-circle about him." Sutton started up the road; Utley said he heard voices. Then he gave the court a vivid description of how Adams threw Sutton on the ground and fell on top of him. "Adams was either pulled off or told to get off, or got up of his own accord." He did not see Adams striking Sutton, but he did recall another person who was "kneeling on him, as near as I can remember holding his shoulders down, and more on the right side of Sutton, and I was more on the left, about Sutton's waist. As I said, Adams got up, and the revolver in Sutton's free hand was taken away from him. There was a struggle for that." Lieutenant Utley could no longer remember whether Sutton's left or his right arm was free, or who took the revolver from the free hand. He was sure Sutton had one revolver left when the struggle ended. It was in the hand that was under him.

Major Leonard knew this was a key point. "Do you know that he had a revolver in that hand?" he asked his witness.

"He had had it when he was covering me."

"All right, go ahead," said Leonard.

"I started to try to reach under him to get hold of the revolver. He had fallen with his arm under him. As I said, I was on the left side. I was reaching under with both hands."

"Which side of him did you reach under?"

"Under his left side, that I remember."

"You say you were on his left?"

"He was lying with his face down, and I was on his left, and I went under this way." He illustrated for the court.

"From his left?"

"From his left, as I remember. I did not get hold of the revolver, and he started drawing his hand out. I tried to follow up. I thought I could follow up quicker."

"Which hand out?" asked Harry Leonard.

"The hand that was under him, Sir."

"Did he draw his hand toward you?"

"He drew it straight up. I don't know which hand it was. He drew it straight up, toward his face, as nearly as I could make out from where I was. About that time I remember hearing somebody call out 'Reddy is shot,' or 'Roelker is shot,' or 'Reddy is dead,' or 'Roelker is dead'; and then Sutton continued this movement of the revolver—of his free hand—and got the revolver apparently clear. I heard the explosion, and indistinctly saw the flash, down by his head. I saw the flash down by his head, the revolver in his hand. His body sort of quivered under me. As I said, I was kneeling on it, and then he did not make any more resistance. I got up and reported to Colonel Doyen."

Lieutenant Utley answered in a loud, clear voice that he did not remember seeing anybody near Sutton's head other than the person kneeling on his shoulders (Bevan), and he was sure that the gun "was in Mr. Sutton's hand when it flashed." But he acknowledged he was probably "not up on the correct definition of suicide. . . . I define it as self-inflicted death," he said. "That is the way I used the term when I reported to Colonel Doyen."

"And if anyone fired a shot at another person and killed himself, would you call that suicide?" Leonard asked.

"Yes, sir," came the response. If that had been the case, Sutton's death was an accident—unintentional on his part and not a real suicide. So it could be argued that Lieutenant Utley had been wrong in telling everyone around the barracks that Sutton had committed suicide. For a change, Henry Davis was satisfied with Utley's answer.

Once the final shot was fired, Lieutenant Utley said he had woken up Colonel Charles Doyen, gone to the hospital, and shortly afterward, ran into Sergeant De Hart in the Company Street between the officers' tents. Utley (who had not heard De Hart's testimony), reported that De Hart told him "he knew where the revolver was that belonged to Sutton." He denied having picked up the revolver on the parade ground. When asked about Private Charles Kennedy, he said that the sentry he spoke to may have been Kennedy. If he told anyone to keep his mouth shut, "it was before the fight. That is, if it was done at all, and I am rather vague on that question. I may have done it before the fight, down there between those two ponds, when

I told the sentry to see that the machines went on across [back across the bridge], and I added to him to keep quiet about it. That was in regard to the fight, the trouble between these two officers."

As for Sutton's reputation among the marines, Lieutenant Utley referred to two incidents. First, one evening Sutton threatened to shoot through the tent of Lieutenant John Potts and then backed down as soon as Utley told him to put his rifle away. The second occasion was the May 20 incident that had come up so often; it turned out that Harold Utley had been the officer-of-the-day that night and the most put out by Sutton's behavior. Finally, he admitted he had not liked Lieutenant Sutton ever since they had both been midshipmen at the Naval Academy.

Major Leonard was still quite intrigued by the fact that Rose Parker had taken it upon herself to interview the officers. What had motivated Harold Utley to go to her room? he asked the witness. And, "What inspired you to talk?"

Davis immediately broke in—"Well, I should say that certainly was one of those mental excursions that you have been objecting to. I cannot understand why what he had in mind in going should cut any figure."

Leonard insisted, "I want to know why he went."

"It may be entertaining. It certainly cannot be enlightening," countered Rosa's attorney.

Lieutenant Utley explained that the men thought responding to Rose Parker's request was the proper thing to do. "Mrs. Parker conversed with us on the subject of her brother's death, and asked us about the feeling toward him. She told us of his having appeared to her in a dream while she was on her way there."

"What?" Leonard asked.

"That Mr. Sutton appeared to her in a dream."

"In a dream?" Leonard seemed amused. From his perspective, both Sutton women were apparently hallucinating.

"Or some sort of an appearance to her. And she told us a good deal about him one way and another." But Lieutenant Utley had no memory of saying anything to Rose about the death of her brother. When this line of questioning ended it was twenty minutes past noon, and the court broke for lunch until two o'clock.

That afternoon, Arthur Birney—now Utley's attorney, as he had volunteered to represent all the accused marines—took some time to examine his new client. Although Utley said he recognized Kennedy, he now said he did not have "the slightest idea" whether he had actually spoken to him on the fateful night. Lieutenant Utley knew he should have done more to prevent the brawl and at first tried to convince the court that he thought Sutton was bluffing and would not carry out any threats he had made. "There was a great deal of confusion and I was probably a good deal excited," Utley reported. No matter who asked him the questions, from this point on, Utley's memory about most of the details of Sutton's last conscious moments did not blow aside the fog of conflicting testimony; the fog became denser.

Utley would also not identify Lieutenant William Bevan as being the man who came on the scene and, kneeling down, held Sutton's shoulders to the ground—nor could he remember how Adams came to get up off Sutton or why. Birney read from Utley's testimony before the original inquest when he claimed Sutton once implied that he might kill himself. But the officer's answer may have been disappointing to Birney; Utley could no longer confirm that Sutton had ever made such a remark to him.

Harold Utley was the first witness to come under fire from Rosa's attorney in his new role as prosecutor, and on this particular day Davis had no backup from Edmund Van Dyke. He began by asking why he had taken such a dislike to Sutton. Utley now explained that he never really knew Sutton and had "nothing personally to do with him" at the Academy by way of association or any other way, nor could he recall hazing him.

"I probably hazed a good many midshipmen without knowing their names," said the defendant.

"And you think if you did haze Mr. Sutton that you did not know him?" Davis was aware that Sutton had fought against hazing at the Academy. He wanted it clear to the court that everything Utley had said about Sutton's plebe year was purely rumor.

"I am positive of it, sir."

Well then, what kind of terms had the two men been on in the Marine Application School?

Utley explained, "As I remember it, we would speak when we met, or in the morning when one of us came to the table; but I never associated with him. By that I mean I never went on liberty with him, or anything of that kind. You might say we were acquaintances, but not friends."

For the next several minutes, Henry Davis went after Harold Utley about matters that could be used in his closing arguments. But now Utley's memory failed him on the subject of any interaction with Private Kennedy; he did, however, volunteer that Kennedy was not attentive to his duties, and "I did not think that he showed any interest in the non-commissioned officers school." Another question troubled Davis. Even though Sutton supposedly "started off with the declared purpose of getting his guns and making a general holocaust, including himself in the affair," none of the three lieutenants who had been in the automobile tried to stop him. What, Davis wanted to know, did Lieutenant Utley think Sutton was going to do when he ran off from the camp? Utley changed his mind and asserted that Sutton probably was not bluffing and would have carried out his threats against Adams or Osterman. Davis had no trouble pointing out the inconsistencies in Utley's testimony. "At the inquest you testified thus. See what you say of it now," said Davis. "'We were all down on the ground trying to get the gun away from Mr. Sutton, and I saw someone else, I don't know who, wrench the gun out of his hands.' Now that was not the gun that was in his hand when he was shot?"

"No," was Utley's response. It was "the gun that was in his free hand."

"The other gun." Davis challenged Utley again. "Now if you testified to that, Lieutenant Utley, you were testifying when the event occurred, to your best recollection, were you not?"

"My best recollection, that is probably better than now." Formerly, Utley had said that Adams was striking Sutton, and he restrained him, and then he heard someone say "get the other gun." In 1907 Utley insisted Sutton shot himself with his left hand, but the lieutenant no longer remembered that. So Davis moved on to the shot that killed Sutton and the mystery of what had happened to his personal revolver just before he died. He got right to the point. Each defendant would be asked the same question. Did Harold Utley give the gun to Sergeant De Hart?

"According to my recollection I did not, sir."

"Very well. You qualify that by 'according to my recollection.' Do you think, Lieutenant Utley, that being present on an occasion of such a tragic nature as this, you could have any doubt about your relation to that gun?" asked Davis.

"Not to the salient points of it, that is, where the gun was actually, you might say, a principal in the affair. While it was still a principal in the affair, I do not think that at the time of the inquest I had any doubt; now it is sometime afterward, and the matter is more or less vague to me, the whole affair."

"Thank you," answered Davis, who would have to postpone further questions until the following morning.

When the proceedings began at ten o'clock on Friday, August 6, the judge advocate, who had with him "some statements that have appeared in the public press," was again on the defensive. ("MAJOR VS. NEWSPAPER," declared one of the *Evening Capital* headlines about the story later that day.) Leonard stood up and explained to everyone assembled in the auditorium that "some of the newspapers have said that I tried to stop the mouth of this witness" because he had brought up regulations that said Utley did not have to testify. There was never any question about Utley testifying, Leonard declared, as much to reporters as the court. "I simply want this to appear on record, in justice to myself."

Harold Utley resumed his seat across from Rosa Sutton and Rose Parker but would not look at them or their attorneys; instead he faced the court. Women crowded into the courtroom, having "given themselves up to a well-defined case of hero worship." Reportedly, they "clustered about the accused marines and whispered words of encouragement into the ears of their white clad young heroes." Edward Willing had been their idol until Lieutenant Utley arrived. But it would be a tough day for the lieutenant and for Henry Davis; both men would lose their tempers. On several key matters, Lieutenant Utley was not able to remember much. Davis zeroed in on what each of the other lieutenants had said about Utley's role in the events of October 13, 1907. Utley claimed to have no recollection of telling Lieutenant Adams to retrieve Sutton's clothes; no recollection of what Bevan said or of Bevan being at the scene of Sutton's death; and no recollection of telling Lieutenant Willing that Sutton was going to shoot somebody. Nor did he remember ordering De Hart to go back to the barracks or picking up the gun that De Hart had thrown away on the parade ground. In fact, Utley did not remember De Hart saying he had thrown the gun anywhere. Lieutenant Utley did agree that he told De Hart to give the revolver over to the officer of the day, but he would not admit ever touching the gun himself. Despite his statement in 1907 that the gun had been in Sutton's left hand, under repeated questioning, he now could not say which of Sutton's hands held the weapon that killed him.

Lieutenant Utley was asked to demonstrate exactly what he was doing with his arm under Sutton at the moment the fatal shot occurred. Afterward, Henry Davis pointed out that Lieutenant Bevan "was between you and Sutton's head, kneeling on the left, with one hand on each shoulder holding him down." But Utley insisted he had no recollection of seeing Lieutenant Bevan near Sutton and said, whoever the man was, he was on the right side of Sutton. Davis observed that obviously one of the lieutenants was mistaken. And then he read again from Utley's 1907 testimony: "I heard someone say get the other gun. I turned toward Mr. Sutton and searched his holster and pockets for the other gun. I did not find it, and turned to the front, when I heard a report and saw the flash." Sutton, in fact, had no pockets in his uniform, and Utley no longer remembered searching him at all.

"Lieutenant, I do not wish to appear too insistent upon this or as consuming time unnecessarily, but to my apprehension this is a very important point," said Davis.

> Within a few hours of this occurrence at which you were present and in which you were an active participant, you testified that you saw someone wrench a gun out of one of Sutton's hands, that you heard somebody say, "Get the other gun," that in the effort to get the other gun you went toward Sutton's feet, you went into his holster, you went into his pockets, and failing to find the gun you turned and looked towards his head and saw the flash. You are now here saying that you were endeavoring to get this other gun by feeling under Sutton's body for it, with your hand in the direction of his, and that you saw his arm reach out as though escaping your endeavor to collect his hand, and then saw the gun go off—absolutely as opposite as the two walls. Now, which is right?

Harold Utley's jaw tightened. Davis was going after him "with a zeal" that incensed him, and he began to answer curtly. He turned to the president of the court, "I would like to ask what he means by which is right. I am testifying as to what I remember. I testified then as to what I remembered then. The testimony that I gave then I have never had a chance to review since I left the Board of Inquest, and I have less recollection of what I testified to then than I have of the actual incidents." Clearly appealing to his fellow marines, he continued.

> To ask me which is right, with my limited knowledge of English, as I understand it is to ask me which actually happened; in other words, am I wrong now or was I wrong then, according to what has been read of my testimony before the Board of Inquest. My recollection now does not coincide with my recollection then, according to the testimony that has been read. I can testify to what I recollect now, but I do not quite understand what he means by asking which is right.

The animosity between Davis and Utley was palpable. "Answer the question to the best of your recollection now," Commander Hood told Utley, "and the Court will give what weight it thinks proper to the testimony."

"To the best of my recollection now, I reached under the left side of Lieutenant Sutton, either that way or this way," Utley demonstrated. "That is going under his left side, reached under his body. I do not remember turning or searching the holster or pockets of Lieutenant Sutton."

Davis would not let up on the glaring inconsistencies between Utley's original testimony given within hours of Sutton's death and what he would

admit to in the summer of 1909. This time Utley was under oath. He read
from the transcript of the inquest again both to help jog Utley's memory
and to get the original testimony in the record of the inquiry. He had done
that several times; the discrepancies in the testimony of the government
witnesses was one of the strongest indications that his client's son might not
have murdered himself. In 1907 Utley stated that he had seen Lieutenant
Bevan on Sutton, a man he knew very well. Davis focused on other ways
the two were at variance.

> Now today and yesterday you say you have no recollection of De Hart be-
> ing there. At the Inquest, when the matter was fresh in your mind, you
> testified to seeing De Hart on his body and sending him off for the hos-
> pital steward. Today you say you were heading in the same direction that
> he [Sutton] was and trying to find this other revolver in his hand under
> his body. At the Inquest you said you were hunting for it in the other di-
> rection, towards his feet. Today and yesterday you say that it was when you
> saw with your own eyes the hand that you were pursuing raised in the air,
> the flash of the weapon which you say killed him, and before the Board
> of Inquest you said that the flash occurred as you turned from your futile
> effort to find the weapon near his feet. Now, Davis said, does anything I
> have said refresh your recollection as to what actually did happen?

"No, sir," came the response. But as the questioning continued relent-
lessly, Utley would repeatedly assure the court that he had never touched
Lieutenant Sutton's hand.

Now Henry Davis wanted to know why Utley had testified "just yesterday" that he had seen Sutton shoot himself. "Do you mean to say that
you saw him aim the weapon at himself and deliberately shoot himself?"

"I mean that my impression was that the shot had been fired by the
pistol in his hand."

"Whether intentionally or accidentally."

"Either intentionally or accidentally."

This was another crucial point. No matter who actually fired the fatal
bullet, Davis wanted the court to know that Harold Utley, who had initiated the suicide rumor, had never claimed that Sutton deliberately killed
himself. "What you meant," Davis paraphrased, "was that you saw the gun
in his hand go off, and the shot from that gun inflicted death on him?"

"Yes, sir, that is my understanding of the word 'suicide.'"

And why, the attorney now changed the subject, had Utley been so
eager to volunteer negative information about Charles Kennedy. Had he
known what Kennedy had said about him?

Utley explained that when he arrived in Boston he had been at sea for twelve days, "where we received no newspapers. As soon as the ship was in, I started for Annapolis almost immediately, and I had seen no newspapers except I believe I had seen some headlines. I had seen something to the effect that I was expected to clear up some question in regard to Private Kennedy, a question that his testimony had raised."

Then Davis tried another tack. Why did Utley say at the inquest that Sutton "informed me that all three of us excepting himself would be dead before sunrise." And now, almost two years later, he accused Sutton of threatening to kill himself as well as the three lieutenants. There was no clear answer. Each time Davis read from the lieutenant's 1907 testimony, he denied that he remembered anything about it. He said he knew nothing about Sergeant De Hart throwing away a revolver. So why, Davis asked, did De Hart seek out Utley and tell him he knew where the revolver was?

"Did it occur to you at that time, or does it occur to you now, that the reason Sergeant De Hart came and told you that he knew where the revolver was, was that he knew that you knew it had gone?" Harold Utley finally admitted he had known the revolver belonged to Lieutenant Sutton but not that he knew it was missing. In fact, he was not sure which revolver De Hart was talking about.

Davis asked the witness to think carefully about the morning after Sutton died. He proposed that Utley had been on duty early that morning when Sunday troop inspection took place right after breakfast. After inspection, Utley left the company, stopped in the parade ground, and picked up something close to the spot where a second base marker now stood on the ball field. Utley remembered nothing of the kind, nor did he recall whether he was on duty or not. He insisted the next time he had seen Sutton's Smith & Wesson was before the Board of Inquest. Then Davis wanted to know how he knew someone had recovered Sutton's pistol. Because, Utley replied, he was on the board of inventory of Lieutenant Sutton's effects. Davis went over and over this topic. The inventory was dated October 13 at ten o'clock, just before the inquest began. It included a revolver. Lieutenant Utley's best recollection was that the gun was produced at the inquest and returned to Sutton's effects, which were collected for his heirs after it ended.

It was shortly after noon when Major Leonard also tried to pin Utley down on a few other matters. Would the witness say a bit more about why Robert Adams was afraid Sutton would not fight with him if the fight didn't take place that night? Because, Utley explained, Sutton was so enraged on the night that he died that he would have been more likely to fight with Robert Adams on the spur of the moment than if it was prearranged in a cold-blooded way. Returning one last time to the scene of the brawl, Leonard tried to get a straight answer about the shot that killed Lieutenant Sutton. Did the shot occur with or without "the intervention of any other person's hand?" he challenged the witness.

"As I remember it, it was without the intervention—"

Leonard jumped in. "Well, but Mr. Utley, don't you remember one way or the other about that?"

"Well, I know that I did not touch either the gun or his hand."

"Do you know or do you not know that anyone else did or did not touch his hand?"

"I don't remember that anybody did, sir."

"But do you remember that they did not?"

"My recollection is that they did not."

"Have you a positive recollection on the subject?" Leonard persisted.

"That is the way I remember it now, yes, sir."

"Positively?"

Utley hedged a bit. "As positively as any of the rest of it."

"Well, are you positive about anything that you have said here?" asked the judge advocate, becoming a bit exasperated himself.

"Yes, sir."

"Then your answer to that question is what? Do you or do you not know whether any other hand intervened in the firing of the shot which produced Mr. Sutton's death?"

"To the best of my knowledge no other hand intervened."

"Have you definite knowledge?" Even Harold Utley began to wear out.

"Yes, sir."

But the witness equivocated once more when Harry Leonard inquired about the testimony of Charles Kennedy. He was now not sure how his prior knowledge about what Private Kennedy had told the court had affected his own testimony. There was no way the young officer was about to incriminate himself.

Following the usual one and one-half hour midday break that brought extra business to the dining room at Carvel Hall, Major Leonard came up with one more question. The gunshot wound Sutton received was on the right side of his head; surely knowing that would help Lieutenant Utley's recall which hand Sutton raised above his head. But he was wrong.

"You mean to say that you were on the man's body and you don't know which hand—"

Lieutenant Utley interrupted, "Yes, sir. That is exactly what I mean."

By the end of the session, the press noted that Lieutenant Utley was visibly annoyed, and Davis was stymied by the "hazy memory" of the witness. Utley had answered many questions but not the important ones. Across the country, newspapers had kept up with Utley's escapades in court. One staff correspondent for the *Evening Star*, which announced "UTLEY CANNOT MAKE VARIED TALES TALLY," observed that three of Utley's co-defendants, Bevan, Willing, and Osterman, "sat on a bench just behind him and grinned at his discomfiture. To them, Utley's predicament seemed a huge joke. They had all spent the best part of a week under similar circumstances. To see Utley 'getting his' furnished them the best fun they have had yet." Davis "badgered" and "hammered" the embarrassed young lieutenant whose face, "already bronzed by exposure to the open waves, turned a deep crimson." The *Army and Navy Journal* reported that at one point he spoke calmly to Davis but with his face "set hard in anger."

In his home state of Illinois, the *Chicago Tribune* characterized Harold Utley as a "willing witness" after his first day of testimony, a man who "is a slow thinker and often pondered over questions," but "for the most part on nearly all essential points his memory was clear and his testimony direct" and "more damaging" to Sutton than that of his peers. And in Springfield, where his mother was riveted to the news, tales of Utley's Annapolis adventure came out on the front page of the *Illinois State Register* in a matter-of-fact style, showing no favoritism to a hometown boy. On August 7, Emma Utley could read the details of Harold's dramatic encounter with Henry Davis and no doubt wished she had been in the Naval Academy auditorium when her son re-enacted his struggle with Sutton. But Rosa Sutton, who characterized him as the "'busy, busy Mr. Utley,'" probably learned from her family in Portland about the *Oregonian* headline, "UTLEY'S REFUGE IS BAD MEMORY."

One other government witness had also been on the *North Carolina* on its journey back from Gibraltar. Dr. Frank Cook made the trip to Annapolis after the recess on the train with Harry Leonard who had been in New Hampshire. Dr. Cook came into the auditorium under a slight shadow— questions had come up about his role as a witness at the first inquest because he was also on the examining board. As he had in 1907, when he testified for only a few moments, Cook explained that he removed Lieutenant Sutton's brain and performed a partial autopsy on it. Major Leonard asked for specific information about the powder burns Cook had found near Sutton's head wound. The surgeon replied, "I cannot, after this lapse of time, remember any singeing of the hair or any powder marks. I don't know; I may have mentioned it if there were any such marks. But there was some mud or dirt which had gotten into the scalp wound and had worked its way a little ways. I remember that part."

Leonard was curious about the "appreciable scalp wound" made before the bullet entered Sutton's head. It was short and a little jagged, Cook responded, possibly due to the "impact of the bullet fired in that direction." Under further questioning the surgeon said that the bullet was "slightly flattened. The hole in the skull . . . was more or less clean cut, but it may have deflected that bullet slightly." Next, the doctor was asked, "If the head of Mr. Sutton had been turned to the left, say, could that bullet have been fired from a revolver directly in front of Mr. Sutton's head and pointed at his head?" "Hardly," answered Frank Cook, adding, "If his head was turned way to the right and he fired that way" (indicating with his hand), "I would expect possibly a glancing blow, grazing, but not into the skull at all." And what if, as so many of the marines had testified, his face had remained buried in the ground? Although it was possible the wound could have been self-inflicted, it was not probable, according to the doctor, unless the pistol was held in such a way "that another finger could have pulled the trigger and changed its direction so it could do that." Moments later Cook would confirm what surgeon George Pickrell had said in his testimony and in a demonstration—Sutton could not have shot himself unless he had used his thumb. But Cook said he could not recall a bruise on Sutton's forehead; nor had he noticed evidence that indicated the lieutenant had been beaten severely enough to have caused his death.

When Arthur Birney took over, Cook revealed that he had not seen evidence that Sutton's teeth had been knocked out, his forehead fractured, or his nose freshly broken. Under cross-examination by Henry Davis, Cook said Sutton's wounds had probably not been washed or dressed before the autopsy. He found no fractures of the bony structure of the skull. At no point could Dr. Cook recall seeing any powder burns or evidence that any part of the brain extruded from the wound, despite Dr. Pickrell's comments to the contrary. He did find mud in the wound. It had been difficult to find signs of tearing up the brain matter because, he explained, the brain is a jelly-like mass that closes up like a sponge if a bullet goes through it.

Rosa Sutton's highly anticipated testimony had been postponed before the week-long recess. But Frank Cook left the auditorium at the hottest point in the afternoon; with only an hour left of the day's work, Harry Leonard called her to the stand.

11

SACRED REPUTATIONS

At about a quarter past three on Friday, August 6, Rosa Sutton made her way around the inquiry table to the witness chair where she would face her attorneys and her daughter; this time her back was to the unfriendly spectators and the men whose futures had been put at risk by her crusade. In a rare gesture of solidarity with the Oregon housewife, a woman in the auditorium shook her fist at Lieutenant Robert Adams. The marines broke out in laughter, and Rosa thought the young men were mocking her. Later that afternoon they would apologize. All eyes were on Rosa Sutton as she waited for the judge advocate to speak. But first he pulled a handful of letters out of his leather bag and placed them on the table. "In these letters," Harry Leonard explained, "very definite and positive allegations of criminality are made against the parties defendant to the inquiry." Rosa's eyes widened as she recognized her broad, bold scrawl on the black-bordered envelopes. How could Major Leonard possibly have the private letters she sent to Harry Swartz in the spring of 1908? She had not even told her own attorneys about them. Swartz, who was now a corporal, had acted as her friend ever since she moved to Washington; Leonard proceeded to ask her to identify her letters to a man who had clearly betrayed her.

The press corps would track down Harry Swartz who insisted that he had not been forced to give the letters to the Navy Department. "All I can say," he told reporters, "is, I was unfortunate. I got into a position where I could not act otherwise from the way I did. I am absolutely not going to talk about this thing anymore." Swartz had agreed to keep Rosa's letters confidential, and he clearly did not like the limelight. When pushed by a correspondent from the persistent New York *World*, he said, "You think all the papers will have this story? . . . I'm in bad enough over it already. I want to let well enough alone. I wish my name could be kept out of the papers."

A reporter inquired whether an officer had requested the letters, but Swartz denied that he had misrepresented himself to Mrs. Sutton and explained to the *Washington Post* that officers rarely have an opportunity to enter rooms "where clerk work is done." "Out of a sense of duty," is the only explanation that had been forthcoming from Annapolis. As it turned out, Swartz never even met Jimmie Sutton. When Mrs. Sutton's wax-sealed letters began arriving in the Marine Corps paymaster's office stamped Portland, Oregon, he could have viewed them as a curiosity. Perhaps he felt sorry for her, but the letters enlivened his office work and surely piqued the interest of his cronies. Once Rosa Sutton confronted the U.S. Navy, there was no way he could keep his unusual correspondent a secret from his superiors.

Rosa had used the former payroll clerk as a sounding board, occasionally grasping at straws and ghostly testimony as evidence for the marines' behavior. Major Leonard knew her emotional, bitter statements did not show her in a good light; his Department may have had the letters for months. He now reminded the spectators and reporters that the United States had gone to "every extreme that it knows of" to bring witnesses from across the world to Annapolis. Either Rosa's charges were based on evidence that she and her attorney would bring before the court, or her statements were not true, "in which event Mrs. Sutton and the Department are entitled to have that fact of record."

Henry Davis was stunned, and as he rose up from his chair, his fury was apparent to all in the room. "This proposition," he protested, "is too extraordinary to bear temperate discussion." He did not know what was in Rosa's letters and said he did not want to. Why hadn't Leonard come to him outside the courtroom? Davis asked, not expecting an answer. "If there is anything in these letters that is incapable of substantiation let him ask, and he will get a man's answer." But for the judge advocate to bring "the words of a mother with a riven heart over the death of her son" into a public forum was indeed "unique and cruel." Davis declared the court could read the letters privately and decide whether Rosa should have her heart and mind probed regarding what she had written "over the gaping grave of her son." Alleging "bad faith" on Leonard's part, he insisted that his client's year-old letters were irrelevant to this inquiry. As her attorney spoke and reporters recorded his distress, Rosa broke down and buried her face in her handkerchief.

Major Leonard was prepared for this outburst. The United States deserved an "opportunity to learn upon what foundation Mrs. Sutton's statements were made," he argued. "Surely Mrs. Sutton would not make the statements without adequate foundation, supportable by the most acceptable and competent evidence." Besides, he continued, underscoring his deference to the three judges sitting at the other end of the table, "the Court is entitled to know these things, not the Judge Advocate only. The Judge Advocate is simply an instrumentality of the Court." "Lest anyone has the wrong idea," Leonard added, "the influence of a gaping and curious public can have no effect on the conduct of the Judge Advocate in this matter." But it would soon be clear, and Leonard would say so himself, that fostering more favorable public opinion toward its position in this case was critical to the U.S. Navy.

Arthur Birney also insisted Rosa's letters to Swartz "be laid before the Court and considered." Acknowledging the widespread press coverage of the case, Birney proclaimed that Rosa had already "sought an open hearing before the public. That is why this Court was convened—that there might be absolute publicity as to all the details of this unfortunate affair, so that there can be now no escape from the purpose of the accuser to have a public hearing." Henry Davis objected strongly. This was not an inquiry into the "bitterness of a mother's heart"; what Rosa saw or said in the past was not admissible as evidence "upon any principle of law or any principle of sense."

As the attorneys sparred over the letters, Harry Leonard fumed over Davis' accusation that he was guilty of "bad faith." Davis, Leonard said, never had understood how this particular court functioned, even though the Department had tried to enlighten him. In a voice "suppressed with emotion," he argued that Davis' accusation should be expunged from the record—"and I so move this Court." Then, looking straight at Rosa's attorney, he went on:

> And I want to invite Mr. Davis' attention, after his eloquent appeal to the Court, to one fact. The hallowed grave of a dead son is no more sacred than the grave of a military reputation; and there are a great many military reputations at stake in this hearing; and they are entitled, as in an honorable old corps, to have every fact that may be adduced brought before this Court and brought before the public.

Commander John Hood now ordered the room emptied. Following a discussion with his two colleagues, he announced that Mrs. Sutton's letters would be read in a private session the next morning in front of no one but "the Court, the parties interested in the trial, their counsel and the stenographer." The word "trial" was technically inaccurate but would now be used freely in the press and in court. Even the president of the inquiry board recognized that the proceeding had taken an unusual turn. But when the court adjourned at 3:45 that afternoon, Rosa and her attorneys were not happy with this new plan.

On Saturday, August 7, the court, the judge advocate, the parties to the inquiry with their attorneys, and the stenographers reassembled; for the first and only time, the inquiry proceeded behind closed doors. Henry Davis won a small victory; his accusation of "bad faith" would remain on the record, although to soften the blow, Hood said the court was satisfied with the "attitude of the Judge Advocate in conducting the trial." The large auditorium that doubled as a theater was eerily silent. There were no reporters scribbling, no photographers flashing their cameras, and none of the spectators who usually sat in the mezzanine at the back of the room or on the ground floor on benches, peering at the men and women around the table in front of the stage. It had been balmy in July when the accused lieutenants testified—in Annapolis it seemed even the weather was loyal to the navy. But Rosa, accustomed to the more temperate climate of the Pacific Northwest, now took the stand during the "equatorial heat wave" of 1909. In New York, people were dying on account of the temperature.

Major Leonard used his one arm to hand Rosa each of the letters she had written to Corporal Swartz. She verified her signatures for the court and probably wished she had never heard of Harry Swartz. Her original letters as well as typed copies of them were the permanent property of the U.S. government, and became Exhibits P-1 through P-4. Henry Davis was still so appalled at this inappropriate evidence that he refused to look at the letters, but Arthur Birney asked for a copy. He had not wanted his own transcript of the testimony, but Rosa's correspondence would prove invaluable for his defense.

Rosa now came under direct examination by the judge advocate. He would go through the letters page by page, insisting that she clarify the statements she wrote in March, April, and May of 1908. Rosa kept returning to the 1907 inquest to bolster her claims, but Leonard was eager to get her inflammatory statements on the record. Reading from what she had told Swartz, he got right to the point: "Now, I notice you say that these men beat your son to death and fired the shot into his head to hide their crime."

"Well, that is my own idea," Rosa explained, totally at ease with her own interpretation of what had happened. "Don't you know, that he was beaten so severely? I could not understand how a man would have an incision in the back of his head an inch and a half long, and his forehead would be broken up so a man would think he had shot himself in the forehead, without being knocked senseless. Then he did not bleed when the shot was fired into his head. I could not understand that." There had been very little blood near the bullet hole in Jimmie's head, and Rosa had asked a doctor about it. "You know we are told that when a man is virtually dead and then shot he does not bleed, but a healthy man bleeds profusely when shot."

Leonard continued, "Is there any evidence within your possession or procurable by you, which will prove or tend to prove that your son's forehead was crushed and his nose broken?"

"The testimony proves that. The hospital steward said he had a hole in his forehead, and one of the officers testified that he supposed he had shot himself in the forehead. You will find that in the testimony." Rosa was certain about what she had read.

Major Leonard kept up the pressure, paying little heed to Rosa's answers. "I notice that you say in your letter that your son was killed by those wild beasts," observed Leonard. "Please state to the Court to whom you referred?"

"The men that were with him there at the time of his death," Rosa said, careful not to accuse any particular officer of murder.

"And you have no other evidence that is unknown to the Court to prove it?"

"Only the letters and the testimony," Rosa responded.

Leonard next went after her assertion that Jimmie had been helpless when the fatal shot was fired. Again she referred to the 1907 testimony that indicated (incorrectly) Jimmie had been drinking and that he was found face down in the ground with a gash in his head and three men on top of him. Despite his dire predicament, no other officer had stepped up to protect her son.

But Leonard was not satisfied. "Have you any evidence which will prove or tend to prove that any officer of the Naval service of the United States knew of a conspiracy to beat your son and did not report that fact to the Naval authorities?"

"No," Rosa replied. As the men around the table listened, the stenographers typed furiously to keep up with her while she blurted out her understanding of what had happened.

> I thought it was strange that four officers would be together and one officer of the four to jump up and offer to fight another officer without knowing the other two officers were going to agree with him, because I believe that is a court-martial offense, to challenge a man to fight, according to the rules of the Navy; and it struck me as clear that with four officers present one officer would not dare to take off his coat and offer

to fight another officer, without knowing the other two were going to stand by him. That is the reason I formed that conclusion.

Leonard let the matter pass but remained as fixated on Rosa's letters as she was on the1907 inquest testimony. "It is alleged in your letter that Marix, meaning Captain Marix, and Utley, meaning Lieutenant Utley, destroyed certain letters in the effects of the late Lieutenant Sutton." At this Henry Davis may have scowled; he was irate at this whole line of questioning. The judge advocate was putting Rosa's words under a microscope and doing it well.

Rosa did not falter. Both she and her daughter had been startled that two officers had gone through Jimmie's possessions without a family member present. Jimmie had a habit of keeping the letters that Rosa sent him and returning them to her, and she also kept his letters. But after he died, she found that some of the letters were missing from his things. There was an envelope in his trunk already addressed and stamped for Portland that, she said now, "was cut open and the letter gone. The envelope was left and on the back of it was 'Will send you some postals in a few days.' It struck me as strange," Rosa told the court, "that the letter should be taken out and not the envelope destroyed; because if a man wanted to destroy the letter he would tear it right up."

Tampering with the U.S. mail was against the law, and Leonard pressed further, relieved that Rosa had no evidence to link a marine with the disappearance of any of her letters. But, she stated emphatically, she had not thought it right that Harold Utley, one of the men present at her son's death, had been in charge of taking inventory. And that is what she had intended to convey in her letter to Harry Swartz. Davis may have relaxed a little. His client did not seem at all intimidated by Harry Leonard.

Now the judge advocate began a different line of questioning, coming to a point of grave concern to his Department. "And you allege in your letters," Leonard asked, "that a certain person or persons were protecting the criminals and by criminals who did you mean?"

"I meant the men who were with my son the night he was killed, and I meant the United States government," Rosa said crisply.

"And who did you mean that were protecting the criminals?" Any man who tried to cover up a crime would be an accessory after the fact, "and the United States wants to know about that."

"Well, I will tell you, Major Leonard, that I was so exercised about it that I meant a clean sweep. I meant the government."

"You meant the United States itself?" Leonard seemed troubled by Rosa's conviction as well as her sweeping claims.

"Yes sir," Rosa replied in a carefully articulated voice. "I meant the Government ought to have investigated the case more thoroughly. I did not mean any one man in particular, because I did not know any of the men here at all."

"And did you mean to indicate particularly that the Department was making affirmative efforts to protect—"

"Oh, no," Rosa protested, not being totally candid as she softened her stance under pressure, "I did not mean that they were making efforts to conceal the crime or protect them, but I just thought in a general way that the Government should have made a more thorough investigation, and I thought they did not do their duty."

"And you have not any evidence in your possession, or obtainable by you, whereby the United States can prove or tend to prove that persons other than the Government itself were endeavoring to protect criminals?"

"No."

"Or conceal criminality?"

"No, I don't think so."

One last time, Leonard pushed Rosa to come up with proof of any criminal conduct on the part of the marines.

"Well, I have some letters," Rosa answered. "I do not know whether they would be accepted as evidence or not. I leave that to my counsel; letters that would lead me to think that somebody saw the crime committed." Leonard encouraged her to ensure that the court had this information, and she agreed.

With that Major Leonard decided he had "nothing further to ask."

Still reeling from this new evidence, and sensing that Rosa preferred to answer questions about her letters in a public session, Henry Davis asked that the court take a recess by noon. At quarter to twelve on this unprecedented Saturday morning, Commander Hood adjourned the court for the weekend. Davis said he only had two or three questions for Mrs. Sutton, but Arthur Birney would need some time to examine this witness. He would face Rosa in an open forum, and he hoped all of America would see how irrational she had been when she wrote to Harry Swartz and accused the marines of a conspiracy to beat up her son.

"TILT OVER LETTERS MRS. SUTTON WROTE," announced the *New York Times* on August 7. If that newspaper or the *Evening Post* (founded by Alexander Hamilton) seemed too sedate, New Yorkers could pick up the *Sun*, the *New York Herald*, the *World*, the *Evening Journal*, or the *New York American* (and others) for more colorful reporting and dozens of photographs. The *Evening Journal* had gone so far as to illustrate dramatic episodes of the Sutton story in comic book fashion. During the coming week, in Boston, Philadelphia, Baltimore, Annapolis, Washington, D.C., Atlanta, New Orleans, and across the country, all the way to Portland, San Francisco, and Los Angeles, Americans became caught up in the feud between the judge advocate and the Suttons' attorney, who was, according to reporters, a "savage fighter when aroused." The *Evening Star* noticed how pleased the defendants were that Harry Leonard had exposed the flimsy evidence behind Rosa's charges, but the real test of this Oregon mother's mettle would be when she confronted Arthur Birney.

Naturally, the press corps had not liked the court's decision to hold a session behind closed doors. On August 8, *New York American* reporter James Dorrance's column also came out in Portland ("Hearst News by Longest Leased Wire"), predictably in the lively and self-conscious *Oregon Daily Journal.* Dorrance observed that while the "afternoon newspaper men were sending from the telegraph offices frantic protest against such secrecy, the Naval board reconsidered and sent word that the Monday session would be open as usual." And several papers cited Rosa's firm desire to have her own examination conducted publicly, agreeing with the *Philadelphia Inquirer* headline that Mrs. Sutton "WANTS NO SECRECY ABOUT INVESTIGATION." Reporters continued to suggest that a compromise would solve the navy's predicament: Sutton was neither murdered nor an intentional suicide but accidentally put the bullet in his own brain while trying to shoot one of the men on his back. If that were the case, Lieutenant Sutton might get to heaven after all.

But Rosa Sutton would never believe her son had shot himself for any reason; her point about Jimmie's "bloodless" wound became the "source of much comment" among those who had been following the case, one that engrossed physicians as well. The *Baltimore Sun* reporter who delved into the matter heard of a local "well-known physician" who also thought there would have been considerable blood if Jimmie had normal circulation when the shot was fired; plus, the reporter observed, Robert Adams' statement that he had "rammed Sutton's head into the earth as hard as he could," and the fact that Sutton was not struggling at all when the final shot was fired, made it unlikely that he fired it.

Rosa reacted to Major Leonard's latest surprise as she had reacted to Jimmie's death—by writing. In the year since she had first contacted Harry Swartz, she had learned how to maneuver in the cutthroat terrain of Washington politics and how to impress reporters with the urgency of her crusade. It was no longer just about Jimmie. Now fully aware of—and a bit

LETTERS ACCUSE MARINE OFFICERS

Charges by Mrs Sutton Admitted After Clash of Counsel.

MRS JAMES N. SUTTON,
Whose Letters Making Serious Charges Against Officers of the Marine
Court Are Admitted as Evidence, But Will Not Be Read in Public.

Will Be Read Today in Closed Court---

"LETTERS ACCUSE MARINE OFFICERS," Boston Globe, *front page, August 7, 1909.*

carried away by—the public interest in her crusade, she framed her goals in the impassioned style of rhetoric used by reform-minded activists of the era. In the only full statement of her views that she made during the inquiry, Rosa went after the naval justice system with language she had not dared to use in the courtroom. She had been offended by Leonard's statement emphasizing the significance of a military reputation. "Has it a tendency to increase the public confidence in our military when officials are permitted to perpetrate and shield outrageous wrongs for the pretended good of the service?" she wrote. "Is it conducive to good government to tolerate in office those who perjure the truth and massacre their fellow man? If those men have done no wrong, why fear for their military reputations? Why are they at stake and why do they need protection?"

The Marine Corps, Rosa said, should be "investigated to the bitterest end," with everything "ushered into the light of honest scrutiny. No official should be such as to fear publicity. The very fact that it dreads exposure is the strongest possible evidence of its self incriminative [*sic*] guilt." Her own awkward eloquence emerged, probably with help at the very least with the punctuation and typing, as she continued: "Governmental actions should be neither secret nor unjust. They should be so manly, dignified and honorable as to welcome observation, challenge criticism and receive the praises of all mankind." Rosa next launched a strongly worded protest against the "exemption of rascals from arraignment 'for the good of the service,'" and she decried the navy's unsatisfactory 1907 investigation that had not called on the chauffeurs, the enlisted men, or the hospital steward to testify. She closed with a passionate appeal to the "noble sentiment and sympathy" of the "faithful fathers and mothers of my country to see that justice is extended [to] me and mine!" and to "the justice, patriotism, heroism and humanity" in "the great American people" who could help her "wage and win this great battle for the holy rights of liberties of men!" She wrote for public consumption but may have been advised by her attorneys or her daughter not to submit her statement to the press. No matter what reporters thought of the case, they would have bristled at the request, written in her handwriting at the top of the typed document, that it be printed "as is or not at all." Their job was to tell the story, not just her story, though in practice that did not always seem to be the case.

When court reconvened on Monday, August 9, Rosa and her daughter steeled themselves for a difficult session. Reporters had been tracking the women all weekend, whenever they came into the assembly room of the Carvel Hall Hotel or into its spacious dining room. The *Evening Capital* issued a warning to the members of its own profession. Women supporting the navy and the Marine Corps were becoming "exceedingly bitter," not only toward the Suttons, but toward the newspaper correspondents. When court had ended on Friday, the wife of a prominent officer proclaimed quite loudly that the "hounds" from the press corps were the ones causing all the trouble. But Rosa Sutton and Rose Parker must not have been disappointed with reporters. As they struggled against the naval establishment on its own turf, they could draw strength from news of other women's gains in making their public voices heard. In fact, a group of Boston suffragists had just suggested a novel campaign to run Chicago reformer Jane Addams (who was exactly Rosa's age) for the U.S. presidency.

On this, the eleventh day of the inquiry, it was already ninety degrees by ten o'clock; Major Leonard was again feeling the heat from the press corps as well as the Annapolis climate—the phantom limb pain on his left side was much more troublesome in high humidity. Once again he was on the defensive, and he responded firmly to the outcry against the closed session on Saturday morning. The court had not met "under a system of star chamber procedure," nor was evidence being concealed from the public, Leonard declared. And because the case was now "a matter of national interest," he moved that the court open its doors and the entire record of Saturday morning be read in public, including Rosa's letters. The court would agree, and the "dean of the press representatives" received a copy of the letters that the judge advocate and a stenographer took turns reading out loud. How strange it must have been for Rosa to hear her emotional prose in these male voices.

From this point on, Leonard would repeat the same theme over and over again—that the navy was accountable to its public. Ultimately, he used it to go after Rosa. "The public and the service are entitled to know," he "thundered," whether or not Mrs. Sutton's charges are based on "hallucination, fancy or dream." And Mrs. Sutton, he added, was not the only mother who deserves sympathy; there were other mothers, those of the defendants, who were entitled to know the basis for the charges against *their* sons.

It was now evident to Americans that Rosa Sutton's visions and her lack of hard evidence would be central to the government's defense. And it was also clear in the debate that followed that the American public, now the "urban masses," informed and to some extent manipulated by the press corps, was shaping the course and the tone of the inquiry itself. In 1909, "public opinion" was a term that applied to a much larger percentage of the population than it had when the concept first originated in the eighteenth century, or even two decades before the Sutton inquiry opened. And the journalists of the day (as now) thrived on the sort of conflict Rosa's crusade embraced—an average citizen speaking truth (at least truth as she saw it) to power. The *New York Times* asserted confidently that "publicity will force out enough of the truth to humble the overbearing spirit of the service." But the navy was a strong and proud institution. Would that confidence prove justified?

Up to this point, Arthur Birney had kept a much lower profile than Davis, and it was now his turn to take center stage. Physically, he was far more impressive than his opponent. At least six feet tall and fit-looking, with silver white hair and a walrus mustache, Birney shared his brother attorney's self-assurance. Like Henry Davis, Birney was a professor as well as a trial attorney and completely at ease speaking in public. He was also an Episcopalian, but Rosa's spiritual quest appeared to hold little interest for him. His brother attorney was childless, while Birney was the father of seven, and harbored firm ideas about how to raise manly sons. Birney knew his harshest judges would not be the men in uniform sitting at the table before him but reporters—in his view they were partly responsible for the inquiry. The proceedings were instituted, he said now, "very largely for the purpose of satisfying the public mind." In fact, Birney admitted, he had deplored "the action of the Court on Saturday in sitting with closed doors." The Navy Department had been satisfied with the original investigation, "but there was spread from Maine to Texas, and from the Atlantic to the Pacific, the charges which these letters contained." Using rhetoric very similar to Leonard's, Birney said that if Rosa's charges "are simply the hysterical ravings of a woman, with no evidence whatever to sustain them, the Court is entitled to know what it is that has poisoned the public mind, to such an extent that these young men came here at the beginning convicted of an awful crime."

After hearing Birney's caustic remarks, Henry Davis grew concerned about Rosa's composure. He urged the court to focus on the task assigned by the Department's precept, namely, to investigate whether Sutton caused his own death. But he too acknowledged the pivotal role of "the public" interest in the case. "Let it be granted for the argument," Davis pleaded, "that this mother hysterically raved, and in her ravings accused these young men of murder." Even so, he argued, the court had heard from every available witness, and the public had followed the testimony as well. If Rosa had been the driving force behind the inquiry based on some ill-advised conclusions, her own scathing remarks would no more enlighten the public than an angry man venting his rage on the street who "stands for nothing

when a grand jury of his fellows has indicted the man he is talking about."
Davis hoped that Birney would spare his client and said that the only reason for bringing the letters into the courtroom was to gratify "a prurient
curiosity or something worse."

"Now at last we stand forth in our true light, and the thorn in counsel's side appears—the re-reading of these letters. Now I say that the public is entitled to know," Leonard responded, admitting that he did have a
prurient curiosity about the case. The court closed briefly and ruled that
the entire record of Saturday, August 7, including Rosa's testimony and the
letters, be read in open session. But perhaps to Leonard's surprise, Rosa was
fully prepared to explain everything she had said to Swartz and "perfectly
willing" to have her examination conducted publicly. And so, for much of
the next hour, she could watch as two men—first a stenographer, then Major Leonard—read her heated prose out loud. Her daughter, Rose, got up
from the inquiry table in the middle of Leonard's performance and left the
room.

Finally, the attorney for the accused lieutenants had his chance to go
after "the accuser" in front of the "largest audience so far"—most of whom
were women. Birney began with questions about Rosa's correspondence
with several people before she came East for the first time on September 7,
1908. She had written surgeon Frank Cook, who declined to discuss the
case with her. But she had not tried to contact the lieutenants her daughter had interviewed. Barely hiding the disdain in his voice, Arthur Birney
established that the only sworn statement Rosa had to support her cause was
William Owens' account of what happened as he drove Jimmie and his fellow marines back to the student officers' camp. The temperature hit ninety-
seven degrees; Rosa was dressed in black silk from head to toe and used her
fan continually. Birney moved on. "In one of your letters you speak of your
son's forehead being crushed. To quote your exact language, you say: 'That
shot was only fired to hide their crime. His forehead was crushed, nose broken, lip cut open, teeth knocked out, big lump under his jaw from a blow
or a kick, and an incision in the back of his head one and one-half inches
long.' Had you read the testimony of Dr. Pickrell, Surgeon U.S. Navy, at
the time you made the statement?"

"I don't think he said very much. I read what he said," Rosa said
tersely, wary of falling into a trap.

"Have you read the testimony of Dr. Cook?" asked the attorney, who,
curiously enough, had questioned Cook that morning about the injuries
Rosa described to Swartz even before Major Leonard introduced her letters
into evidence.

"I read everything in that testimony," said Rosa, no doubt thinking about the inquest.

"Will you tell me where you received any information that your son's forehead was crushed?"

"Why, it says so in that testimony."

"In the testimony?"

Rosa explained, as she had to Major Leonard, that a hospital steward said Jimmie "'had a hole in his forehead.'" She tried as best she could to recall the wording of the 1907 inquest.

"Will you indicate where in this testimony before the court of inquest any such thing as that appears?" Birney asked.

"Well, it is the evidence of one of the witnesses." At this point, Henry Davis came to her defense. "Lieutenant Bevan said it." He read from the 1907 testimony: "'The flash appeared just in front of [Sutton's] head. I supposed he had shot himself in the forehead and the hospital steward stated when he came that he felt the wound in the front part of the head.'"

The more questions Rosa answered, the more evident it became that many of her accusations did indeed have a source other than Jimmie's ghost. Her son's apparition had, it seemed, provided leads about his death that Rosa was able to corroborate from what she read in the 1907 testimony, from letters she received, and, she would later disclose, from her daughter's sleuthing in Annapolis.

Arthur Birney now cited surgeon Frank Cook's statement that the cause of Sutton's death had been the bullet in his brain, and again he pressed Rosa on why she thought her son's skull had been fractured. She gave Birney a fixed gaze. "Mr. Birney, I want to tell you this: I am under oath to tell you what I think to be the truth. I thought those officers were under oath, and I thought every word they uttered was the truth, and from their own testimony I inferred what I did, and they made the statement there that there was a hole in my son's forehead. That is the reason and the only reason I thought his forehead must have been broken."

But Rosa admitted she could not remember who told her Jimmie's teeth had been knocked out. And after reading that Adams had beaten her son in the back of the head, she had mistakenly assumed the one and a half inch incision was there. Birney switched to another topic—one he assumed would leave no doubt in anyone's mind about how unstable Rosa Sutton really was.

"Did you consult a medium?" he demanded.

"I did not."

"You obtained no information from that source?"

"I certainly did not," Rosa said firmly. This was insulting.

"You have said in one of these letters that you had a supernatural appearance from your son?"

"Yes."

Again Birney asked if she had used a medium. He knew that people constantly claimed to hear from dead relatives with the help of mediums—the practice was widespread—and one the court would deem ludicrous. Probably unaware of the Catholic ban on such practices, Birney assumed Rosa had done the same.

"No, sir," Rosa replied. "I told you I did not consult a medium. It was not necessary."

"It was only at your home, then?"

"It was in my own home, in broad daylight."

"His appearance?" To Birney this whole supposition was absurd.

But Rosa was positive about what she had seen. "Yes," she said.

Thwarted from demonstrating that Mrs. Sutton had willingly ventured into the world of the occult, Birney tried another line of questioning. He would prove she did not deserve the sympathy so many reporters and others had given her.

"Now, Mrs. Sutton," said the attorney, "you gave out a great many interviews to the newspapers, did you not?"

"I did not."

"Didn't you?"

"I did not."

"You repeatedly had interviews with reporters or correspondents?"

"I did not," Rosa replied for the third time.

"Not even recently?"

"Recently—what did you mean?"

"Within the last month."

"The only interview I have given out to a newspaper myself was one concerning the offering of evidence or testimony, something like that, to former Secretary Newberry, and he did not pay attention to it. I gave out that interview."

Now Birney thought he could catch Rosa by surprise. "In the newspaper which I have before me, being the Baltimore News of Sunday, July 18, appears this statement attributed to you." Birney read out loud: "'As soon as the first board called it a suicide I began my work to disprove that theory. The family had little hope of my success. Day after day, in black and white, I collected, bit by bit, the evidence I desired. Link by link I forged the chain. It surprised even me, endowed with my mother zeal. Last September I announced my determination to come East.' Did you make that statement?" the attorney asked.

"No, I did not make that statement," Rosa said.

"Were you confronted with the reporter?"

"I may have said that I intended to follow this up, spoke in a general way, and somebody might have heard it; but 'link by link' and all that thing, I never said." Rosa began to realize what Birney was up to. Although reporters often embellished their interviews, the sensational press had become her greatest ally simply by telling the story of Jimmie Sutton's fate with gusto. Rosa was convinced that when Americans learned the details of what happened, they would believe her—even if she had not revealed her own thoughts about it to the press. Newspapers, she told the court, knew enough about it anyway.

But Arthur Birney had something else in mind; he hoped to demonstrate that Rosa was a cold, calculating woman who had ruthlessly pursued his clients from the moment her son died. She was motivated not by overwhelming grief but rather by revenge, a quality unbecoming to a woman. He pointed out to Rosa that the Baltimore paper had placed her remarks as a direct quotation. Still, she gave no ground. So Birney went back to the letters and asked Rosa why she told Swartz that Lieutenants Adams, Utley, and Edward Osterman had conspired to beat up her son. Rosa had several reasons, not all of which would come out that morning. William Owens had sworn that Lieutenant Adams tried to start a fight with Sutton on the way back to the student officers' camp in his machine. Rosa believed Owens and concluded that the fight at the end of the car ride had been agreed on in advance, as no officer "would be goose enough to ask another man to fight when that would mean a court martial if he didn't know that the other officers were going to agree that night." Jimmie had also written a letter home saying some of the marines were out to get him, and Rosa would claim his ghost had told her "my hands are as free from blood as when I was five years old." Although she was wrong about the three men plotting this initial fight with Adams, because Osterman and Utley may well have tried to prevent it, it was only moments later that Adams and Sutton ended up in the fatal brawl.

Throughout Birney's examination of her, Rosa impressed reporters and the men and women in the audience with her confidence. Her daughter had returned a few minutes after she began testifying and watched from a nearby bench in the courtroom, probably smiling to herself. Rose had needlessly worried that her anxious, high-strung mother might snap under the pressure of an inquisition, but she conducted herself well even when Birney began to ask more piercing questions about Jimmie's character.

"In one of those letters you say your son was a brave man and no man would dare to call him a coward without being called to account for it," the attorney stated.

"I don't think there was ever any braver man ever lived than my son," Rosa shot back.

"What did you mean by saying [to Swartz] that no man would dare to call him a coward?"

"I mean to say that he would prove he was not a coward or make him take it back. I don't think you would let any man call you a dirty coward without you resenting it."

So Birney asked Rosa if Jimmie would have forced a man who had insulted him to apologize or else whip him.

Now Rosa was on tenuous ground. She had grown up under the strict tenets of her convent school; her first instinct was that her son should have obeyed the navy's written rules. It was unlikely she knew of the unwritten code of behavior among the men in the service academies—you never reported on one of your comrades. "I don't know," she replied. "He might have reported it. I think that is against the rules and regulations, to force a man to fight by calling him a coward."

"You say 'the man does not live that would have called Jimmie a coward to his face and not have to prove it'?"

"Yes."

"What did you mean by that?"

Rosa replied that her son would have told anyone who called him a coward to apologize and might have reported the insult (rather than fight). Birney had just what he wanted. "And you think your son, whom you designate as an honorable young man, would have reported to his commanding officer if any other officer had called him a coward?"

"I think it is more honorable than fighting." Rosa said, viewing the issue from a mother's perspective. But a man like Arthur Birney would never have advised one of his own sons to appeal to a higher authority when challenged to fight.

"I am asking you what you think your son would have done."

"I cannot tell you what my son would have done; I can only say what I think," Rosa replied. Rosa was determined to appear calm but she was losing patience. Jimmie was no saint, and in fact she had admitted to Harry Swartz that her son could be as wild and cocky as his compatriots. But he had written her that he was getting control of his temper and had stopped fighting. So when Birney asked directly whether Jimmie would have taken an insult, Rosa said no, though he might have tried to avoid a common fist fight.

Now Birney got right to the point; he could make both Rosa and her dead son unsympathetic characters. "Don't you know that he did take part in a number of fist fights?" he asked.

"Before he was a man," admitted Rosa.

"While he was in the service here?"

"He had to do it in the [Naval] Academy, but not in the Marine Corps. I never heard of his doing such a thing in the Marine Corps," Rosa said, striking her fan on the table.

The Marine Corps officers listened carefully as Rosa fielded questions from their attorney, but they avoided meeting her eyes. Somewhat satisfied, Birney now asked Rosa to explain why she thought her son was already unconscious when the final shot was fired. She again referred to the testimony from the inquest, which described him as senseless. Birney contradicted her, "I think you will not find that in the testimony."

Rosa protested and again Henry Davis came to her defense, "Mr. Adams says it himself."

"Does he?" Birney responded. He did not ask for further proof but continued to grill Rosa on the accusations in her letters.

"Then you mean to confine your judgement of this unfortunate event and your judgement that these three men, Lieutenant Utley, Lieutenant Adams, and Lieutenant Osterman, beat your son to death upon the testimony which was taken at the Court of Inquest alone?" When she first wrote Swartz, Rosa had been mistaken about Osterman's role; he had not been present during the second fight that led to her son's death. She had taken the inquest testimony literally because the men were supposed to tell the "sacred truth." And, forgetting again that the men had not been sworn in, she said she could not believe anybody would "lie on their oath." But this second investigation had once more exposed elaborate contradictions in the accused marines' stories and disturbing lapses of memory. With the evidence that she had, was there any chance for justice—or redemption for her son—in this forum?

The defendants, who had grinned openly at each other when Rosa's letters to Swartz were read out loud, began to look somber. Their attorney glanced at them as he continued, glossing over the inconsistencies in their testimony with his next question. "Although these gentlemen absolutely acquit themselves by their testimony and the testimony of their fellows of any such part in it [a murder], you put another interpretation upon it?"

Davis jumped in again. "I object to the question as making an assumption which is not based on the testimony."

Birney backed down. On further questioning, Rosa finally admitted that the marines might not have had a premeditated plan to kill Jimmie "when they started out that night." "But he was killed, unfortunately for everybody, and as he was lying apparently unconscious I didn't see how he could do it himself." Retreating from the accusations in her letters to Swartz, she said the beating was not a long planned conspiracy; it was more of an "understood thing." Perhaps she remembered William Owens' words: "I think, among them, when they got a chance to give Sutton a good licking . . . they were going to do it." Certainly it had been obvious that Robert Adams wanted a chance to fight with Jimmie.

For several more moments, Arthur Birney went through the letters, correcting Rosa's mistakes and challenging her other claims. Some had been purely intuitive and gave him a good example of the type of flimsy evidence she had of his clients' guilt. Less than a week before Jimmie died, a photograph was taken of the officers and student officers at the Marine Corps Application School; Jimmie stood a bit apart from the others, not "shoulder to shoulder like soldiers," and Rosa had been taken aback. But now her impulsive comment proved embarrassing, and she hedged a little. Jimmie's stance in the photograph and the men's expressions were obviously not reasonable evidence that any of them had committed a crime.

Speaking as much to the world at large as to Rosa, Birney again brought up the postmortem appearances of Lieutenant Sutton. "Mrs. Sutton, in your letter referring to the appearance of the spirit of your son to you, you say that he told you that they laid a trap for him and he walked right into it." Rosa had told Swartz that she could prove what her son's apparition had told her. No doubt convinced that the court would share his skepticism, Arthur Birney wanted to know just how she planned to do that. Rosa mentioned the letters she received and the smashed watch she had discovered in Jimmie's effects that read 1:15 in the morning and began to tick when she saw it. She had found Jimmie's jacket without its shoulder knot, and she noticed that his clothes did not show many signs of a struggle on his part. "I think a man would fight very hard if he was afraid to the death, if he had a chance, and I didn't think he would have had much of any clothing on," Rosa said.

By now Arthur Birney was convinced the "accuser" had done enough damage to her own case. When questioned by the judge advocate and by Birney, Rosa could not directly tie his clients to a crime; in any court there would have been reasonable doubt as to their guilt. So much of her evidence was circumstantial or based on intuition. She could never prove that his clients were guilty of murder simply by accusing them of garbled testimony. By focusing on her letters to Swartz, Birney found it easy to damn Rosa with her own words. From his perspective, the case was all sewn up, unless, of course, he had underestimated Rosa's attorney, who still had a couple of witnesses in the wings. Davis, he might well assume, would base his closing arguments on more than the appearances of a ghost.

At twenty-five minutes after twelve, the president called for a recess, leaving those who had been in the auditorium to mull over Rosa's answers during their midday meal. The Washington *Evening Star* went right to press that afternoon; hours later, the paper described Rosa's demeanor for those who had not been in the courtroom. She was a different person on the witness stand than the woman who fifteen months earlier had sent "unmeasured expressions of grief" to a payroll clerk. Rosa's knowledge of the case could match that of the attorneys themselves. The "usually quiet woman was brilliant" on the stand, decided the reporter; she refused to let Arthur Birney embarrass her, and she disappointed the large number of people in the courtroom who had come to support the Marine Corps officers. For the first time there was a great deal of empathy for Rosa in the auditorium (where women outnumbered men three to one). Ninety-nine out of a hundred mothers would have drawn the same conclusions as she had, opined the *Star*, even though she had little hard proof of her statements to give the court.

When court reconvened at two o'clock, Henry Davis gave Rosa an opportunity to explain her relationship with Harry Swartz. She said that from the time she first contacted him in March 1908 he had responded in a "nice and friendly way," and offered to help her. Rosa had not known Swartz before Jimmie died, but he had assured her in a letter that she could write to him in confidence. In fact, Rosa said, just before she left the District for the inquiry in Annapolis, Harry Swartz "took my hand and wished me all success in finding out about his [Jimmie's] death." But she had never given him permission to part with her letters, she declared, with bitterness in her voice. Moreover, she would not have been in touch with Swartz at all if anyone had proven to her that Jimmie had committed suicide. How could she let her son spend eternity in hell if there was any doubt of his guilt? From Rosa's perspective, Jimmie was just as much a defendant in this case as the marines.

Although Rosa had written to the secretary of the navy, Harry Leonard now asked why she had not contacted men who were more senior in the Marine Corps than Swartz. Once again she had jumped to conclusions. She had been confused about exactly what Swartz's position was—he had told her he was a personal friend of Lieutenant Maurice Shearer, so she thought he was a lieutenant too and would know the rest of the officers. She assumed Swartz would have a better chance of getting the truth from men such as Edward Osterman than she did. "I was only after the truth," she told the court. So Leonard asked if she had ever heard from the major general commandant. She had not—in fact she had heard indirectly that he said her son was "'undoubtedly insane.'" And why had she never contacted Charles Lauchheimer, the official custodian of the Corps' records? Rosa's response had its own irony. "You know," she said, "I know nothing about the Marine Corps."

Commander Hood had been thoroughly irritated by a recent article in the *New York American*. And now, just before the four o'clock bells, he asked Rosa if she had quoted a member of his court to the reporter as saying, "'I am heartily tired of this affair. Sutton committed suicide, and there is no use in going on with this thing.'" Rosa had heard somebody make the remark and repeated it to Henry Davis, but she had absolutely not given an interview about it. John Hood saw to it that the record stated that no member of his court had ever spoken these words.

On Tuesday, August 10, Rosa's ordeal in the witness chair was shorter but more difficult to bear. She would not testify again, but Henry Davis asked her to identify for the court Jimmie's letter to Don and his last one to his mother.

Davis was sure these letters would elicit sympathy for Jimmie as a loving brother with great integrity and as a devoted son with a bright future ahead—a different image of the lieutenant than Arthur Birney had created. Over Birney's strong objection, Major Leonard agreed that the letters could shed light on Sutton's true character; besides, Leonard said, all evidence needed to be considered, even if it was only "infinitesimal" in importance.

Leonard read both letters aloud, and when she heard Jimmie's closing words to her, "Hoping this finds you well and happy," Rosa "wept quietly but without concealment." Her daughter, Rose, who had been fighting back tears herself, "patted her on the back." Even the officers "showed deep feeling" when they heard Jimmie's advice to his younger brother: "Walk across hell on a rotten rail to keep your word of honor." A reporter from the *Evening Capital* noticed Lieutenant Adams "wipe his eye furtively." The impact of Jimmie's letters was evident in the silence in the courtroom when Leonard finished. For several moments hardly anyone moved. As soon as the letters were typed into the record, the originals were returned to Rosa.

Within hours, her son's words would appear in major metropolitan dailies across the United States.

Rosa did well in the eyes of reporters. While Leonard and Birney went after her, she proved to be a "perfectly collected, sharp woman," and bore herself well. She "gave as good as she took" and caused the accused officers sitting behind her "to pull long faces." The *Washington Post* reported that she "never showed the slightest sign of embarrassment, proving herself able to cope with every situation. She was never at a loss for a reply . . . and adhered steadfastly to her interpretation of circumstances as pointing to crime." A straightforward article in the *New York Times* filled with passages from her letters revealed Rosa's views about the ghost of her son. But when many papers published long excerpts, they lured their readers with sensational headlines: "SPIRIT OF SON CAME TO MOTHER" (*San Francisco Chronicle*), "MOTHER INVOKES SUTTON'S GHOST" (*Chicago Daily Tribune*), "SPIRIT OF SON TOLD MOTHER OF TRAGEDY" (*Atlanta Constitution*), "WROTE DEAD SON APPEARED TO HER" (*Boston Globe*), and "VOICE FROM GRAVE IN SUTTON INQUIRY" (*Newburgh Daily News*), this last one in a paper that Jimmie's brother, Don, would have seen at West Point.

When she returned to her own seat at 11:15 a.m., Rosa had little time to collect her thoughts—the next witness was her daughter, the "comely sister of the dead Sutton, to whose piercingly brilliant black eyes hypnotic influences are attributed." Rose Parker came to the witness chair smiling, in a formal grey jacket and long skirt, and, as usual, her wide-rimmed black sailor hat. She had taken notes throughout the proceeding and was eager to testify; but she spoke in a barely audible voice, to the frustration of Commander Hood, and the white-frocked women spectators who had to "crane their necks" and strain their "shapely ears" to try to hear her. And this time, while many spectators moved forward, Lieutenants Adams and Utley collected pads of paper and pencils so they could take their own notes.

The navy had little use for Rose, but Henry Davis wanted her impressions on the record, especially those from her private interview with Robert Adams. Perhaps to create more sympathy for her, he asked Rose a few personal questions about her life and her relationship with her brother. It would be up to Rose to give the only direct testimony about her family's Catholic faith.

"Before reaching Annapolis did you or not take any steps with reference to your brother's burial?" Davis inquired.

"Yes, I wired to New York to a friend of mine to come and try and arrange to get a grave for him in Arlington, as I supposed I would have some trouble on account of his being accused of suicide," Rose responded.

"You telegraphed to someone to assist you in getting a grave at Arlington, for the reason you assign?"

"Yes. I did not know whether they would allow a suicide to be buried there or not."

"Was there any reason for his not to be taken to Portland and buried there?"

"Because he was a Catholic, and he could not be buried in consecrated ground, and could not be buried by the Catholic Church if a suicide; and I would not take him home to bury him because I did not want the family to have to suffer the indignity of having him refused to be buried in the family plot." Rose spoke forthrightly, always composed, although tears were streaming down her mother's cheeks, and Rosa lowered her head at the mention of Jimmie's disgraced position in the eyes of their church.

"Mrs. Parker, the creed and belief of the Catholic Church, of which you and your mother are members, as I understand you, is what as to the fate of a suicide?"

"Well, that he cannot be saved, of course."

"In a word—"

"That he goes to Hell."

Rose explained that as a suicide her brother could not have had a priest officiate at his funeral. In fact, she said, he was buried without religious ceremony in Arlington. Davis, who could rightly assume that many if not most of those in hearing distance were Protestant, wanted to be sure the dire impact of a suicide verdict was clear.

"In other words, he was committed to the earth in unconsecrated ground because of this stigma of suicide?"

"Exactly."

Rose also described to the court what she had found among her brother's effects, at which point Henry Davis produced a suitcase with the clothes Jimmie had worn the night he died. As he placed them on the table, Rose recognized Jimmie's Mexican leather holster and cartridge belt as well as a steel pistol that had looked rustier in 1907. When her attorney asked her to identify Jimmie's blue dress trousers, Rose must have winced. "Sutton's Hereafter Is Anxiety of Family" made the headlines, but the public was most curious about Rose's own detective work, above all her session with Robert Adams. Aided by carefully chosen questions from Henry Davis, Rose described her meeting with the officers in considerable detail. Four of them watched from a bench directly behind her; both Robert Adams and Harold Utley seemed to take Rose much more seriously now than they had soon after her brother died.

Rose spoke quickly and enthusiastically. Accustomed to deferring to her imperious mother, she had been waiting for almost two years to make her own statement about what the men said. She confirmed Lieutenant Utley's hostility toward Jimmie and described the reasons that she had asked to see Adams alone. Davis had gotten little information from Adams about the meeting, and he used his questions to place what Rose had written down in her notes about the conversation in the record. Rose recalled that Adams said he took "my brother by the throat in his left hand and beat him in the back of the head with his right." In a soft voice she added that "somebody had come along and kicked him in the ribs."

"Kicked whom?" said Davis, wanting to be sure the court understood how enraged Adams had been seconds before Jimmie had been shot.

"Kicked Mr. Adams," Rose recalled, still describing the fatal brawl; it was William Bevan—the officer of the guard that night—who had needed to kick Adams to get him off her brother. Lieutenant Bevan had told Rose that Robert Adams was so infuriated that he wanted to go back and beat up Jimmie some more, but he (Bevan) would not let him. Adams listened carefully, his face flushing when Rose's account made him angry.

John Hood's partial deafness made it hard for him to hear Rose's words, and he asked her please to speak more loudly. She went on recounting what Robert Adams had told her about his fight with her brother in graphic details that she now repeated to the court.

"And did he say to you in this interview that he, Adams, was then so infuriated—" Davis started to ask.

Rose did not let him finish but broke right in. She said she asked Adams "how in the world he could hit a man when he was down, with two men holding him down for him to hit, and he said he was so infuriated he did not realize what he did, and that he would have hit him more, but that the other officer made him get off." Rosa listened carefully as her daughter spoke, her own fury at Lieutenant Adams likely increasing each time she was forced to relive Jimmie's last moments alive.

"Did he, in this interview, tell you that at the time, while he was [kneeling] on your brother's right shoulder, he heard a report?"

"No," said Rose. "He said he was standing at my brother's right shoulder, he heard a report and a flash, and that they said that my brother had killed himself."

"That who said it?" This was a key point.

"He did not say who said it."

"Did he say 'they' said it?" Davis needed Rose to be very precise on this point.

"No, I think he said some one, one of the two men on his back said that he had killed himself—'Sutton has killed himself.'"

"Did he in this interview say that he saw your brother fire the weapon?" Davis asked, aware that Adams had never admitted seeing the gun fired.

Again Rose went beyond the question in her answer. "He did not. I asked him if he would swear that my brother had committed suicide, and he said well, he did not and he would not, because he did not actually see him do it, but he was reasonably convinced that he did do it."

"Mrs. Parker, did you say this to Mr. Adams in that interview: 'Well, Mr. Adams, when you realized that he was dead, weren't you sorry that you had beaten him so brutally?' And didn't he reply, 'Well, no, Mrs. Parker, because I knew that night that if your brother lived my life would not be worth anything.'"

"Mr. Adams said exactly that," Rose replied.

"Did you then say to him," said Davis, referring again to Rose's notes, "'Mr. Adams, do you realize what you are saying? If you would say that before any jury in the country, they would not hold you guiltless, or you would not get off?' And did he answer, 'Yes; but I am not saying it to a jury, and it is true. I know that if your brother had lived he would have gotten me'?"

"He did say exactly that," Rose replied. To Davis this admission sounded like a motive for murder—or at least a way to establish reasonable doubt about Sutton's suicide. Significantly, Lieutenant Adams had not denied saying these things to Rose; he had testified simply that he had no memory of this part of their conversation. But he agreed he had told Rose that Harold Utley had hated her brother for years.

Rose next described the dinner that she, Dr. J. J. Murphy, and Professor B. Vernon Cecil had with Robert Adams later that evening. Once the lieutenant returned to camp, she had told the two men what transpired in her earlier discussion with Adams. Rose explained that in a futile effort to appeal to Lieutenant Adams' sympathy, she said her brother was a Catholic and that Catholics believed anyone who committed suicide was lost. In fact, she said, her mother, who was sitting just a few feet away while Rose testified, "would never be satisfied if 'suicide' was left to stand."

Henry Davis finished with Rose just in time for the noon recess. Afterward, she would be turned over to Arthur Birney who had little to add when the parties reconvened. He cross-examined Rose for fewer than thirty minutes, primarily about her conversations with the accused lieutenants, becoming exasperated when she answered with far more detail than he expected. At one point, Birney asked Rose if one of the men who came to her quarters, Lieutenant John Potts, had not told her that he thought Jimmie was a coward. Rose admitted that was the case.

So Birney said, "And from that time on you have not fancied Lieutenant Potts." It was not a question.

"No," Rose shot back. "I do like Lieutenant Potts. I have seen Lieutenant Potts when he was not under the influence of liquor and I think he is a very charming young fellow."

She spoke even more readily about Edward Osterman, who had not disliked her brother, "and did not want to fight him and [said] that this fight was thrust upon him, and that he was very sorry that he had ever had any part in it." Trying to poke holes in her detective work, Arthur Birney asked her why she had not sought out either Dr. Cook or Dr. George Pickrell. And Rose revealed that she had not seen a transcript of the inquest until just before she left the East. She had questioned the men who came to see her in Carvel Hall without any detailed knowledge of the first investigation (other than what she may have read in the papers).

Birney turned to Rose's dinner with Lieutenant Adams; he wanted to the court to know they ended the meal on good terms. After all, how could Rose, who paid the check, have been so sociable to a man whom she thought was guilty of murder?

Rose became cautious; she insisted she had borne no ill feelings toward Adams, but she thought he knew a great deal about her brother's death and could help her prove that her brother was not a suicide.

"And that is what you meant when you said a moment ago that he knew how you felt towards him?" asked Birney.

"Exactly."

"That was the extent of your showing him any feeling?"

By this point in her testimony, Rose's animosity toward Arthur Birney began to show. "I had no reason to be ugly," she insisted; in fact, she had been "very pleasant" to Adams. Putting Adams on the defensive would not have worked in her favor as she tried to solicit a self-incriminating confession from the young officer. She knew Robert Adams would never admit to murder, but in 1907 she had thought he might at least back off his accusation of suicide. That was clearly no longer a possibility. Adams had gone to great lengths in his recent testimony and his re-enactments to establish Jimmie's guilt, and Rose Parker no longer had any reason to be so courteous to Robert Adams.

Birney had completed his questions, and Henry Davis had only one more concern. He made sure that Rose told the court that she had given her mother a full report on her trip East. Rose's opinions had obviously had an impact on Rosa's view of the case—and when she corrected her own testimony the following day, Rosa also made that clear.

Reporters noticed that Rose had been a thoroughly self-possessed witness and that she was disappointed that Major Leonard did not call on her once. The following evening, her friends in Oregon could gossip about a prominent photograph of Rose next to one of the officers who might have engineered her brother's death, Harold Utley. The caption in the *Oregon Daily Journal* read "BUREAUCRAT VERSUS PLAIN CITIZEN," and the paper proclaimed "PREJUDICE IN RULINGS BY BOARDS." Correspondent John Lathrop cited an unnamed U.S. senator who called for a "thorough shaking up of court proceedings in the military branch of the government. . . . I know from personal friends . . . that judicial proceedings in the Army and Navy are often farcical." The Sutton hearing, said the senator, showed that there was "an official clique" against the "private and civilian witnesses." Whether or not Lathrop's interview was accurate, he was one of many reporters keeping up with congressional interest in the case—fully recognizing that both Leonard and the Sutton court felt pressure to answer to the branch of the government that funded all the navy's operations.

After Rose testified, the opposing attorneys made brief statements to the newspapers, an "unusual proceeding" for attorneys, observed the *Los Angeles Times*. Henry Davis took a jab at those committed in advance to supporting the findings of the original inquest. Arthur Birney declared that Rosa had no evidence to sustain her charges—they originated in a preternatural vision. Throughout the summer of 1909, Jimmie Sutton's ghost would fortify his mother's convictions while providing the Navy Department with ammunition against her. Few papers went after Rosa's credibility on this point. But Birney would have been pleased to know that an *Oregonian* editor had just drafted a reprimand to the Sutton women for their "Messages from Eternity." "If justice is to be administered on the vision of a dream, it will be the most wonderful thing in the civilized world since dreams and witchcraft were banished. . . . Evidence that eternity sent back any intelligible message other than the ordinary psychical phenomena, is wholly lacking," the editor wrote, "and none has ever been believed by rational minds." Admitting that those involved in the death scene deserved some punishment, the editor gave Rosa's Portland relatives and friends something else to consider:

> The dead tell no tales, and if anybody thinks that Sutton, after his body was in decay, could speak in his old voice or move in his old shape that

Lieutenant Harold Utley and Rose Sutton Parker, "BUREAUCRAT VERSUS PLAIN CITIZEN," Oregon Daily Journal, *August 11, 1909.*

person belongs to the dark ages. If Sutton had been planted under a rose bush he could have appeared again in leaves and flowers, but not as Sutton. . . . Dreams are true only while they last, but the Sutton women are not now dreaming or not supposed to be. Besides, we have only their words for what they allege they saw and heard. The safest persons to believe are those who don't dream.

12

EVERY SCRAP OF EVIDENCE

A s far as the spectators were concerned, anyone who testified after the Sutton women would have a hard act to follow. But when the judge advocate summoned him in the middle of the afternoon on Tuesday, August 10, Henry Lewis Hulbert did not seem worried. He had been a gunnery sergeant in the Marine Corps and acting sergeant major at the barracks on the night of the Sutton tragedy. A veteran soldier with gray hair and a "mustache twisted to a stiletto point in the German style," Hulbert spoke in a businesslike manner. He kept the office records and entered the auditorium with a roster book; Henry Davis hoped that he could prove Charles Kennedy had been on duty when the fatal brawl occurred.

Hulbert said he was sure that Kennedy had been on hospital patrol on October 13, 1907. He even volunteered that "a better class of man [was] picked out as a rule" for the hospital patrol—men authorized to carry a revolver rather than a rifle. Every four hours a change of tours took place, Hulbert recalled, and one began at one o'clock in the morning. But he could not verify that Charles Kennedy had been on that particular tour. The book kept by the sergeant of the guard detailing the precise assignments for the evening in question had disappeared. (It would turn up after the inquiry and corroborate Kennedy's testimony; another guard had been sitting on the book without realizing what it was.) Nevertheless, Hulbert provided the court with some other useful information.

He said that Kennedy had been in Company A, Captain Arthur Marix's company, along with Harold Utley. Soon after Jimmie Sutton's death, the company qualified six men to take an examination for corporal. Five of them passed the exam in the first week of November 1907; only Kennedy failed. According to Hulbert, the examining board was made up of Major Benjamin Fuller and Lieutenants William Bevan and Howard Judson. Captain Marix had recommended Kennedy for the exam. And as far as he was concerned, Hulbert said that he would rate Kennedy a very good man.

But Kennedy's testimony had attracted both interest and empathy from reporters, and judge advocate Harry Leonard had some additional questions for the sergeant major. Kennedy was at times a "straggler" who occasionally broke liberty, said Hulbert; another sergeant major, Charles Eichman, had accompanied Kennedy to Annapolis "because it was thought Kennedy might possibly not arrive here." Leonard wanted to know what the men in the garrison thought about Kennedy's reliability. Naturally, Davis objected. What, he asked, does this man's reputation as to breaking liberty have to do with "whether he tells the truth or not?" The court allowed Leonard's question, and Hulbert would only say that Kennedy had a reputation for "average reliability." Leonard kept at him: what did he mean by "an average reliable marine?"

Davis could barely contain himself. "I hope the answer will not be as it was once given on the witness stand, 'A leetle below par.'"

"Well, sir, I would say that I would consider him a little below par," was Hulbert's reply.

"I thought so," said Leonard, with obvious satisfaction. The *Baltimore Sun* was one of several papers to find this whole line of questioning "somewhat astonishing."

Henry Davis then asked Hulbert directly if he would believe Charles Kennedy on his oath, and the witness gave an affirmative answer. But then Arthur Birney asked him if he thought Kennedy was "good material for corporal." Hulbert became uncomfortable and said he did not; spurred on by this answer, Birney inquired about Kennedy's mental condition.

"I heard one time that Kennedy and Hanner, who was sent to Cuba at the same time, were both more or less crazy," Hulbert observed.

"From what I have heard here, it seems to be a marine affliction," said Rosa's thoroughly annoyed attorney. But the witness then added that most people did not think Kennedy was crazy, just some men said he was "'bugs' more or less." Hulbert was excused just after laughter at this exchange broke out in the courtroom.

Rosa's attorney would tie up several loose ends during the last three days of testimony, saving his best witness for a grand finale. But he first wanted more information about the guns that Sutton had used before he died. Prior questions had focused on the service revolver, the assumption being that Sutton had used it to shoot himself. Several erroneous references had been made in the press describing Sutton's Smith & Wesson, the "little gun," as a

.32 caliber weapon. Colonel Charles Doyen was recalled to the stand, but he was not much help. He did not remember whether Lieutenant Utley or Lieutenant Edward Willing brought the revolvers to him—nor had he ever seen the bullet taken "from the body of Lieutenant Sutton." The revolvers had never been in his personal custody, and it was not at all clear, Davis pointed out, where they had been between the time Sutton died and the beginning of the investigation the next morning. Doyen had only a "dim recollection" that Lieutenant Willing, the recorder at the inquest, had taken them up to the board room. After the inquest, Doyen said he gave the service revolver to the post quartermaster; the Smith & Wesson was placed with Sutton's possessions—at least he thought so. "I saw it there afterwards. I think it was turned over to Mrs. Parker." No one, it seemed, knew exactly when the smaller gun had been returned to Sutton's effects. Doyen gave a muddled description of what probably happened to the bullet taken out of Sutton's head and to the other bullets in the revolvers. The board of inquest "sent down to the barracks to get the armorer to take the cartridges apart, those that were left in one of the revolvers, and he took the bullets out of some of the cartridges from that revolver. There were some bullets wrapped up in paper that probably had been separated from some of the cartridges." As far as he knew, the bullets had been sent back from the board to be locked up in the quartermaster's safe after the inquest. But Colonel Doyen was sure that, about five or six months after the tragedy, he told Lieutenant Maurice Shearer, the quartermaster, "that he could throw them away." Realizing that Doyen knew nothing of any significance on the topic, Major Leonard suggested re-examining Willing.

Lieutenant Willing first explained why the cartridges were opened. "The two revolvers were of different makes, and the [inquest board] took the cartridges apart in order that they may be absolutely certain which bullet killed Lieutenant Sutton, that is, whether it was from the Colt gun or the Smith and Wesson gun." They could tell by the "cannelures or transverse grooves in the body of the projectile. As I remember it, there were two [grooves] in the Smith and Wesson and three in the Colt." Willing's impression was that the cartridges in Sutton's service revolver might have been made of smokeless powder. After lengthy questioning by Henry Davis, Willing stated that Sutton's "private gun was different from the service revolver." "The external shape of the bullet was a good deal the same, but in the base of the bullet there was a good deal of difference as I remember it." The lieutenant was not positive, but he thought that the bullets from the two different guns were not the same length. How he happened to see the bullet that had been lodged in Sutton's brain is unclear, but he told Davis that it was a plain lead bullet with one side of the nose flattened. Apparently, all discussion about these bullets took place off the record at the 1907 inquest.

But by this time, Henry Davis was not convinced Sutton had died from a bullet that came from the service revolver; he observed that both guns had been .38 caliber and that the same bullets could be used interchangeably. So Arthur Birney asked his client whether or not "the bullet which killed Lieutenant Sutton agreed with the cartridges taken from the Colt service revolver." Lieutenant Willing—whose memory had failed him on so many other points—confirmed that it did.

In the last two days before closing arguments, as the audience anticipated the end of the inquiry, courtroom theatrics kept them intrigued. A climactic end to Tuesday's testimony came when Davis unexpectedly asked Robert Adams to demonstrate one more time the position Sutton had been in when the last shot was fired.

Commander John Hood jumped in and told Adams, "Lean over the table. Put your feet on the chair and lay your body on the table." Reporters watched closely, and one described the scene with particular relish: "With superb agility and a boyish impulsiveness Adams was up from his chair and had stretched his tall form across the table." Surrounded by the members of the court, he took off his white duck jacket when it interfered and stood "in decidedly undress uniform his sleeveless undershirt barely concealing the sinewy muscles of his deep torso." He "reached for the revolver lying at the lawyer's side," and with a "catlike suppleness the lieutenant turned his head . . . pulled his right arm from underneath him and with his right arm poised pointed the revolver at the back of his head and pulled the trigger." Then Adams illustrated how Sutton had supposedly turned his head before he pulled the trigger. When the performance ended, Davis went after more details about where he had been when the gun went off.

"You were standing where?"

"At his right rear."

"That is to say, on his right and below the waist toward the feet?"

"Yes, sir, about so, from his feet." For several moments Davis questioned Adams about Willing's position, and, finally, he said, "If Lieutenant Willing was standing between you and Sutton's head, I want to know how you saw him pull his arm out and pull the trigger?"

"I tell you, Sutton's head and Willing were in echelon, if you know what that is. His head was more to the left." But Adams agreed that Willing was forward of him and between him and Sutton's head. Adams was not sure of the distances between the two of them and changed his description from moment to moment. He insisted that he saw Sutton draw his hand out, turn his head, and fire the revolver.

After several minutes of this, Davis' exasperation began to show. "It strikes me as a very remarkable thing that you could see this pistol on that dark night, that you could see this man's arm drawn from under his body on that dark night, that you could see this maneuver and the shooting, and you cannot yet accurately locate the large body of Lieutenant Willing."

Adams protested. He had located Willing as nearly as he possibly could. He saw the shot fired "because he just happened to be standing there looking at him."

Again Davis went over the circumstances of the final shot. Everyone agreed it was very dark, so much so a match was needed to identify features, and Adams had stated that the "uppermost thought" in his mind was to disarm Sutton. But according to Adams' description of Sutton's final moments, no one was attempting to disarm him. In fact, Adams "did not see a soul on his body," but he saw Sutton shoot the revolver with his right hand.

For Davis, this was a crucial point. Just so there was no mistake, he asked one more time if the lieutenant was sure he saw Sutton shoot the gun at the same time that he saw Sutton turn his head.

"I saw him turn his head," said Adams, but then he wavered under intense pressure from Rosa's attorney who asked again if he had actually seen Sutton shoot himself.

"No, I don't think I ever said I knew the bullet entered his head. I think my exact words were that I saw him draw the pistol, turn his head, and saw the flash."

"And didn't you say you knew the pistol shot had entered his head?" Davis had his own ideas why Adams would not give a straight answer.

"I afterward heard that it did, when I was up in camp," came the response.

With this comment, Henry Davis said he would not waste any more time. At 12:43 p.m. the court adjourned early for the day.

On the morning of Wednesday, August 11, embalmer James Weidefeld and undertaker Raymond Taylor took the stand for about fifteen minutes each. Harry Leonard did most of the questioning as Weidefeld described the process he had used in embalming Sutton; he clearly did not have much idea about the condition of the dead man's body or what had happened to his brain. When Sutton was dressed for burial, Leonard wanted to know, how did they get his clothes on.

"Suppose an arm were broken and you had embalmed the body to which the arm belonged, when you raised that arm to put it into the sleeve would the embalming fluid make the arm so stiff that it would not be evident that it was broken?"

"I could not answer as to that," replied the young orderly.

"You don't know?"

"No, I could not say it would make it that stiff," the orderly replied.

Weidefeld's boss, undertaker Taylor, informed the court that he had taken good care of Sutton's remains until he put the body in a casket. But had he not "bothered with Sutton's arms" at all or paid much attention to the body—although he had dressed the body for burial.

"What is the effect of the embalming fluid on a body as to producing rigidity?" asked Leonard, hoping to address Mrs. Sutton's accusation that one of her son's arms might have been broken. But Taylor would only say that the fluid had made the corpse so rigid he had to split the jacket in the back to get it on.

These two Annapolis civilians were followed by a third, Sutton's friend, Naval Academy instructor Gilbert Coleman, who had been overseas for the summer and received a subpoena as soon as he returned to Annapolis. "A dark complexioned young man with black hair and eyes and a heavy marked face," Coleman spoke in a "clear somewhat jerky voice." He reviewed the time he had spent with Lieutenant Sutton and Mary Elizabeth Stewart on Saturday, October 12. Coleman reminded the court of his letter to Rosa on November 7, 1907, written when his memory was fresh. He had learned about Sutton's death when Miss Stewart telephoned him from Carvel Hall the next morning. He also verified that while the three of them were sitting in the large reception room by the fireplace in Carvel Hall, Lieutenant Sutton introduced Lieutenant Edward Osterman to him. Osterman remained there, as far as he could recall, for a few moments. Coleman emphasized that Sutton's condition that night was "one of perfect sobriety," as far as he could tell. Moreover, Sutton was obviously in a happy frame of mind and said some nice things about his mother. In fact, he said, he and Mary Stewart had made plans to dine with Jimmie on Sunday. Coleman's letter to Rosa was put in evidence; he read it out loud to the court before being excused. The next witness would be far less friendly to the Sutton cause.

Twenty-seven year-old Allen Sumner had not expected to testify. Educated at Pomfret and Harvard University, he had come from one of the most privileged backgrounds of all the officers in the Application School in 1907. When he applied to take the Marine Corps exam in 1906, he was the confidential secretary to William Dana Orcutt, vice president and general manager of the University Press. Orcutt lauded Sumner's "many sterling qualities," and added that "his loyalty and discretion, together with his engaging personality have been a value and pleasure to me." The dean of Harvard College, noting that he did satisfactory academic work, described Sumner as "a gentleman through and through."

Sumner was not involved in the brawl with Sutton, but Rosa Sutton had found a printed card with the name of an audit company in Jimmie's effects. On the back was inscribed "Sutton, I am a damn fool. Consider gun business cut out. Allen M. Sumner." She was convinced that Sumner hated Jimmie (possibly he told her so), and she said so to Harry Swartz in one of her letters. Major Leonard, in an effort to leave no stone unturned, had summoned the lieutenant to testify and told the witness to read what he wrote on the card out loud and explain it. He was clearly in a tight spot. Sumner felt Sutton was a "very disagreeable personality and a man to be avoided." He had some trouble with Sutton before they both entered the School of Application, and he claimed that Sutton "was in the habit of not telling the truth." Lieutenant Sumner had been studying for the Marine Corps exams in Washington late in 1906. He wasn't sure of the exact date but said he had gone with Sutton and some other candidates out for drinks at the Willard Hotel and the theater. Sutton was very drunk; he "became very boisterous" and kicked over a red lantern placed as a danger signal in the street, smashing it. According to Sumner, Sutton was almost arrested, but Sumner told the policeman he would look out for him.

The two went to the Hotel Montrose for another drink. "In there Sutton was crowding against me very closely in a way that I did not like, and I told him to keep away from me; and I am not sure exactly how the trouble started. I think it was because I told him that I would not take another drink with him; he became very indignant and in a very melodramatic manner challenged me to a duel to be fought in Rock Creek Park the next morning." Sutton wanted another drink and had one, gradually becoming calmer. Finally, Sumner recalled, he said that

> we were too good friends to fight, but that he would not apologize, and that he knew I would not apologize. So he said that if we both wrote what he would dictate, at the same moment, neither one of us would apologize first. Thinking it was simply a thing to humor him, as he was very drunk, and I wished to get him home without making trouble, I agreed to it, not taking it at all seriously the whole thing. I wrote on that card the words which I have read, and he wrote on a slip of paper the same words, which unfortunately I have lost, as I did not attach any importance to them at the time.

Asked why he had agreed to write on the card, he responded that it was just to humor Sutton until he became sober. Had Sutton ever threatened any member of the Corps? Like the other lieutenants, now defendants, Sumner recounted the incident when he had shot up the camp and Major Fuller took his gun away. Major Leonard wanted to know why he had said that Sutton was in the habit of not telling the truth. At this point, Sumner faltered.

"I meant that several times he had been caught in falsehoods."

"By whom?"

"To my knowledge by different officers."

"Will you state all of those occasions and the circumstances surrounding them?"

"I could not say." Allen Sumner could come up with no examples except one vague instance when Sutton had told him he had been some place, and someone else contradicted him. Major Leonard asked how he could conclude that Sutton was given to lying from one example; Lieutenant Sumner said that was his general impression of Sutton's character. Davis could not have been happy with Sumner's harsh and provocative remarks, and he decided not to cross-examine the witness.

Lieutenant Sumner's testimony had been hard for Rosa and her daughter to hear, but both remaining witnesses would support their side of the case. The first was a man who had been corporal of the guard when Sutton died. The *Boston Post* had published a lengthy interview—spread across the country by wire—in which Archie Todd supposedly said he saw Lieutenant Sutton being shot while running away and being ordered to halt. Todd, the reporter claimed, refused to say who had fired the shot but promised to do so in court. Henry Davis would not comment on the interview, and Major Leonard's reaction was "it's all news to me." But now that the story was out, both men knew Todd would need to testify.

On August 11, Edward H. Butler, the proprietor of an influential evening paper, the *Buffalo News*, sent a telegram to Secretary of the Navy "George Von L Meyer ESQ" referring to Todd's interview.

DO NOT YOU THINK CONSIDERING THE INFLAMED CONDITION OF PUBLIC SENTIMENT IN THIS SUTTON CASE THAT THE CORPORAL OF THE GUARD NOW ON DUTY IN BOSTON SHOULD BE CALLED TO TESTIFY UNDER OATH. THIS CASE IS FAST ASSUMING THE CONDITIONS OF THE DREYFUS CASE & THUS FAR PUBLIC OPINION BASED UPON THE EVIDENCE IS INCLINED TO CENSURE THE ARMY & NAVY RATHER THAN UPHOLD IT IF JUDGE ADVOCATE LEONARDS ATTITUDE IS SUPPORTED BY THE GOVERNMENT KINDLY REPLY BY WIRE COLLECT.

Butler heard by return wire that Archie Todd had already been summoned to Annapolis. Major Leonard sent his own reply stating exactly what he thought of the role of the press corps during the inquiry. An excerpt appeared in the *New York Times*:

> The Department and the Judge Advocate as its representative have used every possible means to bring from the ends of the earth every person who could possibly throw any light on the subject. Witnesses have been brought thousands of miles and no expenses been spared. Yet the amazing charge has been repeatedly made that the Government of the United States was trying to conceal something or shield somebody. There has probably never been a case of great public interest in this country concerning which some newspapers have printed less of the actual testimony and more of the unsubstantial and irresponsible hallucinations.

In the meantime, Archie Todd came right to Annapolis from Wakefield on an overnight train. To the great relief of Henry Davis and his clients, Todd's testimony supported Charles Kennedy's statement that he had been on guard and gone to his sentry post just about the time Sutton died. Harry Leonard read aloud from the *Boston Post* and asked Todd to confirm or deny the statements attributed to him; he denied some and said others were true or partly true. He had seen "a figure with a white shirt, or partly in white running," and he had heard someone cry "Halt and if not I will shoot." Todd had not recognized anyone who took part in the chase, and he had no first hand knowledge about James De Hart throwing away a revolver. However, at breakfast the next morning, he heard that one had been found "behind the second base of the baseball diamond on the parade ground." Like William Owens and Charles Kennedy, Corporal Todd did say he had "wondered more than once why I have not been called to go before the Court of Inquiry and tell what I know." He had not taken any initiative to contact the authorities because, like Kennedy, he was an enlisted man and said, "I didn't think until I was called that it was my place to speak." No one had asked him if he knew anything about Sutton's death until the previous day when a reporter had tracked him down in Wakefield.

"Did you ever see in the public prints or elsewhere that the Government of the United States was making every effort within its power to bring before this Court every jot or tittle of testimony that pertains to this case?" asked Major Leonard.

"I have just read the papers, sir; that's all."

"And did you ever see any statement to that effect?"

"I have not been able to see a paper for the last week, sir," Todd explained.

With that Harry Leonard turned Archie Todd over to Arthur Birney, who questioned him in detail about all the men he had come across on the evening Sutton died. Why had he not volunteered any information? Both civilian attorneys found it hard to believe that Todd had kept quiet simply because he was a noncommissioned officer. But Todd had little else to add, and Major Leonard now called for the Sutton family's last witness.

Dr. Edward Schaeffer, an expert on firearms and gunshot wounds, had worked for nine years at the Army Medical Museum explaining the collection to medical men from across the world. He had also been deputy coroner of Washington, D.C. (and occasionally acting coroner) for five years; he had held inquests, interrogated witnesses, and looked into "all the details of homicide or alleged homicide cases." During that time, the doctor explained, he performed "nearly all of the autopsies that were made in homicide and shooting cases, besides quite a number of suicides which it was my duty to investigate, having always in mind the possible theory of homicide." Over a forty-year career, he had more experience with death from gunshot wounds than the "average medical man" and was an accepted expert who had testified frequently in court and before the grand jury. Given his credentials, it would be a challenge for the defendants' attorney to discredit him—but he would try to find a way to do just that.

Dr. Schaeffer brought a human skull, steel rods, two pieces of wax, an alcohol lamp, and a revolver into the auditorium. Navy surgeon Frank Cook had been invited to stay, and he listened as Davis read his description of the wound he found in Sutton's head. Dr. Schaeffer then warmed the wax with the alcohol lamp, created two wax balls, and placed them on either side of the skull. Using several medical terms that proved a challenge for the stenographers, he illustrated the course the bullet had taken in Sutton's brain with his fingers and the rods (attached by the wax). Guided by Dr. Cook's original description and instructions from Davis, Edward Schaeffer then placed the skull face down on the table.

"My question is," said Davis, who had thought up the idea of this demonstration, "Having the skull in that position, it is a fact, is it not, that a bullet, to have entered the skull from the front, and to have taken that course, must have been fired from a position well in front of the face or skull?"

"Well above the face; not exactly in front of it."

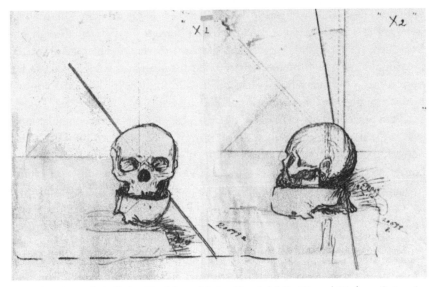

Two drawings of skulls by Dr. Edward Schaeffer. Exhibits X1 and X2 from Sutton Inquiry used to show trajectory of bullet. Courtesy of the National Archives and Records Administration.

Davis clarified. He meant "the front of the head, to the fore of the skull." So that when Sutton's face was "prone to the earth, the missile must have come from the weapon forward here, relative to where my hand is. Is that right?" Davis indicated where he thought the bullet originated. Schaeffer agreed. He emphasized that the size of the weapon was an important factor. The service revolver, assumed to have killed Sutton, was about a foot long, and the doctor confirmed that the position of the hand that held the weapon "must have been low with relation to the center of the skull, and the barrel of the weapon must have been pointing upward, that is in a vertical position." Davis asked what position Sutton's arm would have been in order to use his own his pistol finger to fire this weapon. If he had done so, Schaeffer responded, the dead man's hand would have to have been at least twelve inches from his head. As spectators crowded around the table, Davis asked the doctor whether Sutton could have fired the fatal shot. It was much more likely, the doctor thought, that someone in a standing or kneeling position fired the shot. Next, Dr. Schaeffer produced a revolver himself, one much shorter than twelve inches long, and described the muscles used in pulling the trigger of a gun. "The finger itself possesses no muscles. . . . When we pull the trigger by the fingers, the work is done with the forearm entirely. These muscles bend it down and these bend it back. The muscles involved as I understand it, are flexors and extensors." Even though Dr. Schaeffer's small pistol had an easier pull than a service revolver, he illustrated how difficult it would be to discharge it at his head at the angle used to kill Sutton using his index finger. In fact, he said, only a "professional contortionist" might be able to shoot himself that way.

Dr. Schaeffer was then asked to lay his torso across the rectangular table where the parties to the inquiry were sitting and try to shoot himself. While performing this re-enactment he noticed that it would have been even harder to shoot himself if his whole pelvis had been flat on the ground. Schaeffer tried with his left hand, too (he was left-handed). He could not do it, so both Harry Leonard and John Hood began directing this bizarre scene.

"Try it with your thumb," said Leonard. "Throw the muzzle over backward." Schaeffer could fire a shot with considerable effort with his thumb. But then he explained that lying flat on the ground (as Sutton was) would make the whole action much more difficult, especially with a man sitting on his shoulder. "The motion of the bones and of the muscles connecting the shoulder with the back, and the arm with the shoulder, would be so constrained as to be practically out of their functions. The forearm would still have its freedom, but I think it would be very difficult, if not impossible, for me to raise my pistol into the position in which I have demonstrated to the Court." In fact, said the doctor, any man in Sutton's situation would have been "almost powerless to inflict such a wound on his head."

Davis drove the point home. "Add to that that the man supposed to inflict the wound on himself is apparently senseless or unconscious, or near to being so from a beating. Is there the slightest possibility of a man so situated inflicting such a wound on himself?"

Dr. Schaeffer was cautious—he had his own reputation to think of. "I would not say it was an impossibility, without knowing to what degree his mind was influenced by any injury he had received." But such a man definitely would be at a disadvantage especially in aiming a weapon. In his experience, the doctor observed, the "vast majority of men who shoot themselves, actuated possibly by a desire to produce instantaneous death and avoid pain," would choose the right temple.

Schaeffer's testimony had been compelling, but Arthur Birney would challenge his credibility by bringing up the doctor's age. "How old are you?" he inquired.

"I will be sixty-six next month if I live."

"Are you as supple as you were at twenty-two?"

"Much less so, I regret to say."

"Has your health been good?"

"Excellent."

"Are you as strong as you once were?" Birney asked.

"No, sir."

Now he was getting somewhere. "What is the effect of age upon the muscles?"

"I used to walk to Baltimore on the road at the rate of four miles an hour for ten hours," Dr. Schaeffer replied. "Now I can only make three and a half on the railroad track."

"The sinews are not as strong?"

"In a man who keeps himself in practice the loss of power produced by age is not so progressive," said the doctor, giving as an example a man he had met who at the age of seventy had just walked across the continent. But Schaeffer acknowledged that "he was a very foolish man to have taken that risk at his age."

For his part, Dr. Schaeffer said he thought he still had a good, strong grip.

But not strong enough, thought Birney. "As compared with a youngster of twenty-two?"

"Rather better. I had overgrown my strength and was flabby," the doctor replied, catching Birney off guard, and eliciting laughter from the benches. When asked if his muscles had stiffened, Dr. Schaeffer said, "I was comparing myself with myself." Agreeing that he was no longer an athletic young man, he argued that a pianist his age could be "just as good with his fingers" as at twenty-two because of constant training. And Dr. Schaeffer described the various guns he had and the way he stayed in practice using them.

By this time, it was four o'clock, and Arthur Birney would have the whole evening to think up more questions for the doctor.

On Thursday, August 12, Birney completed his cross-examination, providing welcome comic relief once again. Dr. Schaeffer made it clear that it would have been practically impossible for a man with a forearm near the length of his own to shoot himself under the circumstances in which Sutton had found himself. So Birney asked, "How tall are you?"

"I am five feet eleven and a quarter inches in my stockings."

"Would it be more difficult for a shorter man?"

"The height would not be the determining element, Mr. Birney, so much as the length of the forearm and the length of the fingers."

"A shorter man would probably have a shorter arm, would he not?"

"No, sir, not necessarily. A gorilla has a much longer arm than a man, though he is not as tall. The colored race as a rule have longer arms than white men."

"But among white men?"

"The two are not necessarily connected. I have known men with very short arms who were a good height."

"Was that rather out of the usual?"

"It was." And, the doctor relented; in general a man five feet, eight or nine would have shorter limbs than a man five feet, eleven.

Birney again wanted to be clear on what the doctor meant by saying it was "practically impossible" for Sutton's fatal wound to have been self-inflicted.

"I meant to state that I considered it practically impossible for a man with ordinary length of arm to put a ball into his own skull at an angle of about fifty-three degrees viewed from in front; an angle of about eighty degrees in the anterior posterior line." When Schaeffer tried it, even when he extended his own arm to its full extent, he could only fire the revolver with his thumb.

Birney then shifted to the scalp wound found on Sutton, hoping to connect it to the fatal shot. In his autopsy report, Dr. Frank Cook had referred to a wound about one and one-half inches in length and the [bullet] hole as "about 3/8 of an inch in diameter at the bottom of this." It turned out both Davis and Birney had thought the word "bottom" referred to the point of entrance—that the bullet hole was just below the scalp wound. Thanks to Henry Davis, Dr. Cook was in the courtroom. He had drawn a picture on a little piece of paper to show that the scalp wound actually "radiated from the point of entrance of the bullet." After getting this matter clarified, Arthur Birney asked, over Davis' objection, "Suppose it to be found that there was an incision or scalp wound immediately above the hole of entrance, whether an inch or an inch and half long; what meaning would that have in your mind?" Dr. Schaeffer explained that if the bullet hole was about 3/8 of an inch in diameter, he would "assume that it entered very nearly at a right angle to the surface." Then he continued,

> In order to testify in this case I have refreshed my memory by reference to the very large collection of gunshot wounds of the skull in the Army Medical Museum in Washington. . . . Answering counsel's question, I would not base my view as to the direction in which the bullet impinged on the skull, from the existence of a scalp cut at the top of this wound. I

should like to see if a spicule of bone had been thrown off in that direction, or if there were any other way of accounting for the scalp wound.

"To what would you attribute the scalp wound—to the bullet?" asked Birney.

"I would not know what to attribute it to."

"You would not know?"

"I should not attribute it to the bullet, no," said the witness much to Henry Davis' relief.

"Would you attribute it to some other missile or blow?" Birney knew his opponent thought the scalp wound could have been caused by the butt of a gun.

Schaeffer had not done the autopsy. He could only go so far. "I should not attribute it to the bullet," he said.

Arthur Birney then asked if it would be impossible for a bullet "to go through the scalp away from the point of the hole of entrance into the skull." Schaeffer replied,

> I am speaking of my experience, and I have never met a case where the bullet would traverse the skull, cutting the scalp horizontally, and suddenly turn and enter the skull at right angles, unless there was some hard substance placed right there for it to ricochet on. I should consider that contrary to all the rules or laws governing motion and matter. . . . I have never seen or read of a bullet going under the scalp or cutting through the scalp in a certain direction for an inch or an inch and half, and then turning at right angles and penetrating the hard skull.

Birney did not want to let go of this point. It was key to his defense that the scalp wound be connected to the bullet and not to the butt of a gun. "Do you think it incredible that a bullet should enter the scalp, traverse the scalp for an inch or an inch and a half, and then tip and enter?"

"I have never met such a case in my experience, nor have I read of it; and as to the amount of credibility, I would prefer not to answer," said Schaeffer.

"You did not mean to be understood as saying that it is impossible?"

"Oh, no," the doctor replied. "If it was demonstrated to me by ocular proof that a bullet could do that, I would then believe it; but I would also believe that it was the first time that it ever did occur." When asked for more details about the angle of the bullet, the doctor left the courtroom and returned with two sketches he had made for his own use. He had made the sketches on August 10 and shown them to "Judge Davis" on the eleventh.

At Davis' suggestion they became Exhibits X1 and X2. Using the drawings and his human skull, he described the projectile of the bullet and the way the gun had been fired.

Again Birney challenged him. He asked what Schaeffer's experience had been in firing bullets that struck fluids. Dr. Schaeffer admitted to shooting at fish and snakes in the water, and then, realizing what Birney was after, said he knew a lot about the course a bullet would take after traveling the semi-fluid substance of the brain. He had done a lot of research on cases of this sort. "I studied the autopsy of President Lincoln who was shot in the back of the skull, the very careful description by the surgeons who made that autopsy. The course of the bullet in that case was straight ahead through the fluids." He gave another example and then said he had "a collection of memoranda about 15 inches thick" containing the details of violent deaths. Many were deaths from bullet wounds, though he could not say how many. Dr. Schaeffer had done minor surgery but did not have extensive experience as a surgeon in his own practice.

"Have you fired a revolver in the last three months?" asked Birney.

"Frequently."

"What kind of a revolver?"

"The weapon that I have had here in Court, a Forehand Arms Company revolver, self acting, five shot."

"What caliber?"

".32."

"And how many times have you fired even that little gun?" Birney asked.

"I would not like to state exactly, but maybe several hundred times. When I would go up the river boating I would take it along for some snapshots."

"Just casual shooting from a boat along the river?"

"Shooting at a floating target, for instance like an empty claret bottle; throw it out in the river and it breaks."

"Did you then examined the target to see the effect of the bullet?"

"No, sir, the target went right down."

Henry Davis interrupted, "nobody has any interest in the shape of a claret bottle after it is empty."

"It was empty." Dr. Schaeffer replied.

So Birney became more specific and asked the doctor how much "scientific shooting" he had done in the last one or more years. The doctor could not recall any such case in which he had testified in court recently. In fact, he had not done much of this type of thing since he had been in the coroner's office fifteen years previously. Then the marines' attorney began another line of questioning. He tried to get the doctor to confirm that a person would turn his face away from a weapon when he intended to commit suicide out of instinctive impulse—just as he would if someone else was shooting at him.

Annoyed, Davis said, "I'm not sitting here in stupidity." Birney, who was obviously trying to find a rationale for Robert Adams' new story that Lieutenant Sutton had turned his head to the right just before he shot himself, now admitted as much.

Davis added, "I also direct attention to the fact that everyone else except Lieutenant Adams says just the opposite."

Major Leonard asked the doctor whether or not the course pursued by a bullet "could be at an angle to the line of fire." His answer required him to explain that the brain is composed of a jelly-like substance, "minute blood vessels which would afford practically no resistance."

For several minutes the judge advocate went at this question until Dr. Schaeffer said that under a very unusual circumstance a revolver projectile might not move in a precise straight line through brain substance. Toward the end of the day, an extraordinary scene took place. Major Leonard instructed Lieutenant Adams to get on top of the table a *third* time. Adams took off his coat, lay down on the table face downward, and pointing the service revolver at his head, pulled the trigger a number of times. Leonard then asked the questions.

"Now, Doctor," he began, "as an expert would you say it is possible to do what you have just seen done?"

"That [bullet] would not have hit [Sutton's] head," came the quick response.

"Please do it again," Leonard told Adams. "Fire it all around there, anywhere the notion strikes you." Robert Adams "shot" himself again, holding the revolver in different positions, all within a yard of Lieutenant Sutton's mother and sister.

Even Dr. Schaeffer tried to give him guidance. "Place it at an angle as near as possible to fifty-three degrees from this plane," he said indicating on the skull.

Leonard chimed in with more advice. "Turn your head to the left, then."

And Schaeffer added, "There is the center of the parietal bone (showing Adams the skull), there is the angle, about that way. Now, pull the trigger." Adams pulled the trigger with his finger and also with his thumb; he tried the revolver in several different positions. Anticipating a problem, Dr. Schaeffer glanced over at Harry Leonard.

"If the Judge Advocate will allow me, I know from experience that in that constrained position the trigger finger becomes tired, so that is not a fair test after half a minute."

Leonard had another idea. "Now," he said looking toward the bench on his left, "Mr. Osterman, you come here."

Henry Davis suddenly realized that if more than one man was involved, the table would not be a smart demonstration site. "I submit that if this is to be done it better be done on the floor." So Lieutenant Adams lay down on the floor with Lieutenant Osterman straddling him on his shoulders, Lieutenant Utley straddling him on his back, and Sergeant De Hart sitting on his legs.

The judge advocate directed Adams again. "Now pull your hand out and fire at your head." Adams pulled the trigger three times, pointing the revolver at his head while lying face downward.

After everyone returned to their seats, Davis said to Dr. Schaeffer, "You have just seen the illustration given by Lieutenant Adams on the floor. State if you please whether in any one of these positions in which you saw the revolver when the trigger was pulled the wound appearing from the autopsy description of Dr. Cook would have been inflicted."

"No, sir," came the definite response.

The following morning at shortly after ten, in an effort to be absolutely precise, the doctor added a corollary to this final answer. At one point, when Dr. Schaeffer had held the gun with both hands to Adams' head, the lieutenant tried to pull the trigger with his fourth finger and then changed his hold and fired the weapon with his thumb. In this particular demonstration, Schaeffer believed that the angle of the weapon "corresponded very nearly, with a possible error of a few degrees, to the angle of the weapon as indicated by me, from the direction of the wound." But Robert Adams, in that instance, was not even holding the weapon that fired the imaginary bullet.

Reporters thoroughly enjoyed Edward Schaeffer's performance. "DOCTOR SHOWS BY SKULLS SUTTON WAS NOT SUICIDE," announced the *Los Angeles Times*; in New York, the *Times* reported that an expert on gunshot wounds had shown why "it was quite impossible that Lieut. Sutton could ever have fired into his own head the shot that put an end to his life."

Fourteen days of courtroom testimony were about to end when Birney brought up the subject of the missing witness, Lieutenant Edward Roelker. Acknowledging that his testimony could be important "in view of the great public interest that is being taken in this inquiry," Birney suggested that he read into the record what Roelker said in 1907. Davis objected strongly and won out. He could not remember what Lieutenant Roelker had said, and the witness had not been under oath at the time. (Actually, Roelker's testimony could have helped his client's case—he had testified that Sutton had warned Adams to halt.) Harry Leonard took this opportunity to emphasize that every effort had been made to find Lieutenant Roelker, but he "has vanished from the face of the earth so far as this Department is concerned."

With that, Major Leonard concluded the inquiry. But instead of summarizing the case for the court, he "arose to his full height," his empty sleeve pinned to the left side of his coat, and defended the navy's procedure. "If it please the Court," he began,

> The United States in this case has no argument to submit. The Government, despite the astonishing allegations which it has heard here made to the effect that effort has been made to conceal testimony, to cover the trail of criminals, has used every means within its power to bring before this Court every witness known to it of whom it has heard, of whom it has gained any clue whatsoever. Officers have been brought from the plains of North China, from the jungles of the Philippines, from every point in the United States where they were stationed, from all over the world, from Smyrna, to testify before this Court, to lay before it every fact within their possession. The Government has unearthed, so far as it could, every scrap of written testimony or every scrap of writing which might lead to the production of testimony, every scrap of writing which would produce to the Judge Advocate any clue to testimony, and all those paper writings have been laid before this Court and the clues that they have indicated have been followed so far as the Judge Advocate could, by the use of every effort, to learn of evidence which bore upon the issue.

Unless the attorneys' closing remarks made further comment necessary, Leonard stated that "the Department and the Judge Advocate have no condition of facts that it or he desires to prove. The one aim, the sole object and the single purpose that has actuated every move that has been made in this hearing, was to produce in public before the eyes of the people of the United States everything that bore in any way upon this most unfortunate and to-be-regretted incident that occurred on the night of the 12th–13th of October, 1907." This unusual declaration underscored the pivotal role of the media in the Sutton inquiry. In spite of Leonard's distaste for biased newspaper accounts, he too had used the press corps as a vehicle for his own purposes. Daily coverage of his comments, and of the testimony of every witness, surely proved to the world that this was indeed a thorough inquiry. Major Leonard now asked that he be directed to "hold no further communion with this Court until its findings shall have been arrived at." Once the attorneys had their final say, the judge advocate would merely authenticate the record by his signature.

Commander Hood wasted no time in granting Leonard's motion.

For more than a month, reporters from San Francisco to New York had engaged Americans in the "trial," calling it "remarkable" and "unprecedented" largely because the protagonists confronted each other in a military courtroom. For the citizens who followed it, the investigation had been entertaining, educational, and troubling. By the time testimony ended, both parties had used the media as a sounding board for their own purposes. Some news articles and interviews had been more sensational than others, and some more accurate than others. But no matter what version of the story Americans read, it was clear that several reputations were at stake.

No one knew that better than Henry Davis and Arthur Birney, whose collegial friendship had been severely tested during the previous four weeks. At noon on Thursday, the Sutton court adjourned for the day, leaving both men extra time to prepare their final arguments.

13

"THE FEROCITY OF A TIGRESS"

Friday, August 13, was blissfully cool, barely seventy degrees when court convened, and the largest crowd so far filed through the tall doorways of the Academic Building. Visitors from Washington and men in every branch of the service came to see and hear the finale. While the court heard witnesses from the previous day verify their testimony, spectators were pleasantly distracted by the sounds of the Naval Academy Band playing a popular tune, "Down in Jungle Town," at its regular morning concert. And Henry Edgar Davis considered his audience.

On his right sat Rosa Sutton and Rose Parker. By representing these women, the attorney found himself in an extraordinary position. This was not just an investigation of a possible murder case; if his arguments were persuasive, Jimmie Sutton's soul might finally appear before the tribunal of Christ without the stigma of a mortal sin. Davis was actually a deeply spiritual man, wide open to fresh ideas with a metaphysical approach to the law. From his perspective, the judge advocate's behavior had been high-handed and unreasonable. When he first agreed to be part of this fact-finding process, he never imagined he would present closing arguments as a prosecuting attorney. He could take little comfort from the onlookers, many of whom stood firmly behind the defendants. But Davis could see the members of the press gathered at tables nearby, eager to learn how he had sorted out the confusing testimony of the past three weeks.

Rosa's attorney surely had mixed feelings about reporters. They made mistakes; they misquoted and even invented comments from informants, and they raised issues prematurely that were not always helpful to legal proceedings. Yet these news gatherers and photographers were his clients' primary link with the public. No matter what the court's opinions, reporters would give his arguments a wider forum than could be had in this charming but insular historic city. If he had seen the *Washington Post* that morning, Davis might have been pleased to read that he had been "brilliant in his conduct of the case, and if he is in good form tomorrow there will be an oratorical treat." But Davis' work was cut out for him. The paper also stated, "out of a sense of fair play" for Robert Adams, "no evidence has been developed in the hearing to justify the slightest stigma of hideous crime."

At 10:30 a.m., just as the bell tower struck five bells, Harry Leonard nodded to the Suttons' attorney. When Davis stood up and removed his glasses, a hushed silence fell over the room. "Every eye and ear was given fully" to the attorney, who would speak for more than two hours. He began by informing the court that he had come to Annapolis with "an entirely open mind," but, he said, "my mind is now closed, and what I am about to say is intended to lead the Court to a conviction forced upon me by the testimony that I have heard." Referring to the "wilderness of conflict and confusion" in the evidence submitted, Davis supposed the court "might well wonder that conclusions in some cases are ever possible. And yet," he continued, "I believe that by trying the case along the lines which I have laid down for my treatment of it, confusion will become order and the dark will appear to be light." Rosa was hopeful; for months, this small, intense and animated man had been a loyal ally.

Davis then reviewed the life of Jimmie Sutton, Rosa's "offering to the service of her country." He read out loud Jimmie's last letter to his brother Don urging him to "walk across hell on a rotten rail" to keep his word of honor. And then Davis turned to the letter Jimmie had sent his mother the day before he died, full of optimism and excitement about his upcoming voyage on Roosevelt's Great White Fleet. At this point, Rosa's usual self-possession gave way, and she buried her face in her handkerchief and tried to hide behind her black fan. Before Davis finished, many of the women in the audience would be weeping in sympathy with Rosa. Davis ended his introductory appeal to the heartstrings of the audience with Gilbert Coleman's letter to Rosa about Jimmie's happy last few hours, and, he said soberly, "within an hour of what the letter describes that young man was a corpse."

He turned next to the 1907 inquest board, "summoned as though by the tap of a drum," a board whose recorder had been in the fatal brawl with Jimmie and was himself an officer guilty of "dereliction of duty that night." These three men had made a quick judgment about the cause of Sutton's death; Davis underscored the dire consequences of the suicide finding. Jimmie Sutton had been denied the "hallowing and hallowed words of the priest who to him was God's intermediary." He was now "doomed to an eternity of torment"; his parents no longer had hope of joining him under the "All-Merciful Wing."

There was one more point Henry Davis wanted to make before addressing the testimony of the defendants. For weeks, Rosa and her daughter had been ignored by the navy women in Annapolis. Davis found the inhospitable treatment the two Oregon women received incomprehensible. "I cannot understand why these women, coming here on this mission, should not have been greeted with outstretched hands and flowing hearts, with God-speed on their mission," he told the rapt onlookers. Acknowledging the nation's interest in his client's plight, he drew on the oratorical skill he had been known for since his Princeton days. "Let the walls of this room extend until they reach the horizon. I am willing. And I pray you, sirs, do not let us from now on treat this case as though the words spoken are confined for their sounding forth to the walls within which we sit; and let us not, as did the villages of the poet, 'Take the rustic murmur of our burg for the great hum that sounds around the world.' Let us try the case so."

Davis hoped that the court would ignore the inappropriate evidence that had come up during the inquiry. First, alcohol was not an issue—no drunken brawl had occurred, and "liquor is not responsible, directly or indirectly, for the death of James N. Sutton." Second, the one night, five months before he died, when Sutton had been slightly intoxicated and fired his guns in camp should not have been brought up repeatedly by the government witnesses (with Leonard's prodding) as evidence of a dead boy's unstable personality. Third, Rosa's unfortunate correspondence with Harry Swartz was irrelevant to the matter at hand, and Davis took several moments to explain why. "Months went by. Hope seemed gone, and in the end, or as a means to the end, there came from this mother those frantic letters, pouring her heart out, as she believed, in confidence. Her suspicion had grown with delay. It had become intensified by rebuffs and disappointments. It had turned into conviction, and is it strange that it found its expression in denunciation?" He meant, of course, of the navy. And then, turning to Rosa, he urged the court not to consider her letters. "Let us wipe out this frantic mother's accusations, I care not how you characterize them," pleaded Davis. "We are not trying those, we are not trying her." The inquiry had been convened solely to learn the circumstances of Lieutenant Sutton's death; "every scrap of testimony that could be got from the four corners of the earth (I have the Judge Advocate's assurance for it and I believe it) has been put before this Court to enlighten this question." Its findings should be based on that testimony and nothing else—certainly not

Mrs. Sutton's high-strung language. On this last point, Arthur Birney would strongly disagree. Her accusations, in his mind, were the reason his own clients' honor was on the line.

Could Henry Davis prove to "the world" that Jimmie Sutton was not a suicide—or at least establish reasonable doubt? For about ninety more minutes he argued this case. Ever since Jimmie had written home that some of the marines were out to get him, Rosa thought there had been a plan to beat up her son. Davis reminded the court that Sutton had been "hated by men who, in the providence of God, were in at his death." "He was peculiarly hated by Adams, resentfully hated by Adams, and cordially hated by Harold Utley. It is a fact." "Because," Davis said wryly, "to apply Lieutenant Edward Willing's own naive rule of evidence, 'an officer has said it,' they had been warned that they must not be friends with Sutton; that if they were, it would be at the expense of the friendship of others.'"

"It is beyond dispute," he continued, "because an officer has said it, that Sutton was thought to be too cocky and wanted a taking down." When Sutton offered the other marines a ride back to the barracks from the Carvel Hall Hotel, God gave them a perfect chance to go after him.

Davis focused on the accused: Lieutenants Adams, Harold Utley, Edward Osterman, William Bevan, Willing, Sergeant James De Hart, and the "late Lieutenant [Edward] Roelker" had all been present the night Sutton was shot. If this court could be persuaded that any one of these men wanted to kill Sutton, Davis knew, as Edmund Van Dyke had argued earlier that year, he would have his case. And why, Davis asked, again going after the faulty procedures used in 1907, had other officers and enlisted men with valuable information such as Charles Kennedy not been called before the inquest? Henry Davis laid out certain facts that were beyond dispute.

For one thing, "the first person to show fight was Robert E. Adams, Second Lieutenant United States Marine Corps. He got down from that machine, from the seat where he was sitting beside Will Owens [the chauffeur,] and stripped to fight. What happened is a subject of difference; but that Adams had a fight with Sutton there that night I say the evidence establishes beyond all room for doubt." Even Harold Utley admitted Adams wanted to fight. Central to Henry Davis' argument was the fact that the most incriminating evidence came from the testimony of the Marine Corps officers themselves. "And I beg to say right here, without choler, that everything material in this case that rests on human words is dependent upon the narration of those words by these defendants. The only lips that could speak against them are sealed forever. That Sutton fled to the camp is undoubted. That he was at the mercy of these three defendants is undoubted." Much

less certain was what Sutton had said to the marines. Davis was not convinced that, after Sutton had been pummeled by Lieutenant Osterman, he
had threatened to kill the three men who had been in the car with him. On
the contrary, when Sutton returned to camp, "He did not expect to find
them there. He did not remain in camp and waylay them and lie in hiding
to shoot them as they might approach." Instead, he took off to recover his
cape.

"Then what?" Davis paused. "We have this fatal encounter, and I in-
vite your close attention to the conflicting stories that are told by the sur-
vivors. No two of them agree. No one of them agrees with what he said
to the Board of Inquest, and it all depends upon their tongues."

Davis was troubled by the new information that came out in 1909—
some of it clearly designed to take Lieutenant Adams off the hook. According to Adams, Harold Utley had "ordered him to go back [to the scene
of the fight] and get the clothes—some clothes. When asked whose, nobody's in particular, he just said clothes, and he went. He went alone. And
until this inquiry, no living ear had heard of that." Lieutenant Osterman's
account (in this inquiry) was that Utley invited Adams to go down the road
with him to retrieve the clothes. But, argued Davis, Lieutenant Utley could
not remember saying anything about clothes. Sutton, on the other hand,
did have a reason to go back and find his cloak, and he went with Sergeant
James De Hart. His fatal encounter took place on the way back from this
mission.

Play by play, Davis recounted the discrepancies in the testimony of the
defendants; drawing on Greek mythology, he spoke of their contradictions,
piled one on top of the other like the two giants who tried to pile Mount
Pelion on Mount Ossa in a fruitless effort to overthrow the gods. By piec-
ing together Harold Utley's testimony with that of Adams and De Hart,
Davis concluded that when De Hart and Sutton were on the way back to
camp with his clothes, Sutton was not hunting anyone. Lieutenant Utley
ran into the two men. And then Edward Roelker arrived on the scene, and
there was a semicircle around Sutton made up of Utley, De Hart, and
Roelker. At that point "Utley turned and saw Adams and Osterman in the
distance, Adams coming down the road. And mark you, sirs, what happened. Sutton started to run away; not to fight, but to run away to camp;
as he had already been, he was at the mercy of numbers." And Utley and
De Hart pursued him, at which point Sutton ran into the arms of Adams.
Henry Davis did not see Sutton as running amok but as running away in a
situation where several men rushed him together. After Adams showed up,
they were all "rushing this fleeing man." Once Sutton was down on the

ground, a gun had been in his left hand. This weapon, Davis said, was the smaller gun, a .38 caliber Smith & Wesson. Both in 1907 and in 1909, several of the marines agreed someone had taken the Smith & Wesson from Sutton, leaving the large Colt service revolver with its twelve-inch barrel in his right hand.

Davis now called attention to the inconsistent stories the marines told about Sutton's position. One version was that his arms were both under his chest. Another was that his right arm was under him and his left hand was extended. But most everyone agreed that Sutton's face was pressed down into the ground, so much so that a doctor had to pick the gravel out of his nose—all, that is, except for Robert Adams, who changed his testimony at the 1909 inquiry. This was a point Rosa's attorney would come back to more than once. For the first time, in 1909, Adams said, "I saw Sutton draw his hand from under his body, turn his head to the right and shoot."

Davis glanced at Arthur Birney as he came to a key point.

> I challenge my friend who is to follow me to find the slightest hint or allusion to the turning of Sutton's head, by anybody at any time, anywhere, except on page 104 of this record, when I had Adams under cross examination. Adams never said it before, because it never happened. It is like a thousand other things that occurred to us in our experience. The exigencies of this case required that head to be turned in order that Sutton might shoot himself as Adams said he did. The desperation of that remark is manifest in the point at which it came out. He had to have Sutton's head turn or he could not be shot from the ground the way he was. And I say in passing that had he been shot with a service revolver or any other revolver, four inches from his head or any distance from his head, there would not have been that dull, unfamiliar sound that Bevan heard.

During the inquiry, Adams had been asked to re-enact three times the shot that killed Sutton. Each time, Davis noted, Lieutenant Adams had always turned his own head to the right to try to get the gun in a position that would work. He also changed the way he held the gun on the last day of the testimony when the question arose regarding the possibility of firing a shot like that.

"Every eye saw that," Rosa's attorney proclaimed. "He has twice adapted his testimony to the exigency of the situation in which he here sits." That "is the monument I say, that rises from the plain in this case so that every eye may see it, with the sun flashing on it; and as surely as I am on my feet is that so."

Because of the confusing and often evasive testimony of the government witnesses, other details were cloudy. "What was the situation at the
time the fatal shot was fired?" Davis asked. "No two agree." And during the
entire inquiry no one (including Adams) actually admitted *seeing* Sutton pull
the trigger. For several minutes, Davis quoted from the testimony of the
lieutenants to remind his listeners how their recollections differed from each
other. Then Davis focused on the guns.

According to the marines, Sutton left the student officer's camp with
two different weapons, his personal Smith & Wesson and a Colt service revolver. Lieutenant Utley said the smaller gun had been taken away from Sutton after a struggle. Davis continued, "Under the blue sky of heaven not one
of these men standing there, officer and gentleman though he be, can remember who struggled for that revolver. Each contents himself with saying
that it was not he. Each denies that he took it. So what could have happened
to it? The man who took the gun out of Sutton's left hand," Davis said
solemnly, "is in a grave deeper than that which holds the body of Sutton."

The subsequent fate of the Smith & Wesson was even more disturbing. A mysterious person turned it over to James De Hart, and the sergeant
"was so conscious of its incriminating character that he rejected possession
of it and threw it away" [in the high grasses on the parade ground]. Under
grueling questioning, De Hart had refused to tell the court who gave him
the gun. Looking directly at Lieutenant Adams who was staring moodily at
him, Davis proclaimed, "I say now, here, that the hand that handed that revolver to Sergeant De Hart is stained with blood." He then went further.
"Nobody on God's Earth" will pretend that De Hart has told the truth on
the stand. "Everybody who has heard this testimony, everybody who knows
anything about this case, knows that that non-commissioned officer has
come here and has committed the most flagrant perjury before this court."
Rosa's attorney hesitated. Furious at this accusation, Harry Leonard had
raised his hand to stop the argument. But he was persuaded by the court to
back down and let Davis continue.

Henry Davis reminded everyone in the room that Robert Adams was
the only witness who said that the Colt service revolver was not the gun in
Sutton's right hand when the last shot was fired. Even before the 1907 inquest, Adams identified "the little pistol as the one that had done the work."
Davis gestured emphatically, "In name of God what does that mean?" It
means that "he knew Sutton was killed by that gun." "As surely as I face
you," Davis told the court, "when Sutton met his death it was from a shot
from the Smith & Wesson gun." Not only that, at both investigations Adams
said Sutton had fired three shots from his Colt revolver before being tackled

to the ground. When the shells from the Colt were produced before the board there were three live bullets still in the barrel.

And there was further evidence of Adams' "guiltiness in this case." Some facts "are more potent a thousand to one than any mere words that come from the lips of men," said Davis. For the first time at this inquiry, Robert Adams claimed that Sutton had singled him out and threatened to kill him. The clear implication was that Adams needed a motive of self-defense. While Davis spoke, Robert Adams sat facing him, and his "face was all the while a flush of crimson, and occasionally there was a twitch of anger about his mouth and eyes when the attorney held him up to severe criticism." Occasionally, "when it occurred to him that Mr. Davis was laying too much stress on certain points that servicemen consider immaterial," he would smile.

Another perplexing aspect of the case was the "absolute unanimity with which the officers started that night this suicide story, before the Commandant could get on the ground." Davis now became a storyteller, giving the men and women in the auditorium a respite from his accusations by sharing some anecdotes on the nature of evidence. For example, he said,

> I remember another case where the question was as to the responsibility for a railroad wreck. The point was whether an operator had thrown his red light or his white light. He produced five witnesses to prove that he had thrown the red light. On cross examination every one of them admitted that this man had called attention to the fact that the red light was burning. He had thrown it; but too late. The story was made on a platform like that. Easy enough, perfectly simple.

So then, Davis made the analogy. Why had it not occurred to any of the marines "to leave this question of the manner of Sutton's death open? Why should it occur to them with one tongue that they should begin telling, first the patrol on the hill, and ending with the Commandant, that the man had killed himself?" The only person who equivocated on this point is Lieutenant Adams who would never actually call Sutton a suicide.

Davis also wanted to clarify another point on the trajectory of the bullet. When the Suttons' medical witness, Dr. Edward Schaeffer, testified, the judge advocate had asked if the bullet could have been deflected from its course (making it more plausible that Sutton had pulled the trigger). Both navy doctors had said the wound was clean cut, and Henry Davis had no doubt that the bullet followed a straight trajectory and could not have been shot by Jimmie Sutton. So he urged the court to give strong weight to the testimony of Dr. Schaeffer, who said "it is a physical impossibility for that wound to have been inflicted from the ground with Sutton's head on the ground," even if it had been turned. Dr. Schaeffer's demonstration with the skull and steel rods had proven that.

As Davis neared the end of his remarks, he came back to the issue of reasonable doubt. Applying the standards of a criminal courtroom where he would have been completely at home, he told the three officers at the far end of the table, "You cannot resort to an exception until you have exhausted every possibility of gratifying the rules." For example, to say that "the course of the bullet that killed Sutton was a freak" is not possible under proper rules of evidence. "Nor," Davis continued, "can you make inferences from hearsay into evidence; or make assumptions that Sutton might have used his thumb to pull the trigger of the gun that killed him or turned the weapon upside down." Of course, Henry Davis' instructions carried no weight with the navy court, unless its members decided to listen to him out of good will.

There was no ambiguity in Henry Davis' mind as to the proper verdict, by his standards at least—"You cannot convict a man or find a man guilty of suicide unless you find so from all the facts, beyond all and every reasonable doubt. That is the law's rule. It is mercy's rule. It is the rule of justice. It is the rule of common sense. Reading this testimony as I do read it there is no suicide in this case and there is no room for the hypothesis of accidental killing in this case. And the rest is up to you, sirs."

When Rosa's attorney ended his two-hour oratory, the curious bystanders welcomed the recess. It was a beautiful day, and for several minutes they gathered in the sunshine outside the Academic Building. Rosa and her daughter were grateful for Davis' passionate support. The *Baltimore Sun* credited him with a "masterly argument." He handled the whole subject "without gloves" and "showed not the slightest hesitancy in giving vent to his personal feelings." Davis directed most of his anger at Lieutenants Adams and Utley, and the reporters seemed surprised that Osterman and Willing had not been criticized more severely. Robert Adams emerged from the crowd with his brother, William, looking more somber than usual.

Henry Davis, whose client had been the moving force behind the inquiry, bore the burden of proof. Perhaps that is why, after the recess, Arthur Birney took much less time for his final remarks; he would focus on discrediting Rosa Sutton. Birney was probably quite comfortable in a room filled with women who backed their navy men. But for him, at least in this case, the media was more than an irritation. By giving Rosa Sutton a forum, reporters had tarnished the reputations of his clients and all they stood for as officers. Arthur Birney had not asked for copies of the daily testimony, but he did have Rosa's letters to Harry Swartz. Rosa's charges were preposterous; none of her witnesses had seen the final shot fired. Birney could certainly argue that Mrs. Sutton had no case at all.

Birney's patronizing attitude came through the moment he began speaking in an animated voice that he maintained for the entire hour and a quarter. His own remarks were superfluous, he said. In any ordinary criminal court seeking to prove Adams not guilty—or not proven guilty—he would not even have taken the time to present closing arguments, given the testimony that had been heard. "But," he acknowledged,

> I recognize, with my brother Davis, that this case is being tried in a wider forum than this Court, and I recognize the importance to these young gentlemen, Mr. Adams, my client, and the others who sit with him, that there shall go out from this Court such a declaration of absolute spotlessness in them as shall convince, if human effort can convince, public opinion that it has been heretofore poisoned and is absolutely wrong.

Then he appealed to the court on behalf of his clients' careers.

> We know what an officer's honor is to him. It cannot be stained without the same kind of injury which is done to a woman's honor when it is stained, and these gentlemen appearing here and depending in part upon my weak efforts are entitled under the evidence . . . to such a judgement as will clear their skirts and convince [the world] that there is not a stain upon their honor or the honor of a Corps to which they belong, by retaining them within its fold.

Birney referred to his own civil law background in "the courts of common usage in the country" and his cynicism about the investigation from the outset. Mrs. Sutton's claims, in his estimation, were based entirely upon a vision. Only the renown and eloquence of her attorney gave her any credibility at all. But Arthur Birney informed his audience that both he and Henry Davis had been trained "never to impose our beliefs in any case." Hard evidence, not the personality of the attorney who presents that evidence, was the basis for the argument. Now that Davis had spoken, Birney continued, there should be no question that Mrs. Sutton was, in fact, prosecuting the lieutenants. "People soon forget the result of a trial. People will understand, as they have been made to understand, that these gentlemen are defendants in this case, and consequently accused persons; and if they were not accused before this morning they were accused here then." So Arthur

Birney's job was to see that everyone understood the fallacy—in fact the absurdity—of Mrs. Sutton's unfounded convictions that had been broadcast throughout the land by the press.

Birney spent a good portion of the hour attacking the "frantic ravings" of the "prosecutrix" or "accuser." He focused particularly on two accusations she had made in her 1908 letters to Harry Swartz, ignoring her subsequent retractions. First, Rosa had said there had been a conspiracy between his clients to beat Sutton to death. (Davis explicitly denied any claim that Sutton was beaten to death, though more than one witness suggested Sutton was senseless when he was shot.) Second, Birney went after her suggestion to Swartz that one of his clients was guilty of premeditated murder. These false accusations, Birney told the court, came from "the preternatural vision" of a mother, and they "found their most acute expression perhaps, in the letters which have been introduced here," although, he insisted, these letters made charges that were not new ones.

Henry Davis might argue that "the frantic ravings of a mother ought not to be introduced in evidence here," but, said Arthur Birney, "those ravings have been put in the press over and over and over again until the whole land was filled with the poison." Questioning Rosa's right to have written Swartz at all, he asked, "Is the lady who testified here a fit candidate for a lunatic asylum, or is she a rational being?" Rosa had given an explanation for what she thought was the condition of her son's body, but Birney noted that her description of her son's wounds in the letters had not been entirely accurate. She should have known, he argued, on reading the letter from Colonel Charles Doyen, what the condition of the corpse was. Birney also criticized Rose Parker for not visiting the surgeons or the undertaker when she came to Annapolis to learn more details about her brother's body. Then, referring to Davis' plea for sympathy for Rosa, the marines' attorney twisted his rhetorical knife:

> Heaven forbid that I should minimize the grief of a parent stricken as she; but Heaven also forbid that I should profane the name of sorrow with such outbursts. They are not evidence of sorrow. In view of the pursuit that has been kept up, yea, the malignant, wicked pursuit in the face of all the testimony which was available to her, they rather evidence the ferocity of a tigress than the sorrow of a bereaved parent.

Rosa Sutton's accusations stemmed from "malignant hatred," he asserted; "the application of the term sorrow to such a thing is an insult to American motherhood and womanhood."

So what, he asked, do we have to contrast with this hysterical woman? A few young men who began the evening in the Carvel Hall Hotel acting out a stage of "joyous boyhood." Besides, Adams testified that Sutton insulted him, and what *should* Adams have done? "He naturally resented the foul epithet." "Would you have it otherwise?" Birney asked the judges. Or would you have Adams act like Mrs. Sutton hoped her son would act when she was asked to explain her comment that the man "did not live who would dare to call her son a coward." Rosa had implied she thought Jimmie would have run to "tell the Colonel if called a coward." Rosa Sutton did not really mean this, Birney admitted, but look what kind of reputation she tried to give her son.

Now what would the proper behavior have been? "Lieutenant Adams did the manly thing, the thing which all of us would expect to have done, the thing which I, as a father, would expect my son to do—he resented it. And he acted immediately. If you are familiar with the lines of Marmion by [Walter] Scott, you will remember that Marmion said: 'He rights the wrong where it was given e'en if it were in the gates of Heaven.'" Birney directed his gaze toward the three members of the court in whose hands the fate of his clients lay. "And that is what is expected of men of your profession, and it is expected of young men who come in to join your profession, that they shall protect their honor and not be ready to turn in the position of tell-tale rather than to visit punishment upon the man who impugns that honor."

So, Birney said, with more than a hint of sarcasm, it was fortunate that when Sutton hit Edward Osterman from behind when the men first got into a fight that the lieutenant's mother was not around for him "to go and tell his mama." On the contrary, Osterman resented Sutton's insult, "and the aggressor was fitly punished." Sutton refused to admit that he was whipped or even get up from the ground. As for William Owens' testimony, Arthur Birney had found it amusing. Owens had twice said that Adams rushed at Sutton, but he also admitted he never saw a blow struck. So what did he mean? "That Adams rushed Sutton and then all he did was say 'Boo'?"

Birney's next tactic was to prove what a bad sport Lieutenant Sutton was. "This case has been filled with charges of brutality. Was it brutal for two young men to engage in a fair fight and one of them whip the other one who forced the fight upon him?" Leaving the scene of the initial argument, Sutton "ran to the camp, did what my friend here admits he did; he returned to the camp and armed himself with two revolvers. What for? What for? I waited in vain to hear an explanation of that act, that act which meant murder only." And Sutton lost his temper, accused Birney, in fact, "he yielded to the passions that he declared in the letter to his mother he had subdued, and filled with rage that he had been beaten in a fair fight by Osterman, he armed himself with two revolvers to take the lives of his fellow officers." He did not, Birney asserted, flee back to the camp with no malice in mind.

Arthur Birney assured the court that his opponent's interpretation of the evidence was false. Jimmie Sutton was out to kill one or more of his clients. "He went to seek the man whom he intended to shoot, or the men whom he intended to shoot; and he doubly armed himself to commit the crime which he had declared his intention to commit." And the other marines, according to Birney, were just trying to help Sutton. "They stood about him as friends seeking to induce him to surrender his weapons and go back to camp, he hears Adams coming, and," the attorney exclaimed, interpreting the testimony in a completely different way than his opponent, "these men had not for the moment the presence of mind to overpower him." Sutton was already so in the wrong when he ran off from camp with two weapons that older more experienced officers would have made sure Sutton "would not have left that camp alive, or he would have surrendered those weapons."

Once again, Birney commended Lieutenant Adams for his bravery in a desperate situation. Fixing his gaze on his client, he said,

> It gives me the greatest pleasure to stand here and point to the courage shown by Lieutenant Adams in rushing upon him. Adams with bare fists and in his shirt sleeves rushing upon a man who had a revolver in each hand and was seeking to take the life of Adams. Adams did not turn and flee. But striking with his right fist and clutching at his left hand, he then seized Sutton's right hand, and flinging himself about him, showing the skill of the athlete and accomplished football player, he managed to deprive his antagonist of power to further use his pistols, to fire any more shots at him, and then he threw him to the ground.

This description of Adams' behavior clearly appealed to the men in the room, and to their wide-eyed wives and girlfriends.

Adams had been found savagely beating Sutton in the head when he was down on the ground, and Birney had his own take on the matter. He turned Robert Adams into a hero: "Adams threw himself upon him and threw him down and holding his right arm under his body as well as he might with his right elbow, and holding his left arm above the elbow with his left hand, he did what any man of blood and sinew would do; he pounded him upon the back of the head in order to suppress him." Adams, watching with his peers on the bench near Birney, no doubt also enjoyed this interpretation of the tragedy. Birney continued, underscoring the same point.

"Is Sutton the only man entitled that night to anger and to rage? What a situation! And yet that is the brutality which has been heralded all through this land as the act for which Lieutenant Adams has been so bitterly condemned. Unarmed, with his forearm only at liberty to strike, he struck the man who, doubly armed, was seeking his life."

And what of the other young men, brand new to the armed forces, totally unprepared for this bedlam? "Was not their behavior understandable as well?" Birney's tone softened as he again glanced over at his clients on the bench nearby. "In what a state of excitement were these young men; for the first time in their lives such an incident had occurred, they were taken by surprise, a murderous assault made upon them. They rushed in to attempt to save one comrade and to attempt to disarm another."

Arthur Birney had dismissed the testimony of two of Rosa's witnesses, William Owens and Private Charles Kennedy; he now accused Owens of lying when he said "he had no communication whatever with anybody about this case and then afterwards his letter and affidavit were produced before the Court." As for the inconsistent testimony of the officers, Birney scoffed at Davis for condemning the men "as conspirators and as murderers, for taking part in the killing of Sutton, because they did not pull out a pad, for example, and make a note of every movement that was made." And he went further. His clients were clearly on the spot when confronted by the specter of a man whose soul was not an issue for them but whose death could destroy their careers. So Birney's argument touched on a point that had been key to the investigation: "There never was a case in which men agreed absolutely upon their testimony as to what occurred upon a given occasion when they were altogether," he declared. "Men do not see things at the same angle, men do not recall things in the same way. They forget; memory plays strange tricks."

Recounting some of the testimony, Birney noted that Bevan and Willing, "the two most important witnesses to the actual killing of Lieutenant Sutton," both saw "the flash of a pistol from the right hand of Lieutenant Sutton"; and Willing said he snatched the pistol from Sutton's grasp and "took it with his right hand as it lay there by his head." Even then, Birney protested, Davis had the nerve to "insult the intelligence of this Court by saying that the pistol was not fired from that hand." No court of criminal jurisdiction would tolerate Davis' claims. In fact, after hearing the testimony heard at this inquiry, *any* court would say, "'there is nothing here to be argued. Go free.' That is the situation."

Arthur Birney defended the Marine Corps officers well, using just the right language to reinforce the opinions of the 1907 investigation. In a forceful voice, he declared that Sutton, after all, was the one who committed the crime, any way you look at it. "Criminality! Wrong-doing! Upon whom does it rest, by all the testimony in this case? Upon Lieutenant Sutton, from first to last," Birney exclaimed. Besides, the attorney took on a reassuring tone as he again looked at the officers before him, "these gentlemen have mothers too. Their hearts have been made to bleed, their anxieties have been wrought to the point of desperation at these charges against their sons. They have been charged with crimes as heinous as any in the calendar." Why should they be accused when, "in spite of the lofty sentiments found in his letter to his brother, we find that [Sutton's] reputation was not what that letter indicates it ought to have been." Birney was careful not to get into Sutton's one poor fitness report from Benjamin Fuller; in civilian courts, that would be inadmissible evidence. But he found holes in any testimony made on behalf of the Sutton cause. "If I were to use a pet phrase of my friend, [Davis,] I should say that the evidence of guilt in this case does not rise to the dignity of suspicion." The only evidence worth mentioning, "heaven save the mark when I say evidence," allowed Birney, might be that of Dr. Schaeffer, but the attorney did not actually deal with Schaeffer's testimony except to make little of it; no man except one "fit for the insane asylum" could believe these defendants were guilty. Reasonable doubt was not even an issue.

The one thing Arthur Birney would concede was that possibly Sutton took his life "in the attempt to murder one of his associates." If Sutton had not been killed, he argued, he would be in a penitentiary for attempting to commit murder. If Mrs. Sutton is here to clear the memory of her son, and Davis is here "to clear the memory of Lieutenant Sutton from the infamy of suicide, you must find that Lieutenant Sutton met his death while criminally attempting to take the life of another." Either way he was guilty of self-murder. Birney did not give an inch. Practically every day, newspapers print stories of one man killing another and then turning the weapon on himself. So Birney's strategy was to leave the court with the image of Jimmie Sutton as an enraged young man, "driven to a pitch of insane fury at the moment he heard that Lieutenant Roelker was dead. . . . And there he was, in that condition of furious insanity which he had brought upon himself at that moment, and informed that that man who had been endeavoring to prevent him from doing this act, was lying dead beside him."

Addressing the court directly, he expressed confidence that it would see things his way, and he made a final plea on behalf of his clients. "If the regulations of the service permit you to do so, in your findings declare that there is not only no guilt upon their garments, nor blood upon their hands, but that there is absolutely nothing here to stain their honor or to discredit them" and, he added, no excuse or evidence for "the terrible charges that have been brought against them." Quite the contrary, Rosa Sutton had been pursuing them "for now nearly two years, pillorying them in the press, in spite of her denials of interviews, publishing them broadcast as criminals." The "accuser" (Birney almost never used her name) knew, "if she is sane, if she has the brains which the Almighty blessed her with at her birth, if she is rational, [then] she knew when she made these charges that she could not support them."

The marines' attorney closed, "glad of the opportunity" he had to work on behalf of "some of America's fine young men." He was also glad to have been able to take part in a case that "should relieve from discredit or dishonor officers in whose hands from time to time . . . will be the honor of their country." And then he left those in the courtroom with a barb at Davis. "I am glad to know that in this case there has been nothing developed out of anything except the imagination of my fertile-minded friend upon the other side, anything to indicate the commission here of any crime for which the naval service of the United States has any cause to be ashamed of its representatives who sit here."

When Arthur Birney sat down, it was close to three o'clock. The judge advocate kept the crowd—and the impatient reporters—together a few moments longer; it was his last chance to clear up any misconceptions the public might have about his own role in the case. He began with the observation that his remarks over the previous weeks had filled thirty-eight pages of the transcript, and though he was loath to say anything more, it would be "unworthy of my cloth" as the representative of the U.S. government if he did not comment further on Henry Davis' remarks. Leonard assured those present that the "facts are what the Government is after, and are what it has sought without sensation from the beginning of this case." And then, recalling Davis' comments about how inhospitably Mrs. Sutton and Mrs. Parker had been treated, Leonard said that he had come to aid the women in their search for facts and to help the defendants as well.

In an open show of partisanship, Leonard complained that, while the defendants that he was presumably there to prosecute ("not to persecute mind you but to prosecute") had laid all the facts they knew before him, Davis had been no help at all. On the contrary, Davis had even sullied the reputation of a helpless enlisted man [Sergeant De Hart], a man who "has no voice to lift, to protest against it." All the while Davis claimed to be "garbed in the ermine of judicial unbias." And now this man [De Hart] "must go forth from here charged with perjury, notwithstanding my learned brother's statement that the presumption of innocence rises to confront any man who charges another an[d] offers no proof." Finally, the judge advocate indicated that he had no personal knowledge of or interest in "that witness" [De Hart] except as a fellow officer.

Davis interrupted to assure the court that his criticisms had not been directed at Leonard. But the judge advocate had the last word and used the opportunity to go after Lieutenant Sutton and his mother in eloquent rhetoric. "If it please the Court, there are two aphorisms to which I desire to give utterance, and with that I leave the matter. One is, as counsel has well said, 'The wicked flee when no man pursueth.' ["But the righteous are bold as a lion" (Proverbs 28:1).] The other is, with Mr. Kipling, 'The clamor of the insolent accuser wastes the one hour we needed to make good.'"

The record of the proceedings of the fifteenth day of this inquiry was now read out loud and approved. Commander John Hood announced, "there being no further business before the Court in open session, it will now adjourn, to meet again in informal closed session, to prepare its finding." And at 3:35 p.m. military men and civilians left the auditorium for the last time—reporters and photographers doubtless moving toward the doors at a faster clip than anyone else in the room.

Rose Parker, quite alone in the courtroom with her family's attorneys, remained stoic and stared at the floor while Arthur Birney and Harry Leonard spoke. The morning session had been too much for her mother to bear. Rose may have been relieved that her mother had not heard Birney's attack on her integrity and her sanity, and Jimmie's character as well. Both women returned to Rosa's apartment at the Burlington where they could read about Birney's remarks in the Annapolis and Washington papers soon enough. Across America, reporters gave a blow-by-blow account of the bitter charges put forth by the attorneys. Davis was credited with a "masterly argument," Birney with "intense feeling" and a "surprising outburst of eloquence." Referring to the oratorical skill Henry Davis used in building up a monument of Adams' changed testimony, the *Washington Post* mentioned that Arthur Birney had ignored much of what Davis said and, in that way, gave the monument a "humorous tumble."

Rosa's family in Oregon would be pleased with Davis' defense and appalled by the story of Arthur Birney's "savage" attack that came out in the

Oregonian. Jim Sutton rarely remarked on the case, but several papers published his reaction to Birney's accusations. For the first time in public, he tried to lend some credibility to his wife's paranormal experiences. He chose this moment to describe how his wife, his oldest daughter, and his sister, Margaret Ainsworth, had indeed each seen his son in their dreams on Tuesday, October 15, 1907, wearing a white shirt. The women were nowhere near each other when Jimmie's ghost told them that he had been struck on the head with a gun. The incident made an indelible impression on his father. "So that even I, skeptical as to dreams and visions, perceived that my boy's spirit demanded that his memory be purged of the stain of taking his own life."

Jim Sutton continued, "The inquiry has shown that he was in his shirt sleeves and wore such a bandage when buried as my wife dreamed. If the Naval board does not at least admit he was no suicide, we will stop at nothing short of a congressional investigation." Rosa would, of course, agree with her husband. She also told the press she would carry the case further should the Department of the Navy conclude that her son committed suicide. If necessary, Rosa would not hesitate to keep her word.

14

THE COURT, THE CORPS, AND PUBLIC OPINION

The voluminous transcript of the Sutton court testimony was tangible proof that this time the navy had been thorough, but it was a lot to master. On Saturday, August 14, Commander John Hood took the unusual step of sending a copy to the acting secretary of the navy, Beekman Winthrop, before his court had deliberated. By then Herman Pechin and Frederic Irland from Smith and Hulse Law Reporters had typed 1,491 legal-sheet pages of testimony and closing arguments. With the added indexes and twenty-nine exhibits, the record was close to six inches thick; eventually, the navy would bind it in two volumes with chestnut-colored leather spines and stiff board covers. But on this first weekend after the inquiry, while Americans waited for the "great Sutton case" to be decided, an express messenger from Annapolis brought the bulky packages into the cavernous State, War, and Navy Department Building. Rosa Sutton's letters to Harry Swartz stayed with the transcript, as did Edward Schaeffer's drawings of a skull showing the trajectory of the bullet that allegedly killed her son.

Monday, August 16, began with such heavy rain that the streets in Annapolis flooded; on West Street, where William Owens worked, "the water was up to the horses knees in some places" (and surely covered the wheels of the auto that Owens drove). But after weeks of drought, farmers throughout Anne Arundel County were greatly relieved that at least some of their crops had been saved. That morning, John Hood, Wendell Neville, and Henry Norman Jensen, following navy regulations to the letter, met in private (possibly in the court-martial room in the Academy Administration Building where the parties had met on the first day) to consider all they had heard during the past month. Commander Hood had correctly forecast that it would not take long for the men to make up their minds. At 2:30 that afternoon, the court sent for its judge advocate, who had spent the weekend

241

in Washington; he would copy down their seven pages of Findings, Opinions, and Recommendations with a thick-nibbed fountain pen in black ink,
using his ornate longhand.

Major Harry Leonard returned to the nation's capital, guarded by a
Marine Corps sergeant, in order to present the material to Winthrop the
next morning. The navy secretary's views on the matter would be strongly
influenced by the advice of his judge advocate general, Edward H. Campbell, who trusted Leonard. The two navy attorneys met with Winthrop for
about an hour, at which point Captain Campbell took the papers back to
his office to make sure that proper procedures had been followed during the
inquiry and to prepare the Department's endorsement. Campbell assured
the press that he would devote much of Tuesday to mulling over the details,
and perhaps, to protect his court from pesky reporters, he insisted that its
members had been sworn to secrecy. Major Leonard was eager to return to
New Hampshire; he would send Campbell thirty-eight pages of excerpts of
his words from the transcript—a "compilation of the arguments in the Sutton case in order that should you desire to know at any time what was the
attitude of the Department's representative on any occasion you will not
have to go through the entire record." At the end of his note, he wrote
breezily, "*Au revoir*, very cordially, Henry Leonard."

Between August 14 and 18, reporters in Maryland and Washington, D.C.
(even more than elsewhere), engaged in speculation about what the navy's
conclusions might be and about the possible impact of various findings on
both parties involved. Interested readers now learned the rudiments of military justice, as they had just about everything else, from their newspapers.
Among the topics reviewed by the press were the following: what a Court
of Inquiry was (although this one had taken on several aspects of a trial);
how it worked; the role of the judge advocate general and the secretary of
the navy in final decisions; the rights of the Marine Corps defendants; and
the options available to Rosa Sutton. Because the two-year statute of limitations had not quite passed since Jimmie Sutton's death, the accused officers risked severe punishment. But at least one paper would boldly ask
whether they can be held as accessories to murder should Sutton be convicted of murdering himself. A widely expressed theory was that the court
would say Sutton caused his own death accidentally.

The *Washington Post* filled several inches of column space with commentary on the spiritual implications of another suicide finding after the reporter consulted with Catholic clergy. Mediation by the Church on behalf
of Sutton's soul was a possibility but unlikely; however, "the laws of the

church do undertake to enforce stern discipline among the living, and for that purpose the decisions of the regularly constituted courts are accepted" in order to "measure out judgment at the portals of yonder life." Because a coroner's verdict was a definitive guide for the Catholic Church on the cause of death, the *Post* stated, the decision of the 1907 Board of Inquest had been conclusive; Sutton's grave could only have been consecrated after the intervention of a bishop who believed the government had erred. But this time, the paper argued, if the finding was not suicide, the "churchly barrier to the hallowing of [Jimmie Sutton's] last resting place could be removed."

Readers in Maryland learned from their *Baltimore Sun* that many people in Annapolis regarded "the suicide theory" as "a joke, in the face of the fact that a man in an angry and fighting mood, such as Sutton is alleged to have been in, would never think of deliberately taking his own life." But most newspapers either suggested or stated that the navy would not attribute Sutton's death to any of the Marine Corps officers, even if their behavior had been reprehensible. Reporters correctly assumed that the speed with which the Department finished its discussions meant it was satisfied with the work of its court.

On Wednesday, August 18, immediately after the Department had signed off on the findings, a copy was sent to Henry Davis. The document began with a comment on the evidence the court had "carefully weighed." Given the two-year time gap and the "excitement under which the principal witnesses were laboring," the court acknowledged that the testimony is "peculiarly mixed and contradictory in details." Nevertheless, certain facts stood out, "clearly, distinctly, and beyond dispute or cavil." These facts were, first, that "a quarrel took place in which filthy language, unbecoming [to] an officer and a gentlemen, was used by Second Lieutenant Sutton towards Second Lieutenant [Robert] Adams in the presence of their senior, Lieutenant [Harold] Utley, about 1 a.m., 13 October 1907: that Lieutenants Utley and [Edward] Osterman intervened and prevented a fight."

Five more facts stood out. The second was that Sutton was the aggressor in the fight with Osterman. Third, the court found, in effect, that again Sutton was at fault and when "ordered under arrest by his senior officer, Lieutenant Utley, [he] failed to obey such [an] order, ran away to his, Sutton's, tent, threatening to shoot all present, and armed himself with two .38 caliber revolvers, one a Smith and Wesson commercial, and one a service Colt." The fourth fact established during the inquiry was that Sutton, when armed with these two revolvers, ran amok, "threatening all who came in sight, after first defying his senior officer, Lieutenant Utley, and the officer of the guard, Lieutenant [William] Bevan, who had also ordered him under arrest." A fifth conclusion of the court was that Lieutenant Harold Utley and Sergeant James De Hart should be credited for trying to persuade Sutton to disarm. And finally, when Sutton was "overpowered and thrown to the ground by Adams, [he] was killed by a revolver shot, from a service Colt revolver, held in his own right hand, and fired by himself, without the intervention of any other hand."

Henry Davis was no doubt disappointed, though he was probably not surprised. Just as Arthur Birney had done, the court ignored or dismissed his arguments and his witnesses—including William Owens. The testimony supporting the "facts" came only from the accused marines; of course, only they had been eyewitnesses to the final shot, although what they actually saw was hard to fathom. The reality was, in terms of hard evidence, that one could argue doubt existed on both sides of the case. But Davis read on. The court had been authorized to give its "Opinions" as well. The gist of these was that Lieutenants Utley, William Bevan, and Edward Willing failed in their duties that night for not disarming Sutton. Nevertheless, the court found "no possible charge of criminality lies against any of the participants in the fray except Lieutenant Sutton himself, and that Lieutenant Sutton is directly and solely responsible for his own death, which was self-inflicted, either intentionally or in an effort to shoot one of the persons restraining him, and his death was not caused by any other injury whatever." Its last opinion, directly aimed at Rosa Sutton, was the harshest by far, and it infuriated Henry Davis: "The charges of wilful murder and conspiracy to conceal it, made by the complainant Mrs. Sutton, mother of Lieutenant Sutton, are purely imaginary and unsupported by even a shadow of evidence, truth, or reason." Unkind, indeed, and a direct attack on Rosa's visions, but how could Davis prove this judgment wrong? Answering that question had been the Sutton family's dilemma for almost two years.

The one remaining task assigned to this court was to make recommendations for further action. Commander Hood, Wendell Neville, and Henry Jensen stated that, given their inexperience, no further proceedings should be taken against the marines. The document was signed by Commander Hood and Major Leonard. But it did not stand alone. Added to it was a two-page "Minority Report" written by the president (and hand copied by Leonard), in which Hood underscored the unacceptable conditions in the Marine Corps at the time of the Sutton incident. After agreeing with the report, Hood asserted, "Lieutenants Utley, Adams, Osterman, Willing and Bevan showed a deplorable lack of knowledge of their duties and obligations as officers holding commissions in the Marine Corps."

Hood argued vehemently "against the practice of commissioning, and putting into positions of responsibilities" young men without proper training. Moreover, he stated, "Lieutenants Willing, Bevan and Utley should have been brought to trial at the time for neglect of duty: and Lieutenants Adams and Osterman should have received milder punishments for engaging in a brawl unbecoming [to] officers and gentlemen." But no further proceedings would be taken against the officers because of "their youth and inexperience" and "because of their being in a sense, the victims of a system for which they themselves were not responsible."

Henry Davis could take some comfort in Commander Hood's words, which "stung the pride" of the Corps. When these documents were sent to the Navy Department, Beekman Winthrop added his own "thorough disapproval of the lax state of discipline" at the Marine Corps training school. This laxity, he wrote above his signature, had brought "serious discredit" on those in charge and "on the Marine Corps as a whole." Yet, he reportedly told the *Baltimore Sun*, while he was not concerned about whether or not Lieutenant Sutton intended to kill himself, his Department's "legal authorities" were convinced that the court's opinion "falls little short of declaring Sutton's death to have been the result of an accident."

But Winthrop also assured the public that he was confident the chaotic situation would not be repeated and that "splendid discipline prevails at this time." Immediately after Sutton died, discipline had been tightened up at the Marines Corps officer training school by Colonel Charles Doyen. "[Edward] Roelker was the first to get a lesson," said two Maryland newspapers, and he was dismissed by a court-martial. In 1908, the school had been relocated to Port Royal, South Carolina, and placed "under the direction of Lieutenant-Colonel Cole, who is regarded as an able officer." Although plans had reportedly been in the works to move the school for a number of years to provide better quarters for the student officers, more than one newspaper attributed its relocation directly to the Sutton tragedy. Once the school was no longer in Maryland, Charles Doyen's responsibility for it ended. But he remained in charge of the barracks and popular in Annapolis. The press said he was well respected by the Department as a "capable and efficient officer." Although Doyen would serve with distinction in World War I, the behind-the-scenes story at Marine Corps headquarters in Washington had been far more complicated between 1907 and 1909 than either reporters or Rosa Sutton's attorneys realized.

On August 18, Commandant George Elliott received a memorandum from the judge advocate general, Edward Campbell, officially dissolving the Sutton Court of Inquiry, information he received with considerable relief.

Elliott had found the case troubling all summer long. The intense public spotlight on his Corps only exacerbated his own serious personal and professional problems. He was almost sixty-three years old and had been commandant since October, 1903 (and major general since May 1908). His frequent headaches, ear pain, depression aggravated by drinking, and occasional explosive fits of anger had helped to create hostility between Elliott and his more reflective, scholarly adjutant and inspector. Charles Lauchheimer showed little respect for the commandant, gossiped about him behind his back with his subordinates, and most damaging of all, criticized Elliott in front of Massachusetts congressman John Weeks. Lauchheimer's close friendship with Weeks, a former Naval Academy classmate, not only irritated Elliott but also was symbolic of a larger problem in Washington—tight alliances between Marine Corps officers and politicians, such as the men who served on the House Committee on Naval Affairs. Their dispute would come to a head in the early spring of 1910.

A Court of Inquiry, with none other than Commander John Hood as its judge advocate, placed both men's behavior under scrutiny in March and April. In its Findings and Opinions, the court found that, dating back at least to 1907, there had been "an extraordinary lack of military discipline existing at the Headquarters," affecting "practically all the commissioned officers on duty there." Among the officers who received reprimands was Colonel Charles Doyen, Lauchheimer's "counsel," who gave "confusing and evasive testimony" about the adjutant and inspector's confrontation with his commandant—and who then acknowledged his own "ignorance of the proper customs of the service and the military respect and subordination due from a junior to a superior officer."

This leadership crisis at Eighth and I Streets may help to explain why so little about the marines' response to Sutton's death came out in the papers in 1907; the *Baltimore Sun* came up with its own theory about the matter. Elliott and other authorities had realized conditions were unacceptable after Sutton died, but they "kept quiet for the sake of the Corps, not wishing to subject the service to any further public scandal." Admiral Willard H. Brownson, commandant of midshipmen at the Naval Academy when Sutton, Edward Roelker, and Utley were there had "concurred in this view." And so, said the paper, had Navy Secretary Victor Metcalf. "Personally and quietly many other officers admitted this, and secretly blamed the authorities for 'not cleaning out the Marine School.'" The authorities, had, however, made sure the school would never again be located in Annapolis.

The tensions at Corps headquarters did not trouble Charles Doyen nearly as much as the far more public Minority Report Commander Hood added to the Findings in the Sutton case. Hood's document led the Department of the Navy to send letters of censure to the men who made up the hierarchy of command at the Marine Application School on the night Sutton died: Charles Doyen, Benjamin Fuller, Edward Willing, William Bevan, and Harold Utley. These letters would remain in the officers' files for the remainder of their careers, to be reassessed each time they came up for promotion. Both Doyen and Fuller tried to have the blot created by the Sutton case removed from their records. They were assured by the navy that the censure implied disapprobation, not a punishment. But, particularly for Charles Doyen, the Department's letter was unacceptable. And his response to it reveals a great deal about the inner workings of military justice.

He received the letter on August 20, on the same day the *Baltimore Sun* published its lengthy analysis of the case. The Department placed the responsibility for the poor state of discipline at the school squarely on the "lack of vigilance" and "direct personal supervision" by Colonel Doyen. Possibly because of his many prior health problems, Doyen was intensely anxious about his own standing in the Corps. His extreme defensiveness in this instance may help to explain why he had been so willing to publicize what his students said about Sutton's character and suicide. Admitting that his military reputation was "one of his most prized possessions," Doyen wrote, the court and the Department had unjustly assailed it "to the service and the country at large." He protested this censure repeatedly until 1914, often in eloquent language, but never with the results that he hoped for. After his initial brief response, he laid out all his objections to the Department in a twenty-four-page memorandum on September 16, 1909. Colonel Doyen decided that the censure had, in effect, made him a defendant and that, consequently, the navy had disregarded his constitutional rights and "ignored the instructions" contained in Charles Lauchheimer's Forms of Procedure "by which it should have been guided"—for example, "at no time was he called before the Court and informed that a *prima facie* case had been made against him." Reaching outside the realm of military law for a remedy, Doyen cited part of the Sixth Amendment to the Constitution, which states that in all criminal prosecutions "'the accused shall be informed of the nature and cause of the accusation, be confronted by witnesses against him, . . . have compulsory process for obtaining witnesses in his favor, [and] have the assistance of counsel for his defense.'" And, Doyen underscored, "it is therefore submitted *as a conclusion of law that the minority opinion of the Court is unconstitutional, illegal, and void, and should have been disregarded by the Department."*

Colonel Doyen also asserted that discipline at his school had been under control except for the night of the fatal brawl. After all, the "officers were but a few months in the service, unaccustomed to military discipline and restraint," and extreme measures would not have been appropriate. His men should be forgiven for their error of judgment; when confronted "by a man in an abnormal mental condition," they acted just as civilians "would have been legally justified to do." (Colonel Doyen had given Robert Adams, Harold Utley, and Edward Willing excellent ratings on their fitness reports for the period between July and December 1907, making no mention of the tragedy.) Doyen closed by noting that no one had brought these accusations against him two years earlier. In fact, he said, no one had accused the superintendent of the Naval Academy of poor control over discipline when James Branch died after his fight with Minor Meriwether Jr., a matter that "was aired in the public press almost as widely as was the Sutton incident."

Charles Doyen was not above trying to pull political strings himself when his reputation was at stake. Congressman John Weeks, chairman of the Committee on Expenditures in the State Department, was not only an ally of Charles Lauchheimer; Colonel Doyen was also a former classmate and, according to Weeks, one of his "oldest and best friends in the service." The congressman was obviously loyal to his Marine Corps comrades. On September 21, he wrote to the Department of his "unqualified confidence" in Doyen's "military capacity" and said, "[I] know that he has borne the reputation, from that view point, of being one of the best officers in the Marine Corps." The congressman requested that Secretary George Von Lengerke Meyer give the matter his personal attention before making a decision on the "fairness of the censure" against Doyen caused by the Sutton inquiry.

The Department's response to Charles Doyen's request was to define the nature of the court itself: "A Court of Inquiry does not perform any real judicial function and its proceedings were not a trial in any sense, but merely an investigation." But the court did have the power to render an opinion on collateral matters, not just the main facts revealed in the evidence. And one matter was clearly the state of discipline at the Application School. Nevertheless, Charles Doyen continued to protest with lengthy correspondence until February 1914 when Acting Secretary of the Navy Franklin D. Roosevelt turned him down.

The pivotal role of the media and public opinion in Doyen's, and the navy's, perception of the Sutton case stands out in this correspondence. On

February 17, 1913, Doyen told the secretary of the navy that he had waited to protest further for "public interest to die out" and hoped "to avoid any possible further embarrassment to all parties concerned by keeping [public interest] agitated." And again in March, he complained that the 1909 reprimand had been "published in the press throughout the country to his official detriment and personal humiliation." Doyen remained quite outraged that he had not been given a right to produce evidence on his own behalf to counter the censure. Finally, in August of 1913, he took a new tack, suggesting to Navy Secretary Josephus Daniels that the injustice done to him in 1909 had been inadvertent on the part of the inexperienced judge advocate general (Campbell), and the newly appointed assistant secretary of the navy (Winthrop), who naturally acted on his JAG's recommendation. The colonel included a strong accusation in this letter—one that corroborates the *Baltimore Sun*'s impressions of the case: "The Department has refused to acknowledge its error because if it became known that there was any irregularity in any part of the proceedings of the [Sutton] Court or the Department's action there on [*sic*]; the case which had already become embarrassing to the Department, by congressional action and the newspapers, would become still more so." Still, the reprimand stayed with his record.

Benjamin Fuller, who was serving at Camp Elliott in Panama during the Sutton inquiry, received a censure for his "inadequate disciplinary action" when Lieutenant Sutton fired his revolver in camp. Major Fuller also asked that his censure be removed, though he did not become obsessive about it. And when his initial request was denied, he too sent a longer explanation— four pages, not twenty-four—for his actions. Like Colonel Doyen, he resented being made a party to the inquiry with no chance to defend himself before a judgment was made. Fuller wrote that in May 1907 Sutton had only been on duty for thirty-three days and had "shown no inclination toward serious misbehavior." Sutton had hardly shot up the camp; he was "somewhat under the influence of liquor," had shot his gun off in the air a few times to make noise, and threatened the other officers with an "entirely unloaded" pistol. "The next morning he expressed contrition for his conduct and on account of his youth, his having just begun his military service, and as it was his first offence, he was admonished and suspended from duty for ten days." That, Fuller argued, "was the severest punishment that I was authorized to inflict." A court-martial had not been warranted, and "considering the conduct of Lieutenant Sutton was very good from that time until the 13th of October it is not clear that any punishment short of dismissal would have had a greater effect than did the suspension." Unlike the other officers at the inquiry, Fuller had given Sutton the benefit of the doubt. Fuller was convinced that the two-year statute of limitations for disciplinary action had run out by August of 1909. Beekman Winthrop informed him that the censure was merely a statement of disapproval and said the Department has the "undoubted power to criticize adversely the conduct or procedure of any subordinate officer. The incident is considered closed." With that definitive response, the future commandant let the matter die.

Neither the American people nor Henry Davis had any inkling of these complex internal politics at Marine Corps Headquarters. But reporters did have easy access to Henry Davis' response to the navy's opinions and recommendations. Davis declared, with a touch of irony, that the findings were "all that could have been expected from the manner in which the investigation was conducted by Major Leonard." He thought the case might continue in a civil court, "which makes the inquiry a mere curtain raiser to the main performance." Rosa Sutton's attorney actually had quite a bit to say, and his lengthiest response came out in the Washington *Evening Star* on August 20. Davis was not fighting to save his own reputation as much as he was appalled by the injustice of it all. His decision to make a public statement was motivated by his genuine concern that "those who know only so much of the case as the press has found it possible to publish may be led to think that the determination of a body of officers in the military service of the country must be a righteous result." Chastising Major Leonard for being "derelict in his duty" and for his "eminently unjudicial" language, he examined each of the court's conclusions and reiterated many of the arguments he had presented in his closing remarks. Davis again stressed the irregularities that occurred when Leonard put a devoted mother on the stand and presented her personal letters to Swartz to the court. He also referred to Robert Adams with no ambiguity: "The significance of the fact that Lieutenant Adams, the only witness who stated that he saw Sutton in the act of shooting himself, identifies the Smith and Wesson [the smaller gun] as the revolver used by Sutton in the alleged act [of suicide], is too obvious for comment." Moreover, Davis claimed, only Lieutenants Adams and Willing were in a position to have had this smaller gun and then given it to James De Hart who was so uncomfortable that he tossed it into the grass.

Strong public reaction to the Department's findings was not confined to Henry Davis. Millions of Americans found the full text in their papers; soon afterward they could read the response of the parties to the inquiry, and in several cities, newspapers published editorials on the case. Rose Parker remained circumspect when the "verdict" was read to her, saying "that is rather rough isn't it? . . . but I cannot say that I am surprised." Then she added, "Neither my mother nor I can say anything about the matter at this time." Across a continent, Jim Sutton vowed that the family would continue its fight. According to the *Washington Post*, he saw the verdict as a "whitewash." "'I realized,'" he said, "'when we entered upon our efforts to obtain a rehearing into the death of my son, that we were up against a stone wall. I believe three important facts have been brought out by the investigation, however. First, that they were unable to prove my son a suicide; second, that the investigation proved to be a farce; and, third, that the affairs in the Marine Corps at Annapolis as conducted are in a deplorable condition and should be investigated.'" That same Thursday, the *Oregonian* quoted him as saying, "the great mass of Americans" is satisfied that Jimmie did not commit suicide; "We have made [the navy] sit up and maybe we will make them sit up a little more."

Arthur Birney was jubilant and found the court's conclusions to be exactly what they should have been, though he no doubt was less pleased with Hood's Minority Report. Reportedly, he met with the accused marines right after court adjourned. The young officers decided not to bring a suit against the Sutton family for the unjust treatment they had received. Both Robert Adams and his brother had already told the press they thought the inquiry was a "useless waste of time." Harold Utley may have felt the same way, but he would need to reassure his mother when she learned that he had received a censure and "failed in his duty as senior officer present." As for Edward Roelker, he had still not turned up. Thankfully, his family's response to their own tragedy remained out of the harsh glare of publicity.

President Taft had been informed of the decision at his summer home in Beverly, Massachusetts, before it was made public. On August 18, the *Baltimore Sun* speculated as to why: either the Navy Department wanted to be sure the president was comfortable with another suicide verdict "so that Mrs. Sutton might not bring political pressure to bear through the President for further action," or so that Taft could "anticipate any political or legislative movement in Congress to force a court-martial of the other officers present." The following day, the *Sun* learned that, as far as the Annapolis Sutton case was concerned, the president would rely on the Navy Department. "Most of his information concerning it thus far has come from the newspapers. He commented today upon the public interest in it, as indicated by the reading matter and pictures of the principles printed." But it had not been before him for any action; "If it should come up it would be treated as are all breaches of military discipline upon which the action of the president is required."

America's self-conscious press corps had generated interest in the case for weeks, and several papers now published their own opinions about the inquiry—often correctly reassuring their readers that Rosa Sutton's battle was not yet over. In its exhaustive commentary, the *Baltimore Sun* considered the options available to her. On August 20, the *Sun* delved into other repercussions of the tragedy, placing it in the context of long-standing tensions in Annapolis among marines and midshipmen. But the friction that resulted in Lieutenant Sutton's death had more to do with the internal dynamics of his particular Marine Corps class than the marines' rivalry with Academy men in 1907.

Editorial comments could be slipped into news stories; more formal editorials came out in a number of papers and the *Army and Navy Journal*. A contemporary journalism handbook described the power of early twentieth-century editors in language especially suited to the story:

> The official known as the editor-in-chief is in command of every department outside of the business management and mechanical production of the paper. . . . He is, theoretically, at least, the supreme authority, the court of appeal, and the court of final resort, subject only to the owners of the newspaper, who make the policy. Occasionally he is the principal owner, or one of the owners, or indirectly represents the owners, in which case he is, in fact, general in command of the journalistic army under him.

In Philadelphia, this "general in command" of the *Inquirer*, or at least one of his editorial writers, thought the case came to "a most lame and impotent conclusion" because the naval inquiry had tried to avoid "any damaging discoveries"; Major Leonard had shown bias throughout the proceedings and clearly thought that in 1907 Sutton "got no more than he deserved and that this attempt to place the responsibility for his death was in the nature of an outrage. It was an attempt with which he had not the slightest sympathy and its failure he made it evident he would welcome." The court had ignored unfavorable testimony, and although the *Inquirer* praised the Minority Report of Commander Hood, "upon the whole the Sutton inquiry will not increase the respect of the public for trials of this class."

To the *Washington Post*, the court's position seemed "the logical determination." Sympathy was expressed for the "bereaved and distressed mother" because the American people "will not too promptly forgive the behavior of the officers." Moreover, the paper said, the "Sutton case should be taken to heart by the whole Marine Corps, and the unfortunate circumstances be ever in the mind as a warning to those who think lightly of the responsibility of the uniform." The *Army and Navy Journal* also stated that the findings were "a logical deduction from the evidence presented" and applauded the court for not being distracted by the "chicanery of lawyers or the abuse indulged in by plaintiff's counsel." Major Leonard had also "acquitted himself with credit." In Hartford, Connecticut, a brief editorial comment in the *Courant* was rough on Rosa Sutton for denouncing the Court of Inquiry (something her attorney did but that, in fact, Rosa was apparently careful not to do).

The *New York Times* saw the verdict as "UNSATISFACTORY BECAUSE IN-CONCLUSIVE." "After it was revealed that Mrs. Sutton 'knew' her son was murdered by certain fellow officers of his in the Marine Corps because his ghost had appeared to her and told her so, and that she had practically no other evidence to present," the verdict was "almost inevitable." But, the editor wrote, the findings were unsatisfactory, "as the determination of such bodies so often are to civilian minds." The paper did not question the intentions of the members of the court, though "military law has its own method of procedure as well as its own objects," but, the *Times* conceded, even though "we are to understand that the discipline of the corps and that of the Marine School of Application has now been reformed and safeguarded," action was not taken against the men present, leaving the public with an inadequate verdict and an excuse for "turning to other arbiters in search of justice." The implications of this last remark, in terms of the public's stake in the case, were clear.

Editorial comment in the Oregon press spanned a range of issues and viewpoints. The *Oregon Daily Journal* had made up its mind, even before the attorneys gave their closing arguments. In a one-line "Comment," the paper said, "The suicide theory in the Sutton case is preposterous." Once the verdict came out, the paper assured its readers that a "wave of protest in the country over" would result and that in Washington, D.C., the "almost unanimous sentiment" was that the navy's conclusions would "mightily injure the military arm of the government." But the more reserved *Oregonian* saw the inquiry as a mixed blessing because it exposed appalling behavior on behalf of young Sutton and his compatriots. While the naval investigation had certainly disappointed the Sutton family, the editor suggested, perhaps it would convince Congress to remove Sutton's companions from the Corps and take the authorities to task. The family's efforts are "bound to work for the improvement of the Marine School and better conduct of the Marine Corps." For "there is no place for carousing and combat within the military and the marine service." Certainly all of Jimmie Sutton's friends and relatives who saw the editorial could agree with that.

They could also think about the aggressive role of the press corps in the case, should they happen to read the *Portland Evening Telegram*. This verdict, the editor wrote, would "arouse deep and widespread indignation." At first the case attracted very little notice. But soon it was clear that there was an attempt "to suppress evidence that might lead to the bringing forth of the truth, regardless of whom it helped or harmed." During the inquiry, which the paper called the trial,

> this opinion became more deep-seated, and what was at first suspicion in the end became conviction that the court was not going to give the Sutton family a square deal, but that it was going to shield at all hazards the "officers and gentlemen" who participated, as most people now believe, with murderous effect, at that last fatal and disgraceful orgy. The verdict which is today officially announced emphasizes in the most extraordinary way this popular conviction.

Noting that the Sutton family had already spent $10,000 (other sources would suggest more), the *Telegram* had strong ideas about the next step for journalists. The Suttons have "gained enormously in the fact that the popular verdict is decisively in their favor." There is no way, the editor declared, that Sutton could have "killed himself while lying on his face, with two men sitting on him and his arms beneath him." Looking at the armed forces as a whole, "who see themselves as an aristocracy in a class by themselves," the *Telegram* suggested that some of the inferior officers' testimony had "been tampered with and co-erced. The straight story was not allowed to come out." And, "the public is afraid that the same standard exists among older officers as prevailed among the young officers. Therefore what is needed is an investigation that will go to the bottom of things." Obviously, it could not be conducted at private expense. And so, the editor proclaimed, "an agitation should be begun by the American press" to call for a congressional investigation into "the conduct and standards of all our military institutions of training and learning." Rosa Sutton would certainly take these sentiments to heart.

Further editorial comment was stirred up by the investigation of Don Sutton's injuries at West Point—a situation that President Taft had been involved in once the army's lengthy investigation ended. These elaborate proceedings had been conducted without eager reporters clustered in the court-martial room. Still the papers had published whatever they could find out during the summer of 1909. Two days after the Annapolis Sutton verdict became public, President Taft dismissed seven cadets from West Point for the hazing incident. Across the United States, Taft's decision made the headlines. But Rosa Sutton had tried to stay out of the New York investigation, at her son's suggestion. In fact, she had expressed her sorrow for the boys who attacked Don at West Point, saying it was too bad "their punishment should be so severe." She also told the *New York Times* that letters from Don indicated that he "is getting along splendidly."

Some members of the press were less charitable to the perpetrators than Rosa. A year earlier, not long before Rosa Sutton had arrived in Washington to make her case, President Theodore Roosevelt reversed himself and reinstated several West Point cadets who had been dismissed for hazing. This action had undermined the authority of Military Academy Superintendent Hugh Scott who, along with several members of Congress, had fought fiercely against hazing. Roosevelt's actions had "struck a blow at discipline in the Academy from which its friends feared that it would never recover. As commander in chief of the army, Mr. Roosevelt did more to demoralize it by autocratic decree and flagrant favoritism than all the presidents who preceded him." Calling Roosevelt's actions a "wretched farce," the New York *Sun* and the *Newburgh Daily News* complemented William Howard Taft for his action in Don Sutton's case. And, on August 21, in a piece titled "ARMY AND NAVY ETHICS," *Post-Dispatch* readers in Saint Louis read that dismissing "the guilty West Point cadets was the only possible punishment short of incarceration for assault." Even if the verdict from Annapolis was correct, "the people are privileged to know if they are maintaining bullies and brawlers in their training schools." What has happened to cause such "moral deterioration of picked men?" Hopefully, the paper stated, these are only "instances of individual misguidedness."

The Department of the Navy's conclusions about the death of Lieutenant Sutton moved a number of citizens to write to public figures. It is impossible to tell how many of these letters were sent, but the handwritten letters that survive in one Sutton case file represent the unfiltered voices of Americans, some more well educated than others, but all passionate about what they had learned from their newspapers. They wrote the judge advocate, the secretary of the navy (or the secretary of war), and even the court directly. One New York businessman who had tried to obtain a copy of the transcript took it upon himself to mail Navy Secretary George Meyer some sample editorials, claiming to have nearly "a hundred others" that he would send the Naval Affairs Committee when Congress convened. "The editorials in all the papers of the country must convince the Government that the people are not satisfied with the decision of the court of inquiry," he wrote.

On the day of the court's decision, Thomas Donally, a New Yorker living at 202 East 31 Street, demanded to know "how you have the Bare face to publish before this world that James N. Sutton met his death by accidental shooting or by suicide when it has been proven in court that those who were his enemies committed scornful murder is it to befriend them because they were his enemies and to hide their crime that you are trying to conceal." Another man, James Wallace, "One of the citizens of the U.S.A.," respectfully sent his concerns to Major Leonard. Wallace was positive that the inquiry had proven that Sutton had been murdered and that facts had been suppressed by the officers involved and by cowardly higher officials. The United States and the public had, in effect, been betrayed, and "it's specifically proven that several officers—lately called defendants—ought to be in jail or on the gallows but not parading as U.S. officers of the navy." "It will be a good thing," Wallace wrote, "to have the matter placed before Congress." If the officers were not expelled from the navy, he warned, "you will see how the citizens will take it up and how they will get rid of such scoundrels."

On August 18, Frank White wrote to the secretary of the navy from Brooklyn, New York, to express his dismay at the "whitewash," obvious to "all fair minded people" and an insult to their intelligence. "I haven't met a single man that does not believe that Lieutenant Sutton was murdered and I fail to see according to the evidence as published in the papers how any unbiased person could come to any other conclusion." Discipline must be enforced to "protect the Honor of the American Navy and the men who enlist under its banner from murder." Secretary Meyer [Beekman Winthrop was acting secretary] received a more empathetic but equally concerned response from a New Yorker who called himself (or herself) "Justice." This citizen, who also claimed to speak for many people, had "studied the case in all its aspects" and had the optimism to think his or her voice could make a difference. "You acted as a very just man when you ordered the reopening of the Sutton case," the letter began,

> and nine people out of ten . . . are of the opinion that the decision of the Court should not meet with your approval—You hear on all sides in the case, in the cities, on the streets, that it is a case of whitewash . . . the officers of the Court acted as if they were said attorneys for the accused. It is strongly, almost unniversally [sic] in the public mind, that after following the evidence as presented to the Court, that young Sutton was done to death by the coterie of officers accused.

The letter writer urged that the men be dismissed from the service and (agreeing with Rosa's theory) said that they had not intended to kill her son but "having done so by brutal treatment, the shot was fired into the head to cover up their crime."

Finally, Howard England, "a citizen of the United States and a Priest of the American Episcopal Church" (St. Paul's Church in Washington) emphatically protested "against the outrageous decision." Once again the newspapers were the source of his irate response.

> I read all the evidence as presented through the daily papers, and the harsh and unreasonable language as used in the decision was certainly uncalled for, to say the least. A majority of the people I talk with think young Sutton was deliberately killed, and the Department is bringing discredit upon the Government and the service in trying to whitewash these ruffian officers. The whole affair is disgraceful.

These Americans' patriotism, and their sense that they spoke for a large number of their fellow citizens, is clear. But loyal navy men understandably had concerns that the press coverage had not always been fair, and civilians were not always sure which branch of the military was involved in the Sutton case. An *Army and Navy Journal* editorial stated bluntly that there was nothing the Marine Corps training school had in common with the Naval Academy and that neither the army nor the navy could be held responsible for the officers' behavior "whether commendable or otherwise." A Naval Academy alumnus (Class of 1880) with similar sentiments strongly objected to the suggestion that the Sutton case had "anything whatever to do with the United States Naval Academy." He thought that misconceptions stemmed from the fact that many men who had "fallen by the wayside" at the Academy secured appointments "through political influence or otherwise" as second lieutenants in the Marine Corps. The true story was, of course, more complicated than either of these writers realized. Of the four men in the Marine Application School Class of 1908 who had spent time at the Naval Academy, Jimmie Sutton was now dead, Edward Roelker had disappeared, and a third, Harold Utley, now censured, was the officer Rosa Sutton had once accused of masterminding the brawl that led to her son's death.

One other marine connected to the Sutton case who had disappeared from the news by the early fall of 1909 had been the subject of some curious correspondence before the inquiry began. On July 2, Beekman Winthrop sent a note to Pennsylvania governor Edwin S. Stuart in Robert Adams' home town of Harrisburg. "I am in receipt, by reference from the President, of your communication of June 28, in the interest of Mr. Harry M.

Swartz, who is taking the examination for entrance to the U S Marine Corps as a second lieutenant." Winthrop said he would forward the governor's letter about Swartz's promotion to the Marine Examining Board. A month later, Pennsylvania congressman Thomas S. Butler, then chairman of the Committee on Pacific Railroads, sent a telegram to Winthrop expressing his own great interest "in the success of Harry M. Swartz" in his effort to receive a Marine Corps commission, and Butler wrote, "[I] will be indebted to you for anything that you may be able to do for him." Unfortunately for him, Swartz failed the Marine Corps exams in mathematics, history, and geography, leaving Winthrop with no other options to help him. Butler thanked the secretary for his efforts, saying he had known Swartz for some time, and he would have made an efficient officer. "For this reason, I interested myself in his behalf."

On August 11, the *Washington Post* reported that Harry Swartz admitted he had tried unsuccessfully to secure a promotion in the Marine Corps. But he insisted no one had promised him anything in exchange for turning over Rosa's letters to the government. Although the paper did not look into the matter further, the fact that Swartz's efforts began just as the navy organized the second Sutton inquiry seems an unlikely coincidence. And Pennsylvania's governor and its congressman, Thomas Butler, had reason to be grateful to Swartz. After all, distinguished Pennsylvania politicians had enthusiastically endorsed two of the defendants in the Sutton case when they first applied for the Corps: Edward Willing and Robert Adams, the latter's connections going all the way to the governor's mansion. At the beginning of the twentieth century, as events would demonstrate even more clearly in the coming months, Washington was still a very small town.

15

JIMMIE SUTTON'S
BODY AND SOUL

Rosa Sutton may have said little to the press after the Navy Department announced its findings, but she remained focused on her sacred mission. On August 21, she wrote to the highest official of the Roman Catholic Church in the United States. She addressed His Eminence with a self-confident tone, without the appropriate formality and, as usual, did not pause for much punctuation:

> Dear Cardinal Gibbons
>
> In view of the evidence produced will you instruct or give your consent to Rev Father Griffith of St Augustines Church to consecrate my sons grave? Please let me hear from you at once as I am leaving the City and this must be done on Wednesday next Hoping God will give me the strength to stand all this sorrow I am your obedient child
>
> Rosa B Sutton Aug 21st 1909—"The Burlington"
>
> P.S. I might add I have not consulted Father Griffith but I know he <u>does not</u> think my son was a suicide

When he heard from Rosa Sutton, seventy-five-year-old James Cardinal Gibbons had long since reached the pinnacle of his career; in the summer of 1909, he was the only American cardinal. A former Civil War pastor and army chaplain, Gibbons had been the archbishop of Baltimore since 1877 and a member of the College of Cardinals since 1886. On his death in 1921, the unprecedented outpouring of condolences from all over the globe gave credence to the *New York Times*' assessment: that he was, indeed, "one of the wisest men in the world." The *New York Herald* echoed this praise: "In the sense that Francis of Assisi is everybody's saint, James Gibbons

*James Cardinal Gibbons, ca. 1907. Portrait by
Bachrach. Courtesy of the Associated Archives at St.
Mary's Seminary and University, Baltimore, Md.*

was everybody's Cardinal," and regardless of their beliefs, Americans held the
cardinal "in the highest respect and esteem." These Americans included both
Presidents Roosevelt and Taft. Theodore Roosevelt told Cardinal Gibbons
he was "'the most respected, and venerated, and useful citizen of our country.'" Pope Leo XIII was so pleased with the growth of the American
Catholic Church under Gibbons' tenure that he wrote to him, "'the state of
your churches . . . cheers Our heart and fills it with delight.'"

Intensely patriotic, the cardinal was deeply committed to American
values—chief among them its constitutional government that guaranteed
personal liberties, including freedom of religion. A tolerant man and a
peacemaker among immigrant Catholic groups, the cardinal represented the
American Catholic Church to the world at large. Despite some small foibles,
Gibbons was never aloof or arrogant. Those who knew him admired his
character, his unassuming nature, and his simplicity. He never rode when he
could walk and always showed "intense interest in people no matter what

their station in life." A century ago, he was the "public face of the American Church," a "small, neat man, his silver hair perfectly in place, he seemed always gracious, never pompous, impeccably conservative, but instinctively fair." In other words, he had exactly the empathetic qualities that could benefit Rosa Sutton.

Cardinal Gibbons' views on most matters with moral, spiritual, and even political import were widely covered in the news throughout his long tenure from 1886 until his death at eighty-seven. In 1908, for example, the *New York Times* reported his concern that the people of America showed "less respect for religion than fifty or sixty years ago," and statesmen rarely cited the scriptures as they had in the past. Fully aware of reporters' power to inform and motivate citizens on a daily basis, Gibbons welcomed press coverage of his speeches and activities; newspapers, he thought, were ideal mediums to be put to use for the benefit of religion. In *The Ambassador of Christ*, Gibbons suggested his priests look for ways to make the press serve the Church because so many people regarded it as an "oracle" that "went far toward molding the opinion and forming the judgment of millions who had only a vague idea of Christianity."

Not surprisingly, Rosa Sutton's request to Cardinal Gibbons intrigued reporters. Between August 24 and August 26, a flurry of articles came out in Baltimore and Washington with conflicting information about the timing of the cardinal's response. The *Washington Post* and the *Evening Star* both claimed (apparently in error) that Gibbons was in Portland, Oregon, when Rosa wrote him and had consulted with Jim Sutton. Given the exhaustive coverage of the case in Gibbons' "favorite paper," the *Baltimore Sun*, there is no doubt that he was familiar with her story and with "the evidence" she referred to in her letter. But the chancellor of the archdiocese of Baltimore, Reverend P. C. Gavan, told the *Sun* on the night of August 25 that His Eminence was "in retreat at St. Mary's Seminary with the secular clergy" and had not yet responded to Rosa's request, which he had received a few hours before beginning the retreat.

But by the time Reverend Gavan's comment came out, papers in Washington, Baltimore, Annapolis, and Portland had already announced that Rosa had been granted her wish. Apparently satisfied that her son had not taken his own life, at least not intentionally, Cardinal Gibbons brought immense joy to Rosa Sutton. Gibbons was a savvy politician who knew how caught up his own flock had been in Mrs. Sutton's spiritual dilemma. Regardless of his reasons, and there may have been more than one, it was thanks to His Eminence that preparations could finally begin for Rosa's son to lie in consecrated ground. He would, however, need to contact the bishop of Virginia, who had jurisdiction over such matters in Arlington Cemetery.

"Victory has come to Mrs. Sutton at last," the *Washington Post* declared in a long article reassuring its readers that a mother's heart had finally been "softened by gladsome tidings." The *Post* then touched on another equally intriguing topic that had preoccupied the press during the week after the inquiry; Rosa Sutton wanted to see her son. Her success, according to the reporter, now came on two fronts: "The happiness which came suddenly and like a ray of sunlight through a cloud was increased twofold yesterday by the war department which has jurisdiction over the National Cemetery at Arlington, where the slain officer is buried, granting permission to have the body exhumed and an autopsy performed." The article continued with the same dramatic prose: "Mrs. Sutton and her daughter, Mrs. Parker, who has been her staff during the siege of sorrow and battle for a dead son and brothers' name and memory, in their hour of happiness have not laid aside their armor or in any way given up the struggle to put before the world all the facts concerning the death of lieutenant Sutton on that memorable night of October 13, 1907."

And so, for Rosa, two goals could now be accomplished at once. For almost two years she had been convinced that someone representing the family should examine Jimmie's remains. During the inquiry her views had hardened, and her mission transformed—it was no longer exclusively a spiritual one. (If that had been the case, the support of Cardinal Gibbons would have satisfied her.) Rosa had been ridiculed by the naval court, her sanity and integrity questioned in a public forum. Perhaps the most devastating insult was Arthur Birney's contention that her crusade was an insult to American motherhood. Now, more than ever, she hoped to find concrete proof of what so many people believed and what Jimmie's ghost had told her. At least she might show the world that he was badly beaten and perhaps that his right arm was broken. An autopsy might even demonstrate that the bullet came from too far away for a suicide or that he had died from other wounds.

But it was Washington in August, and it turned out that Rosa would have to exercise some patience. Many high-ranking officials were away, and even Henry Davis planned to take a vacation. Davis had written the quartermaster general for permission to exhume Sutton's remains on August 20; within three days authorization came through from the War Department, accompanied by detailed instructions for a very private exhumation— anyone who leaked information about it to the public or the press would face "peremptory dismissal" from the service. But then the matter became more complicated—"certain questions having arisen"—and on the 25th, army captain and quartermaster Evan Humphrey wrote to Mrs. Sutton a second time, confirming what she had learned in a telephone call that morning: the Department had decided to postpone granting her request. It was an awkward situation for the government agencies involved; bureaucratic debates over details such as where the autopsy would take place and who would be in charge continued for two weeks. At all times great respect was shown for Mrs. Sutton, who was still staying at the Burlington.

Initially, the navy hoped that surgeon Raymond Spear would oversee the autopsy and potentially the dissection of Lieutenant Sutton's remains; the assumption was that his body would be sent to the anatomical room at the Naval Medical School Hospital at the foot of 24th Street in Georgetown for a medico-legal examination. Both Secretary of the Navy Meyer and Secretary of War Jacob Dickinson were out of town, and according to the *Evening Star* on August 25, "The officers in charge do not care to assume full responsibility in the case," which "has assumed national importance." Planning the exhumation attracted the constant scrutiny of the press. Between August 20 and September 10, reporters undoubtedly annoyed the men trying to arrange this delicate procedure in the most efficient way possible. A dispatch from Washington in the *Oregonian* said that publicity had been the reason for the delay to begin with. Rosa Sutton, now a veteran at using the press, discussed every communication she received from the army and the navy, and shared her dismay at the sudden delay in the exhumation.

Once the army consented, the acting judge advocate general, Henry Morrow, decided it would only be fair to have the accused officers represented, "considering that their own liberty and possibly their own lives might be at stake as the result of this investigation." But the marines waived their right to be present and approved an order to have navy surgeon Raymond Spear stand in for them. Spear, whose medical degree was from Jefferson Medical College in Philadelphia, was thirty-six in 1909 and a career navy doctor. On June 22, 1900, he had been promoted to passed assistant surgeon; three years later he received his commission as a surgeon. A navy press release written when he died stated that Captain Spear, who served on board numerous ships and at the Naval Hospital, "was one of the outstanding Surgeons in the Medical College of the Navy." Dr. Spear was to "make such examination and report as may be possible without in any way touching the remains, as it is not considered desirable for any person in the Navy to in any way lay hands upon them." Finally, by the second week of

September, the acting secretary of war, Robert Shaw Oliver, and the navy secretary, Beekman Winthrop, signed off on a new date requested by Henry Davis—September 13. The procedure would take place in a storehouse behind the elegant, historic Lee Mansion that stood high on a hill overlooking the Potomac River.

Rosa Sutton, meanwhile, had found "one of the best-known surgeons of Washington" willing to examine Jimmie's remains. George Tully Vaughan, like Henry Davis, had excellent professional credentials. By 1909, the year he turned fifty, he was renowned for his pioneer work in heart surgery and had published a textbook that would become a classic. And Rosa had also shrewdly chosen a man with strong military connections in more than one branch of the service. Between 1902 and 1906, Vaughan was assistant surgeon general of the public health and marine hospital service. He took his career, his military service, and his lineage all very seriously, declaring in his will that he came from the "best blood of Wales, England, Ireland and Scotland," a point that he made not to be boastful but "for the information of my descendants." At the time of the autopsy, George Vaughan had been chief surgeon and head of the department of surgery at Georgetown University Hospital for more than ten years.

The acting secretary of the navy, William S. Cowles, sent specific instructions to Raymond Spear on August 25 as to how he was to handle himself during the autopsy. Secretary Cowles confirmed that Mrs. Sutton had requested that her son's remains be inspected, and the surgeon designated by her (Vaughan) should determine "the nature and scope of the investigation." Spear was to be present from the time the casket was opened and to "witness the inspection of the body by her representative, giving such assistance as possible working in cooperation with him." Secondly, Spear was advised, "as the representative of the Navy Department, it will be very desirable that you determine as far as practicable, under the circumstances, whether or not other wounds or injuries other than the pistol shot wound existed at the time of Lieut. Sutton's death, which might have caused death or which would have made it impossible for him to have shot himself with a pistol held in his right hand."

Cowles further instructed his surgeon to take measurements of Sutton's skull and prepare sketches of it (as Dr. Schaeffer had done) so that the "fractures and points of penetration may be accurately located." Cowles wanted Spear to "determine, if possible, the caliber of the shot which penetrated the skull" and "whether or not there are powder marks in the point of entrance of the bullet, thereby being able to form an estimate as to the distance of the muzzle of the pistol from the head at the time the shot was fired." The surgeon was to make detailed notes for the Department, keeping in mind that if any condition indicated that the wound was not self-inflicted, Dr. Spear might be called on to testify about the condition found. Finally, Cowles told Spear to hold an attitude of "absolute neutrality, maintaining no theory, and making no effort to establish facts in defense of or against any person, but merely to ascertain as far as practicable the condition of the body at the time of death."

As inspector of National Cemeteries, D. H. Rhodes was in charge of the procedure—a highly unusual one for any cemetery, including Arlington. (Rhodes had supervised the disinterment of the body of Major Pierre Charles L'Enfant before it was transported from Riggs Farm to Arlington.) He described the day's events in a nine-page letter to the depot quartermaster to assure the War Department that its orders had been followed precisely.

By 11:30 that Monday morning, workmen had opened and cleared Lieutenant Sutton's grave; when Rhodes saw the condition of the shipping case that held the casket, he asked the workmen to dig the hole "6 inches wider and longer than the original dimensions," to "facilitate the prompt removal of the remains intact," and to accommodate a new casket, should one be needed. A watchman stationed nearby made sure the men were not disturbed. Two noncommissioned officers and fifteen soldiers from Fort Myer would also report for duty to see that the proceedings went smoothly. Promptly at noon all the entrances to Arlington Cemetery closed; the cemetery would be off limits to the public until Lieutenant Sutton's body was re-interred that evening.

Dr. Vaughan had chosen a place for the autopsy in one end of a storehouse about five hundred feet northwest of Lee Mansion. At about noon, workmen cleared and cleaned a space thirty feet square "on the ground floor of that building." According to Rhodes,

> An old paulin was then spread on the concrete floor and the central part of this was covered with a layer of sand. An improvised operating table was then arranged and placed on the areas covered with sand, this table being covered with oil and cloth. The necessary tools, disinfectants, water, soap, etc. were assembled ready for use and a number of chairs were placed nearby in case they should be needed by Mrs. Sutton, her friends and representatives.

Rhodes had arranged to have a Red Cross ambulance bring a new metallic casket for the late Lieutenant Sutton that would be "placed in a room nearby, and was then unpacked and opened ready for immediate use." He acknowledged that Dr. Spear would not perform the autopsy, "nor assist thereat in any manner whatsoever," but that he would be present simply as an observer and representative of the Navy Department.

Rosa Sutton was by now the only member of Jimmie's family in Washington. Rose Parker left the day of the autopsy, most likely to join her husband who was stationed in Minnesota—he had probably not seen her since July. Shortly after 1:30 p.m., Rosa—with attorneys Henry Davis and Edmund and Harry Van Dyke, her two friends, and Dr. Vaughan with his assistant Dr. H. E. Gaynor—arrived at the cemetery's main West Gate. Only those officially authorized, including about a dozen newspaper correspondents vouched for by Davis or by Mrs. Sutton, were allowed in. The somber party passed through a military cordon to the grave where Rhodes, the superintendent of Arlington Cemetery Major Harrison Magoon, the receiving depot quartermaster, Major Moses G. Zalinski, and Raymond Spear waited.

A few moments later, on this warm, clear day, eight laborers raised the casket from Lot 2102. Mrs. Sutton, dressed in black, her head covered with a wide hat and mourning veil, watched from her carriage with her two friends as her son's remains were placed on a horse-drawn army ambulance. At the sight of the oak box containing the coffin, according to a sentimental reporter from the *Washington Post*, "Mrs. Sutton was seen to wipe a tear from her eyes and her frame gave a slight tremor," before she resumed her composure. Only her slightly moist eyes showed "the battle her will was waging with her mother emotions." The small funeral cortege wound its way across the cinder path for approximately a mile until it reached the storehouse, at about 2:05 p.m., according to Rhodes. The party waited outside while the casket was brought into the improvised autopsy room; a cordon of troops would guard the storehouse as they had the grave.

Mr. Rhodes opened the fragile case and removed the lid of the casket, which "fell into pieces." He reported, "The remains were enclosed in a metal-lined casket having a glass panel which extended over the head and chest." Rhodes had to get help from one of his "regular men" to remove some rusty screws and clamps. A *Washington Times* reporter described the frail American flag covering the casket—its "silken fiber had become a little faded and mildewed. The remnants were used in wiping the moisture from the glass covering above the dead marine's face." Once the glass was cleaned, Dr. Vaughan then motioned to Rosa Sutton, who had asked to see Jimmie's face but would not stay for the autopsy. Those present dropped back as she entered the room and stared intently at her son for the first time in four years. A few tears appeared on her face "and then, as if remembering that this was an autopsy of possible vindication and not one of grief, she regained her wonderful self-control."

Unshaken by the odor of decomposition, Rosa spent several minutes bending over the glass and staring at Jimmie's drawn face, the swelling under his left jaw, and a large bluish-red discoloration over his right eye. His thick dark brown hair looked normal but had been partially shaved to reveal a wound three inches above his right ear. Her eyes moved to his damp dark blue service blouse and, perhaps, to his badly macerated hands that lay on his blue wool trousers. Rosa became calm and in an official tone began pointing out his injuries to the surgeons and her attorneys. Once again, she said she was convinced that her son was murdered. "I want members of the press to notice the large bruise on the forehead," Rosa directed. After a few moments, Henry Davis "touched her on the arm. This movement startled her somewhat, but she betrayed no emotion until the party was ready to leave the room. It was then that she straightened herself to an almost rigid position and with clenched hands walked to her carriage. Entering the carriage, she was at once driven from the scene." After she left the storehouse, newspaper reporters were allowed to view what Rosa had seen, per her instructions. They would not be present during the autopsy.

It was almost three o'clock when Rosa and her friends reached the grave site to wait while the autopsy was performed by Dr. Vaughan and his assistant. Henry Davis was not able to stay for the entire afternoon, so Edmund Van Dyke took an active role in the proceedings. His brother Harry observed, as did Rhodes. The Van Dyke brothers had wanted to have the surgeons remove a small amount of tissue and "a section of the skull"—the "crown piece." Rosa refused, saving the War Department the trouble of debating the matter, since the body was now the property of the U.S. government. Although the Van Dykes had requested that a photographer come to record an image of Jimmie's skull, he did not arrive in time and was sent back to Washington. But Dr. Spear, as instructed, carefully watched everything that happened and made notes and sketches in a small notebook that would be the basis for a lengthy confidential report to the Navy Department.

As soon as "the glass lid of the casket was removed, the body lost its dark pink color and assumed that of a chalk like whiteness." The surgeons told the reporters that this change was due to the air. Dr. Vaughan, his assistant, and Mr. Rhodes lifted the body from the casket and placed it on a platform at 3:01 p.m. Immediately the doctors noticed that the body was in "a remarkable state of preservation." This fact is mentioned repeatedly in Dr. Spear's report as he describes each phase of the autopsy. For example, when Dr. Vaughan examined the chest, "the muscles and skin were in an almost perfect state of preservation and normal in color." The skin on Jimmie's legs was "almost the same as it had been in life." The doctor found no bones broken anywhere in Jimmie's body. After he examined the entire body, Dr. Vaughan "removed the stitches that held the two flaps of the scalp together" and examined the bullet hole "three inches above the tip of the right ear." Sutton's hair had been cut to about half an inch long around the wound. No one examined it under a magnifying glass, but it did not appear singed to the naked eye, according to Dr. Spear. Sutton's scalp and hair were both "in an excellent state of preservation."

Spear continued, "The wound was bluish-black in appearance; from its center there were several small radiating tears about one-eighth to one-fourth of an inch in diameter." Then he described the tear in the scalp and an extensive scalp wound around the point at which the bullet entered. This, he said, was at least partially caused by the original autopsy and removal of Sutton's brain. According to the navy surgeon, "the scalp wound was plainly situated, then on an outward curve of the skull, such a curve as is found on a sphere." But the bullet wound itself was the focus of Dr. Vaughan's work. As Spear explained, it

> was charred by powder infiltration, hairs were driven into the wound and the edges were black. There was a blackish, moist material that looked like disintegrated powder in the scalp wound. The edges of the tear in the scalp were black and slightly everted. The subcutaneous tissue, the fascia and fronto-occipital aponeurosis near the wound were blackened and infiltrated with powder. Around the bullet wound was a distinct black area. This area was about one inch in diameter and circular in shape with the bullet wound in the center.

And Vaughan found that "no powder marks were visible on the well-preserved scalp."

As for the back of the head, there was a small half-inch cut in the posterior flap of the scalp situated in the mid-line. Dr. Spear decided it had "every appearance of having been made at the time of the incision of the scalp for the removal of the brain." Besides, "the hairy scalp was further examined and Dr. Vaughn [sic] stated that he found no wound or contusion." Sutton's brain had been removed during the original autopsy and replaced with plaster of paris. The dura and bone beneath the plaster of paris was in a perfect state of preservation; "some blood in the posterior fossa looked as if it had freshly clotted." Dr. Vaughan found a small sliver of lead lodged in the occipital bone; he performed a lengthy examination of the skull cap, and Van Dyke again "held the skull cap up from the inside and saw the Brand-downward." Spear wrote that he could not see this Brand, and he sharply criticized Edmund Van Dyke's performance as the attorney "now became an active participant in the autopsy."

Van Dyke "called attention to the linear wound in the scalp and stated that the bullet had ploughed through the scalp from above downward. He instructed Dr. Vaughan in the significance of a "Brand" and pointed one out at the bottom of the bullet wound toward the ear, the idea being that the pistol had been held by some person, above the head. "Van Dyke has much to learn about pistol wounds," Spear wrote. "He failed utterly to interpret the significance of the charred and torn scalp, the blackened area about the wound, the absence of powder grains in the skin adjacent to the wound, the powder infiltration of the subcutaneous tissues, etc., etc." Dr. Spear next described the attorney's detective work, noting that he "took the skull cap and made a tracing on a handkerchief, of the bullet wound. He sketched in what he thought was the 'Brand' at the lower margin of the wound."

By the time the body was turned over and Jimmie's back muscles and skin were also found "in an excellent state of preservation," evening shadows began to descend over the cemetery. The body was turned on its back again, and the doctor sewed up the autopsy wound in the head. At 5:20 p.m., Jimmie's remains were placed in the new hermetically sealed metallic casket; the lid was screwed on, and the casket—once again covered by an American flag—was placed in a wooden burial box. While it was carried to the Red Cross ambulance and conveyed to the grave, Major Zalinski relieved the detail of troops from further duty.

Before the autopsy, Rosa Sutton had been advised not to view her son's body, but she told reporters she would have done it if it had meant her death. The *New York Times* stated that she was not surprised that her son's remains were so well preserved: "It is the mercy of God. It proves that Jimmie came to me after his death and told me he had been murdered. He said a view of the wound on the forehead would prove it. God has preserved the body that I might see for myself. I am now more than ever convinced my son did not kill himself, could not have done it, and I mean that justice shall yet be done for his memory."

The autopsy had taken close to three hours, and at six o'clock that Monday evening, Rosa could finally focus on her son's redemption. An Irish priest had waited with Rosa and her friends throughout the autopsy. The Reverend Father Alonzo J. Olds was one of the founders of Saint Augustine Roman Catholic Church, the oldest African American church in the nation's capital. A colleague of Reverend Paul Griffith, whom Rosa originally thought would perform the burial rites, Father Olds had come to Washington from Boston along with his mother (whose name was Rose).

"The brightest moment of the entire afternoon for Mrs. Sutton—and she reflected her happiness in her face—was when Father Olds advanced, attired in his priestly robes," and came "slowly towards the open grave, and, as the coffin was prepared for lowering, sprinkled the holy water upon it and began the soft musical chant of the Latin ritual used by the Catholic Church." The *Washington Times* reporter continued his eyewitness account. Rosa Sutton "drank in every word" and the "light of motherly triumph" shone in her eyes as Jimmie Sutton was again laid to rest. For twenty-three months Rosa had prayed she would hear the words that were now likely spoken in Latin by Father Olds: "God through Your mercy the souls of the faithful are at rest. Bless this grave and appoint Your holy Angel as its guardian. Absolve from all the bonds of sin the soul of him whose body is buried here so that he may rejoice for ever in You with Your Saints. Through our Lord. Amen."

Father Olds sprinkled the new coffin and the grave with holy water and incensed them. He then probably intoned the antiphon, "I am the Resurrection and the Life." Jimmie Sutton's casket was lowered into his grave, "just as the evening gun at Fort Myer announced sunset." Again came the words "I am the Resurrection and the Life" as more holy water was sprinkled on the coffin. "Grant this mercy, O Lord, we beseech Thee, to Thy servant departed, that he may not receive in punishment the requital of his deeds who in desire did keep Thy will, and as the true faith here united him to the company of the faithful, so may Thy mercy unite him above to the choirs of Angels. Through Jesus Christ our Lord. Amen."

"Eternal rest grant unto him, O Lord," said the priest.

"And let perpetual light shine upon him," Rosa no doubt responded. "May he rest in peace."

"Amen."

Rosa finally broke down when the first clod of earth was placed on the grave; she and her friends stayed "until the grave had been re-filled and mounded" to place numerous bouquets and other "floral offerings" on it. Just as the sun set, a Wagnerian scene unfolded, which reporters described with relish. Her surgeon, her attorney, and her friends stepped back as she approached the grave and stepped waveringly up to the foot of the newly made rounded mound that again hid her son and the wounds of which he died. Two floral wreaths she carried—white and green—one a crown and the other a cross. The crown bearing the word "Jimmie," was placed at the head and the cross, bearing the word "Mother," was placed at the foot. There at her dead son's feet she stood, gowned in black, faltering and, with the tears that always before had been held bravely back coursing over her cheek, she murmured a prayer. "This crown for a martyr," she said, "and this cross an emblem of what I bear for my boy."

Before the flowers on Jimmie's hallowed grave could wilt, Americans were caught up in the results of the autopsy. They were not clear cut. No evidence had been found to prove that Jimmie had died from any wounds other than the bullet. However, early news articles stated unequivocally that Vaughan's examination proved Jimmie did not commit suicide. "HOLE IN SUTTON'S HEAD CLEAN CUT—AUTOPSY ADDS STRENGTH TO MURDER THEORY—SHOT FIRED FROM DISTANCE—POWDER MARKS AND BURNS NOT FOUND ON BODY, SKULL BRUISED AND CUT, SCARS OF BATTLE CLING TO CORPSE—ALL OF BONES SOUND—FAMILY DOCTOR SAYS SUICIDE CONTENTION IS EXPLODED," proclaimed multiple headlines that the Sutton family and their friends woke up to in their morning *Oregonian*. The Portland story, which came from the *Oregonian* News Bureau in Washington, also made a point that others did not, namely, that both Sutton's brain and the bullet in it had been destroyed immediately after Sutton's death; therefore, "the surgeons were unable today to cast any light upon the effect produced by the blows which Sutton received on his head." The *Washington Post* was one of several papers with newspaper men on the scene. According to the *Post*, the autopsy confirmed that Sutton was a powerful man physically. His face "bore marks of having received a severe beating," and the contusions over his right eye caused a "slight indentation" in the forehead, which "were caused by blows struck by a blunt weapon."

Rosa's attorneys were reportedly delighted with the results. Edmund Van Dyke, who almost a year earlier had spent several weeks preparing the initial arguments on Rosa's behalf, now once again became Rosa's primary advocate. He argued that the shot was fired at least five feet from Sutton's head, and the "condition of the wound in the head caused by the bullet showed conclusively that it was impossible for Sutton to have fired the shot which ended his life." He also believed that "If the muzzle of the revolver had been held close to Sutton's head, the ball would have shattered the skull. Furthermore, the ball would have drilled clean through this skull and come out at the opposite side. As it was, the ball was embedded in Sutton's brain." Van Dyke did not think the blow on Sutton's forehead could have killed him. But in New York's *Evening Journal,* he is quoted as saying that there was a wound that cut into the scalp about three-quarters of an inch and shattered the skull, located on the top of the head, and no mention had been made of it in the former autopsy. It was evidently a terrific blow and must have been made with the butt of a revolver. This wound, he conjectured, also could have caused Sutton's death.

When Dr. Vaughan completed his report, Henry Davis gave at least part of it to the newspapers for publication. The doctor did not comment on the shooting but focused on the nature of Sutton's wounds. The report, however, "is accepted by Mrs. Sutton and her attorney as so thoroughly satisfactory that they regard it as sufficient proof that Sutton could not have killed himself and promptly announce that they will take steps to fight the case to the end." The doctor allegedly told a *Baltimore Sun* correspondent that "the hair around the bullet hole in the head was singed, and that there was a serious scalp wound at the rear of the skull." The printed excerpt from Dr. Vaughan's report stated that the edges of the bullet wound

> were black and a few particles resembling powder grains were picked from them. There were no indications of powder burns outside the side of the wound, but the hair seems to have been clipped in this region. Leading from the bullet hole in the scalp backward and upward toward the median line of the head, was a wound about one and one half inches in length with dark colored edges and extending through the entire thickness of the scalp. It looked as if it might have been done with a blunt instrument. About the center of the line drawn across the scalp was another cut about three quarters of an inch long, not extending through the scalp.

When he gave out Dr. Vaughan's statement for publication, Henry Davis said to a *Washington Post* reporter, "At present, I have no comment to make upon either this report, or the supposed report of Dr. Spear." Within two days of the autopsy, however, the press correctly began to forecast that Dr. Spear would back the navy's verdict.

The text of Spear's report, which he sent to the judge advocate general, Captain Campbell, on September 16, would never be made public, but the *Baltimore Sun* was sure "it contains findings that are calculated to confirm the testimony given before the recent court of inquiry." Spear had, in fact, gone to considerable effort to do just that. In his opinion, "the wound that caused the death of Lieutenant Sutton was self-inflicted, by a service

.38 caliber revolver, which was held in his right hand forward of the right ear. The muzzle of the revolver was within one-half inch from his scalp." The navy doctor went into great detail as to the reasons why he thought the bullet was fired close to Sutton's head.

> The muzzle of the pistol was either under one-half inch from the scalp when it was discharged, or it was at a distance of over four feet from the scalp. . . . The burned wound, the blackened area around the bullet wound and the tearing and blackening of the subcutaneous tissues above the wound, all place the muzzle of the revolver when it was discharged, at the closer range, i.e., under one-half inch.

As for what Spear called "the longitudinal tear in the scalp," his assertion was exactly what the Department hoped it would be. He insisted, in contrast to Dr. Vaughan (and Dr. Edward Schaeffer, the Sutton's witness), that this "was really a part of the bullet wound, the blackened tissues and everted edges testified to its having been produced by a force acting from under the surface of the scalp."

Spear also concluded in his official report that "the body of the pistol was below and in front of the bullet wound in the head and without question and by no possibility could this bullet wound have been produced by a pistol held near or upon the top of the head and pointing downward." The statement is puzzling, because Dr. Spear had in hand the navy's 1907 autopsy report stating that the "'direction of the bullet of the shot was downward, backward and to the left.'" On this point Spear wrote that the gun was "held at least forward of the right ear and pointed slightly backward." In conclusion, Dr. Spear said Vaughan's autopsy showed no injuries to indicate that anything other than a bullet wound killed Lieutenant Sutton, nor did the corpse reveal any injuries that would have prevented Sutton from firing the fatal shot.

Raymond Spear carefully addressed every point raised by William Cowles' instructions. He even had his own men re-enact the death scene and contended Sutton could indeed have shot himself. He "had them hold a .38 caliber service revolver while lying flat in the position testified to at the Courts of Inquiry in the case of Lieutenant Sutton, and found that they could discharge the pistol while holding it forward of the ear and pointing it slightly backward; this can be done easier by using the thumb to pull the trigger than by the use of the index finger."

The autopsy had shown that Jimmie Sutton was badly beaten, but Dr. Spear stated that he was not beaten to death before the bullet entered his now-missing brain. Without photographs or the complete text of Dr.

Vaughan's findings, it is hard to know how close he thought the gun was to Sutton's head when the bullet entered his skull. Dr. Raymond Spear confirmed the press excerpts from Dr. Vaughan describing the black edges of the wound. And so it was likely that the gun was indeed fired within six inches of Sutton's head. However, neither doctor could have been sure who held the gun at the moment the shot was fired. After the *Evening Star* said that Spear would prove the suicide finding by showing why the bullet was shot from close range, Henry Davis made a point that had been raised indirectly at the inquiry. If Spear's report is correct, Davis said, then the shot that killed Sutton came from a weapon too close to his head for him to have fired it.

16

POLITICS AND THE PARANORMAL

Once Lieutenant James N. Sutton had been laid to rest a second time, a question on many people's minds was "What next?" in the Sutton melodrama. Reporters assumed that Rosa would pursue her campaign. "MRS. SUTTON READY TO CONTINUE FIGHT," announced the *Washington Times* on September 14; the following morning the paper outlined Rosa's prospects on the congressional front. Rose Parker sent the article to her sister, Daysie, who was by then living in Los Angeles. Their mother had made it clear that she would do whatever was necessary to ensure that the Sutton cause was "not a dead issue."

James William Good was one congressman clearly dissatisfied with the navy's findings. The forty-three-year-old attorney from Cedar Rapids, Iowa, began his first term as a Republican Representative to the Sixty-First Congress with President Taft's inauguration on March 4, 1909, and he would remain in Congress until 1921. (Good became Herbert Hoover's secretary of war.) Congress had been on a recess since August 5, while some of the most critical testimony before the Sutton court took place, and well before its findings were made public. The *Washington Times* speculated that when Congress finally resumed for its second session on December 6, Good would play a key role in the "now famous case." Good had apparently been interested ever since the Navy Department agreed to a second investigation. He did not know the family personally, but, the paper asserted, he was sure that Lieutenant Sutton had not taken his own life. When the navy verdict proved to be just as he had expected, Good declared his intention to introduce a resolution for another investigation by a congressional committee, in all likelihood the Committee on Naval Affairs. It seems that Representative Good had already talked with his colleagues in Congress before the court's adjournment at the end of August "and convinced himself that such a resolution as he proposed would pass without serious opposition."

Although Arthur Birney had reportedly demanded "that the case be dropped right now," Rosa was also optimistic about the chance that Congress would support her efforts. She planned to stay in Washington through the winter and told the *Times* that, if her family took the congressional route rather than using the civil courts, at least the "officers implicated in the midnight campus fight" might be dismissed from the service. She also said the Suttons' support in the Senate came not only from Jonathan Bourne but also from Senator-elect George Earle Chamberlain, the former governor of Oregon.

But, in the end, Good would not be the man to initiate a resolution to investigate Sutton's death once more. That task fell to a man whom he probably knew well, William Wallace McCredie, a brand new Republican Representative from Rosa's birthplace in Washington State. A Pennsylvania native, McCredie grew up in Iowa and studied law both in Iowa City and in Portland, Oregon. Between 1904 and 1909, he had been a judge in the Superior Court of Vancouver. Throughout his career, he kept his ties with Portland and Vancouver. (In 1904 he was part owner of the Portland Baseball Club.) Elected to fill a sudden vacancy, William McCredie only served in Congress from December 6, 1909, until March 3, 1911. But he was the representative to propose House Joint Resolution 186 on April 1, 1910. It called for a joint commission—of both Houses of Congress "to be composed of three members of the Senate, to be appointed by the President thereof, and three Members of the House of Representatives, to be appointed by the Speaker"—that was directed "to make a thorough and complete investigation as to the facts and circumstances attending the death of Lieutenant James N. Sutton." The members of the commission would hopefully solve the mystery of Sutton's death and make appropriate findings and recommendations "in order that the ends of justice may be fully observed and such steps taken as may be necessary to prevent the recurrence of such scenes as were enacted at the institution kept, maintained, and supported by the people of the United States." For much of the preceding decade, members of Congress had struggled with the concerns expressed in this statement.

If approved, the six-member commission would examine the record of both the 1907 Sutton inquest and the 1909 Court of Inquiry. In effect, McCredie's recommendation was for another full-blown investigation; the resolution also specified that any witness who "refuses to answer any question pertinent to the investigation herein authorized, shall be deemed guilty of a misdemeanor," punishable by a fine of up to one thousand dollars and imprisonment "in a common jail for not more than one year nor less than one month." The hearings were to be "open to the public," and all the commission's conclusions were to be reported to Congress.

In 1910, the men assigned to congressional committees to draft and analyze legislation were chosen on the basis of several criteria, including special competence and experience, party loyalty, policy views, and above all, the seniority or electoral position of a member in Congress. In general, the more seniority a member had, the more prestigious his committee assignment. At the second session of the Sixty-First Congress, nineteen men sat on the House Committee on Naval Affairs. The members represented a wide range of states from New York to California and Massachusetts to Louisiana. The Committee's chairman was George Edmund Foss from Lieutenant Harold Utley's home state of Illinois. Neither McCredie nor Good was a member of the Committee, nor was anyone on it from Oregon or Washington State.

On the tenth of May, just under six weeks after receiving the resolution, Foss wrote the secretary of the navy to request digests of the evidence from both Sutton investigations. His request was forwarded to Commandant George Elliott, who, naturally, asked Major Henry Leonard to prepare the material. Secretary George Meyer sent Foss Major Leonard's summaries on May 27. The former judge advocate created an eight-page abstract of the testimony given in 1907. It is a synopsis of the events that occurred in the hour prior to Sutton's death as told by the Marine Corps witnesses. Leonard also noted that, prior to October 13, Sutton had been "reckless in the use of firearms" and threatened to shoot other officers. Once again, this reference to Sutton's now-infamous actions on May 20, 1907, was used as the rationale for the marines' behavior on the tragic night. But members of Congress did not have Benjamin Fuller's account of what had actually happened, nor his comments about Sutton's subsequent responsible behavior. It was buried in the navy's correspondence files; probably no civilians had seen it.

Leonard's digest of the evidence before the 1909 Court of Inquiry is twice as long, just over sixteen pages. It was, he explained in a cover note, merely a summary of a record "comprehending approximately 1800 pages of information." Not every matter brought out in this record has been set forth in the digest, only the "important facts" established by the weight of the evidence. (Major Leonard placed page numbers from the inquiry transcript in brackets after each statement of fact in the digest.) The "important facts" were again those brought out by officers. Their testimony was apparently assumed to be true because an officer said it. There is no ambiguity and no reference to any conflict of opinion among the witnesses. For example, the "facts" Leonard presented about the car ride back to the Marine Barracks on the fateful night were that Sutton used provocative language and threatened Robert Adams. Driver William Owens' conflicting testimony had been ignored. The congressmen read in Leonard's report that James N. Sutton was responsible for the entire fracas and unquestionably shot himself in the head. The inquiry Rosa had fought for might as well not have happened—except for the final paragraph of Leonard's summary, an indictment of Rosa's credibility and that of Lieutenant Sutton's alleged ghost.

The Naval Affairs Committee learned that "the complainant, Mrs. Sutton, . . . founded her allegations that Sutton died otherwise than by his own act upon the supposed supernatural appearance of said Sutton to his said mother in Portland, Oregon on the date on which his death occurred." Sutton, the document continues wryly, "informed his mother that his death did not occur as a result of his own act; this notwithstanding the fact that the said Sutton had, at the time aforesaid, departed this life." The postmortem visits of Jimmie Sutton to his mother, and her "unsupported suspicions," were, according to Harry Leonard, all that was worth mentioning of Rosa Sutton's long crusade.

Congress had not been in session during the second half of the inquiry, and the members of the House Naval Affairs Committee could have asked for the entire court transcript. But like the large majority of bills, House Joint Resolution 186 received an "adverse report." Beyond these two digests, there are no congressional records on this matter other than the calendar of the House Naval Affairs Committee. However, one fact may have had some bearing on the Committee's inaction. Veteran congressman Thomas S. Butler from Pennsylvania (the home state of two of the most high profile defendants) was a senior member of the Committee—a year earlier he had tried to help Harry Swartz secure a promotion. The congressman's son was Smedley Butler, an ambitious and impetuous man who joined the Marine Corps at sixteen and became one of its most well-known officers. During the Boxer Rebellion in China, a fellow marine had saved Butler's life and lost his own arm in the process. That man was his close friend, Harry Leonard.

A few congressmen requested information about the Sutton inquiry after it ended, but the family's efforts in Washington fell apart when this joint resolution failed in 1910. However, an intriguing story appeared on May 22 in the *Los Angeles Times*. Under the headline "SISTER OF DEAD CADET ANNOUNCES HER MOTHER'S CAMPAIGN PLANS" is the following:

Miss Daysie Mae Sutton, sister of Lieutenant James N. Sutton, whose tragic death at Annapolis two years ago threatened to develop into a "Dreyfus case in America," yesterday, at the Angelus Hotel, affirmed the statement that her mother, Mrs. J. N. Sutton, would run for Congress as a means of influencing legislation toward reopening the investigation into the causes of her son's death.

Rosa apparently intended to stop in Los Angeles on the way to Portland where she would open her campaign. "S. Creed Cross, according to Miss Sutton, will take the stump in behalf of Mrs. Sutton and make addresses, not only in Oregon, but in every State on the Pacific Coast."

Daysie, "a woman of remarkable intellect and rare personal charm," went on to say that the testimony already given in the case would show in a criminal court that her brother could not have committed suicide. But she told the reporter, "The young men implicated are too well connected, their interests too well represented in Washington, to give any hope of vindication." Oregon election figures for 1910 do not indicate that Rosa ran for office. She may, in fact, have changed her mind now that Jimmie's soul could rest in peace. By August of 1910 she had returned to Portland after an absence of almost two years.

Rosa claimed she rarely saw Jimmie's ghost once she returned home. But she had not forgotten Harry Leonard's accusation that her version of the truth was based on "hallucination, fancy or dreams," or Arthur Birney's suggestion that she belonged in a lunatic asylum. Like Charles Doyen, she took the navy's censure personally—largely because it had been spread across America. Her fight now took on a new dimension. She turned to a man who, like James Cardinal Gibbons, had strong views about life after death, though he approached the subject from a very different perspective.

While Rosa was a young girl studying her catechism under the watchful eyes of the Sisters of Providence, millions of Americans were absorbed by Spiritualism (also called "spiritism"), the belief that living people can communicate with the spirits of those who have died through human mediums. Spiritualists did not focus on the concept of salvation, nor did they emphasize a personal God. But they did acknowledge that there could be several heavens. Public curiosity about the movement was intense. Across the United States people flocked to séances and sittings with mediums. Some went for the entertainment value; others believed mediums could receive messages from beloved family members—for instance, those who had died during the Civil War. The men and women who lived through the war experienced a cultural void and sought new ways of coping with a changed world.

Once Spiritualism spread among clergy and laymen in Europe, England, and America, the movement attracted serious attention from scholars and scientists. There were skeptics who studied the subject in order to challenge the claims of those who believed in communication with the dead. But others were more open-minded, and they determined to apply the scientific methods of the age to the study of paranormal phenomena. The task of these psychical researchers was complicated by the large number of fraudulent activities and claims that captured the popular imagination. In Great Britain and the United States, psychologists found psychical research to be an interesting alternative to an approach that attributed mental illness and unexplainable phenomena (such as telepathy or spirit communication) to physiological causes.

In 1882 a group of distinguished men and women in London founded the Society for Psychical Research (SPR). Several of its members were Cambridge educated, and some were wealthy enough to contribute their own funds to the work of the society. Their goal was to systematically investigate the work of mediums and the claims of Spiritualists. Seven years later the International Congress of Experimental Psychology in Paris approved a Census of Hallucinations that the SPR sponsored. Some 410 census takers asked 17,000 people in England and Wales, "'Have you ever, when believing yourself to be completely awake, had a vivid impression of seeing or being touched by a living being or inanimate object, or of hearing a voice; which impression, so far as you could discover, was not due to any external physical cause?'" In response, 1,684 people said yes—far more women than men. After further study of the affirmative answers, the conclusion of the researchers was that approximately 10 percent of the population had sensory hallucinations while they were awake. If an external event (such as the sudden death of someone) caused such a hallucination, the experience was a form of apparition; communication from someone without a direct causal connection would be considered telepathy or "'feeling at a distance.'"

Across the Atlantic, the wealth of stories and novels that explored what William Dean Howells described (in the year Jimmie Sutton died) as "the borderland between experience and illusion" revealed Americans' widespread interest in ghosts and other elements of the supernatural. Howells observed that Americans may appear to focus on the material world but "really live more in the spirit than any other. Their love of the supernatural is the common inheritance from no particular ancestry." But, he added,

"It is evident in the southern part of the country and in New England, or among those descendants of the German immigrants [such as Rosa Sutton] who brought with them to our Middle States, the superstitions of the Rhine Valleys or the Hart Mountains." Gradually, as the widespread influence of Spiritualism itself began to wane, psychical researchers in the United States began the serious study of various manifestations of spirits that captivated so many Americans' imaginations.

Psychologist William James was one of several intellectuals who were curious about psychic phenomena in the decade before World War I. By the time he retired from teaching at Harvard in 1907, he had become a leading figure in a debate that preoccupied many American intellectuals of his era, one studied in depth by Louis Menand: the "general confusion of psychic phenomena, religious beliefs, and science." For much of his life James had tried to prove his "instinctive belief that the universe has a spiritual dimension," and he became "the first man to forward the cause of psychical research in the United States." In 1885, James met an American woman, Leonore Piper, one of the most famous trance mediums in the history of psychical research. He had been encouraged to visit Mrs. Piper because his mother-in-law and sister-in-law told him of her unusual ability to provide names and facts in her trances. A twenty-eight-year-old Boston housewife, she impressed James, who wrote that "she has supernormal powers." Conscientious and professional in her approach, Mrs. Piper added an aura of respectability to the belief in communication with spirits. Her trances led scholars to wonder whether spirits communicated directly with mediums or if mediums acquired the information they revealed because of mental telepathy with the sitter. As he got to know her, Mrs. Piper became William James' "white crow," and her fame spread among psychical researchers in both America and England. Throughout his career, James remained open to the concept that there were many forms of consciousness. There is, he wrote, "actually and literally more life in our total soul than we are at any time aware of." And, citing British scholar Frederic Myers, he agreed that "'each of us is in reality an abiding psychical entity far more extensive than he knows—an individuality which can never express itself completely through any corporeal manifestation.'"

In the year he met Mrs. Piper, William James also became a founding member of the American Society for Psychical Research (ASPR). A number of well-known men served as officers in the association, or as members or associate members, among them Francis Parkman, Theodore Roosevelt, Henry Holt, Charles Sanders Peirce, and a scholar who received the first American PhD in psychology under William James, G. Stanley Hall. But support for the society did not necessarily mean belief in telepathy or spirit manifestation; it suggested, rather, the sort of intellectual curiosity that characterized Henry Davis' open-minded approach to the spiritual world. The field would always be controversial, and its critics insisted that researchers produce, in G. Stanley Hall's words, "'a single fact that can be demonstrated regularly in a laboratory.'"

One of the ASPR's first sponsors and vice presidents, Hall helped define both child psychology and educational psychology, and he was instrumental in the establishment of another organization, the American Psychological Association. He became its first president in 1892. While he was not optimistic about what psychical research could discover about telepathy or direct communication with the dead, Hall did hope it would demonstrate "'the utter inadequacy of current psychology in dealing with the unconscious.'" Although the original ASPR had folded for lack of financing and "sympathetic intelligentsia" in the United States, scholarly interest in the paranormal continued; by the end of the nineteenth century a number of academic psychologists referred to psychical research in their lectures. It would take James Hervey Hyslop, one of Hall's former students and a man also well-known to William James, to revive the ASPR between 1906 and 1907. Three years later, Dr. Hyslop would become intrigued by the postmortem appearances of Lieutenant James N. Sutton as well.

Hyslop was born on a small Ohio farm in 1854 and raised in a conservative denomination of the Presbyterian Church. His brother, Charles, and his sister, Anna, died of scarlet fever when he was ten, and he lost his mother in 1869 when he was only fifteen. These frightening experiences, exacerbated by his failed relationship with an unsupportive father, led the reflective and insecure young man to devote much of his later life to the question of whether or not the dead communicate with the living. Hyslop won a fellowship to work with G. Stanley Hall at Johns Hopkins University and completed his doctorate in 1887. In 1889, he joined the department of psychology and philosophy at Columbia University, where, over the next ten years, he advanced to become a professor of logic and ethics. When he was in his thirties, James Hyslop also met Mrs. Lenore Piper, and his interest in psychical research intensified. Impressed by an "epochal" report by British researcher Richard Hodgson, Hyslop's initial skepticism about the possibility of an afterlife began to crack. In 1898, two years after his father died, he held several sittings of his own with Mrs. Piper, taking elaborate precautions to keep her from recognizing him. He also interviewed other mediums. Hyslop finally came to the conclusion that Mrs. Piper really was com-

Dr. James H. Hyslop. This image is reproduced from a portrait of Dr. James H. Hyslop, who was president of the American Society for Psychical Research from 1907 to 1920. It was painted by Henriette Roos. Courtesy of the American Society for Psychical Research, Inc., New York.

municating directly with spirits because of the "extraordinary hits" that her messages "contained about his own family life." At the same time, like William James, he became fascinated by "exceptional occurrences [i.e., apparitions, mediumistic phenomena, telepathy] which seemed to suggest a broader view of the mind–brain relationship" than the scholarship of his day would acknowledge.

After 1900, James Hyslop's career took a new turn as once again tragedy transformed his life. His wife, Mary Fry Hall, whom he married in 1891, died, leaving him with three young children. In the next year he developed what he described as "nervous prostration and tuberculosis, with stomach complications." William James feared that the illness was "'the end of him for worldly purposes.'" Hyslop did recover, but he remained frail, and his interest in the paranormal drew criticism from some of his fellow scholars at Columbia. Ultimately, after the 1902 fall semester, he left his teaching position for health reasons. Following a few months of recovery in the fresh mountain air of Vermont, he became the first American academic to devote himself full time to psychical research. For the remainder of his life, Hyslop determined to use scientific procedures to examine paranormal phenomena. A prodigious worker, he produced thousands of pages of methodical reports, often written in a cumbersome and repetitive style but always dispassionate and impartial, though by then he was an admitted Spiritualist. His "special genius was for the amassing and weighing of facts" and for collecting reliable data. He did have a number of detractors, but by 1907, he had been instrumental in founding a new American Society for Psychical Research, and he was the dominant figure in the field.

The new society encouraged both psychological and psychical research, but it struggled with a lack of funds and prejudice from the scientific community. Nevertheless, during the first two decades of the twentieth century, James Hyslop labored, not entirely successfully, to establish psychical research as a credible field in the face of academic skepticism and clearly fraudulent popular superstition. Men in his field appreciated Hyslop far more than others in the academic community. He could be rigid and short fused, and he was reluctant to share control of the ASPR with men unsympathetic toward his views. His own contribution to the ASPR remains somewhat controversial. But there is no doubt that Hyslop created an organization for "the rational study of unusual phenomena . . . that embodied the best traditions of reflective and empirical science." William James, while frustrated by Hyslop's difficult personality, wrote of his high respect for Hyslop's work, although, he said, the facts "are yet lacking to prove 'spirit return.'" (James pulled his support from the Institute for Psychical Research.) But Hyslop's work remains of great interest to survivalists and researchers in Great Britain as well as in the United States. According to British scholar and former president of the London SPR, Henry Habberley Price, researchers like James Hyslop demonstrated that the chance of survival after death "is not the vanishingly small thing that most educated people are wont to assume."

James Hyslop conducted hundreds of interviews during the course of his career and directed field investigations in different regions of the United States. When Rosa Sutton wrote to him on September 10, 1910, the tone of her letter distinctly showed "a desire for help in a distressful situation." Hyslop was intrigued and responded promptly "to ask for a more detailed report of her experiences and such corroboration as might be possible." Eager to make sense of her visions, Rosa responded in a long letter from Portland on October 5. Hyslop included it at the beginning of his published report, "The Case of Lieut. James B. [*sic*] Sutton." The only information he removed from her letter was Rosa's digressions revealing her "animadversions" to the government and "desire for justice." As was his usual custom, James Hyslop proceeded cautiously, aware that skeptics would say that Rosa's experience before the devastating telegram arrived was a coincidence, not a premonition.

Late in October, Dr. Hyslop wrote to Oregon psychical researcher George Thacher to request that he call on Mrs. Sutton. Would he investigate her claims that she had seen "visions" of her dead son? Thacher was curious but also cautious. Hyslop asked him to learn as much as possible about Rosa's previous psychical experiences, to try to verify them, and also to beware of retro cognition—she could be adding details to her stories that she had learned after the apparitions had appeared. One of Thacher's most complex challenges was that most of Rosa Sutton's "visions" that were under consideration had appeared three years earlier. Both he and Hyslop were acutely conscious of the gravity of the matter, given the investigation by the navy. Both would study the legal documents connected with the case, though Thacher's comments on the naval inquiry were not part of the published report. Their goal was not to challenge the Court of Inquiry's findings but rather to determine whether or not Rosa's postmortem visits and messages from her son could have been authentic, and, if so, was what Jimmie had told his mother true? Thacher's approach was to attempt to corroborate Rosa's claims through witness testimony, through verification of her facts, and through getting to know her (and the Sutton family) over a long enough period of time to evaluate both her personality and her psychic capabilities.

George Thacher had his first meeting with Rosa on November 6 and "found her to be a woman of unusual intelligence and apparently vigorous health." But, he wondered, had she been so torn by grief in 1907 that her sanity and mental balance had been in question? Between November 1910 and February 1911, he became acquainted with Rosa and Jim Sutton as well as Daysie and Louise, their two children who were then living at home. (Rose was in Europe and Don at West Point.) Within six weeks he had become practically a member of the Sutton household.

He spent most of each day in their home for more than sixty days, speaking with them and examining various documents and a "mass of letters." He soon decided that Rosa's shock and grief at Jimmie's death was not of the pathological sort, nor had the tragedy caused a "split of personality whatever that may be." In the case of Mrs. Sutton, "there is no alternating personality and a lack of capacity for self-control. . . . She as well as two sisters and her brother whom I have become acquainted with are noticeable for good physical and mental development." Thacher concluded that Daysie and Louise were also perfectly normal physically and mentally. Moreover, he wrote, both of the Suttons' sons were athletes, "and the survivor [Don] has made a record this year as the best basket ball player in the West Point team and has been given the credit in the newspapers for winning several games for West Point. He was a popular member of the Multnomah Athletic club of Portland before going to West Point."

George Thacher also obtained written descriptions of three occasions that occurred long before her son died when Rosa claimed to hear voices from the dead, experiences that were verified by her husband and her sisters Mary and Eliza. Because the Suttons were living in Los Angeles at the time, he was especially impressed by the 1890 incident when Rosa heard directly from her late mother that she had died before anyone in her family told her the news. After several weeks with the Suttons, Thacher noted a "telepathic rapport between Mrs. Sutton and one of her daughters [Daysie]." But he also observed her family's doubts about her dreams and visions; when Rosa told her stories, "she was shown no mercy." In fact, "the members of the family indulge in a frankness of speech which is rather unusual," Thacher wrote, "and Mrs. Sutton's dreams are generally received with impatience. They strike a slightly discordant note into happy hearted nonsense and chaff in which the younger members of the family like to indulge. One of the daughters remarked to me, 'Mamma has too many dreams.'" Thacher then commented on the family's ambiguity about Rosa's visions.

> Mrs. Sutton does not possess the spirit of Griselda and so the members of the family, probably in a spirit of self-defense, sometimes exclaim rather contemptuously when a vision is related, apparently to counteract its effects and to ward off any discussion as to the deeper significance of such occurrences. On the other hand, they do in serious moments frankly admit that there have been some very strong coincidences between Mrs. Sutton's dreams and the events that they describe. They regard these things as remarkable and unquestionably cherish an undercurrent of feeling that "there is something in it" but they declined absolutely to admit that the claims of spiritualism are even partially proven by the coincidences that they have personal knowledge of.

The skepticism of Rosa's family only made her paranormal experiences more credible for George Thacher, who also found another point critical to his research: "The family are Catholics and anything like spiritualism as a faith is repugnant to them." He concluded that some of the visions, or parts of them, which Rosa Sutton told him about could be subjective, but for others, there was no apparent reason for their origin other than genuine communication from the dead.

Satisfied that a professional investigation of Jimmie Sutton's postmortem appearances could be enlightening, Thacher conducted formal interviews and obtained signed statements from Rosa and Jim Sutton and six other family members, as well as four of Rosa's women friends and three of their adult children. His subjects recalled what Rosa had told them in October 1907 before she heard any details from the navy or from her daughter Rose. Thacher found his fourteen witnesses to be "respectable, intelligent persons and their voluntary statements show, I think, that they do not attempt to tell more than they clearly remember." He was fully conscious of the limitations of evidence based on oral testimony. Exhibiting the prudence his employer would expect, and language similar to that of twenty-first-century scholars, he wrote that his witnesses "show very conclusively I think, that one does not ever remember an event, but does remember the impression or mental picture which the event produced." At times, he acknowledged, when a memory is not perfectly sharp and clear, the impression is only a "partial picture of the events which produced it." More than a dozen people had confirmed that Rosa had visions of her son. These witnesses, who signed statements for George Thacher, also agreed to let him use their names should his report be published. "The remark of one indicates the mental attitude of all. She said, 'It's true, why shouldn't I be willing to say so?'"

Once he secured a statement from Rosa, George Thacher had a "long conversation" with her husband about her "dreams," as he called them. Jim Sutton told Thacher about some of Rosa's previous experiences in which she had no normal means of getting the information she had received. Jim Sutton "is not a spiritualist," Thacher observed, yet over time Jimmie's father had clearly become curious; "he described some mediumistic séances that he had attended and how in some instances he had detected the mediums in fraudulent practices." Jim Sutton's first impression of his wife's visions was "that she had the intuitive perception of a mother concerning all matters affecting her children." His second theory, Thacher reported, "admits the possibility of spirit return to a limited extent, still giving the mother's acute perceptions considerable credit in the matter of receiving impressions." Far less comfortable with the mechanics of writing than his wife, Jim Sutton asked Thacher to draft a statement based on their conversation, which he then reviewed and signed. For him as well as for several other witnesses, the tangible evidence of Jimmie's broken watch would be particularly memorable.

Twelve days later, Thacher began meeting with other family members, each of whom would add another piece to the puzzle of Jimmie's postmortem appearances. Rosa's brother, George W. Brant, confirmed that both Rosa and Jim had told him that "Mrs. Sutton saw their son in a dream or vision after the news of his death came, and that he told her that they had killed him; that there were three or four mixed up in it and that they jumped on him. There were other things told me but my recollection about them is not clear." Thacher also spoke with Rosa's sisters, Eliza Bruin and Mary Hodgson, her brother-in-law Nephi Hodgson, and her daughters, Louise and Daysie. Eliza, Mary, and Louise all recalled the incident about the watch. There seemed to be no rational explanation for how Rosa had known her son's watch had been smashed immediately after he died.

But relatives do not always make the best witnesses, and Thacher canvassed the Suttons' friends who had paid their respects at Hoyt Street in the days immediately after they learned the tragic news. Only then was he satisfied that Rosa's visions could be corroborated by other people. She had somehow known about the wound on her son's head, the bandage on his forehead, the lump under his jaw, his smashed watch, and his missing shoulder knot before Rose Parker returned from Annapolis. George Thacher would also tell Hyslop that he had met three other people who claimed to have seen an apparition of Jimmie Sutton, but they preferred to remain anonymous.

Despite her tendency to exaggerate, Thacher seemed to enjoy Rosa, and more than once implied she could have been a medium herself. "She has a happy disposition naturally, and a sense of humor which is sometimes denied to members of her sex. She has the mental traits of mediumistic persons including a lively imagination and a certain nervous irritability at times. She is exceptionally bright and shrewd." Rosa had several unusual experiences that Thacher observed first hand. He asked her to write memoranda of them while he gave careful consideration to her family life. One of the "best incidents" came on December 16, 1910. George Thacher arrived at the Sutton home in the early afternoon, and Rosa told him that she had experienced a vision before waking in which she was asked to step into a room. She saw a coffin and exclaimed, "Who can that be in that coffin?" Rosa continued, "I stepped nearer and saw the smiling face of Sister Dorothy. She smiled at me very sweetly and said, 'your sister Mary will know.'" Rosa informed Thacher that Sister Dorothy was her teacher in the convent school in Vancouver. She had been her sister Mary's teacher for a much longer time. She told him that it was her impression that Sister Dorothy had died about six months previous. When George Thacher called Mary Hodgson to verify this account, she too thought Sister Dorothy had been dead for six months. So it seemed at first that the vision or dream was not of the premonitory type.

But on January 4, 1911, an obituary for Sister Dorothy appeared in the *Morning Oregonian*. She had died on the previous day in Portland's St. Vincent's hospital—less than three weeks after Rosa's vision. The story became even more interesting. Rosa described to Thacher the coffin and the setting of Sister Dorothy's funeral before it took place. On the evening of the funeral, while George Thacher and Jim Sutton were smoking and talking, Jim Sutton also confirmed that Rosa had told him some of these surprisingly accurate details. Thacher verified the incident by talking with the people in charge of St. Vincent's hospital and others who knew about the "convent school in Vancouver." This experience, Thacher decided, was definitely a vision "of the genuine premonitory type."

Rosa Sutton spent a great deal more time with George Thacher than her husband, but when Thacher recounted an experience he had with a friend, Mrs. J. Youmans, Jim Sutton became fascinated. Thacher had known Mrs. Youmans for a long time. She "was not a professional medium," and he had never detected in her any attempt to deceive others or herself. She was "the subliminal type of medium," a woman who goes into a trance during which certain personalities talk for her. In this case, the "trance personalities" were three young girls between ten and twelve years old. One day, before he knew anything about the Suttons, Thacher had met with Mrs. Youmans who told him something unusual would happen to him on November 6. It turned out that was the day he met Rosa for the first time. When he heard this story, Jim Sutton, who was now less skeptical about his wife's paranormal experiences than he had been when their son died, asked Thacher to bring Mrs. Youmans to the Sutton home.

The sitting occurred on November 13, about a week after Thacher met the Suttons. Mrs. Youmans did not know whose house she was visiting, and Thacher did not believe that Mrs. Youmans came up with her impressions because she remembered what had been reported in the press. During the sitting, the voices she heard did touch on several aspects of the tragedy. Possibly impressed, Rosa unexpectedly gave Thacher a letter to hand to Mrs. Youmans. He knew nothing of the contents of the letter. One of her trance personalities said, referring to whoever wrote the letter, "something happens in his family that softens up his conscience. Help to send this boy of ours back." Rosa then asked George Thacher to read the letter. He would report to Dr. Hyslop the following:

> The writer, who did not sign his name, said that he knew that Jimmie Sutton was murdered and that he wished most fervently that the truth could be brought out. He expressed sympathy for the family, there was no attempt to disguise the handwriting. Mrs. S. received it in 1909. Mrs. Sutton as the result of a good deal of trouble has got the signature of a young man who was present on the night of the tragedy. A comparison of the handwriting indicates quite strongly that he was the writer of the letter.

Dr. Hyslop would follow up on this intriguing bit of information.

After three months with the family, probably in March 1911, Thacher decided that Rosa Sutton "unquestionably" has visions that correspond to events "of which she could have no information in normal fashion. These the psychical researcher calls veridical hallucinations." He would inform James Hyslop of "two facts concerning the family. They are above the average in intelligence and they are not Spiritualists in any sense of the word." In fact, "Mrs. Sutton's experiences, or impressions, in connection with the death of her son at Annapolis" were as genuine as her other well-documented experiences, including ones he had witnessed himself. "There is also no doubt of the fact," he wrote, "that Mrs. Sutton believes so firmly in the veridical nature of these communications (though she is a devout Catholic) that she has been sustained in one of the bravest and most persistent fights ever made by a woman to rehabilitate her son."

But even if many people found Rosa's supernormal experiences both memorable and credible, Thacher's work had only just begun. He also studied "a mass of testimony filling 1500 typewritten pages and various documents and correspondence," related to the inquiry. He found Rosa's knowledge a great help in sifting through these legal documents. Admitting that she sometimes confused her facts "with the implications from these facts," he said Rosa had "mastered every detail of the hearings before two naval courts." But Rosa had no legal training and was "inclined by temperament to overstatement rather than understatement." Thacher's purpose in reviewing all of this material—as was Hyslop's when he received it—was to make sure that none of the official records disproved what Rosa had learned in her visions. Thacher found that transcripts of both naval investigations, with the autopsy report, showed "very conclusively that Lieutenant Sutton received a scalp wound an inch and a half long on the top of his head, which laid open the scalp to the bone, before the fatal shot was fired." Rosa claimed that Jimmie's spirit described a blow on his head, a bruise on his forehead, and a lump on his jaw as well as someone jumping on his body. These statements were confirmed in court or at the autopsy. So Thacher encouraged psychical researchers to examine the official legal and medical records of the case, ones that he shipped to Dr. Hyslop. By then, George Thacher was caught up in the drama himself:

> Here is the material for the study of the old question which the tragedy of the Prince of Denmark suggests in a purely literary form. Here is a tragic death of a promising youth in the 20th century. Here are a grief stricken mother and father demanding from the powerful officials of a great democracy that the stigma of suicide be removed from the name of their son, and that justice be done. Is the story of the [spirit] testimony worth while?

Even more critical to George Thacher and James Hyslop, if Rosa Sutton's visions were real, what could they tell us about another profound question: "Do the so-called dead communicate with the living?" Dr. James Hyslop would not form his own opinions about Rosa Sutton until he received the voluminous box of documents from Oregon in the spring of 1911. He would study the material himself and attempt to solve the mystery of the unsigned letter that asserted Jimmie Sutton had been murdered. That April, Assistant Secretary of the Navy Beekman Winthrop received two typed letters from James Hyslop written on the letterhead of the American Institute for Scientific Research—Section B—American Society for Psychical Research. The first, dated April 4, reveals how carefully Hyslop approached this case. "In accordance with the suggestion of your secretary todday [*sic*] I write a request to get some tracings of the handwriting of Ex-Lieut. Edward P. Roelker. It is not his name that is desired so much as samples of his regular handwriting. I should also be pleased to have his address, if that is now accessible." Hyslop explained this unusual request as follows:

> I am interested in the scientific side of some experiences of Mrs. Sutton, the mother of the Lieut. Sutton of unfortunate fame and accident, and it concerns the possible testimony of Lieut. Roelker. Someone wrote a letter to Mrs. Sutton claiming to be a true friend of Lieut. Sutton and did not sign his name to it, only "A true friend." There seemed to friends of Mrs. Sutton that the handwriting of the writer was that of Lieut. Roelker and it is my desire to have some samples of Lieut. Roelker's handwriting to compare with a photograph of the letter sent to Mrs. Sutton and which she thinks is that of Lieut. Roelker.

The letter, he allowed, "might be a hoax," and he tried to reassure the secretary of the navy that he was not interested in "the civil questions involved" but only hoped to determine whether or not Rosa had genuine psychic experiences. "Some of them were corroborated in a way that makes it hard to impeach them," he said. "This sensational incident which would interest the public I do not think capable of either proof or disproof, in my reading of the testimony." Hyslop added that it was "his obligation as a scientist" that compelled him to write. Twelve days later, Hyslop, who had omitted the fact that the mysterious letter accused the marines of homicide, reminded Winthrop of his request. He received a response written on April 21. Winthrop said that the only papers "which can be conveniently located in the Marine Corps bearing the signature of former Lieut. Roelker" are "two endorsements, the signatures on which are entirely different." He offered to have Hyslop come to Washington to look at these signatures. But Beekman Winthrop neglected to mention the lengthy form that Edward Roelker had filled out when he applied to the marines. And, of course, there could have been material at the Naval Academy as well. But by April 24, James Hyslop had decided that it would not "avail anything" to see these apparently inconsistent signatures. (George Thacher had already seen an example of Roelker's signature and decided the letter appeared to be in Roelker's handwriting.) So he wrote to Winthrop, "It is probable therefore that I shall drop the matter where it is, and thanking you for the opportunity to see the writing mentioned." More than three years after his friend's death, Edward Roelker had still never been found.

Hyslop then edited Thacher's report and made several comments of his own. As he saw it, the real issue for the psychic researcher is the "credibility of any and all the incidents described by Thacher." Greater than normal "obligations for caution" on the part of the researcher are required because, Hyslop said, "the presumption will always be that the findings of the Court of Inquiry are not easily to be set aside." This point was critical. Hyslop did not assume Rosa's psychical experiences were real—quite the opposite: "We are obliged to settle whether this statement of the communicator [the ghost] is true or not by the evidence produced for or against the verdict of suicide" in the courtroom. "That is, the whole case turns on the question whether the evidence adduced to prove Lieut. Sutton's suicide is true or false." Did any evidence at the inquiry negate Rosa Sutton's allegations?

Do ghosts lie? People who believe in spirit communication, Hyslop observed, assume that spirits send messages that are peculiarly sacred and unquestionable. Skeptics attack the *fact* of communication from spirits, not what their message is. "But in fact there is no reason for supposing that spirits, granting their existence, are or should be either any more veracious or as having any better judgment of fact than the living. They may be as liable to error in statement as living people whether the error be intentional or unintentional." So all communication from the dead needs to be weighed with reservations until verified by their coincidence with independent mental or physical facts. In arguing this third point, Hyslop cited British psychical researcher Dr. Richard Hodgson who thought that the spirits of those who died violent deaths could well be in some sort of disturbed mental state when communicating.

Dr. Hyslop reviewed the broad outlines of the story of what happened to Jimmie Sutton and drew on his training as a professor of logic and ethics. The testimony of disinterested parties in Annapolis such as William Owens contradicted that of those who might be suspected of homicide. Hyslop saw "no motive for the alleged suicide . . . established by the evidence and no attempt made to establish it." Like attorneys Edmund Van Dyke and Henry Davis, Hyslop emphasized the inconsistency in the testimony of the Marine Corps witnesses. Moreover, he said,

> the examination of the body after exhumation two years later showed wounds and conditions which had no proper consideration in the earlier inquest and the direction of the bullet, as also shown in the original autopsy, was against the theory of suicide as testified, and the direct testimony of some witnesses [such as Dr. Edward Schaeffer] made it appear impossible.

As had Henry Davis, Hyslop thought it curious that the witnesses ignored the possibility of accidental suicide or justifiable homicide. According to James Hyslop, a much stronger case could have been made for justifiable homicide than Sutton's intentional suicide. Even if this was the case, there was not adequate evidence for this view. All of the parties testifying as defendants would have been "deeply implicated in any verdict against suicide." While it may be possible that Sutton committed suicide, Dr. George Vaughan and "most students of the evidence" "deem it improbable." (This is the one clear statement of Dr. Vaughan's final conclusion that exists.) Because of his reputation as a meticulous researcher (in spite of the controversial nature of his field), there is no reason to believe Hyslop misled his readers. So had Mrs. Sutton seen an apparition of her son—one that gave her accurate information? Hyslop weighed the recollections of Rosa, her family, and her friends against the testimony in the navy's courtroom. While there is no positive proof that the ghost's accusations of murder were accurate, he said, "circumstantial evidence coming from unwary admissions and the testimony of disinterested parties points toward homicide. It is a case where science can announce no proved verdict and the individual will have to be left to his own judgment." But Sutton could have been murdered. So, he said, "It is merely the legal aspect of the case that requires us to say that nothing can be proved. Apart from legal technicalities which may be necessary for the protection of human rights in situations where passion cannot be allowed any reign, I think most readers of the evidence would accord homicide a strong claim in the case."

Dr. James Hyslop left his readers with five points and his final conclusion. The first two points provide the skeptic's view. Retro-cognition could explain why Rosa Sutton used the names of Lieutenants Robert Adams and Harold Utley in her 1910 narrative about what Jimmie told her in 1907. The witnesses who confirmed what she said may not have realized that she was naming names. Second, any mother—especially a Catholic mother—might be so horrified by a suicide verdict that her exclamation about her son not committing suicide must be taken with some reservations. But, third, Hyslop said, some incidents in her narrative defy explanation; they are "so well confirmed by other testimony than her own that chance coincidence is perhaps the only alternative to the supernormal." Fourth, there is the corroboration by more than one witness that certain details, such as the beating, the broken watch, the lump on the jaw, and the loss of his epaulet, were mentioned to them long before they were verified as facts. This, he argued, outweighs the suspicion of retro-cognition. Finally, Dr. Hyslop was impressed by the fact that Rosa's previous paranormal experiences had been verified by several reliable individuals. "On the whole, therefore," Hyslop decided, "I would say that there is much to sustain the contention of Mrs. Sutton." The evidence for Lieutenant Sutton's suicide is "not at all satisfactory"; none of it indicates that Rosa could not have had the psychical experiences she said she had when learning about the death of her son. "While the evidence does not absolutely prove the case [of communication from the dead], Hyslop concluded, it deserves serious consideration and will put the case among those which may collectively prove much for psychical research."

With that remark, Professor Hyslop left his readers to decide for themselves.

James Hyslop's experiences with mediums and other paranormal phenomena fascinated reporters, as had the activities of both the London and the American Societies for Psychical Research. The *New York Times* took a special interest in the topic. Dozens of articles and, on occasion, editorials about the field came out every year between 1907 and 1911. And Hyslop's report on the Sutton case piqued the interest of Edward Marshall, who read it just before it was published. It was obvious to Marshall and his editor that Hyslop's account would appeal to a much wider audience than the selective readership of the *Journal of the American Society for Psychical Research*. (The report came out as an issue of the *Journal*.) So, on November 12, 1911, a clear, cool Sunday, hundreds of thousands of New Yorkers, travelers, and out-of-town subscribers woke up to a feature article that filled the entire front page of the *Times Sunday Magazine* (seven columns) and half of the next page. It included photos of Rosa, Rose Parker, Jimmie, and a scene from the Court of Inquiry. All were positioned under a photo of Bancroft Hall at the Naval Academy which was spread across the top of the page. The article's large headline proclaimed, "WEIRD CLAIMS OF SPIRIT TESTIMONY IN NAVAL TRAGEDY. MOTHER OF LIEUTENANT SUTTON, WHOSE DEATH AT ANNAPOLIS CAUSED A SENSATION, SAYS HER SON'S SPIRIT HAS RETURNED TO HER SEVERAL TIMES—SOCIETY FOR PSYCHICAL RESEARCH INVESTIGATES THE CASE." Marshall began with a seductive first few paragraphs:

> Here is an amazing case in which spiritism charges murder though the verdict of the courts is suicide; a case in which the nation is interested because the crime, whatever may have been its nature, occurred in or near the grounds of the Government Naval Academy at Annapolis, Md., and involved directly those only who were connected with that famous institution.
>
> I am enabled here to give to the world for the first time the details of the part which spiritism has played in the affair from the beginning to the present time; a part so utterly astonishing that it is without a parallel in history.
>
> The claim that into this sad story of a young man's untimely death the supernatural had forced an entry came with such force to the Society for Psychical Research from the dead boy's mother that the society, at large expense of time and money, made an exhaustive expert study, which has just been completed, of the whole affair.
>
> The result of this investigation does not throw the story out of court as false, but the society preserves the carefully judicial attitude of one still unconvinced. Details of the study of the case will form a large part of the society's next annual report. Among the psychicists the case ranks in its importance with the recently alleged communications with the spirit of the late Prof. [William] James.
>
> The case is that of the alleged return to this plane, seeking justice for itself, but not revenge, of the spirit of the late Lieutenant James B. [*sic*]

WEIRD CLAIMS OF SPIRIT TESTIMONY IN NAVAL TRAGEDY

Mother of Lieut. Sutton, Whose Death at Annapolis Caused a Sensation, Says Her Son's Spirit Has Returned to Her Several Times---Society for Psychical Research Investigates the Case.

New York Times, *November 12, 1911. Courtesy of the* New York Times.

Sutton, United States Marine Corps, who met a violent end of some sort at Annapolis, Md., on the night of Saturday Oct. 12, 1907, or early in the morning of the 13th.

Marshall then summarized, with lengthy quotations and paraphrased sections, most of George Thacher's research and James Hyslop's comments. He emphasized the judicious way in which Hyslop drew his conclusions. There are a few errors in the article, and Marshall is more cautious than Thacher and Hyslop in reporting their results. The *Times* did not publish the names of any marines accused by the Sutton family, although Hyslop's report would do so. But it was clear to its readers that Hyslop and Thacher thought Rosa Sutton was both sane and rational.

Both men were eager to have others study their records. Toward the end of World War I, Hyslop completed a comprehensive volume that outlined his thoughts about survival after death, something he then regarded as "scientifically proved." He observed that war time awakens the public interest in the meaning of life and death, and in contrast to academics, "the public will go straight to the heart of the matter." For, "No one can act rationally in life without hope." And "there is no proof that can be made more helpful to man than a belief in survival." Close to seventy-five years later, on the centennial of the American Society for Psychical Research in 1985, Hyslop's biographer would observe that among the many reports of apparitions he investigated in pursuit of this question, there was "one remarkable veridical case," that of Lieutenant James N. Sutton.

Rosa Sutton would have been pleased by the Thacher/Hyslop report, even more so when the *Times* placed it before the public. Jimmie was her first son, she wrote in her official statement for Hyslop, and "there was always a peculiarly close sympathy and love between us." But her goals could not have been achieved without the support of her husband and several other men who recognized the larger implications of her case: Edmund Van Dyke, Jonathan Bourne, Henry Davis, and James Cardinal Gibbons. With the press corps as a catalyst, they had helped her win a distinctly American brand of justice.

Encouraged by the optimism characteristic of an age when faith in progress inspired Americans, Rosa Sutton had found a path toward redemption for Jimmie and salvaged her own reputation. It was, after all, the era of Theodore Roosevelt's Great White Fleet and the Wright brothers' daring flights. A week before Father Olds blessed Jimmie Sutton's grave, Commander Robert Peary cabled that he had planted the Stars and Stripes on the North Pole. Women achieved suffrage in Rosa's birth state of Washington in 1910. Over the next two years, similar victories would follow in California, Oregon, Arizona, and Kansas. Rosa Sutton had used her right to enter a public forum with ferocity because she and her sons believed in the system that had let them down. By 1910, she was no longer torn between her visions and her faith. As she wrote to James Hyslop when she attended mass in Washington, D.C. in June, "Just at the elevation, I said to myself, 'Oh my Heavenly Father, I don't see why Jimmie had to die,' and he came to me and said, '*To purify the Navy, Mamma.*'"

EPILOGUE

Here's health to you and to our Corps
Which we are proud to serve.
In many a strife we've fought for life
And never lost our nerve.
If the Army and the Navy
Ever look on Heaven's scenes
They will find the streets are guarded
By United States Marines.

—final stanza, The Marines' Hymn

When Rosa Sutton wrote that Jimmie died "to purify the Navy," she also made sense of her own three-year effort to hold the U.S. government accountable, an exercise in "active liberty" that might not have been possible for a housewife a generation earlier. Rosa was born less than seventy-five years after the ratification of the Constitution; by the time her daughter Rose turned twenty-one in 1901, changes in American society had made it possible for all citizens to have a stake in the news and to use the media to express outrage against real or perceived injustice. America's armed services and institutions of professional military education faced scrutiny that was more intense, more frequent, and broader in scope than ever before. Rosa's hopes of reforming the navy—more specifically the Marine Corps—foreshadowed the goals of civilians and military men in the decades to come. Discipline at the Marine Corps Application School clearly improved immediately after Lieutenant Sutton's death; during the inquiry, members of Congress were shocked by the conditions that existed at the Marine Barracks in 1907. And so the press assured its readers that a Marine Corps shake-up would take place. Woodrow Wilson's secretary of the navy from 1913 to 1921, Josephus Daniels, a Democrat and newspaper publisher, did institute a number of reforms. Over time, the officer corps that was accused of arrogance during the inquiry at Annapolis (and the hazing investigation at West Point) would become more egalitarian. As General George C. Marshall reminded an audience of historians at the start of World War II, in our democracy with a government that is "'truly an agent of the popular will, military policy is dependent on public opinion, and our organization for war will be good or bad as the public is well informed or poorly informed regarding the factors that bear on the subject.'" A century after Lieutenant James N. Sutton died, America's military officials—often in response to adverse public opinion—do engage in self-examination. Today they face new challenges in meeting the needs of a diverse society and a public with opportunities to evaluate military education and justice through an ever-present media that is no longer confined to print.

The mission of professional military education remains a vital one. Junior officers must be trained to play a critical role in handing down the values and traditions "that are an integral part of the warrior ethic." Some of the questions being asked in the twenty-first century were also relevant in 1909. How can leadership and character best be taught? What is the appropriate temperament for success as a military leader? How much stress, austerity, and rigorous discipline is needed for professional military education to achieve its goals? According to a 1997 assessment, especially because of the "growing role of the media," military leaders must become proficient at managing issues related to communication; a decade later, candor remains "critical in an environment intended to build a culture of honor and integrity."

Today the moral education of midshipmen at the Naval Academy—future Marine Corps or naval officers—is a high priority. The advice given in 2005 by Brad Johnson and Gregory Harper in *Becoming a Leader the Annapolis Way: 12 Combat Lessons from the Navy's Leadership Laboratory* would have pleased Rosa Sutton and Henry Davis. The officers in Sutton's Marine Corps Application School class demonstrated a genuine commitment to service in the effort they made to meet the requirements for a commission in the Corps. But, as Johnson and Harper assert, there is no such thing as "natural born leaders," and the differences in maturity among the new second lieutenants required commanders with knowledge of human nature and a willingness to use it that was not widespread in 1907. All of the student officers involved in the case entered the Marine Corps with potential, stamina, drive, and curiosity. But some did not have the empathic skills essential for effective leadership. Lieutenant Harold Utley exhibited more self control than either Lieutenants James Sutton or Robert Adams; his confidence appears to have come at the expense of humility. Other qualities deemed significant by Johnson and Harper include self-awareness and the ability to remain calm and exhibit grace under pressure. Lieutenants Sutton and Adams in particular appeared insecure and prone to outbursts of anger, a trait that Jimmie Sutton, apparently, worked hard to control.

One cause of the stormy relationship between Sutton and Adams may be found in an op-ed piece by David Brooks in the *New York Times*:

> Plato famously divided the soul into three parts: reason, eros (desire) and thymos (the hunger for recognition). Thymos is what motivates the best and worst things men do. It drives them to seek glory and assert themselves aggressively for noble causes. It drives them to rage if others don't recognize their worth. Sometimes it even causes them to kill over a trifle if they feel disrespected.

For reasons that predate their Marine Corps experience, both Adams and Sutton hungered for acceptance in October of 1907; the mutually supportive dynamic between them quickly disintegrated, partly as a result of peer pressure at the Marine Corps Application School. Anger management is a great challenge for those who must instill pride in would-be warriors. Johnson and Harper emphasize that anger has "genuine evolutionary value." It is a "primitive drive for self protection"; physically, "the body responds with a burst of brain neurotransmitters that arouse both hypersensitivity and aggressiveness." But when hypersensitivity gets out of hand, as both Edmund Van Dyke and Henry Davis suggested it had for Lieutenant Adams in the moments before the tragedy (and it had for Sutton as well), the consequences may be fatal. Training now exists at the Academy to improve the emotional intelligence of future leaders in both the Marine Corps and the navy.

Another concern central to the Sutton story that still plagues the navy and the Marine Corps is the issue of misplaced loyalty, one made more complicated by the insularity of officers from the civilian world. How often do officers or enlisted personnel justify either silence ("I cannot recall") or false testimony in a military court proceeding because it is best for their unit (let alone best for an individual officer's future)? From its educational institutions to its justice system, the U.S. military still tends to close ranks against outsiders in the face of criticism; this response may cause more public outcry than the original offense warranted. The debates between attorney Henry Davis and judge advocate Harry Leonard during the Sutton inquiry revealed the difficulty civilian and military bars had in understanding each other. Rosa Sutton was an alien in the naval courtroom; the mutual mistrust between civilian and military personnel comes through at the inquiry and in the media coverage of the case—one that Eugène Fidell might describe as the "perceived outrage of the moment." Then as now, the journalists, scholars, and politicians who critique military justice and call for transparency in its proceedings are usually civilians themselves—a fact that must exacerbate the self-protective attitude of those in charge of the armed services. But the system is changing, however slowly—as it must "if it is to survive and thrive." Over the past century, even as the news media continue to underscore the pitfalls of excessive defensiveness, the navy has tried to address some of these issues head on.

Following World War II, millions "left the service believing [military justice] was harsh, arbitrary, and above all, far too subject to command manipulation." Once the armed forces were merged into one Department of Defense between 1947 and 1948, the Articles for the Government of the Navy and the army's Articles of War were no longer practical. The resulting federal statute, the Uniform Code of Military Justice, provided for a fairer treatment of enlisted personnel in all branches of the armed services. Courts-martial became judicial tribunals rather than instruments of command (although commanders still have authority to select their members). Service men and women now have extensive appellate rights, and the Court of Military Appeals (now the Court of Appeals for the Armed Forces), with its three civilian judges who do not have life tenure, has been and is critical "as both an instrument and a catalyst for change." Historian Jonathan Lurie observes that since 1951 this court has been "consistent in affirming the general principle that due process does indeed apply to the military." At the same time, Supreme Court justices, such as William Rehnquist, have emphasized that "'the different character of the military community and of the military mission requires a different application'" of First Amendment protections.

This "different character" can be seen in what Cathy Packer identifies as the "military civilian free-speech dichotomy." The obedience to commanders so essential for an effective fighting force goes hand-in-hand with specific limits on service members' freedom of expression. At the U.S. Naval Academy, the Military Academy, and the Marine Corps Application School (now the Basic School and the Officer Candidate School at Quantico), young men (and more recently women) learned these rules the moment they arrived. Following World War II, the *Manual for Courts-Martial* (*MCM*), a guide for all of the armed services, spelled out several examples that Packer mentions. No disrespect may be shown to superior commissioned officers—or, for that matter to the president, vice president, members of Congress, the secretary of defense, and other high-ranking officials including governors. Adverse criticism that is not contemptuous or abusive is not considered a violation of these rules, but "provoking" words or "reproachful words or gestures" are. One *MCM* article specifically stated that "the truth or falsity of the [offensive] statements is immaterial." Another said that an officer disciplined for using denunciatory language must remember that "truth is no defense." These regulations do indicate that in certain areas the military establishment must place loyalty above truth; this same attitude was evident a century ago in the code of loyalty among Naval Academy midshipmen; it played into the values of the marines—enlisted men and line officers—who testified in the Sutton case.

However, seasoned officers have always encouraged young men to aspire to the highest standards of integrity and morality. When Jimmie's brother, Don, graduated from West Point in 1913, he heard Secretary of War Lindley M. Garrison tell the class, "Life is no dress parade. Military life holds few occasions of a theatrical character." "Beware of arrogance," he cautioned them in ageless rhetoric, "of the use of power merely because you possess it; of intolerance; of narrowness of view" and, "last and greatest of all, of injustice." The words of retired Brigadier General Horatio G. Gibson, the second speaker at Don's West Point graduation, added advice that would have made Rosa Sutton smile if she read it (his parents could not afford to go): "Be ever courteous to women—homely or comely, aged or youthful, richly or poorly endowed." And, Gibson said, "never forget your mother, nor that which you learned at her knee when she lifted your little hands in prayer to the Great Being who rules this Great Universe and heeds the sparrow's fall . . . for you will find nothing so grateful and consoling as the kindly regard and sympathy of a true woman."

For the American press and its readers, Rosa Sutton came to represent every mother who had lost a son in the military and sought the facts about his fate. This dilemma resonates as strongly today as it did in the decade before World War I. In 2006, America's journalists followed three families whose sons died in Iraq under questionable circumstances. Two of these young men's mothers appeared on a PBS weekly news program, *NOW*, on March 17 and November 17. Their battle "to get the truth from the military" (in this case the army) has followed a course strikingly similar to Rosa Sutton's crusade as is evident in their language and the hurdles they faced. Freed from the limitations of pen and paper, these women telephone and e-mail, seeking answers in the face of inconsistent and false information. Peggy

Buryj filed a Freedom of Information Act request for army reports about Jesse, only to learn that he died from friendly fire from Polish troops—a point now contested by another soldier from her son's unit. Karen Meredith sought help from a member of Congress and finally learned that her son, Ken Ballard, died from "an accidental discharge by an unmanned machine gun." Both felt the "fierce discontent" that Theodore Roosevelt referred to in 1906, which, with their sense that they have the right to know exactly what happened, has fueled their response to tragedies that are part of today's discourse about secrecy in the government. "I should not have had to beg, scream, cry, call politicians, play the political game," said Buryj. "I shouldn't have to be going to the media."

Neither mother, overwhelmed by a very private grief, wanted to use the media, nor did the parents of Patrick Tillman, who seek answers three years after their son died in Afghanistan, in a case more highly publicized than most because of his decision to leave a successful National Football League career to join the army. Yet, a front page story in the *New York Times* describes the "long, sometimes raw, letters to military leaders, demanding answers about the shooting" that Tillman's father, Patrick, has written. His former wife told the reporter how she has been going "over and over and over this. . . . I am beyond tears. It's killing me." Mary Tillman has contacted officers who might know something about her son's death and has lobbied for help from Congress. A United States Defense Department investigation concluded early in 2007 that nine army officers provided misleading or inaccurate information about Tillman's death. On April 24, congressional hearings probed further. Mary Tillman and Pat's brother, Kevin, spoke about the smokescreen that has obscured the facts about Pat's death as well as what they see as the army's attempt to dupe the public in order to instill patriotism. In their response to this savvy and distraught mother, congressmen underscored the critical need for justice and the public and parents' right to know the truth about this incident and others like it.

As was true of Rosa and Jim Sutton, these parents are all patriotic and immensely proud of their sons, who, in turn, were proud to be in the military service. Then, as now, mothers fought hard to help their sons achieve their dreams. They have made progress, but their grief has been hardened by anger and skepticism about an institution that depends on the absolute loyalty of its recruits. Not long ago, a young Marine Corps officer and classics major, Nathaniel Fick, was struck by the "timelessness" at the base at Quantico. The dedication of his book, *One Bullet Away: The Making of a Marine Officer* (2005), is to a captain killed in action in 2004 and "the brave mothers of United States Marines." These mothers know their bravery comes at a price. "Men love to believe that women love warriors," author Richard Rayner wrote in 1997. But there are maternal truths that may never exist in complete harmony with the Corps' warrior ethos. Rosa Sutton, whose crusade for justice took place before America had ever been caught up in a world war, would say that is a good thing.

MILITARY REPUTATIONS

The officers whose lives were touched by the Sutton case served at a time when America had just become a "quasi imperial power," with both economic and missionary interests in the Caribbean, Mexico, Central America, China, and the Pacific. Marines and navy men played a lead role in this expansion, and some officers served more effectively than others. John Adrian Hoogewerff, the president of the 1907 inquest board, became a rear admiral and retired after forty-seven years in the navy. Wendell C. Neville, a member of the Sutton court in 1909, had a superb career that ended suddenly with his death when he was major general and commandant of the Corps in 1930. He was succeeded by General Benjamin Fuller, who had been acting commandant during Neville's illness; Fuller served until his retirement in 1934. The judge advocate, Henry Leonard, became a lieutenant colonel who earned several awards and decorations before retiring from the Marine Corps in 1911 on account of the injury he had received in China eleven years earlier. He was recalled to duty in the office of the judge advocate general during World War I. He later became a respected attorney, director of the National Metropolitan Bank of Washington, a Republican National Committeeman from Colorado, and an enthusiastic rancher. For many years he divided his time between Georgetown and Colorado Springs. He was sixty-eight when he died in 1945. And the Sutton story would not be complete without a look at the fates of Lieutenants Robert Adams, Harold Utley, and Edward Roelker.

Lieutenant Adams left Annapolis for New York City at the end of August 1909. He would spend thirteen more years in the Corps, many of them productive but distressing ones. Adams was plagued by gastrointestinal and other health problems that had flared up in the fall of 1907 and became increasingly severe over the next decade. His stomach trouble and inability to digest food became debilitating after he returned from a U.S. military expedition to Cuba in 1911. Nevertheless, he continued on duty, although he suffered from depression and anxiety. It was then that he wrote, "I went to New York, on account of my nervous condition, they put me under the charge of a psychiatrist, who thought my condition was entirely mental nervousness." The causal relationship between his "nervous temperament" and his stomach problems was unclear. Adams had been disciplined once for insubordination, and he also received commendations for his performance in 1916 and 1917. Toward the end of his military career, he began to study criminal and civil law. His last position in the Corps was, ironically, that of judge advocate of a general court-martial at the Brooklyn Navy Yard, a job he performed with "exceptional ability and usefulness," demonstrating a temperament that was "alert, forceful, active, painstaking." According to his official medical report in 1920, Robert Adams suffered from "marked tremors of the fingers," was "hypochondriocal [*sic*] in speech and manner," and had a "history of projectile vomiting." But he had been promoted to major by 1920, and he retired, in good standing, for health reasons in November of that year. He had not married by the time he left the service, and he died in 1947 in Atlantic Highlands, New Jersey.

Lieutenant Harold Utley's career took a far more favorable turn; in many respects, he exemplified the Marine Corps of the era. America's imperialistic foreign policy involved not only the protection of interests abroad but also intervention in Honduras, Panama, Cuba, Haiti, Santo Domingo, and Nicaragua. Harold Utley served in Cuba, Santo Domingo, and Haiti and won several awards including a Distinguished Service Medal for his courageous performance as commander of the Eastern Area in Nicaragua in 1928–1929. His official record was no doubt gratifying to him and to his mother. But a fair assessment of Utley's career, which is beyond the scope of this book, should take into account the documents accompanying an examination of his "moral fitness" while in Nicaragua. When Harold Utley arrived in the Eastern Area in Nicaragua, tension already existed between the civilian population and the marines because of allegations of prisoner abuse. (One lieutenant, M. R. Carroll, "had used a so-called electric chair to torture prisoners and extort confessions from them." This officer and other marines had shot an escaping prisoner. A second officer, a captain, had also been charged with torturing prisoners at the post of El Gallo.) About two months after Utley took command, "the civil population" again reported Carroll for "alleged inhuman conduct with regard to prisoners." Utley finally ordered an investigation to be headed by Lieutenant Maurice Shearer, probably his former classmate. Ultimately, Carroll received a formal reprimand and was transferred from foreign duty to the United States.

Utley also ran into serious difficulties with a local businessman in Nicaragua, who, with others, sent letters in April 1929 protesting Utley's arrogant and self-absorbed behavior toward civilians. Utley was, allegedly, a heavy drinker, according to one report, "disgracing himself in the uniform he wore by his drunken acts on the dance floor," guilty of crude behavior toward women, and of deliberately using his auto to scare the horses and annoy a riding party from which he had been excluded but his wife had not. Utley denied these charges and insisted that his personal reputation was "good in all respects." However, after the investigation, he was relieved of his command and replaced by Edwin McClellan (another former classmate at the Marine Application School). McClellan testified that he was sent to Puerto Cabezas because of the "friction of Major Utley with the Manager and other officials of the Lumber Co., and [because Utley] was also mixed up with liquor and women or a woman." McClellan found the charges to be true once he arrived but had been told to keep the matter confidential; he said that one reason a court-martial had not been held was that it would "bring considerable discredit upon the Brigade after the matters were discussed in court." The deleterious effect of Utley's behavior and activities on "public opinion" was quite obvious to him.

Among the documents appended to this investigation is a copy of a letter from the major general commandant to the secretary of the navy "withdrawing approval of award to Major Utley for service in Nicaragua." Like those in the Sutton inquiry, the credibility of the charges against Major Utley depended on whom one believed. One solution to problems with command overseas was evidently to bring the offending officer back home. Harold Utley was reassigned to duty in the United States in January 1930. For three years he was an instructor and director of the Field Officers Course at Quantico; he then spent his last three years before retiring in 1936 in Newport at the Naval War College. Utley did become a lieutenant colonel on Christmas Day 1932. (He returned to command the Marine Barracks in Newport between 1941 and 1944.) He died of heart disease on July 8, 1951.

Lieutenant Edward Roelker's fate remained more of a mystery than that of Jimmie Sutton. Despite his parent's best efforts, he never seemed entirely happy in military settings. His discharge from the Marine Corps in 1907 seems unduly severe, even though he had been disciplined previously for intoxication. Roelker chose to represent himself at the investigation and could have been embarrassed to face his parents after the dismissal. On the evening in question—as several men testified—he was much more sober than his fellow officer, Allen Sumner. But once dismissed, Roelker had no recourse to appellate review. Perhaps Charles Doyen was eager to use Roelker as an example after the Sutton fracas, as reporters suggested. (His Examining Board files are missing, and journalists' accounts of his whereabouts in 1909 may or may not be accurate.) If Roelker was alive in 1909, he may indeed have written Jimmie's family that Sutton had been murdered. The sources do not reveal whether suicide, homicide, or a new identity factored in the tragic disappearance of Edward Roelker.

The Virginia Military Institute has a notation in Roelker's alumnus file, dated January 15, 1929: "Roelker disappeared from the records many years ago." In 1922, the year Rear Admiral Charles R. Roelker died, Edward "Red" Roelker's sister Mildred wrote that her brother disappeared "not long after his departure from the V M I and his family have no knowledge of him, subsequent to the time of his disappearance." She preferred to keep the incident confidential as it was "extremely painful to his relatives." And it was heartbreaking to Parthenia Roelker, who no doubt suffered just as much as Rosa Sutton over the loss of a son—in her case, a loss without closure or even a final resting place.

SEPARATE HEADSTONES

Rosa and Jim Sutton's marriage did not survive the calamity of their son's death. Part of the cause was a complete breakdown in communication; part of it was financial. At first, Rosa refused to leave the house on Hoyt Street, forcing Jim Sutton to declare bankruptcy. Her two expensive years in Washington had not helped matters; their divorce became final after a bitter separation on February 10, 1915. (There were clearly some areas of Rosa's life not governed by Catholicism. She had married out of her faith and, although divorce was epidemic at the turn of the last century and soundly denounced by James Cardinal Gibbons, she was the one to file for divorce.) Afterward, Jim Sutton lived in a rooming house in Portland not far from Hoyt Street. On Sunday, November 14, his fifty-ninth birthday, he told his landlady he was dying of a broken heart and asked if she would mind if he died in her home, "where I now feel welcome." He had ordered a suit to be buried in, he said, and he did not want to be cremated. The next day, just before two in the afternoon, Jim left his associates at the East Side Freight Office of the Southern Pacific and Oregon-Washington Railroad and Navigation Company by saying, "I'm not coming back." He boarded the Belmont jitney to go home. Shortly afterward, a friend who caught the jitney at Twentieth and Morrison streets greeted Jim Sutton. There was no response; Jim had had a fatal heart attack. Dr. James Hyslop would have found it intriguing that Sutton had a premonition of his own death. Noting the tragedies that had befallen the Sutton family, the *Oregon Daily Journal* reminded its readers that, eight years earlier, Jim Sutton's son had died "a mysterious death" at Annapolis.

By the time Jim died, Rosa Sutton had agreed to the sale of 784 Hoyt Street, and she subsequently lived in an apartment in Portland. But she soon moved to Los Angeles to be near her daughter Daysie and her two young grandchildren. Between 1912 and 1930 she helped Daysie raise her son and daughter, making sure they became Catholics. Rosa died after a long illness on May 23, 1937; she is buried in the San Francisco National Cemetery, at a former army base, the Presidio. (Her brother, Louis, and son-in-law, Hugh Parker, are also at the Presidio.)

While her parents' marriage was disintegrating, Daysie Sutton met the love of her life—a man from Iowa who became a miner and celebrated humorist in Arizona. Dick Wick Hall adored the Arizona desert, and he is credited with co-founding the town of Salome (west of Phoenix) and making it famous through the *Salome Sun*, his nationally syndicated (originally mimeographed) news sheet about desert life. (The town still celebrates Dick Wick Hall Days every fall.) Hall died suddenly in 1926, and two years later his wife contracted breast cancer. She died on May 12, 1930, leaving her sister Rose as the guardian of her by-then-adolescent children.

The Suttons' oldest child outlived all of her siblings. Rose decided that she had been too young when she married an army officer, and she divorced Hugh Parker. She spent several years studying and writing in Europe before marrying a widower, Robert Randolph Hicks, a Wall Street attorney and Virginia gentleman, in 1919. They raised Black Angus cattle on farmland in northern Virginia where they built a manor house in 1928–1929—one that reflected her love of Europe. They hung onto it through severe financial losses in the Depression; it is now open to the public as Poplar Springs Inn. Both Randolph Hicks, who died in 1951, and Rose, who died in 1958, are buried on the property.

Few records or Sutton family papers have been found about Louise Sutton. She and her sister Rose, who was twelve years older, disagreed over the custody of Daysie's children. Between 1930 and 1937, their husbands carried the expenses of Rosa's deteriorating health. Louise married three times; her second was a happy marriage to Hugh Parker, her former brother-in-law. After he died, Louise and her third husband, Durwood Bailey, made their home in Santa Monica.

It seems fitting to close with the Sutton's youngest son, Don Sutton, who entered West Point in 1909 a few months after Wilbur Wright's historic flight in western France. Don was caught up in America's growing passion for aviation. After graduating in 1913, he served as a post commander in Massachusetts, and then, on June 16, 1915, he became a first lieutenant in the Army Signal Corps. He resigned from active duty in the army just before the United States entered World War I. Don became a businessman, but long-term success evaded him. In 1936, Don, who was divorced, moved to Mexico where he purchased several gold, silver, and mercury mines. At the age of fifty-four he married nineteen-year-old Luz Maria Centeno Soriano, and on March 11, 1944, she gave birth to a son, Don's only child. During World War II, the Mexican government confiscated Don's mines; Rose and Louise sent him their gold jewelry, but it was stolen by a day laborer. Don became depressed, and on a September Sunday in 1946, while his young wife was at church, he committed suicide by drinking a bottle of cyanide. He is buried in Mexico City. His son, James R. Sutton, who was named after his Uncle Jimmie, has served in the air force and as an FBI special agent. He was a senior research intelligence analyst in the Terrorism Task Force created after September 11, 2001. Since 2006, Jim Sutton has been director of the Highway Watch Information Sharing and Analysis Center at the Transportation Security Administration Operations Center in Virginia.

AUTHOR'S COMMENT

In a brittle fragment of what was once a Sutton family Bible, there is a page bordered in red and gold titled "Deaths." Only one entry appears in Rose Sutton Parker's handwriting, "James N. Sutton Jr. Oct 13th 1907." It includes a penciled comment: "Beaten to death by his Brother officers in U S Marine Corps." Although they were not able to prove it in a courtroom, Rosa Sutton and her daughter, Rose, never stopped believing Jimmie had been murdered.

After a decade of living with the historical sources, I do not believe Lieutenant Sutton committed suicide, nor do I think the evidence fully supports Rose's remark that his death was caused by a beating, not a bullet. Had he not been shot, he could have died from another head wound, and he may well have been unconscious when he was shot. But there is no reason to doubt the testimony that he was alive—though barely so—when he was first found by Colonel Charles Doyen and Dr. George Pickrell. An argument can be made that, in the heat of fury, Lieutenant Robert Adams killed Lieutenant Sutton. He is certainly the most likely person to have fired the fatal shot. The inconsistencies in his statements, especially the new pieces of information that he recalled in 1909, are the most troubling. The fragile nature of human memory, and the many factors that bear on the accuracy of eyewitness testimony, make it impossible to prove beyond a reasonable doubt that any of the accused marines committed perjury. And so there is insufficient evidence to convict Adams or anyone else. On the other hand, attorneys Henry Davis and Edmund Van Dyke, Dr. Edward Schaeffer, and James Hyslop all present persuasive arguments based in part on logic and common sense that Sutton did not shoot himself, either intentionally or accidentally. The re-enactments by Robert Adams and by three doctors revealed how hard it would have been for Lieutenant Sutton to kill himself in the circumstances in which he found himself (in spite of Dr. Raymond Spear's alleged attempts to successfully repeat the same re-enactments after Dr. George Vaughan's autopsy). However, the most credible descriptions of the apparently fatal bullet hole, in Dr. Spear's autopsy report and newspaper accounts citing Dr. Vaughan's report, indicate that the bullet was fired at close range (less than six inches away) or while the gun was in contact with Sutton's head. But that information does not prove who pulled the trigger. (If Adams did, it would have made sense for him to hold the muzzle near Sutton's head.) In any case, Edmund Van Dyke was likely incorrect in his statement to the press—assuming he made it—that the shot was fired from more than five feet away.

The slipshod investigation that occurred within hours of Lieutenant Sutton's death may, in fact, not have been a deliberate cover-up by the three members of the naval inquest board. John Hoogewerff, Frank Cook, and Benjamin Fuller could have simply chosen the easy way out; they took the testimony of the young marines who were present at Sutton's death at face value, ignoring their inconsistencies and failing to seek out others who might shed more light on the case. The board's haste was inexcusable but not surprising in the context in which it occurred. On the other hand, an intentional cover-up of all the facts by one or more of the student officers and by Sergeant James De Hart—who no doubt felt trapped into lying—is far more probable. That fact was probably clear to the 1909 court, which was well aware how little hard evidence the Suttons had.

So why did the navy agree to reopen the Sutton case? Part of the reason was obviously political pressure exerted through Senator Jonathan Bourne. But the threat of scandal in this era of insatiable reporters was of grave concern to men whose reputations were sacred to them. I believe that Private Harry Swartz began sharing Rosa's blunt letters with his superiors in the Marine Corps before the winter of 1908–1909. These letters may have given him something to brag about. Rosa's obsessive determination to see the matter through—so clear in these letters—could have caused the Department's change of heart. If that was the case, Harry Swartz inadvertently helped her cause by the fact of his betrayal. Loyalty to the Corps above all else was a value he had learned well.

A PERSONAL NOTE

Rosa and Jim Sutton were my mother's maternal grandparents. After my mother died in 1987, I found a puzzling black enamel locket among the jewelry she inherited from her Aunt Rose. It has a flaming Sacred Heart in the center that is crafted of seed pearls and gold; inside is a faded photograph of a young officer and a lock of chestnut hair. Many years later, I realized that the locket is a classic piece of mourning jewelry from the Progressive Era, and the photograph in it is Jimmie Sutton. (Newspaper photographs reveal that Rose Parker wore it at the inquiry.) In the spring of 1996, I came across some newspaper clippings about the case and a carbon copy of Rosa Sutton's passionate response to Major Leonard's statement that "the hallowed grave of a dead son is no more sacred than the grave of a military reputation." No one had ever told me about Jimmie's controversial death, nor had I known my mother was raised as a Catholic. Rosa's psychic experiences were clearly awkward for the family, and the tragedy too difficult to discuss.

I recall hearing little about Rosa, except for my mother's occasional reference to taking care of her ailing "Gram" when she was barely thirteen. But as a young child, I was close to my great aunt, Rose Sutton Parker Hicks. Not long after her brother Don died, she suffered a stroke that paralyzed her right side. Even though she was in a wheelchair, I remember her clever, mischievous, and spirited nature and the way she struggled to write with her one good hand. Older friends have made unsolicited comments to me about her mesmerizing eyes—a feature that so intrigued reporters in 1909.

For much of the past decade, the research for this book has been a personal as well as a professional journey. A few occasions have been especially moving. On a rainy Memorial Day in 2001, I visited Jimmie Sutton's modest grave at Arlington Cemetery—it is not exactly where site number 2102 should be and was, therefore, hard to find. Today, almost hidden under the boughs of a huge fir tree, it is surrounded by the impressive markers of other more distinguished officers. I have also been inside the auditorium in Mahan Hall at the Naval Academy where the inquiry took place, and I walked around what was once the Sutton house on Hoyt Street in Portland, Oregon, trying to imagine its better days. (I was not allowed inside.) It was most intriguing to find the originals of Rosa Sutton's letters to Harry Swartz attached to the inquiry record in the National Archives. And, finally, in 2005, I had the good fortune to meet the step-granddaughter of Major Harry Leonard. Ellen Rublee and her husband, George, an attorney and former marine, have been most generous with their hospitality and their support for this project. Mrs. Rublee's grandmother married the former judge advocate when her mother was barely three years old. (He had no children of his own.) She spent many hours riding horseback with him and recalls her "Uncle Harry" well. He remained extremely disciplined throughout his life. When the Rublees invited me for dinner, I was touched to find Leonard's monogrammed silverware at my place setting. I hope that my great-grandmother and her step-grandfather, who represented such sharply opposing worlds, somehow know of our friendship.

Hundreds of unread documents including court transcripts and the Marine Corps officers' Applicant for Commission and Examining Board files at the National Archives await future scholars. Their career and medical histories humanize the marines whose private battles were often as difficult as the ones they faced in the service of their country.

A NOTE ON THE SOURCES

Although this account is based primarily on newly discovered documents from a century ago, a number of secondary sources proved invaluable in deciphering them—highlights of these appear below. A full bibliography follows the notes. Additional information and images related to the Sutton case can be found on the author's website (www.RobinRCutler .com).

MEMORY AND TRUTH-TELLING

Several authors helped to shape the framework for this book by posing important questions and answers about the eternal search for verifiable truth. These include two works by Daniel L. Schacter, *Searching for Memory: The Brain, The Mind and the Past* (1996) and *The Seven Sins of Memory (How the Mind Forgets and Remembers)* (2001); see also Elizabeth F. Loftus, *Eyewitness Testimony* (1996); Peter B. Ainsworth, *Psychology, Law and Eyewitness Testimony* (1998); Bernard Williams, *Truth and Truthfulness: An Essay in Genealogy* (2002); Harry G. Frankfurt, *The Importance of What We Care About* (1988); and Sissela Bok, *Lying: Moral Choice in Public and Private Life* (1999, reprint) with her *Secrets: On the Ethics of Concealment and Revelation* (1989, reprint). Sidney Axinn, *A Moral Military* (1989), provides perspective on the ethical issues confronted by those who lead and follow in our armed services, and Joyce Appleby, Lynn Hunt, and Margaret Jacob, *Telling the Truth about History* (1994), do the same for historians. And, last but not least, Walter Lippmann, in *Public Opinion* (1922), who wrote, "The hypothesis, which seems to me the most fertile, is that news and truth are not the same thing, and must be clearly distinguished."

THE DECADE

An excellent introduction to the Progressive Era with a comprehensive bibliographical essay, updated in 2000 and organized by topics, is John Whiteclay Chambers II, *The Tyranny of Change: America in the Progressive Era, 1890–1920* (2004, reprint). The period between approximately 1890 and 1920 has had many labels, and scholarly analysis of the era continues to generate controversy, as Chambers notes; his chapter 9, "The Meaning of the Progressive Era" is essential reading. Also helpful were Steven J. Diner, *A Very Different Age: Americans of the Progressive Era* (1998); Michael McGerr, *A Fierce Discontent: The Rise and Fall of the Progressive Movement in America: 1870–1920* (2003); and Edward Wagenknecht, *American Profile: 1900–1909* (1982). The indispensable multi-volume work by Mark Sullivan has been condensed and edited by Dan Rather, *Our Times: America at the Birth of the Twentieth Century* (1996), and for a global perspective, Alan Dawley, *Changing the World: American Progressives in War and Revolution* (2003). On individual presidencies, see (as a start) Edmund Morris, *Theodore Rex* (2002); Lewis L. Gould, *The Presidency of Theodore Roosevelt* (1991), with its comprehensive bibliographical essay; and Paolo Enrico Coletta, *The Presidency of William Howard Taft* (1973). Jonathan Lurie is now working on a new biography of Taft. And see bss.sfsu.edu/cherny/gapesites.htm for H-SHGAPE's (Society for the History of the Gilded Age and Progressive Era) list of websites for the Gilded Age and Progressive Era.

MILITARY JUSTICE

Jonathan Lurie correctly notes that today the law governing our armed forces does not need to be "'fundamentally arcane and inaccessible'" (*Military Justice in America*, 2001, xii). As a start, consult the superb articles in Eugene R. Fidell and Dwight H. Sullivan, eds. *Evolving Military Justice* (2002); and the seven entries under "Justice, Military" in *The Oxford Companion to American Military History*, ed. John Whiteclay Chambers II (1999). For bibliographical references, see Thomas C. Mackey, "Military and Martial Law Issues," in *A Guide to the Sources of United States Military History*, ed. Robin Higham and Donald J. Mrozek, Supplement IV (1998); and Donald G. Nieman, "Military Law, Martial Law and Military Government," in Supplement I of the same series (1981). The following sources (in alphabetical order) also help define the issues and place the proceedings of the Sutton Court of Inquiry in a broader context: S. T. Ansell, "Military Justice," *Cor-*

nell Law Quarterly 5 (November 1919): 1–17; Walter T. Cox III, "The Army, the Courts and the Constitution: The Evolution of Military Justice," *Military Law Review* 118 (Fall 1987): 1–30; *Forms of Procedure for Courts and Boards in the Navy and Marine Corps* (1910); *A Guide to Military Criminal Law* (1999); Jonathan Lurie, *Military Justice in America: The U.S. Court of Appeals for the Armed Forces, 1775–1980* (2001; this is a revised and abridged edition without notes of Lurie, 1992 and 1998); Thomas C. Mackey, "The Judiciary and the Military," one of several useful articles in the *Encyclopedia of the American Military, Vol. 1* (1994); D. B. Nichols, "Military and Civil Legal Values: *Mens Rea*—A Case in Point," *Military Law Review* 28 (1965): 169–93; Cathy Packer, *Freedom of Expression in the American Military: A Communication Modeling Analysis* (1989); Robert Pasley Jr. and Felix Larkin, "The Navy Court Martial: Proposals for Its Reform," *Cornell Law Quarterly* 33 (1947): 195–234; James E. Valle, *Rocks and Shoals: Naval Discipline in the Age of Fighting Sail* (1980); and William Winthrop, *Military Law and Precedents*, 2nd ed. (1920; first published in 1886, this classic was found in Jimmie Sutton's trunk after he died).

THE MARINE CORPS AND THE UNITED STATES NAVAL ACADEMY

The United States Marine Corps (USMC) History Division and its historical reference branch are now in Quantico, Virginia, as is the Library of the Marine Corps, the Alfred M. Gray Research Center, and the new National Museum of the Marine Corps and Heritage Center near the USMC base (www.usmcmuseum.org). Research information can be found through the website www.mcu.usmc.mil. Military records relating to individual Marine Corps officers and naval investigations before World War I remain at the National Archives Building in Washington, D.C. The United States Naval Historical Center (www.history.navy.mil) also has biographical information on naval officers and suggestions for reading on its websites; the United States Naval Academy (www.usna.edu/library) has an excellent site with a guide to the collections at Nimitz Library.

Essential secondary works on the Marine Corps include Allan R. Millett, *Semper Fidelis: The History of the United States Marine Corps* (1991); J. Robert Moskin, *The U.S. Marine Corps Story* (1992); Thomas E. Ricks, *Making the Corps* (1997); the late Karl Schuon's, *United States Marine Corps Biographical Dictionary* (1963); and Jack Shulimson, *The Marine Corps' Search for a Mission: 1880–1898* (1993).

Shulimson has written a comprehensive study of exactly why marines still feared "for the existence of their Corps" and "constantly defined, redefined and justified their roles and missions to both themselves and everyone else." A key problem was the "inherent insecurity of the Marine officer" about his place in the American armed services (*The Marine Corps' Search for a Mission*, 1993, 208). By the beginning of the twentieth century, some of these problems began to be resolved. See also Merrill L. Bartlett and Jack Sweetman, *The U.S. Marine Corps: An Illustrated History* (2001). For the history of the Application School between 1908 and World War I, Eugène Alvarez's unpublished manuscript, "The Cradle of the Corps: A History of the United States Marine Corps Recruit Depot, Parris Island, South Carolina, 1562—2002," is at the Parris Island Museum, Marine Corps Recruit Depot. A copy is also at the Marine Corps Historical Center, Quantico, Virginia.

On the Naval Academy in this era, begin with Jack Sweetman, *The U.S. Naval Academy: An Illustrated History*, 2nd ed., revised by Thomas J. Cutler (1995); also Peter Karston, *The Naval Aristocracy: The Golden Age of Annapolis and the Emergence of Modern American Navalism* (1972); John P. Lovell, *Neither Athens nor Sparta? The American Service Academies in Transition* (1979).

THE NEW JOURNALISM

Useful contemporary books about the newspaper industry in this decade include John L. Given, *Making a Newspaper* (1907); James Edward Rogers, *The American Newspaper* (1909); Nathaniel C. Fowler Jr., *The Handbook of Journalism* (1913); William Salisbury, *The Career of a Journalist* (1908); and Grant Milnor Hyde, *Newspaper Reporting and Correspondence* (1912). Walter Lippmann found Given's book to be the "best technical book I know, and should be read by everyone who undertakes to discuss the press" (*Public Opinion* [1922] [1997]: 205n1).

General surveys include Michael Emery and Edwin Emery, *The Press and America: An Interpretive History of the Mass Media*, 7th ed. (1992); Frank Luther Mott, *American Journalism: A History of Newspapers in the United States through 250 Years, 1690 to 1940* (1941), and *A History of American Magazines 1885–1905*, vol. 4 (1957); Matthew Schneirov, *The Dream of New Social Order: Popular Magazines in America: 1893–1914* (1994); and Michael Schudson's works, especially *The Good Citizen: A History of American Civic Life* (1998) and *Discovering the News: A Social History of American Newspapers* (1978). J. Anthony Lukas wrote a superb chapter on the impact of the press in this decade in *Big Trouble: A Murder in a Small Western Town Sets Off a Struggle for the Soul of America* (1997). A number of books provided insights about journalism as a profession: Timothy E. Cook, *Governing with the News* (1998); James S. Ettema and Theodore L. Glasser, *Custodians of Conscience: Investigative Journalism and Public Virtue* (1998); Bill Kovach and Tom Rosenstiel, *The Elements of Journalism: What Newspeople Should Know and the Public Should Expect* (2001); Barbie Zelizer, *Taking Journalism Seriously: News and the Academy* (2004).

WOMEN IN THE PROGRESSIVE ERA

The literature on the subject is vast, and many suggestions are included in the books listed above by Chambers and Diner. But on the themes in this story see Aileen S. Kraditor, *The Ideas of the Woman Suffrage Movement: 1890–1920* (1981); Elisabeth Griffith, *In Her Own Right: The Life of Elizabeth Cady Stanton* (1984); Paula Baker, "The Domestication of Politics: Women and American Political Society, 1780–1920," *American Historical Review* 89, no. 3 (June 1984): 620–47 (Baker's survey includes hundreds of useful references in the notes); Robyn Muncy, *Creating a Female Dominion in American Reform: 1890–1935* (1991); Theda Skocpol, *Protecting Soldiers and Mothers: The Political Origins of Social Policy in the United States* (1992); Nancy Woloch, *Women and the American Experience* (1999); and more recently, four very accessible works: the lively volume by Gail Collins, *America's Women: 400 Years of Dolls, Drudges, Helpmates, and Heroines* (2003), with its own comprehensive bibliography; Eleanor Clift, *Founding Sisters and the Nineteenth Amendment* (2003); Jean H. Baker, *Sisters: The Lives of America's Suffragists* (2005), and her "Getting Right with Women's Suffrage," *The Journal of the Gilded Age and Progressive Era* 5, no.1 (January 2006): 7–17. Two contemporary sources rarely cited that provide fascinating information on century-old perspectives are Emma F. Angell Drake, *What a Young Wife Ought to Know* (1908), and her *What a Woman of Forty-Five Ought to Know* (1902), which describes some of the emotional struggles women Rosa's age went through during menopause a century ago.

HISTORY OF AMERICAN CATHOLICISM

A well-written recent history is Charles R. Morris, *American Catholic: The Saints and Sinners Who Built America's Most Powerful Church* (1997). Also useful is Jay P. Dolan, *The American Catholic Experience: A History from Colonial Times to the Present* (1987), and his *In Search of an American Catholicism: A History of Religion and Culture in Tension* (2002); John T. McGreevy, *Catholicism and American Freedom* (2003); Robert A. Orsi, *Between Heaven and Earth: The Religious Worlds People Make and the Scholars Who Study Them* (2005), especially chapter 3, "Material Children: Making God's Presence Real for Catholic Boys and Girls and for the Adults in Relation to Them"; and for perspective on the Oregon church, Patricia Brandt and Lillian A. Pereyra, *Adapting in Eden: Oregon's Catholic Minority: 1838–1986* (2002), and Wilfred P. Schoenberg, *A Pictorial History of the Catholic Church in the Pacific Northwest* (1996).

The repository for most of James Cardinal Gibbons' papers, including all his incoming correspondence, is the Associated Archives at St. Mary's Seminary and University in Baltimore. The most comprehensive biography of Gibbons' life is still that by John Tracy Ellis, *The Life of James Cardinal Gibbons, Archbishop of Baltimore, 1834–1921*, 2 vols. (1952); Ellis' definitive biography includes a full assessment of the man and his personality at the end of volume 2. For his own words, start with James Cardinal Gibbons, *A Retrospect of Fifty Years* (1916) and his classic, *The Faith of Our Fathers: A Plain Exposition and Vindication of the Church Founded by Our Lord Jesus Christ* (1980 [1876]), 111th printing.

PARAPSYCHOLOGY

R. Laurence Moore's *In Search of White Crows: Spiritualism, Parapsychology, and American Culture* (1977) remains one of the most balanced surveys of this controversial field. Two recent books based on exhaustive research are Barbara Goldsmith, *Other Powers: The Age of Suffrage, Spiritualism, and the Scandalous Victoria Woodhull* (1999); and Deborah Blum, *Ghost Hunters: William James and the Search for Scientific Proof of Life after Death* (2006). Also useful are Seymour H. Mauskopf and Michael R. McVaugh, *The Elusive Science: Origins of Experimental Psychical Research* (1980); Vanessa D. Dickerson, *Victorian Ghosts in the Noontide: Women Writers and the Supernatural* (1996); Christine Wicker, *Lily Dale: The True Story of the Town That Talks to the Dead* (2003); Sylvia Hart Wright, *When Spirits Come Calling: The Open-Minded Skeptic's Guide to After-Death Contacts* (2002); Ray Hyman, *The Elusive Quarry: A Scientific Appraisal of Psychical Research* (1989); Richard S. Broughton, *Parapsychology: The Controversial Science* (1991); and Carlos S. Alvarado, "The Concept of Survival of Bodily Death and the Development of Parapsychology," *Journal for the Society of Psychical Research* 67 (April 2003): 65–95.

An unparalleled collection of primary sources about the history of psychical research can be found in the archives of the American Society for Psychical Research in New York City. See also the journal of the society, which began publication in 1907. The Eileen J. Garrett Library of the Parapsychology Foundation Library in Greenport, New York, and the foundation's excellent website (www.parapsychology.org) are sources for dozens of references to other credible sources. The foundation also has books for sale, including pamphlets that provide an introduction to the field.

SCENE SETTING

The Oregon Historical Society, the Historic Annapolis Foundation, the Maryland State Archives, and the Historical Society of Washington, D.C., and their websites should be the first stop for anyone seriously interested in the history of Portland, Oregon, Annapolis, or the nation's capital. Important sources include the following:

Portland, Oregon

E. Kimbark MacColl, *The Shaping of a City: Business and Politics in Portland Oregon 1885 to 1915* (1976), and his expanded version, *Merchants, Money and Power: The Portland Establishment 1843–1913* (1988), are excellent introductions to Portland and its politicians such as John H. Mitchell and Charles Fulton. Polk's *Portland City Directory* for 1909 is much more than a list of names; it also includes a listing of businesses, individuals, and advertisements and an essay on the city's population. See also Joseph Gaston, *Portland, Oregon: Its History and Builders*, vol. 3 (1911); Lawrence H. Larsen, *The Urban West at the End of the Frontier* (1978); for the 1905 fair, Carl Abbott, *Portland and the Lewis and Clark Exposition*, rev. ed. (1996); and Percy Maddux, *City on the Willamette* (1952). For the former Columbia University where Jimmie Sutton spent a year, see James T. Covert, *A Point of Pride: The University of Portland Story* (1976).

Annapolis, Maryland

A comprehensive social and political history of Annapolis has yet to be written. However, the town is justly proud of its architectural history; the Historic Annapolis Foundation has a new center focusing on this history called History Quest (www.annapolis.org). Although most research to date has focused on colonial Annapolis, for the early twentieth century, see William Oliver Stevens, *Annapolis: Anne Arundel's Town* (1937); Mary Elizabeth Warren, *The Train's Done Been and Gone: Annapolis Portrait, 1859–1910* (1976); Michael P. Parker, *President's Hill: Building an Annapolis Neighborhood: 1664–2005* (2005); and Marsha M. Miller and Orlando Rideout V, eds., *Architecture in Annapolis: A Field Guide* (1998). The *Annapolis City Directory for 1910* is the first annual directory for Annapolis.

Washington, D.C.

See Carol M. Highsmith and Ted Landphair, *Union Station: A Decorative History of Washington's Grand Terminal* (1988); Paul H. Caemmerer, *Historic Washington, Capital of the Nation* (1948); James M. Goode, *A Century of Washington's Distinguished Apartment Houses: Best Addresses* (1988); W. Andrew Boyd, ed., *Boyd's Directories of the District of Columbia* (1902–1911); Letitia W. Brown and Elise M. Lewis, *Washington in the New Era, 1870–1970* (1972); Kathleen Collins, *Washingtoniana Photographs: Collections in the Prints and Photographs Division of the Library of Congress* (1989); Douglas E. Evelyn and Paul Dickson, *On This Spot: Pinpointing the Past in Washington, D.C.* (1992); Thomas Froncek, ed., *The City of Washington: An Illustrated History* (1977); Charles Suddarth Kelly, *Washington, D.C., Then and Now: 69 Sites Photographed in the Past and Present* (1984); Pamela Scott and Antoinette J. Lee, *Buildings of the District of Columbia* (1993); Wayne Andrews, *Architecture, Ambition and Americans: A Social History of American Architecture* (1964), especially "The Age of Elegance," chapter 5.

The Congress

For the committee system see George S. Blair, *American Legislatures: Structures and Process* (1967); William J. Keefe and Morris S. Ogul, *The American Legislative Process: Congress and the States*, 8th ed. (1993); and Barbara Hinkley, *The Seniority System in Congress* (1971). On the House Naval Affairs Committee, United States Congress, *Official Congressional Directory: For the Use of the United States Congress*, 61st Congress, 2nd Session, 3rd ed., compiled by A. J. Halford (1910).

NOTES

All quotations from primary sources, including the dialogue from the 1909 inquiry in part II, are the exact words used in the documents with their orig- inal spelling and capitalization. Quotations from in- terviews that are cited inside newspaper articles are indicated with a single quote inside a double quote.

ABBREVIATIONS USED IN THE NOTES

Inquest — Record of Proceedings of a Board of Inquest Convened at the U.S. Naval Hospital, U.S. Naval Academy, An- napolis, Md., October 13, 1907, in the Case of James N. Sutton, Second Lieu- tenant, United States Marine Corps, Found Dead in the Grounds of the Naval Acad- emy, at Annapolis Maryland, on the 13th of October, 1907. General Correspon- dence of the Office of the Secretary of the Navy, July 1897–August 1926. General Records of the Department of the Navy, 1798–1947, File 20971, Record Group 80. NAB.

Inquiry — Record of Proceedings of a Court of Inquiry in the Case of James N. Sutton. Parts I and II. Case Number 5140. Proceedings of Courts of Inquiry, Boards of Investigation and Boards of Inquest, Records of the Of- fice of the Judge Advocate General (Navy) 1890–1941, Record Group 125. NAB.

MEB — Proceedings of Naval and Ma- rine Examining Boards. Records of the Office of

the Judge Advocate General (Navy), 1890–1941, Record Group 125. NAB.

NAB — National Archives Building, Washington, D.C.

OBC/NHC — Officer Biography Collection, U.S. Naval Historical Center

RG 24 — Records of the Bureau of Naval Personnel. NAB.

RG 80 — General Records of the Depart- ment of the Navy, 1798–1947. NAB.

RG 92 — Records of the Quartermaster General, 1800–1914. NAB.

RG 125 — Records of the Office of the Judge Advocate General (Navy), 1890–1941. NAB.

RG 127 — United States Marine Corps General Correspondence File, 1904–1912. NAB.

RG 405 — Records of the United States Naval Academy, Nimitz Li- brary.

Thacher — George H. Thacher, "The Case of Lieutenant James B. Sut- ton" [sic], *Journal of the Amer- ican Society for Psychical Re- search* 5, no. 11 (November 1911): 597–664. Introduc- tion by James H. Hyslop, 597–600, and "Comments" by James H. Hyslop, 651–64.

USMC — United States Marine Corps

USNA — United States Naval Academy

PROLOGUE

xi   *"May there not"*: William James, "Pragmatism and Common Sense," lecture 5 in
*Pragmatism: A New Name for Some Old
Ways of Thinking* (first published in
1909), *William James' Writings,
1902–1910*, New American Library
edition (New York: Literary Classics
of the United States, 1987), 559–71.

xi   DEATH BY SUICIDE: A. S. McLemore to
James M. Sutton, October 13, 1907,
copy in his handwriting with penciled
notation "sent Sunday 1 p.m." Second
typewritten copy in same file. File
19706, RG 127, NAB.

xii   *Jack London wrote*: John Whiteclay Chambers II, *The Tyranny of Change: America
in the Progressive Era, 1890–1920*
(1992; repr., New Brunswick, N.J.:
Rutgers University Press, 2004), 80.

xii   *"the fully admitted right to speak in public"*:
Lisa Grunwald and Stephen J. Adler,
eds. *Letters of the Century: America,
1900–1999* (New York: Dial Press,
1999), 26. These two women "and
their female collaborators accomplished a titanic change in public attitudes." Jean H. Baker, "Getting Right
with Women's Suffrage," *The Journal of
the Gilded Age and Progressive Era* 5, no.
1 (January 2006): 16.

xiii   *"If we cannot get justice"*: See chapter 4.

xiii   *"one of the most remarkable"*: *Baltimore Sun*,
July 26, 1909.

xiii   *"There is nothing"*: John L. Given, *Making a
Newspaper* (New York: Henry Holt,
1907).

xiii   *had become a neighborhood*: Michael J.
Sandel, *Public Philosophy: Essays on
Morality in Politics* (Cambridge,
Mass.: Harvard University Press,
2005), 13.

xiv   *"belated, reluctant and coerced"*: *New York
Times*, July 19, 1909.

xv   *"hallucination, fancy and dreams"*: Inquiry.
See also Inquiry testimony in chapter
11.

xvi   *the record of the 1909 investigation*: Inquiry.

xvi   *"an altercation with"*: Inquiry, Exhibit I.

xvii   *had begun to fascinate*: See, for example, the
seven definitions of memory in *Cen-
tury Dictionary: An Encyclopedic Lexicon
of the English Language* (New York:
Century Co., 1890), 3705.

xvii   *"men do not recall things"*: Inquiry. See
chapter 13.

xvii   *"endless number"*: Hermann Ebbinghaus,
*Memory: A Contribution to Experimen-
tal Psychology*, chapter 1, at
psychclassics.yorku.ca/Ebbinghaus/
index.htm.

xviii *"memory and history"*: William Cronon,
"The Competing Truths of History
and Memory," foreword to *Remember-
ing Ahanagran: A History of Stories*, by
Richard White (Seattle: University of
Washington Press, 1998), x.

CHAPTER 1: "YOU MUST CLEAR MY NAME"

1   *"ardent swain"*: "Marine School of Appli-
cation, Where Lieut. Sutton Met His
Death," *Evening Star* (Washington,
D.C.), July 25, 1909, section 2.

1   *"very good-sized gun"*: Inquiry, 713–14,
718, 721.

1   *"shot himself in the head"*: Charles Doyen's
account at the 1907 Inquest, 8–10; see
also the 1909 Inquiry, 424–54. In 1909,
Doyen recalled that Utley said, "Lieutenant Sutton has killed Lieutenant
Roelker and then shot himself" (425).

2   *hospital corps*: This account comes from the
1909 Inquiry, 392ff.

3   *"in the dead house"*: Inquiry, 394.

3   *Dr. Pickrell*: George Pickrell to the Superintendent, October 13, 1907, File 525,
James Sutton, General Correspondence, 1907–1927, RG 405, USNA.

3   *"for the purpose of"*: Acting Secretary of the
Navy to Charles J. Badger, July 1,
1907, File 900–32, RG 24. See "Rear
Admiral Charles J. Badger," Officer
Biography Collection, Operational
Archives Branch, United States Naval

Historical Center, Washington Navy
Yard, Washington, D.C. Hereafter
OBC/NHC. Badger to John Adrian
Hoogewerff, File 19706, RG 127.

3   *"REGRET TO REPORT"*: (Charles) Badger to
Commandant Marine Corps, October
13, 1907, File 525, James Sutton,
General Correspondence, 1907–1927,
RG 405.

4   *complications related to appendicitis*: "Medical
Record for Promotion of Surgeon
Frank C. Cook, U.S. Navy, since March
3, 1903," Cook's Proceedings of Naval
and Marine Examining Boards File. See
also "Record of Service of Surgeon
Frank C. U.S. Navy (since Last Promotion) November 28, 1916," RG 125.

4   *"as the cerebellum"*: Inquiry, 1006–7, and
his full testimony, 1006–31. The death
certificate was read into the record
(1011). Cook said the words were
probably taken from the report of the
autopsy but he did not make out the
death certificate.

4   *"all you know"*: Inquest.

4   *undertaker Harry Raymond Taylor*: Inquiry, 1260–66, for Taylor's account.

4   *his most demanding task*: Inquiry, 1251–57, for this paragraph.

5   *But a century ago*: the Oregon Historical Society's copy of the *Portland Block Book* for 1907 shows the location of 784 Hoyt and the Suttons' prior home. Index Map, vi, vol. 1 (Portland, Oreg.: Portland Block Book Company Publishers, 1907). Microfilm 427 from the Tax Records gives the lot size and details. This description comes from photographs taken in 1906–1907 in Sutton Family Papers, and those taken by the author in 2001.

5   *"one of the most"*: Three front page newspaper stories summarized James Sutton's life when he died. "James N. Sutton, Railroad Man, Died Suddenly in Jitney," *Oregon Daily Journal*, November 15, 1915; "James N. Sutton Dies in Jitney," *Oregonian*, November 16, 1915; "Shadow of Tragedy Again Passes over Family of Sutton," *Portland News*, November 16, 1915.

6   *a more congested*: Jim Sutton's long-standing financial worries come out in *Rosa B. Sutton vs. James N. Sutton*, Summons, Circuit Court of the State of Oregon for the County of Multnomah, filed August 19, 1914, Multnomah County Records Office, Portland, Oreg.; and *Rosa B. Sutton vs. James N. Sutton*, Complaint, Circuit Court of the State of Oregon for Multnomah County, February 19, 1915, Judgment No. 59952, Case No. E1400, Multnomah County Records Office, Portland, Oreg.

6   *especially on holidays*: For Rosa's family life and personality, see Thacher, 597–664, introduction by James H. Hyslop, 597–600, and "Comments" by James H. Hyslop, 651–64. Hereafter Thacher.

7   *Rosa's oldest brother*: Louis Brant "was a Cadet at West Point and later a Major in the US Army." *Clark County Pioneers: A Centennial Salute* (Vancouver, Wash.: Clark County Genealogical Society, 1989), 132. West Point records confirm this.

9   *Rosa lay awake*: Rosa B. Sutton to James Hyslop, October 5, 1910, in Thacher, 597–99; "Mrs. Sutton's Statement," November 10, 1910, Thacher, 619–23.

9   *"when my father told mother"*: "Statement of Louise Sutton," Thacher, 628–29.

9   *"I have lost my mind"*: Thacher, 598. For a slightly different description of this occurrence, see Thacher, 621.

10   *"as soon as we receive them"*: *Oregonian*, October 14, 1909.

10   *"It's my shoulder knot"*: Thacher, 621.

10   *unusual experiences*: All of which are described at length in Thacher, 603–8, and verified by other family members including Jim Sutton.

10   *her husband was not*: "Statement of James N. Sutton on Nov. 10, 1910, Concerning the Impressions of His Wife, Rosa B. Sutton, at the Time of the Death of Their Son Jimmie, at Annapolis, on Oct. 13, 1907, Which Were Related to Him at the Time of Their Occurrence at 784 Hoyt St., Portland, Ore," Thacher, 624–26, appendix D.

11   *"face and head"*: Thacher, 27.

11   *"they got me at last"*: Thacher, 630–31.

11   *into a pioneer family*: See *Clark County Pioneers*, Joseph Brant, 132; Joseph Adolphus C. Brant, (one of Rosa's brothers), 133. Joseph and Louisa Brant, their daughter Rosanna who died at two, and their son Albert Brant are all buried in St. James Church Cemetery in Vancouver, Plot 116. See also Edmond S. Meany, *History of the State of Washington* (New York: MacMillan, 1909).

12   *these dedicated women*: Brant records in the "Day Student Accounts: 1857–1913," for Providence Academy, Vancouver, Wash. Sisters of Providence Archives, Seattle, Wash., several notations about Rosa Brant, between December 10, 1867, and June 25, 1868. Also useful is *Catholic Church Records of the Pacific Northwest*, vols. 1 and 2 (Vancouver, Wash.: French Prairie Press, 1972).

12   *They spent their days*: Jay P. Dolan, *The American Catholic Experience: A History from Colonial Times to the Present* (Garden City, N.Y.: Doubleday & Co., 1987 [1985]), 215–16.

12   *a "web" of relationships*: Robert A. Orsi, *Between Heaven and Earth: The Religious Worlds People Make and the Scholars Who Study Them* (Princeton, N.J.: Princeton University Press, 2005), 5; and Dolan, *American Catholic Experience*, 144–45.

12   *second-class citizens*: Dolan, *American Catholic Experience*, 203, 238.

13   *"that profound peace"*: James Cardinal Gibbons, *The Faith of Our Fathers: A Plain Exposition and Vindication of the Church Founded by Our Lord Jesus Christ* (Rockford, Ill.: Tan Books and Publishers, 1980), introduction, xi, xv. First published in 1876, by 1917 the book had been through eighty-three revisions and had been translated "into nearly all the languages of Europe."

13   *"nothing is so essential"*: Gibbons, *Faith of Our Fathers*, xvi; he cites Matthew 16:26.

13   *"The Church has"*: Gibbons, *Faith of Our Fathers*, 54.

13   *these shepherds held*: Gibbons, *Faith of Our Fathers*, 318–20. Chapter 29, "The Priesthood," reveals why it was so essential to have a priest perform funeral rites and consecrate the deceased's grave.

13   *God forbade Catholics*: *Catechism of Christian Doctrine for Academies and High Schools*, Intermediate No. III, Rev. M. Muller's (C.S.S.R) Series (St. Louis, Mo.: Benziger Brothers, 1877), 108.

14   *But Jimmie also knew*: These terms are Gibbons' phrases for hell and heaven (*Faith of Our Fathers*, 175). Catechisms vary in the specific answers they give to questions and use simpler language when they are designed for young children.

15   *An Annapolis reporter*: *Evening Capital* (Annapolis, Md.), October 14, 1907, and October 16, 1907.

15   *Elliott stated*: Brigadier General Commandant, G. F. Elliott to the Secretary of the Navy, October 14, 1907. The letter also informed Mr. Victor Metcalf that Mr. Sutton had been notified by telegram ("a copy enclosed"); he requested that the body be prepared for burial and "held pending the arrival of his sister." File 19706, RG 127.

15   *"The board having examined"*: Charles Badger to the Secretary of the Navy, October 15, 1907, File 19706, RG 127.

16   *Sutton agreed*: J. N. Sutton to Brig. Gen. Geo. F. Elliott, November 11, 1907, refers to this correspondence. File 19706, RG 127.

16   *Less than two years earlier*: "Recent Deaths," *Army and Navy Journal*, November 11, 1905, 292. Minor Meriwether's and Sutton's class at the Naval Academy (1908) dedicated their yearbook, *Lucky Bag*, to Surgeon Cook and Commander Hoogewerff.

CHAPTER 2: "FULL OF ANIMAL LIFE AND SPIRIT"

18   *To President Theodore Roosevelt*: See Theodore Roosevelt, *The Works of Theodore Roosevelt in 14 Volumes: Presidential Addresses and State Papers*, part 1 (New York: P. F. Collier & Son, n.d.), 71. Remarks made "at the Centennial Celebration of the Establishment of the United States Military Academy, West Point, June 11, 1902." Roosevelt's comments applied not only to West Point but also to its "sister college that makes similar preparation for the service of the country on the seas."

18   *it had an excellent*: The annual *Reports of the Board of Visitors to the United States Naval Academy* provide detailed information on life at Annapolis. In their 1904 *Report*, the board noted, "During the past generation the Naval Academy has become a school of engineering" (8–9). RG 405, Records of Boards, 1836–1942.

18   *His candidate was a limber*: James N. Sutton Jr., Applicant for Commission File 13977, United States Marine Corps General Correspondence File, 1904–1912, RG 127. Details about his appearance are in the form he filled out in 1905; on his former neighbors, the Hincks family, see Thacher, 630–31.

19   *Jimmie's prior education*: The family lived in Los Angeles for seven years between the time Jimmie was five and twelve; he spent at least a few months there at St. Vincent's Academy for boys. File 13977, RG 127.

19   *"Force will make me"*: "Gossip of the Town," *Columbiad* 1, no. 5 (February 1903), 75. His sister, Rose, also referred to this boyhood nickname, "Sunny Jim." Inquiry, 1165.

19   *at a preparatory school*: "Candidates Colony in Annapolis," United States Naval Academy Special Collections Vertical File, Preparatory Schools. See also undated letter from Robert L. Werntz to prospective candidates.

19   *The classes worked—at least initially*: Documents related to Jimmie's exams, Midshipman Personnel file of James Sutton, Records of the Office of the Superintendent, 1845–1950, Correspondence, 1845–1950, General Correspondence, 1907–1927, File 525, RG 405.

21   *Days filled with*: The midshipmen gave their own impressions of their plebe year in the 1907 *Lucky Bag*, 179. RG 405, USNA.

21   *source of great concern*: John P. Lovell, *Neither Athens nor Sparta? The American Service Academies in Transition* (Bloomington: Indiana University Press, 1979), notes "the great deference by all academy personnel" toward members of Congress, 231, and 232–33 on the Board of Visitors.

21   *After the death of*: Early in 1906, a subcommittee of the Committee on Naval

Affairs of the House of Representatives conducted a thorough investigation of discipline at the Academy and included details about conditions in the previous two years. See United States Congress, House Committee on Naval Affairs, *Hearing before a Subcommittee of the Committee on Naval Affairs of the House of Representatives at the United States Naval Academy, Annapolis, Maryland, on the Subject of Hazing at the Naval Academy*, February 15–24, 1906 (Washington, D.C.: Government Printing Office, 1906) (hereafter USC Hazing). The following discussion is based in part on the summary on pages 439–52. Throughout 1906 the *Army and Navy Journal* repeatedly published articles on the subject of hazing, and many revealed the friction among administrators in both service academies and members of Congress.

21 *the demeaning tasks*: USC Hazing, 440.

21 *"full of animal life and spirit"*: USC Hazing, 445–46.

22 *"an ordinary enough"*: This description comes from a long article in the *Evening Capital* (Annapolis, Md.), July 28, 1909.

22 *He showed off*: Jimmie had written home on December 12, 1904, "'I have got the name of being the bad man of the Plebe class, the uppers have dubbed me "Tracy," the bad man.'" Thacher, Hyslop's Editor's Note, 651. Also Gary Meier and Gloria Meier, *Oregon Outlaws: Tales of Old-Time Desperadoes* (Boise, Idaho: Tamarack Books, 1996), 167–78.

22 *"if you knew him well"*: Quoted in the *Evening Capital* (Annapolis, Md.), July 29, 1909. This young man was interviewed in one of three sequential articles about the Sutton case in the Annapolis paper.

22 *sensitive and reflective side*: The poem, "Reverie," is one of three documents that still exist in Jimmie's own words. The *New York American* published it on July 12, 1909.

23 *"the reach grows long"*: *Washington Post*, August 4, 1909.

23 *He resigned on*: Paul Morton to J. N Sutton, Late Midshipman, June 3, 1905. Midshipman Personnel File of James N. Sutton, Administrative Records, 1845–1930, Relating to Midshipmen and Cadets, 1846–1925, General Records, RG 405.

23 *not clearly defined*: Jack Shulimson, "Military Professionalism: The Case of the US Marine Officer Corps, 1880–1898," *Journal of Military History* 60, no. 2 (April 1996): 231–42.

23 *This expansion was*: *Annual Report of the Secretary of the Navy 1905* (Washington D.C.: Government Printing Office, 1906), 14. On the history of the Corps, Alan R. Millett, *Semper Fidelis: The History of the United States Marine Corps* (New York: Free Press, 1991), is indispensable. His book includes extensive notes and a useful essay on sources.

25 *"comes of an excellent"*: Unless noted otherwise, all the correspondence related to Sutton's application for the Marine Corps can be found in File 13977, RG 127.

25 *Archbishop Christie informed*: "Most Rev A. Christie to the Secretary of the Navy, USA," December 19, 1905," File 13977, RG 127.

25 *The requirements may*: See "Circular for the Information of Persons Desiring to Enter the US Marine Corps as Second Lieutenants," Attached to letter in File 13977, RG 127.

26 *recalled his former roommate*: *Philadelphia Inquirer*, July 12, 1909.

26 *that he was always called*: This description of Edward Roelker and the correspondence related to his Marine Corps application can be found in File 16334, RG 127. His nickname is confirmed in the class yearbook *Lucky Bag 1908*.

27 *she fully intended*: Mrs. C. R. Roelker to Superintendent Scott Shipp, May 15, 1903. See file of Edward P. Roelker, Class of 1906, Virginia Military Institute Archives, Lexington, Va.

27 *He performed poorly*: Administrative Records, 1845–1930, Relating to Midshipmen and Cadets, 1846–1925, Conduct Roll of Edward P. Roelker 1904–1906, RG 405.

27 *the academic ones*: Roelker's application file includes his form, but the file is very thin. His only endorsements were from each of his parents and Hon. William Loeb, writing for Roosevelt. After Loeb wrote Charles J. Bonaparte, March 7, 1906, he received a thank you note on March 8 from Parthenia Roelker. File 16334, RG 127. The Marine Corps Examining Boards File for Roelker is missing from the NAB.

27 *Roelker's family navy*: Parthenia Porter Roelker to Mr. Wm Loeb Jr., March 15, 1907; she had heard unofficially that Edward passed his Marine Corps exams and, impatient for the official response, asked for confirmation. She received one from Truman Newberry four days later dated March 19, 1907, File 21514, RG 80.

28 *the nickname "Highcock"*: The nickname stayed with him even though he did

not graduate. *Lucky Bag 1907*, 134. Each midshipman was given a nickname in the yearbook along with a descriptive quotation, many of which seemed tongue-in-cheek. Utley's was taken from Shakespeare: "Can the world buy such a jewel."

28   "*The whole nation was aroused*": Before graduation they would recall the congressional investigation of "hazing and fighting in all its degrees" in their yearbook, *Lucky Bag 1907*, 183.

29   *how anxious he was*: Shelby M. Cullom to Chas J. Bonepart [*sic*], July 29, 1906, File 17545, RG 127. Newberry's response and all correspondence related to Utley's application is in this file unless otherwise noted. Between 1904 and 1907 (and for the rest of her life) Emma Utley's world centered on her son. Joseph Utley died on February 16, 1908, and was clearly very ill when Senator Cullom made his remarks.

30   *a lengthy explanation*: Emma Utley to Truman Newberry, August 3, 1906, File 17545, RG 127.

30   *the next examinations*: Harold Utley to the Brigadier General, Commandant, November 28, 1906, File 17545, RG 127.

31   *troubled by health problems*: Charles A. Doyen, United States Marine Corps Historical Center, Operational Archives Branch, Officer Biography Collection. Charles Doyen's military and medical history is fully documented in Doyen File, Proceedings of Naval and Marine Examining Boards, Records of the Office of the Judge Advocate General (Navy), 1890–1941, RG 125.

31   *covered every detail*: "Regulations for the Government of Student Officers at Marine Barracks and School of Application, Annapolis, Md., at time of death of Lt. Sutton, U.S.M.C.," copy in File 51158, RG 127. The title of this typewritten document is handwritten. These rules deal with daily life and personal habits, and should not be confused with the printed official copy of the academic regulations found in File 20971, RG 80

32   *He took the first course*: Benjamin H. Fuller, United States Marine Corps Historical Center, Operational Archives Branch, Officer Biography Collection; Karl Schuon, *United States Marine Corps Biographical Dictionary* (New York: Franklin Watts, 1963), 81–83; Conduct Roll of Benjamin H. Fuller, 1885–1889, Administrative Records, 1845–1930, Relating to Midshipmen and Cadets, 1846–1925, RG 405; and Benjamin Fuller file in RG 125.

32   *Five days a week*: *Regulations and Course of Instruction at the School of Application, United States Marine Corps, Annapolis Md.*, Approved by the Brigadier General, Commandant, U.S.M.C., July 1, 1904. Approved by the Secretary of the Navy, July 18, 1904 (Washington, D.C.: Government Printing Office, 1905), copy in File 20971, RG 80, and RG 125; Barton D. Strong, Midshipman, USN, "A History of the Marine Barracks, Annapolis, Maryland," U.S. Naval Academy Course Paper, U.S. Naval Academy Archives, Special Collections, Vertical File, U.S. Marine Corps Barracks, Annapolis, Md., 1964.

33   *His evaluation only*: Utley's "Report on Fitness of Officers," April 18–June 23, 1907, RG 125.

33   *He had shown*: Sutton's "Report on Fitness of Officers," April 18–June 23, 1907, RG 125; B. H. Fuller to the Brigadier General, Commandant, May, 21, 1907, RG 125; B. H. Fuller to Secretary of the Navy, October 21, 1909, File 20971, RG 80.

34   "*nobody else around*": Inquiry, 27, testimony of Robert Adams about what Edwin McClellan told him.

34   "*dreamed all his life*": Reverend Isaac L. Wood to Mr. Chas J. Bonaparte, June 8, 1906, File 14905, RG 127. Written on the stationery of Grace Methodist Episcopal Church.

34   *A year later he*: "William J. Adams," *Commemorative Biographical Encyclopedia of Dauphin County, Pennsylvania, Containing Sketches of Prominent and Representative Citizens, and Many of the Early Scotch-Irish and German Settlers*, 1896, 487. Marriage Records of Grace Methodist [Episcopal] Church, Harrisburg Pennsylvania; Harrisburg Cemetery Records; Adams family records found by Jean Pugh and Warren Warbaugh, archivist, Dauphin County Historical Society.

34   "*He is finely educated*": Robert Emmet Adams (application) to Navy Dept. Secretary's Office, May 26, 1906; J. C. Delaney to Honorable Secretary of the Navy, May 23, 1906, Applicant for Commission File 14905, RG 127.

35   *he was a superb athlete*: Photocopy of page from the *1906 Record*, University of Pennsylvania Yearbook, indicating Adams' athletic accomplishments; he used the nickname "Bob." University Archives and Records Center, University of Pennsylvania, Philadelphia.

35   *he had scored third*: M. E. Olmstead to Brig. Genl. George F. Elliott, May 8, 1907, File 14905, RG 127.

35   "*made a call on a girl*": Inquiry, 27.

35   *he also told her*: Rosa B. Sutton to Mr. H. M. Swartz, May 3, 1908, Inquiry, Exhibit P-3.

36   *he wrote his brother one*: Jim Sutton to Don Sutton, Inquiry, EX T-1.

36   *"I have taken out"*: After Sutton's death "the insurance was paid." Letter quoted by Hyslop in Thacher, 634–35.

36   *Jimmie requested duty*: His letter requesting duty in the Philippines is in File 18801, RG 127.

36   *he had written his father*: The September 30, 1907, letter from Jimmie stated, "I feel in my bones something is going to happen, but it is the feeling most people laugh at." Quoted by Hyslop in Thacher, 635. And Rosa B. Sutton to

Mr. H. M. Swartz, April 9, 1908. "In one of Jimmie's last letters to his father he says Daddy I feel in my bones they are going to get me[.] It is the feeling men usually laugh at but never mind if I have a fair chance they will surely know I've been there." Inquiry, Exhibit P-2.

37   *"the dream of his life"*: Rosa B. Sutton to Mr. H. M. Swartz, May 3, 1908. Inquiry, Exhibit P-3.

37   Western Life *described these*: Walldon Fawcett, "Coal for the Battleship Cruise," *Western Life* 1, no. 6 (December 1907): 78.

37   *Jimmie Sutton wrote to his mother*: Jim to his Mum, Inquiry, Exhibit T-2.

CHAPTER 3: "SISTER COMING FOR REMAINS"

39   *The city's population*: Portland's population grew 80 percent in four years, reaching 207,214 in 1909. E. Kimbark MacColl, *The Shaping of a City: Business and Politics in Portland, Oregon, 1885 to 1915* (Portland, Oreg.: Georgian Press, 1976), 307. The *Portland City Directory* for 1909 (Portland, Oreg.: R. L. Polk & Co., 1909) puts the population at 255,000, up from 96,600 in 1899.

39   *In all of Oregon*: Percy Maddux, *City on the Willamette* (Portland, Oreg.: Metropolitan Press, 1952), 151, 154.

40   *"fine clubs and hotels"*: Cited in MacColl, *The Shaping of a City*, 221–22.

40   *"Rose City"*: Charles N. Black, "Portland Rose Carnival: The First Annual Rose Festival of Portland, Oregon," *Western Life* 1, no. 2 (August 1907): 89. Black was chairman of the Press and Publicity Committee.

40   *"a popular headquarters"*: MacColl, *The Shaping of a City*, 227–28. The quotation is from Burton Hendrick in an article from *McClure's Magazine* a few years later.

40   *a new beginning*: On Harry Lane, see MacColl, *The Shaping of a City*, 299–303; and MacColl, *Merchants, Money and Power: The Political Establishment 1843–1913* (Portland, Oreg.: Georgian Press, 1988), chapter 19.

42   *"PLEASE WIRE PARTICULARS"*: Jas. N. Sutton to A. S. Mclemore, File 19706, RG 127, 10:06 p.m.

44   *Rose sent her own wire*: Rose Sutton Parker to Captain Boyd, USMC Annapolis, October 13, 1907. Records for a Captain Boyd have not been found. She might have meant to wire Charles Badger. For their correspondence, see Office of the Superintendent, General Correspondence, 1907–1922, File 525, RG 405.

44   *Rose probably took*: Rinaldo M. Hall, *Oregon, Washington, Idaho and Their Resources*, promotional booklet (Portland: Oregon Railway and Navigation Co. and Southern Pacific Co., 1905), 69–70.

44   *the premonitions and dreams*: The story of this dream came out in several papers in 1909, such as the *New York American*, July 11; and in Jim Sutton's statement to George Thacher in 1911.

44   *The* Evening Capital: *Evening Capital* (Annapolis, Md.), October 16, 1907.

45   *her first impressions*: Mary Elizabeth Warren, *The Train's Done Been and Gone: Annapolis Portrait, 1859–1910* (Boston: David R. Godine in association with M. E. Warren, 1976), 22, 63. The remainder of this paragraph is drawn from Warren's excellent compilation of contemporary photographs and facsimiles from newspaper stories, with introductory essays by experts on the historic city.

46   *"nose seemed to be"*: Inquiry, 1162–63.

46   *no structure in Annapolis*: A New York City hotelier purchased the property late in 1901 and named his new venture after "Richard Carvel," the title character in a story by American novelist Winston Churchill. Warren, *Annapolis Portrait*, 65.

47   *"to the right of the office"*: Inquiry, 1161, 1164.

47   *she almost tripped*: This story, which may be more charming than accurate, appeared in two sensational papers on July 24, the *Denver Post* and the New York *Evening Journal* with illustrations. According to the *Journal*, Ulsin also warned Rosa that Jimmie had been murdered.

47   *officer's limbs*: For Raymond Taylor's testimony, see Inquiry, 1260–66.

47   *the last person to arrive*: Inquiry, 1171.

48   *readers of the Evening Capital*: J. B. Aleshire, Quartermaster General, U.S. Army to Mr. James N. Sutton Sr., October 23, 1907: "This lot is not intended for general family use," J. B. Aleshire wrote in a letter informing Jim Sutton of the grave site, "but there is no objection to the interment therein of the widow of the officer if so desired." File 240418, RG 92. See also *Evening Capital* (Annapolis, Md.), October 21, 1907.

48   *"No salute was fired"*: *Washington Post*, October 22, 1907.

48   *was buried under bouquets*: 1907 Photograph of Sutton Grave, *New York American*, Newspaper Photograph Morgue, Harry Ransom Humanities Research Center, University of Texas at Austin.

48   *the* Army and Navy Journal: *Army and Navy Journal*, October 19, 1907.

49   *she later recalled*: Inquiry, 1170, 1173, 1199.

49   *compiled an inventory*: Inquiry, Exhibit O. It is not clear whether or not they opened his locked trunks.

50   *red mud on the knees*: Inquiry, 1166.

50   *a gold pocket watch*: Inquiry, 1166–68, for Rose's description of her meeting with Arthur Marix and Utley. Their inventory is Exhibit O.

50   *the missing shoulder knot*: Inquiry, 1167, "I never received that shoulder knot."

The knot may have stood out in her mind because of her mother's dream about it.

50   *a special point*: Inquiry, 1169.

50   *he had not understood*: Inquiry, 1191, 1170. Edward Osterman's comment, 1192.

50   *sent his card to*: Inquiry, 140.

50   *"after having been with a man"*: Inquiry, 1172. The following description of Rose's meeting with Robert Adams is her account at the 1909 inquiry, which she based on the notes she took in 1907. Inquiry 1170–84.

51   *"a shrewd-looking woman"*: Inquiry, 140–42 (Adams testimony).

51   *Utley had hated*: Inquiry, 1181.

51   *"if your brother had lived"*: Inquiry, 1178.

52   *"to have a drink on"*: Inquiry, 1179.

52   *"did not commit suicide"*: Inquiry, 1183–84, 1196.

52   *"not at all satisfied"*: Inquiry, 1189.

52   *was mentioned in the* New York Times: *New York Times*, October 14, 1907. A brief article that also included several errors.

52   *his joyful letter*: Rosa B. Sutton to Mr. H. M. Swartz, April 9, 1908, Inquiry, Exhibit P-2.

52   *"the crystal was shattered"*: "Mrs. Sutton's Statement," in Thacher, 622.

53   *Jim Sutton recalled*: Thacher, 625.

CHAPTER 4: "WE ARE NOT SLEEPING"

54   *during her lifetime*: In 1900 fewer than 3 percent of Americans attended college; 20 percent of these students were female. But 60 percent of high school graduates were women, according to Jean H. Baker, *Sisters: The Lives of America's Suffragists* (New York: Hill and Wang, 2005), 188.

54   *celebrated women's accomplishments*: On the day Rosa learned that her son had died, the *Oregonian* published a large feature on "Women as Lawyers at the Highest Bar," those admitted to practice before the Supreme Court since 1879 (October 13, 1907). See also "What Women Are Doing in All Parts of the World," *Washington Post Sunday Magazine*, July 18, 1909, and "Has the Masculinized Woman Come to Stay? The Trend of the Feminine Mind Towards Man's Work and Costume," *Oregon Sunday Journal* (with the slogan, "She Flies with Her Own Wings"), July 18, 1909.

55   *"It is the mother"*: Excerpts from Roosevelt's speech were published under the headline "Mothers Supreme, Says Roosevelt," in the *New York Times* on March 11, 1908.

55   *Coleman wrote*: The letter is Exhibit W, Inquiry. On April 11, 1907, he had been given a prescription by Dr. J. J. Murphy for complete rest due to obstinate insomnia; it was approved by the head of the Department of English and Law. Gilbert Coleman File, General Correspondence, 1907–1927, Correspondence, 1845–1950, RG 405.

56   *"apparently entirely disinterested"*: *Oregonian*, July 13, 1909.

57   *she pieced together*: The following comments about what the marines said in 1907, and on Rosa's likely response on reading it, are based on the thirty-seven-page inquest transcript. Inquest, File 20971, RG 80.

58   *Rosa received a letter*: Doyen's letter is Inquiry, Exhibit Q.

59   *she was curious*: This line of thinking comes out in her testimony. See chapter 11.

59   *She slept with*: Thacher, 630.

59   *she began writing*: Rosa Sutton's four letters to Harry Mabry Swartz accompany the Inquiry transcript as Exhibits P-1, P-2, P-3, and P-4.

59   *She explained that*: Rosa B. Sutton to Mr. H. M. Swartz, March 13, 1908. Enve-

lope postmarked "Portland, Ore. Mar 14, 3 p.m. 1908," sent to Swartz at the Paymaster's Office, Inquiry, Exhibit P-1. Rosa at first became confused and referred to the receipt as a letter "from which I judge you and Jimmie were good friends."

60   *letter dated April 10*: This time she wrote to him in Washington at P.O. Box 835. Rosa B. Sutton to Mr. H. M. Swartz, April 9, 1908. She dated her letter April 10, but it is postmarked April 9. She probably received his letter about the 7th. Inquiry, Exhibit P-2.

61   *she wrote another letter to*: Rosa B. Sutton to Mr. H. M. Swartz, May 3, 1908, Inquiry, Exhibit P-3.

62   *This mysterious benefactor*: The unidentified New Yorker also apparently talked to undertaker Raymond Taylor who said that the embalmer "had left his employ" not long after Jimmie died, and he could not remember the man's name. "Now what does that look like[?] Maybe he can be made to remember," Rosa wrote. Rosa B. Sutton

62   to Mr. H. M. Swartz, May 3, 1908, Inquiry, Exhibit P-3.

confirmed her worst: William Owens' letter is attached to Rosa B. Sutton to Mr. Harry M. Swartz, May 16, 1908, Inquiry, Exhibit P-4.

63   *she sent one to Harry Swartz*: Rosa B. Sutton to Mr. Harry. M. Swartz, May 16, 1908, Inquiry, Exhibit P-4. This is the last letter that exists from Rosa to Swartz, but she was obviously in contact with him subsequently.

63   *"several vessels came"*: The Fleet—or at least some of it—came nearby but never to Portland; the ships did "pass by the mouth of the Columbia on May 20th 1908" on the way to Puget Sound. Passenger cruises took residents from the city to the mouth of the river to see the famous battleships. And that is likely the date when Rosa experienced another of her "visions." E-mail from Dave Pearson, Columbia River Maritime Museum, Astoria, Oregon, January 24, 2006.

63   *"immediately after their arrival"*: "Mrs. Sutton's Statement," Thacher, 622.

CHAPTER 5: "THAT NO INJUSTICE MAY BE DONE"

65   *Swartz met her*: This fact came out at the inquiry and was reported in the *Washington Post*, August 10, 1909.

66   *"the most discriminating tastes"*: The *Book of Washington* (Washington, D.C.: Washington Board of Trade, 1930), 300.

66   *he was engaged in*: In 1890, Edmund Van Dyke entered the law offices of Hon. Samuel Shellabarger and Hon. Jeremiah M, Wilkins to study law, remaining there until 1898. Henry B. F. MacFarland, *American Biographical Directories: District of Columbia: Concise Biographies of Its Prominent and Representative Contemporary Citizens, and Valuable Statistical Data, 1908–1909* (Washington, D.C.: Potomac Press, 1908), 481.

66   *had already submitted a statement*: *Baltimore Sun*, July 23, 1909.

67   *His analysis would be crucial*: "In the Matter of the Death of James N. Sutton, Late Second Lieutenant, United States Marine Corps, in the Grounds of the Naval Academy, at Annapolis, Md., on the 13th of October, 1907. Notes on the Evidence before the Board of Inquest. E. W. Van Dyke, Attorney for Mrs. Rosa B. Sutton, the Mother of the Deceased," File 20971, RG 80. The following summary of Van Dyke's analysis is drawn from this document.

69   *"that no injustice"*: Jonathan Bourne to Truman H. Newberry, January 30, 1909, File 20971, RG 80.

71   *Newberry observed*: File 20971, RG 80.

71   *had been new at his job*: Edward Campbell File, Naval Historical Center, Operational Archives Branch, Officer Biography Collection, Washington Navy Yard, Washington, D.C.

71   *he informed Newberry*: Edward Campbell, Memorandum for the Secretary, February 9, 1909, File 20971, RG 80.

71   *a letter from Rosa Sutton*: Inquiry, Exhibit N.

72   *"the facts may warrant"*: File 20971, RG 80.

72   *"if the relatives of Lieutenant Sutton"*: Truman Newberry to "My Dear Senator," February 10, 1909, File 20971, RG 80.

72   *"the case is closed"*: *Baltimore Sun*, July 20, 1909.

73   *"the most impressive pageant"*: *New York Times*, February 23, 1909.

73   *A resident of Portland*: "Shall Bourne Run?" summarizes his views and accomplishments as a senator (Bourne File, Oregon Historical Society); apparently Senator Bourne's wife kept or destroyed his correspondence with Theodore Roosevelt, Taft, and others. What was not destroyed went to the University of Oregon, at Eugene. See

George Putnam, "Sidelights on Jonathan Bourne, Father of Ore. Political System," *Capital Journal*, September 22, 1955, Biography File, Oregon Historical Society. See also *Biographical Directory of the United States Congress, 1774–1989*, bicentennial edition (Washington, D.C.: Government Printing Office, 1989); and *Guide to Research Collections of Former United States Senators: 1789–1995*, compiled by Karen Dawley Paul (Washington, D.C.: Government Printing Office, 1995), 56. Finally, see Leonard Schlup, "Republican Insurgent: Jonathan Bourne and the Politics of Progressivism, 1908–1912," *Oregon Historical Quarterly* 87, no. 3 (Fall 1986): 229.

73   *Bourne also played golf*: *Oregon Daily Journal*, August 10, 1909. See also "The Kitchen Cabinet of the President," *New York Times*, August 8, 1909, which refers to the senator as part of Taft's "Golf Cabinet"; and "The Most Intimate Friends of President Taft," *New York Times*, May 29, 1910.

75   *"I would personally"*: Jonathan Bourne to "My dear Judge," March 17, 1909, File 20971, RG 80.

75   *Meyer was close to*: On George Meyer's career, see Paolo Enrico Coletta, ed., *American Secretaries of the Navy* (Annapolis, Md.: Naval Institute Press, 1980), 495–522; and his book, *The Presidency of William Howard Taft* (Lawrence: University Press of Kansas, 1973).

75   *"She will have the right"*: Secretary of the Navy Meyer to "My Dear Senator," April 5, 1909, File 20971, RG 80.

75   *"a democratic society"*: Eugene R. Fidell, "The Culture of Change in Military Law," in *Evolving Military Justice*, ed. Eugene R. Fidell and Dwight H. Sullivan (Annapolis, Md.: Naval Institute Press, 2002), 164.

76   *maintain military discipline*: James E. Valle, *Rocks and Shoals: Naval Discipline in the Age of Fighting Sail* (Annapolis, Md.: Naval Institute Press, 1980), 29; and William Herbert Page, "Military Law: A Study in Comparative Law," *Harvard Law Review* 32 (1919): 349–73.

76   *"military exigencies require"*: "Military Courts Defended," *Army and Navy Journal*, July 27, 1907. The editorial was written to address criticisms by the press.

76   *a document enacted*: Robert Pasley Jr. and Felix Larkin, "The Navy Court Martial: Proposals for Its Reform," *Cornell Law Quarterly* 33 (1947): 197–98. In "content and phraseology" the Articles are not far removed from Oliver Cromwell's articles of 1649.

76   *"are wholly absent in"*: "Military Courts Defended," *ANJ*, July 27, 1907.

76   *"simply instrumentalities"*: S. T. Ansell, "Military Justice," *Cornell Law Quarterly* 5 (November 1919): 6. Samuel Ansell was a strong advocate for reform following abuses of the system in World War I.

76   *adjuncts of command*: Ansell, "Military Justice," 6.

77   *"above the law"*: Ansell, "Military Justice," 8.

77   *Secretary Meyer sent a memorandum*: "Memorandum for the Commandant of the Marine Corps," File 20971, RG 80 (copy in File 19706, RG 127). George Elliott responded on April 7 to the assistant secretary of the navy; he had already sent orders to the two officers serving "on the Asiatic Station," Lts. Adams and Osterman, File 20971, RG 80.

77   *he came before a general court-martial*: Record of Proceedings of a General Court-Martial in the Case of Edward P. Roelker, Case Number 16845, Proceedings of Courts of Inquiry, Boards of Investigation and Boards of Inquest, Records of the Office of the Judge Advocate General (Navy) 1890–1941, RG 125.

79   *Parthenia Roelker accepted a subpoena*: E. H. Campbell returned the subpoena to Harry Leonard as "he cannot be found." File 20971, RG 80. See also *New York Times*, July 20, 1909.

79   *easy traveling distance*: Commandant George Elliott wrote the secretary of the navy to confirm this fact on June 24, 1909, listing the officers and their current whereabouts. File 20971, RG 80.

79   *members of the Sutton court*: The order convening the Court of Inquiry went out on July 6. Commander John Hood received his instructions as president from W. P. Potter, acting secretary of the navy. File 20971, RG 80.

79   *he had no separate authority*: William Winthrop, *Military Law and Precedents*, 2nd ed. (Washington, D.C.: Government Printing Office, 1920; first published in 1886), 170. Among his many tasks, the president was responsible for order during the session—including order in the audience. As an individual he could make no ruling—he could only announce one as the conclusion of the court (171).

79   *These three men*: The navy and the Marine Corps have records on the careers of these men. See note on sources. Academy superintendent Charles Badger was asked his advice as to who should serve on the court. J. E. Pillsbury to Badger, June 29, 1909, File 20971, RG 80.

80   *"a full statement of all the facts"*: W. P. Potter to Commander John Hood, Memorandum, July 6, 1909, File 20971, RG 80, and Inquiry, Exhibit A.

80   *"behave with decency"*: Winthrop, *Military Law and Precedents*, 177–78. At least this is the behavior expected at a court-martial.

80   *"Get a detail"*: File 20971, RG 80.

80   *A Washington native*: One from Columbian (George Washington) University in 1891, and a second from the same university, an LL.M, in 1898. A few details about Leonard's life before 1898 appear in three obituaries and are attached to his profile in the Leonard Reference File, Archives and Special Collections Branch, Library of the Marine Corps, Gray Research Center, Quantico, Va. Once he received a commission in the Marine Corps in 1898, the records are more extensive, with several documents in RG 80, and a few in RG 127. For his professional service, see the Leonard File, Proceedings of Naval and Marine Examining Boards, Records of the Office of the Judge Advocate General (Navy) 1890–1941, RG 125.

80   *He hoped to be judge advocate*: Letters recommending Leonard for the position of Navy JAG, written in October 1907, can be found in File 16419, RG 80.

80   *"able, energetic and enthusiastic"*: Report on the Fitness of Officers, January 1, 1909, to June 30, 1909, Leonard File, RG 125.

80   *the pain he still fought*: W. W. Rockhill (American Legation, Peking, China) to Captain Henry Leonard, Military Attaché with enclosures, May 7, 1907, Leonard File, RG 125; "Medical Record of Captain Henry Leonard, U S Marine Corps, Since July 23, 1900," Leonard File, RG 125; "Record of the Proceedings of a Marine Retiring Board Convened at the Marine Barracks, Washington, DC in the Case of Major Henry Leonard," September 26, 1911" (includes a "Statement of Major Henry Leonard" in which he describes the nature of the pain he felt at the site of his missing arm), Leonard File, RG 125.

81   *he had no personal interest*: Yet "prejudice or interest, however conspicuous or controlling, on the part of the judge advocate, cannot of course impair the *legal validity* of the proceedings." Winthrop, *Military Law and Precedents*, 186. For the duties of the judge advocate, see 188–204.

81   *"the mother of the deceased"*: File 20971, RG 80.

81   *On July 6, he wrote*: Henry Leonard to the Major General, Commandant, July 6, 1909, File 8656, RG 127.

81   *with the Department's blessing*: Beekman Winthrop notified Commander Hood and Lieutenant Adams of this fact on July 13, 1909. File 20971, RG 80. Almost immediately the newspapers took notice of Adams' unique status at the investigation. For example, "Adams to Have Counsel," *Evening Capital* (Annapolis, Md.), July 15, 1909.

81   *Arthur Alexis Birney came from*: "Death of Arthur A. Birney," *Washington Law Reporter* 44 (September 8, 1916): 561. Birney died suddenly on the golf links of the Washington Country Club on Labor Day in 1916 at the age of sixty-five. See *New York Times*, September 6, 1916. Birney received his law degree from the University of Michigan in 1873. See also *Cyclopædia of American Biography, Revision to 1914 Complete*, ed. Hon. Charles Dick and James E. Homans, vol. 1 (New York: Press Association Compilers, 1915); Allen Johnson, ed., *Dictionary of American Biography*, vol. 1 (New York: Charles Scribner's Sons, 1964); *Who Was Who in America*, vol. 1, 1897–1942 (Chicago: A. N. Marquis, 1942); *Who's Who in the Nation's Capital, 1921–1922*, first edition (Washington, D.C.: Consolidated Publishing Company, 1921); A. R. Safford, *Encyclopedia of Virginia and the District of Columbia of the Nineteenth Century: Eminent and Representative Men of Virginia and the District of Columbia of the Nineteenth Century* (Madison, Wisc.: Brant and Fuller, 1893), 48–51.

83   *"such competent evidence"*: Henry Leonard to E. W. Van Dyke, Esq., July 5, 1909. On the same day, Leonard sent a copy of this letter to Edward Campbell who had obviously authorized him to contact Van Dyke. File 20971, RG 80.

83   *considered by his contemporaries*: "Death of Mr. Henry E. Davis," *Washington Law Reporter* 55 (April 1, 1927): 201.

83   *fifty-four-year-old Davis*: Henry Edgar Davis was known as "Harry" later in life, and as "Jeff" at Princeton where he won several prizes for his oratory skill. The Seeley G. Mudd Manuscript Library, Princeton University, Princeton, N.J., has a few documents including one that gives his height and weight the year he graduated (five foot, six inches, 135 pounds). "Obituary of Henry E. Davis, '76," by Henry L. Harrison, Class Secretary, in the *Princeton Alumni Weekly*, April 8, 1927, summarizes his

career and his dedication to the university. He was class vice president for forty-five years, and president beginning in June 1926. See also *Who's Who in the Nation's Capital, 1921–1922.*

83   *enjoyed challenging cases*: Newspaper Obituary (source unknown) in Davis file from the Seeley G. Mudd Manuscript Library, Princeton University. Davis' parents came from "pioneer Maryland families"; after he graduated from Princeton with highest class honors, he began Harvard Law School but left because of illness. He completed his legal training in Washington. He loved Washington, D.C., and was a well-known authority on

the "history of the law in the District of Columbia and the history of local courts."

83   *from his office in the Jennifer Building at*: Henry E. Davis to Hon. Beekman Winthrop, July 17, 1909, File 20971, RG 80.

85   *received a quick response*: E. H. Campbell to Henry E. Davis, July 17, 1909, File 20971, RG 80. On the same day, Edward Campbell authorized Harry Leonard to permit the court reporter to give Davis a copy. The copy would not include the finding and opinion of the court.

85   *this "remarkable" drama*: Baltimore Sun, July 26, 1909.

CHAPTER 6: "A WIDER FORUM"

86   *America's newspapers*: Few important facts came out in other parts of the country that did not also appear in the *Capital*, or one or more of the following: the *Baltimore Sun* (a book could be written just from the *Sun*'s coverage), the *New York Times*, the *Washington Post*, the *Evening Star* (Washington, D.C.), and the *Oregonian*. However, entertaining details and photographs were plentiful in New York's sensational papers, the *Evening Journal* (New York), the *World* (New York), and especially the *New York American*.

87   *with each passing decade*: Michael Schudson, *The Good Citizen: A History of American Civic Life* (Cambridge, Mass.: Harvard University Press, 1998), 178–82; and Timothy E. Cook, *Governing with the News: The News Media as a Political Institution* (Chicago: University of Chicago Press, 1998), 31–37.

87   *The number of high schools*: Michael Emery and Edwin Emery, *The Press and America: An Interpretive History of the Mass Media*, 7th ed. (Englewood Cliffs, N.J.: Prentice Hall, 1992), 156.

87   *"Usually reporters strive to"*: John L. Given, *Making a Newspaper* (New York: Henry Holt, 1907), 211 (error in page number, the book gives it as 213).

87   *leased wire services*: The AP, founded in the mid-nineteenth century, "took its final form in 1900." The United Press Association was founded by Edward Wyllis Scripps in 1907; Hearst began his International News Service in 1909. Emery and Emery, *The Press and America*, 181–82, 243.

87   *Americans could choose*: Emery and Emery, *The Press and America*, 155.

87   *Newspaper readership*: Matthew Schneirov, *The Dream of New Social Order: Popular*

Magazines in America: 1893–1914 (New York: Columbia University Press, 1994), 5.

87   *free rural delivery*: Emery and Emery, *The Press and America*, 181.

87   *The figure would soon climb*: In 1850 a large journal would have had fifty thousand subscribers; by 1909 any one of the "modern" New York dailies could have a circulation of nearly half a million. James Edward Rogers (Chicago: University of Chicago Press, 1909), 17. In March 1897, "The combined circulation of its [the *World*'s] morning and evening editions touch the million mark." Frank Luther Mott, *American Journalism: A History of Newspapers in the United States through 250 Years, 1690 to 1940* (New York: Macmillan, 1941), 546.

87   *Taft held weekly meetings*: Cook, *Governing with the News*, 47–49. Mott points out that Taft "inaugurated the policy of regular weekly press conferences to which all accredited correspondents were invited, though he did not always adhere to the plan" (*American Journalism*, 608).

87   *"only in the present day"*: Rogers, *The American Newspaper*, vi, vii, 23. America was a nation in many respects thanks to the telegraph and the telephone as well as newspapers; for the first time it was possible "'for all men to understand one another,'" according to William Allen White. See Michael J. Sandel, *Public Philosophy: Essays on Morality in Politics* (Cambridge, Mass.: Harvard University Press, 2005), 13.

88   *"the newspapers reflected"*: Rogers, *American Newspaper*, 42.

88   *Now that citizens*: "The very notion of public opinion was a product of this pe-

riod," J. Anthony Lukas wrote in *Big Trouble: A Murder in a Small Western Town Sets off a Struggle for the Soul of America* (New York: Simon & Schuster, 1997), 634–35. For an earlier navy case sensationalized in the New York press, see Buckner F. Melton Jr., *A Hanging Offense: The Strange Affair of the Warship Somers* (New York: Free Press, 2003).

88 *"gain adherents"*: Given, *Making a Newspaper*, 217.

88 *Suicide was widespread*: Kim Townsend, *Manhood at Harvard: William James and Others* (New York: W. W. Norton, 1996), 32, and chap. 1 for a discussion of William James' thoughts on suicide.

88 *"squeeze a suicide"*: Given, *Making a Newspaper*, 170, and see 9. In 1909, in New York City alone, more than 325 suicides were reported in the *Times*, according to the paper's index. And note the chapter "Is Life Worth Living?"— a question asked by William James, many of whose colleagues and associates contemplated suicide. Townsend, *Manhood at Harvard*, 32–37.

88 *the path-breaking leadership*: On the *Times* see Emery and Emery, *The Press and America*, 235–39; and Schudson, *Good Citizen*, 177–79.

89 *Don testified*: Proceedings of the Board of Officers Convened at West Point, New York, by Special Orders No.180, Current Series, Headquarters, June 25, 1909, United States Military Academy, Special Collections and Archives, West Point, 2–3.

90 *acquired the nickname "Hero"*: "Hero" appears as Don's official nickname in his Class of 1913 West Point yearbook.

91 *"opinion in this quaint little Maryland city"*: *New York Times*, July 12, 1909.

91 *He told the press*: *New York Times*, July 12, 1909.

91 *"There are numerous stories afloat"*: *New York Times*, July 12, 1909.

91 *"define the issues"*: As in "Pros and Cons Told," *Baltimore Sun*, July 19, 1909.

91 *"It seems very strange"*: *Evening Star* (Washington, D.C.), July 28, 1909.

91 *the San Francisco Chronicle*: The *Chronicle* headline "ARMY AWAITS NEW SENSATION" reflects the tendency of the press to occasionally mix up the services.

92 *quoted A. Wollett Webb*: *New York Times*, July 18, 1909; *Washington Post*, July 18, 1909. Mention of Webb appears in several other papers including the *Los Angeles Times* (July 18, 1909), which said that he had received a summons to appear as a witness before the Board of Inquiry.

92 *from every angle*: Just about every paper used speculated about Sutton's relationship

with Mary Elizabeth Stewart. The *St. Louis Post-Dispatch* (July 10 and 13, 1909) claimed that she and Lieutenant Sutton "were engaged to be married." According to the *Baltimore Sun*, July 19, 1909, half a dozen letters from Mary Elizabeth Stewart were taken to Annapolis by the attorneys.

92 *Jimmie's recent friendship*: Rose Parker surely met Miss Stewart and Gilbert Coleman in Annapolis. That may well be why her mother wrote to both of them.

92 *A New York* World *reporter wrote*: *World* (New York), July 12, 1909.

93 *"ardently in love"*: *Chicago Tribune*, July 11, 1909. The *Evening Capital* (Annapolis, Md.), July 10, 1909, and other papers note that she arrived in Annapolis on October 6, 1907, to visit her brother.

93 *"MISS STEWART SAW NO GLOOM"*: *New York Times*, July 15, 1909; the *Chicago Tribune* also backed off from the romance on July 15, quoting Mary as saying they danced together at one of the hops but saw each other infrequently after that.

94 *she received at least two letters*: *Evening Journal* (New York), July 22, 1909.

95 *The St. Louis Post-Dispatch was more blunt*: *St. Louis Post-Dispatch*, July 11, 1909, part 2.

95 *Mrs. Roelker said she felt sorry*: *New York American*, July 9, 1909.

95 *The Baltimore Sun found it*: Once out of the service "he could quietly disappear from the face of the earth." *Baltimore Sun*, July 19, 1909.

95 *"every known means"*: *Baltimore Sun*, July 18, 1909.

95 *The thirty-one-thousand-plus readers*: *Oregon Daily Journal*, July 9, 1909. The paper published the previous day's circulation on its front page. It cost two cents, but the price went to five cents on trains and newsstands. Some of its stories came through "United Press Leased Wire."

96 *headlined its similar piece*: "I Don't Know Much About Christianity," *New York American*, July 14, 1909; *Chicago Tribune*, July 10, 1909; see also *New York Times*, July 15, 1909.

96 *surmised a New York Times reporter*: See *New York Times*, July 11 and 12, 1909. Also, William Owens was "shying at the newspaper fraternity," *Evening Capital* (Annapolis, Md.), July 10, 1909. Owens' story came out in *New York American*, July 8, 1909; *Boston Globe*, July 19, 1909; *Atlanta Constitution*, July 19, 1909; *World* (New York), July 14, 1909; *Oregon Daily Journal*, July 10, 1909; *Chicago Tribune*, July 10,

1909; *St. Louis Post-Dispatch*, July 10, 1909, July 13, 1909, July 19, 1909; *Cincinnati Enquirer*, July 19, 1909.

96   *largely responsible for the inquiry*: New York *Times*, July 12, 1909, and July 17, 1909.

96   *stirring accounts of Rose's sleuthing*: New York *American*, July 11, 1909.

96   *comparable* Chicago Tribune: *Chicago Tribune*, July 11, 1909.

97   *Rosa Sutton was the leading lady*: For this paragraph, see the *Chicago Tribune*, July 12, 1909; *World* (New York), July 12, 1909; *New York American*, July 13, 1909.

98   *Old friends of the Suttons*: *Los Angeles Times*, July 18, 1909.

99   *according to the* Philadelphia Inquirer: *Philadelphia Inquirer*, July 13, 1909; also *Los Angeles Times*, July 13, 1909.

99   *Meyer assured the* New York Times: *New York Times*, July 10 and July 16, 1909.

99   *"Officers, particularly those of the Marine Corps"*: *New York Times*, July 17, 1909.

99   *the "reluctance on the part of"*: *Atlanta Constitution*, July 19, 1909.

99   *"more charitable to"*: *Philadelphia Inquirer*, July 14, 1909.

100   *Correspondent John E. Lathrop*: *Oregon Sunday Journal*, July 18, 1909. On July 19, Lathrop wrote a lengthy summary of the entire case.

100   *"WRAITH of Lieutenant Sutton"*: *Cincinnati Enquirer*, July 20, 1909.

100   *"against her doctor's orders"*: *Baltimore Sun*, July 19, 1909.

100   *wished them well*: *Evening Capital* (Annapolis, Md.), August 9, 1909.

102   *"TO WIPE OUT THE MYSTERY"*: *New York Times*, July 19, 1909.

CHAPTER 7: A SERIOUS AND GRAVE AFFAIR

103   *described the colorful scene*: *World* (New York), July 20, 1909.

103   *"lane of clicking cameras"*: *World* (New York), July 20, 1909.

103   *"as dark as her jet black hair"*: For example, the *New York American*, July 20, 1909; *Washington Post*, July 19, 1909.

104   *"an active little man"*: *World* (New York), July 20, 1909.

104   *"greeted the swarm"*: *Evening Star* (Washington, D.C.), July 19, 1909.

104   *the Navy Department's precept*: Inquiry, 1. Precise rules governed every step of the Court of Inquiry. The precept and organizing papers are Exhibits A, B, C, D. The transcript capitalizes many words that are not capitalized today; in all dialogue and quotations from the inquiry, I use the original capitalization.

105   *whose official job it was*: The official language does not do justice to Leonard's real job—at least as it would evolve in this proceeding. For the texts of the oaths for the members of the court, and the judge advocate, see *Forms of Procedure for Courts and Boards in the Navy and Marine Corps*, published by Authority of the Secretary of the Navy (Washington, D.C.: Government Printing Office, 1910), pages 191ff. According to the New York *Evening Post*—then a serious and not a sensational paper—Major Wendell Neville "administered the oath of service to Major Leonard." July 19, 1909. Normal procedure would have had Hood do it. The transcript states that he did. Inquiry, 2.

105   *Major Leonard offered one to Birney*: Inquiry, 2–3. Exhibit E, attached to Inquiry, is the letter authorizing the stenographer to provide Henry Davis with a copy of the day-to-day testimony that he agreed to pay for himself.

105   *the court recessed*: Inquiry, 3.

105   *The Academic Building*: A detailed description of the building is available from the Public Works Office, USNA, Real Estate Records, 106: Mahan Hall, Inventory by Sally K. Tompkins, June 1980.

106   *a Naval Academy dance*: Robert Adams recognized the building as soon as he began to testify; the dance was in the same auditorium. Inquiry, 6.

106   *An upright piano, a music stand*: "Photograph by *New York American* staff photographer of 'scene in court at yesterday's Sutton inquiry,'" *New York American*, July 20, 1909.

106   *a fact that pleased the "townsfolk"*: *New York Herald*, July 14, 1909.

107   *Among the spectators*: *Evening Capital* (Annapolis, Md.), July 21, 1909.

107   *"a score of young girls"*: *New York American*, July 21, 1909. See also *St. Louis Post-Dispatch*, July 25, 1909.

107   *On this first day*: *Baltimore Sun*, July 20, 1909.

107   *"The ghost of Lieutenant James Nuttle Sutton"*: James French Dorrance, one of the few who used a byline, wrote the opening piece in the *New York American*, July 20, 1909.

107   *the first of these was Robert Adams*: For Adams's initial testimony, see Inquiry, 6–148.

107   *Reporters noted the heavyset*: Washington Post, July 20, 1909. See also *Philadelphia Inquirer*, July 21, 1909; *Baltimore Sun*, July 20, 1909. Photographs of Robert Adams appeared in many of the big-city dailies surveyed. Full descriptions of his appearance—not very flattering—appeared in the New York *World* (July 20 and July 25) and the *St. Louis Post-Dispatch* (July 24).

107   *"shall be the truth"*: Major Leonard would administer the oath to every witness; the wording he must have used can be found in the *Forms of Procedure for Courts and Boards in the Navy and Marine Corps*.

108   *"whose incredulity"*: World (New York), July 20, 1909.

108   *"clustered in the pew-like seats"*: World (New York), July 20, 1909.

109   *"[indicating]"*: It is not possible to know exactly what Adams's motions were, but when the court transcript includes the word "indicating" I have left it in.

109   *a sturdy orderly*: New York Times, July 20, 1909.

110   *"eyed the witness closely"*: New York Times, July 20, 1909.

112   *"momentarily confused"*: New York Times, July 20, 1909. Summaries of his testimony appear in all the big-city papers. Most placed the story on their front page.

113   *"concentration rather than apprehension"*: Army and Navy Journal, July 24, 1909.

113   *"visibly affected"*: New York American, July 20, 1909.

115   *"was a dead shot"*: Oregon Daily Journal, July 19, 1909.

115   *"to have him hanged"*: Denver Post, July 20, 1909.

115   *"TRAP ADAMS IN DENIALS"*: Evening Journal (New York), July 20, 1909; see also the *New York Times* for the same day.

116   *"fixed her eyes upon him"*: Philadelphia Inquirer, July 21, 1909; and New York American, July 21, 1909.

119   *"who has a rather harsh voice"*: Denver Post, August 9, 1909.

121   *"with almost parrot-like repetition"*: Evening Capital (Annapolis, Md.), July 20, 1909.

CHAPTER 8: "AN OFFICER SAID IT"

123   *Harry Leonard emphasized*: "Compilation of the [Government] Arguments in the Sutton Case," informal untitled document from Henry Leonard to Edward Campbell, received August 20, 1909, File 20971, RG 80.

124   *he was found to be*: Dean of the faculty Frederick Maglott to Whom It May Concern, April 22, 1904, File 17434, RG 127.

124   *he was not as tall*: Philadelphia Inquirer, July 21, 1909; *Atlanta Constitution*, July 20, 1909. Edward Osterman was five foot, nine and a half inches tall.

124   *"nervous air"*: Evening Star (Washington, D.C.), July 21, 1909; *New York American*, July 21, 1909.

124   *to give only the facts*: For Osterman's initial testimony and the surrounding dialogue, see Inquiry, 144–219, on July 20.

125   *a St. Louis reporter*: This anecdote came out in a late edition of the *St. Louis Post-Dispatch* on the evening of July 20, 1909.

126   *"highly educated"*: Hon. William Pinckney Whyte to Truman H. Newberry, October 17, 1906; Hon. Sydney E. Mudd to Truman H. Newberry, October 20, 1906; Applicant for Commission, File 14663, RG 127.

127   *senator Isidor Rayner*: And he defended Winfield Scott Schley at a naval Court of Inquiry into his conduct at the Battle of Santiago. According to the *Baltimore Sun*, Rayner had received a scathing letter from Rosa Sutton right after she arrived in Washington in September 1908 calling her son's death the "blackest crime in the whole history of the Navy."

127   *Bevan said that he first encountered*: For William Bevan's testimony, see Inquiry, 220–32, on July 20; 233–313, on July 21.

128   *An* Evening Capital *reporter*: Evening Capital (Annapolis, Md.), July 21, 1909.

128   *"high strung" judge advocate*: Evening Star (Washington, D.C.), July 21, 1909.

129   *"their shapely bonnetless heads"*: World (New York), July 22, 1909.

131   *"the first cousin of Mrs. John Jacob Astor"*: New York American, July 22, 1909. John Jacob Astor IV married Philadelphia beauty Ava Lowle Willing, the daughter of Edward Shippen Willing on May 1, 1891. In 1909, he divorced Ava. See also *Boston Globe*, July 22, 1909; and Justin Kaplan, *When the Astors Owned New York: Blue Bloods and Grand Hotels in a Gilded Age* (New York: Penguin, 2006).

131   *When he applied to the Corps*: Applicant for Commission, File 12946, RG 127.

131   *with glowing references*: Edward Shippen to the president, undated handwritten letter received on August 18, 1906. Senator Boies Penrose to Charles J.

Bonaparte, October 16, 1906. He wrote again on January 9, 1907 to the Secretary of the Navy Victor Metcalf. The acting secretary to President Roosevelt, Rudolf Forster, also wrote to Bonaparte, October 9, 1906. Willing's Applicant for Commission, File 12946, RG 127.

131   *when he took the witness stand*: Applicant for Commission, File 12946, RG 127. For Willing's testimony, see Inquiry, 317–69, on July 21; 372–91, on July 22.

132   *"black eyes were rapid fire"*: New York American, July 22, 1909.

132   *"How can they let him sit there"*: New York American, July 22, 1909.

132   *"a large slow young man"*: Evening Star (Washington, D.C.), July 22, 1909.

132   *"long and earnest discussion"*: New York Times and Chicago Tribune, July 22, 1909, among others.

133   *according to a headline*: "SUTTON'S MOTHER AND SISTER SNEER," Hartford Courant (Connecticut), July 22, 1909.

134   Washington Post *suggested*: Washington Post, July 22, 1909.

135   *Navy surgeon George Pickrell*: For Pickrell's testimony, see Inquiry, 392–423, and see chapter 1.

135   *"took the revolver in his right hand"*: Evening Star (Washington, D.C.), July 22, 1909; Cincinnati Enquirer, July 23, 1909; and Atlanta Constitution, July 23, 1909.

136   *Rosa's attorney raised*: For Charles Doyen's testimony, see Inquiry, 424–56.

137   *The papers would describe him as*: San Francisco Chronicle, July 23, 1909. See also the Sun (New York), Evening Star (Washington, D.C.), and Chicago Tribune for the same day.

137   *"retracting his own opinions"*: For James De Hart's testimony, see Inquiry, 457–513, on July 22; 518–53, on July 23.

137   *"many a glance of apprehension"*: New York American, July 23, 1909.

138   *Major Leonard "roared"*: The dialogue is from the transcript. Reporter James Dorrance describes Harry Leonard as "the government inquisitor."

139   *"Mrs. Parker kept her big, keen"*: Evening Star (Washington, D.C.), July 23, 1909.

140   *De Hart testified that*: Lieutenant Willing testified that he picked up the gun.

140   *"Everything that he could deny"*: New York Sun, July 23, 1909.

140   *"steadfast in his"*: Washington Post, July 24, 1909.

140   *But* New York American *reporter, James Dorrance*: James Dorrance, in the New York American, July 23, 1909.

141   *was still en route*: Baltimore Sun, July 19, 1909.

141   *Describing the young man*: Baltimore Sun, July 20, 1909.

141   *Two days later a report said*: Oregon Daily Journal, July 22, 1909.

142   *another bit of information*: Baltimore Sun, July 20, 1909.

CHAPTER 9: "SUTTON MYSTERY DEEPER"

143   *"lanky stripling"*: Evening Star (Washington, D.C.), July 24, 1909.

143   *he identified himself*: For William Owens' testimony, see Inquiry, 555–87, on July 23.

145   *friend, Edward Griffith*: For Griffith's testimony, see Inquiry, 603–17, on July 23.

145   *"with a memory"*: Evening Capital (Annapolis, Md.), July 23, 1909.

145   *"decidedly the best"*: Baltimore Sun, July 24, 1909.

145   *"impressed everyone"*: Evening Capital (Annapolis, Md.), July 25, 1909.

145   *"prearranged affair"*: Baltimore Sun, July 24, 1909.

145   *"frank and intelligent"*: Washington Post, July 24, 1909.

145   *"bears an excellent reputation"*: New York American, July 24, 1909.

146   *the* Evening Capital *published*: Evening Capital (Annapolis, Md.), July 24, 1909.

147   *there were reported rumblings*: New York American, July 26, 1909; see also Baltimore Sun, July 27, 1909.

148   *A Portland paper named*: Oregon Daily Journal, July 26, 1909.

148   *A Baltimore Sun correspondent*: Baltimore Sun, July 27, 1909.

148   *reporters did track down*: Philadelphia Inquirer, July 25, 1909; see also San Francisco Chronicle, July 25, 1909; Denver Post, July 25, 1909; New York Times, July 25, 1909; Oregonian, July 25, 1909.

149   *but John Anthony*: Inquiry, 672–76. Anthony testified after a few final questions had been asked of Owens and Griffith, 646–72. Dr. Albert McCormick also testified briefly, but he never examined Sutton.

149   *"dropped into the situation"*: New York Times, July 27, 1909; see also New York American, Philadelphia Inquirer, and the Baltimore Sun on the same day.

149   *Marine private Charles Kennedy*: For Kennedy's testimony, see Inquiry, 699–771.

149   *"keen brown eyes"*: Baltimore Sun, July 27, 1909.

150 *bulldozing the witness*: Baltimore Sun, July 27, 1909.

151 *blueprint of the scene*: Inquiry, 772. The blueprint is attached to the record.

151 *"with a measuring line"*: New York American, July 27, 1909. The *Army and Navy Journal* also describes this visit to the parade grounds (July 31, 1909).

152 *"fixing the responsibility of it"*: The Sutton letter to the secretary of the navy dated February 8, 1909, would be read into the record twice. Inquiry, 780–82, 803–5.

152 *"hostile feminine eyes"*: Washington Post, July 28, 1909.

153 *I have sedulously avoided*: Inquiry, 787–88.

155 *"You have a right to be present"*: Inquiry, 805.

155 *"in grave peril of irregularity"*: Inquiry, 791.

156 *"crying farce"*: Washington Post, July 28, 1909.

156 *"carefully planned coup"*: Cincinnati Enquirer, July 28, 1909.

156 *a twelve-page letter*: File 20971, RG 80.

157 *But Davis' request*: File 20971, RG 80. *New York Times*, July 31, 1909, ran a long piece on why the navy would not accept Davis' protest.

157 *"'I do not know whether'"*: Baltimore Sun, July 28, 1909.

157 *He told his office staff*: Washington Post, August 1, 1909.

157 *The New York* World *printed*: World (New York), July 28, 1909.

157 *a* New York Times *editorial*: New York Times, July 29, 1909.

158 *"THE CITY OF BROKEN HEARTS"*: Evening Capital (Annapolis, Md.), July 28, July 29, and July 30, 1909.

158 *the reporter speculated*: Evening Capital (Annapolis, Md.), July 29, 1909.

158 *a Marine Corps housecleaning*: Evening Capital (Annapolis, Md.), August 2, 1909; "MARINE CORPS SHAKE-UP," Baltimore Sun, August 1, 1909.

158 *the* Army and Navy Journal *editorial*: Army and Navy Journal, July 31, 1909. The Journal continued its campaign of keeping reporters honest and accurate in their interpretations of the case even after the inquiry ended. See, for example, the August 28 issue.

158 *submitted a long report to*: Hazing Investigation Board, Proceedings, June 23, 1909, Records of Boards and Committees; Records of the U.S. Military Academy, Record Group 404; National Archives—Affiliated Archives: Record on Deposit at U.S. Military Academy Archives, West Point, N.Y.

159 *refuse to answer any questions*: Harold Utley's new situation created speculation in several newspapers including the Philadelphia Inquirer, August 6, 1909, and the New York Herald, August 5, 1909.

159 *"THE DILEMMA IN THE SUTTON CASE"*: New York Times, July 30, 1909.

CHAPTER 10: "TO THE BEST OF MY RECOLLECTION"

160 *The following morning*: For this scene, see Evening Star (Washington, D.C.) and Evening Capital (Annapolis, Md.), August 5, 1909, New York Herald and Baltimore Sun, August 6, 1909.

160 *"white uniformed officers of court"*: Evening Star (Washington, D.C.), August 6, 1909.

160 *an* Evening Star *reporter*: Evening Star (Washington, D.C.), August 5, 1909.

160 *"darling of the corps and"*: Denver Post, August 6, 1909.

160 *Two stenographers*: Inquiry, 807.

160 *his coolness toward them*: Evening Star (Washington, D.C.), August 5, 1909.

161 *"there has been a charge of crime"*: Inquiry, 807.

161 *Leonard disagreed*: Inquiry, 809. For Utley's testimony, see Inquiry, 810–931, on August 5; 933–1004, on August 6.

161 *"was counted on to blow aside"*: Denver Post, August 5, 1909.

165 *Davis had no backup*: Baltimore Sun, August 6, 1909.

167 *"I simply want this to appear"*: Inquiry, 933–34.

167 *Women crowded into the courtroom*: Denver Post, August 6, 1909.

168 *"with a zeal" that incensed him*: New York Times, August 6, 1909.

170 *The inventory was dated*: Inquiry, Exhibit O. Harold Utley would be questioned about the inventory both by Henry Davis and Harry Leonard for several moments. Although the punctuation in the inventory is missing a comma and states "revolver[,] belt and holster," Utley admitted that after the inquest Sutton's Smith & Wesson was added to his effects. He and Captain Arthur Marix, the instructing officer at the time, completed the inventory on Monday, October 14. Inquiry, 985–87.

172 *"hazy memory"*: Washington Post, August 7, 1909.

172 *One staff correspondent for the* Evening Star: Evening Star (Washington, D.C.), August 6, 1909. See also "LIEUT. UTLEY ADDS TO THE MAZE OF CONTRADICTIONS," Evening Post (New York), August 6, 1909.

172   *his face "set hard in anger"*: Army and Navy
        Journal, August 14, 1909.
172   *the* Chicago Tribune *characterized*: Chicago
        Tribune, August 6, 1909. The paper
        mistakenly gives his first name as
        Howard.
172   *the* Illinois State Register: "SUTTON'S
        DEATH TOLD BY UTLEY–GRAPHIC
        STORY OF TRAGEDY IS GIVEN BY
        SPRINGFIELD BOY," *Illinois State Regis-
        ter*, August 6, 1909.

172   *Emma Utley could read the details*: "LIEUT.
        UTLEY AGAIN ON STAND," *Illinois State
        Register*, August 7, 1909.
172   *"busy, busy Mr. Utley"'*: New York American,
        August 5, 1909.
172   *the* Oregonian *headline*: Oregonian, August
        6, 1909.
172   *Dr. Frank Cook made the trip*: Baltimore Sun,
        August 5, 1909.
172   *Cook explained that*: For Cook's testimony,
        see Inquiry, 1006–31.

CHAPTER 11: SACRED REPUTATIONS

174   *In a rare gesture of solidarity*: Washington Post,
        August 7, 1909.
174   *"In these letters"*: Inquiry, 1036.
174   *Swartz, who was now a corporal*: Baltimore
        Sun, August 10, 1909.
174   *"I was unfortunate"*: Oregonian, August 10,
        1909. The paper took this statement
        to mean that Harry Swartz "had to
        give up all letters." See also *Evening
        Star* (Washington, D.C.), August 10,
        1909; *New York World* (New York), Au-
        gust 10, 1909.
175   *explained to the* Washington Post: *Washing-
        ton Post*, August 11, 1909; according
        to the New York *World*, August 10,
        1909, he declared "his lips were
        sealed." Swartz's superiors had al-
        legedly warned him not to discuss the
        case because he might become a wit-
        ness. *Evening Capital* (Annapolis, Md.),
        August 10, 1909.
175   *"in which event Mrs. Sutton"*: Inquiry, 1036.
175   *his fury was apparent to all*: For Henry Davis'
        reaction and the ensuing debate, see
        Inquiry, 1037–45. See also *Washington
        Post*, August 7, 1909.
175   *Rosa broke down*: Baltimore Sun, August 7,
        1909; *Los Angeles Times*, August 7,
        1909.
176   *"suppressed with emotion"*: New York Herald,
        August 7, 1909.
177   *the inquiry proceeded behind closed doors*: In-
        quiry, 1046–60, for the testimony on
        Saturday August 7. On Monday, Au-
        gust 9, 1909, the *New York American* re-
        ported that a letter Rosa wrote to
        Colonel Charles Doyen had been read
        in court on Saturday morning, but it
        was not put into evidence.
177   *"equatorial heat wave"*: "FIVE DIE AS MER-
        CURY CLIMBS TO 93 MARK," as an
        "equatorial heat wave" struck the
        city Saturday. *New York Times*, August
        10, 1909. It was "a sweltering Satur-
        day." *New York American*, August 9,
        1909.
181   *"savage fighter when aroused"*: Evening Capi-
        tal (Annapolis, Md.), August 9, 1909;
        Baltimore Sun, August 7, 1909.

181   *the* Philadelphia Inquirer *headline*: Philadel-
        phia Inquirer, August 8, 1909; by Sun-
        day, August 8, Rosa asserted she was
        ready to back up everything she said,
        and "perfectly willing to have my ex-
        amination conducted publicly" and
        show "every effort to have all the re-
        maining sessions open to the public."
        Washington Post, August 8, 1909.
181   *Reporters continued to suggest*: Baltimore Sun,
        August 13, 1909; *Oregonian*, August 8,
        1909.
181   *The* Baltimore Sun *reporter*: Baltimore Sun,
        August 10, 1909.
183   *In the only full statement of her views*: "Mrs.
        James Nuttall Sutton replies to the
        statement that her son's death should
        not be investigated 'for the good of
        the Marine service.'" Undated original
        carbon copy found by the author
        among the few surviving Sutton fam-
        ily papers. The text of the document
        makes it clear that it was written to-
        ward the end of the inquiry, in August
        1909.
183   *not to submit her statement*: I have not found
        the document or parts of it cited in
        any newspaper.
184   *the wife of a prominent officer*: Evening Capital
        (Annapolis, Md.), August 9, 1909.
184   *a group of Boston suffragists had*: "'Jane Ad-
        dams of Chicago future president of
        the United States,' will be the slogan
        before many months have passed, ac-
        cording to the advocates of equal suf-
        frage. Boston has been chosen as the
        starting point of the startling and
        novel campaign by which the women
        hope to gain prestige if not actually a
        president." The article cited William
        Dean Howells and Alice Stone Black-
        well. The latter said Miss Addams
        "would have as much tact as Taft, as
        much zeal for right as Roosevelt, and
        a greater breadth of mind than either
        of them." Jane Addams, however, did
        not take the comments seriously. *Los
        Angeles Times* and *Chicago Tribune*, Au-
        gust 9, 1909.

184   *he responded firmly*: For Rosa's testimony, see Inquiry, 1061–11, on August 9. Although it was clear that the letters would soon be published, and some had leaked to the press, Rosa's testimony on Saturday morning was not released until Monday morning, August 9. By then, the letters to Harry Swartz were "famous." *Philadelphia Inquirer*, August 10, 1909.

184   *"dean of the press representatives"*: *Evening Capital* (Annapolis, Md.), August 9, 1909.

184   *he "thundered"*: *Evening Capital* (Annapolis, Md.), August 9, 1909.

185   *"publicity will force out enough"*: *New York Times*, July 29, 1909.

185   *the court had heard from*: There were still a few more witnesses—including Davis' best witness—but no one else who had been at the scene of the tragedy.

186   *the "largest audience so far"*: *Baltimore Sun*, August 10, 1909.

189   *Rosa impressed reporters*: *Washington Post*, August 10, 1909.

191   *striking her fan on the table*: "With an emphatic rapping of her fan, she adhered steadfastly to her interpretation of circumstances as pointing to crime." *Washington Post*, August 10, 1909.

191   *who had grinned openly at each other*: *Evening Star* (Washington, D.C.), August 9, 1909.

192   *a photograph was taken*: A copy appeared in the *New York Herald* on August 11, 1909.

194   *to identify some papers*: These items included a bill of lading made out by Lieutenant Sutton anticipating his trip on the Great White Fleet, Inquiry, Exhibit U; the two letters of Lieutenant Sutton to his brother and his mother, Inquiry, Exhibit T-1, T-2.

194   *"wept quietly but without concealment"*: *Philadelphia Inquirer*, August 10, 1909.

195   *"perfectly collected, sharp woman"*: *Evening Star* (Washington, D.C.), August 9, 1909.

195   *The* Washington Post *reported*: *Washington Post*, August 10, 1909.

195   *A straightforward article*: "MRS. SUTTON WROTE THAT SPIRIT OF HER SON CAME TO HER AFTER DEATH AND ACCUSED OFFICERS," *New York Times*, August 10, 1909.

195   *"comely sister of the dead Sutton"*: *Evening Star* (Washington, D.C.), August 10, 1909.

195   *she spoke in a barely audible voice*: The *Evening Star* (Washington, D.C.) and *New York Herald* are two of the papers that comment on Rose's soft voice, August 11, 1909.

195   *so they could take their own notes*: *Baltimore Sun*, August 11, 1909.

195   *It would be up to Rose to*: For Rose Parker's testimony, see Inquiry, 1159–1200.

196   *and Rosa lowered her head*: *New York Herald*, August 11, 1909.

196   *"SUTTON'S HEREAFTER IS"*: *Evening Star* (Washington, D.C.), August 10, 1909.

197   *his face flushing*: A number of people noticed that Robert Adams had a tendency to blush making it hard for him to hide his feelings. *New York Herald*, August 11, 1909.

200   *photograph of Rose*: *Oregon Daily Journal*, August 11, 1909.

200   *made brief statements*: *Los Angeles Times* and *Oregonian*, August 11, 1909; *Evening Star* (Washington, D.C.), August 10, 1909.

200   *drafted a reprimand*: *Oregonian*, August 12, 1909. Four days earlier, another *Oregonian* editorial decided that Sutton had probably been killed "by his own hand, by accident, in a scuffle with several of his fellows." And, the editor said, "The course pursued by the unfortunate young man's mother is not unnatural—since she is the mother. But it can hardly be deemed wise. The son, clearly, was an irascible and boisterous young man, who didn't get on well with his fellows and seem to be at variance with every member of the party. After the tragedy they naturally wished to excuse themselves, as far as possible, and their testimony needs sifting." But "there is no need to suppose he was murdered, or that he intentionally killed himself" (August 8, 1909).

CHAPTER 12: EVERY SCRAP OF EVIDENCE

203   *A veteran soldier*: *Evening Star* (Washington, D.C.), August 11, 1909.

203   *Hulbert said he was sure that*: For Henry Lewis Hulbert's testimony, see Inquiry, 1201–15.

204   *Baltimore Sun was one of several papers*: *Baltimore Sun*, August 11, 1909.

205   *he was not much help*: For Charles Doyen's testimony, see Inquiry, 1215–26.

206   *with particular relish*: *Evening Star* (Washington, D.C.), August 11, 1909.

206   *He "reached for the revolver"*: *Baltimore Sun* and *Washington Post*, August 11, 1909.

207   *James Weidefeld and undertaker Raymond Taylor took*: For Weidefeld's testimony, see Inquiry, 1250–57; for Taylor's testimony, see Inquiry, 1260–66.

208   "*A dark complexioned young man*": *Evening Star* (Washington, D.C.), August 11, 1909.

208   *When he applied to take the Marine Corps exam*: All of this correspondence is in Allen Sumner's Applicant for Commission File 16240, RG 127. Massachusetts Governor Curtis Guild's endorsement of the son "of one of my oldest and dearest friends, now deceased" was unqualified.

209   *a printed card*: The calling card became Exhibit S in Inquiry.

209   *He was clearly in a tight spot*: For Sumner's testimony, see Inquiry, 1275–94.

210   *The Boston Post had published*: The sensational interview came out in papers that Jimmie's family could have seen in Oregon and West Point. "MISSING WITNESS SAYS SUTTON MURDERED," a "United Press Leased Wire" from Boston, *Oregon Daily Journal*, August 10, 1909; see also *Oregonian*, August

11, 1909, and *Newburgh Daily News* (West Point, N.Y.), August 10, 1909.

210   *sent a telegram to Secretary of the Navy*: The telegram is in File 20971, RG 80.

211   *An excerpt appeared in*: *New York Times*, August 12, 1909; *Oregonian*, August 12, 1909.

211   *Todd's testimony supported*: For Archie Todd's testimony, see Inquiry, 1295–1331.

212   *Dr. Edward Schaeffer*: For Edward Schaeffer's testimony, see Inquiry, 1340–59, on August 11; 1366–1409, on August 12.

220   *Reporters thoroughly enjoyed*: *Los Angeles Times*, August 12, 1909; *New York Times*, August 12, 1909.

221   "*arose to his full height*": *Evening Capital* (Annapolis, Md.), August 12, 1909. Photographs reveal that Harry Leonard was at least six feet tall. This is one of only a few references to Leonard's missing arm in the press coverage.

221   *defended the navy's procedure*: For Leonard's remarks, see Inquiry, 1405–8.

CHAPTER 13: "THE FEROCITY OF A TIGRESS"

223   *the largest crowd so far*: *Baltimore Sun* and *Oregonian*, August 14, 1909.

223   *a deeply spiritual man*: See Henry Edgar Davis, "The Law Spirit: Its Source and Its Sway," in *Annual Address Delivered at the Tenth Annual Convention, Cape May, New Jersey, June 28, 1904* (Harrisburg: Pennsylvania Bar Association; Seeley G. Mudd Manuscript Library, Princeton University, N.J.). Copies of this and other writings and addresses by Davis can be found at the Historical Society of Washington, D.C., and the Library of Congress.

224   *a hushed silence fell*: *Evening Capital* (Annapolis, Md.), August 13, 1909.

224   *He began by informing the court*: For Davis' closing remarks, see Inquiry, 1415–55.

224   *she buried her face in her handkerchief*: *Baltimore Sun*, August 14, 1909.

224   *weeping in sympathy*: *Evening Star* (Washington, D.C.), August 13, 1909; *Evening Capital* (Annapolis, Md.), August 13, 1909.

229   *who was staring moodily at him*: *Evening Capital* (Annapolis, Md.), August 13, 1909.

230   "*all the while a flush of crimson*": *Evening Star* (Washington, D.C.), August 13, 1909. The *Evening Capital* (Annapolis, Md.) said that Adams had a letter in his hand.

230   *he would smile*: *Baltimore Sun*, August 14, 1909.

231   *reporters seemed surprised*: *Baltimore Sun*, August 14, 1909.

232   *in an animated voice that*: For Arthur Birney's closing remarks, see Inquiry, 1456–87.

238   *He began with the observation*: "Concluding Statement by the Judge Advocate," Inquiry, 1488–91.

239   "*no further business*": Inquiry, 1491.

239   *Davis was credited*: *Washington Post*, August 14, 1909; *Baltimore Sun*, August 14, 1909.

239   "*humorous tumble*": *Washington Post*, August 14, 1909.

239   *appalled by the story*: *Oregonian*, August 14, 1909.

240   "*So that even I*": "3 SAW SUTTON IN DREAMS," *Washington Post*, August 14, 1909; *Evening Star* (Washington, D.C.), August 13, 1909.

240   *She also told the press*: *Washington Post*, August 14, 1909.

CHAPTER 14: THE COURT, THE CORPS, AND PUBLIC OPINION

241   *took the unusual step*: *Evening Capital* (Annapolis, Md.), August 16, 1909. See also *Evening Star* (Washington, D.C.), *Baltimore Sun*, and *Washington Post*, August 16, 1909. The transcript and accompanying documents became

part of the pre–World War I Military Records housed in the National Archives Building after 1939.

241   *while Americans waited*: *Washington Post*, August 14, 1909; and the "famous case," *Cincinnati Enquirer*, August 17, 1909.

241   "*up to the horses knees*": *Evening Capital* (Annapolis, Md.), August 16, 1909.

241   *had correctly forecast*: *New York Times*, August 13, 1909.

242   *Findings, Opinions, and Recommendations*: The Findings, Opinions, and Recommendations of the Court are at the back of Inquiry transcript and take up about seven handwritten pages.

242   *returned to the nation's capital*: Following the appropriate procedure as described in William Winthrop, *Military Law and Precedents*, 2nd ed. (Washington, D.C.: Government Printing Office, 1920; first published in 1886), 204. See also *New York Times*, August 17, 1909. The members of the court "expressed great relief" that the case had ended.

242   *The two navy attorneys met*: *Evening Star* (Washington, D.C.), August 17, 1909.

242   "*compilation of the arguments in*": Henry Leonard to Edward Campbell, August 20, 1909, File 20971, RG 80.

242   *one paper would boldly ask*: *Baltimore Sun*, August 18, 1909. This question was raised immediately after the verdict was announced.

242   *widely expressed theory*: *Washington Post*, August 15, 1909.

242   *The* Washington Post *filled*: *Washington Post*, August 18, 1909.

243   *Readers in Maryland learned*: *Baltimore Sun*, August 16, 1909.

243   *Reporters correctly assumed*: And they also predicted the case was not over yet. *Evening Star* (Washington, D.C.), August 16, 1909; *Baltimore Sun*, August 16 and 17, 1909. The *Evening Capital* (Annapolis, Md.) suggested that the officers accused of murder might proceed in the courts against Mrs. Sutton, August 17, 1909, but many papers began projecting what Rosa's next step would be.

245   "*stung the pride*": *Baltimore Sun*, August 20, 1909.

245   "*the lax state of discipline*": Beekman Winthrop's dismay was noted by the press and the *Army and Navy Journal*, August 21, 1909.

245   *he reportedly told the* Baltimore Sun: *Baltimore Sun*, August 19, 1909.

245   "*splendid discipline prevails at*": *Baltimore Sun*, August 19, 1909.

245   *the school had been relocated*: Conversation with Stephen Wise, Curator of the Parris Island Museum, Marine Corps Recruit Depot near Port Royal, South Carolina, December 1, 2005. In fact, discipline was so tight in the relative isolation of Parris Island, and Cole such a heavy task master, that some of the new officers compared it to Devil's Island.

245   *plans had reportedly been in the works*: *Army and Navy Journal*, January 6, 1906. The

student officers had been "quartered in the garret of the enlisted men's barracks in rooms formed by partitions of canvas" during the colder months. Commandant George Elliott hoped to find better accommodations for them.

245   *more than one newspaper*: For example, *World* (New York), August 19, 1909; *Evening Capital* (Annapolis, Md.), August 20, 1909; *Baltimore Sun*, August 20,1909.

245   *Charles Doyen's responsibility*: *Evening Capital* (Annapolis, Md.) and *Baltimore Sun*, August 20, 1909.

245   *Elliott received a memorandum*: Memorandum Dissolving the Sutton Court, File 19706, RG 80.

246   *Their dispute would come to a head*: Beekman Winthrop, Acting Secretary of the Navy, to Major General George F. Elliott, Commandant U.S. Marine Corps, July 15, 1910. This lengthy document explains to Elliott all the opinions of the court and its suggested solutions. Elliott File, Proceedings of Naval and Marine Examining Boards, RG 125. See also Wayne A. Wiegand, "The Lauchheimer Controversy: A Case of Group Political Pressure during the Taft Administration," *Military Affairs* 40, no. 2 (April 1976): 54–59.

246   "*lack of military discipline*": Beekman Winthrop, Acting Secretary of the Navy, to Major General George F. Elliott, Commandant U.S. Marine Corps, July 15, 1910, Elliott File, RG 125.

246   "*confusing and evasive testimony*": Beekman Winthrop, Acting Secretary of the Navy, to Colonel Charles A. Doyen, July 15, 1910, Doyen File, RG 125.

246   Baltimore Sun *came up with its*: *Baltimore Sun*, August 20, 1909.

247   "*one of his most prized possessions*": C. A. Doyen to the Secretary of the Navy (thru Commandant, U.S. Marine Corps), August 21, 1909, File 20971, RG 80.

247   *a twenty-four-page memorandum on*: Charles Doyen to the Honorable Secretary of the Navy, September 16, 1909, File 5118, RG 127. A second copy appears in RG 125; much of Doyen's correspondence about this matter is also in File 20971, RG 80.

248   *excellent ratings*: However, Lieutenant Harold Utley was suspended for seven days on October 27 for neglect of duty. See Utley, MEB File, RG 125; Edward Willing, MEB File, RG 125; Robert Adams, MEB File for these reports.

248   *On September 21, he wrote to the Department*: John W. Weeks to Hon. George von L. Meyer, September 21, 1909, File 20971, RG 80. C. A. Doyen to the

Secretary of the Navy (thru Major General, Commandant), October 29, 1909, objected to the fact that the court also disregarded the fifty-ninth article of the Articles for the Government of the Navy, which provides as follows: "The party whose conduct shall be the subject of inquiry, or his attorney, shall have the right to cross examine all the witnesses." File 20971, RG 80.

249 *"public interest to die out"*: Charles A. Doyen to the Secretary of the Navy, February 17, 1913, File 20971, RG 80.

249 *"published in the press throughout the country"*: Charles A. Doyen to the Secretary of the Navy, March 18, 1913, File 20971, RG 80.

249 *he took a new tack*: Charles A. Doyen to the Honorable Josephus Daniels, August 16, 1913, File 20971, RG 80. Charles Doyen continued to have a successful career in the Corps and served with great distinction in World War I. He became a brigadier general, but in 1918 he was brought back from France, a victim of the devastating influenza epidemic; he died at Quantico.

249 *"inadequate disciplinary action"*: The Department cautioned Major Benjamin Fuller that "undue leniency is as hurtful to the proper conduct of a military command as undue severity." Beekman Winthrop to Major B. H. Fuller (thru commandant, U.S. Marine Corps), August 20, 1909, File 20971, RG 80. Duplicate in File 51378, RG 127.

249 *he too sent a longer*: Fuller's response came from Panama at Camp Elliott. B. H. Fuller to the Secretary of the Navy, October 21, 1909, File 20971, RG 80.

250 *merely a statement of disapproval*: Beekman Winthrop, Acting Secretary of the Navy, to Major B. H. Fuller, November 1, 1909, File 20971, RG 80.

250 *Henry Davis' response*: New York Times, August 19, 1909.

250 *Rose Parker remained circumspect*: New York Times, August 19, 1909.

251 *According to the* Washington Post: Washington Post, August 19, 1909.

251 *the Oregonian quoted him*: Oregonian, August 19, 1909.

251 *decided not to bring a suit*: Army and Navy Journal, August 21, 1909.

251 *"useless waste of time"*: Baltimore Sun, August 13, 1909.

251 *Taft had been informed*: The president's response was also reported in the Cincinnati Enquirer on August 19, 1909.

252 *A contemporary journalism handbook*: Nathaniel C. Fowler Jr., The Handbook of Journalism (New York: Sully and Kleinteich, 1913), 11.

252 *"a most lame and impotent conclusion"*: Philadelphia Inquirer, August 19, 1909.

252 *"the logical determination"*: Army and Navy Journal, August 21, 1909.

252 *the "Sutton case"*: Army and Navy Journal, August 19, 1909.

253 *brief editorial comment*: Hartford Courant (Connecticut), August 19, 1909. The Courant suggested that both Rosa Sutton and Harry Thaw's mother, who went after the judge in her son's insanity case, "should be taken in hand by real friends, if they have any, and told that the limelight is the worst thing for them these days."

253 *"UNSATISFACTORY BECAUSE INCONCLUSIVE"*: New York Times, August 20, 1909.

253 *"wave of protest in the country over"*: "SUTTON VERDICT MOST UNPOPULAR AT WASHINGTON," Oregon Daily Journal, August 18, 1909.

253 *But the more reserved* Oregonian saw: Oregonian, August 23, 1909.

254 *"deep and widespread indignation"*: Portland Evening Telegram, August 20, 1909.

254 *Taft's decision made the headlines*: For example, see the stories in News of the Highlands (West Point, N.Y.), August 21, 1909; Newburgh Daily News (West Point, N.Y.), August 19, 1909; "SEVEN WEST POINT CADETS DISMISSED FOR PARTICIPATING IN HAZING OF ROLAND [sic] SUTTON, BROTHER OF MARINE OFFICER," New York Times, August 20 and 21, 1909; Los Angeles Times, August 20, 1909; Evening Star (Washington, D.C.), August 19, 1909; Washington Post, August 20, 1909.

255 *"is getting along splendidly"*: New York Times, August 20, 1909. See also Washington Post for the same day. On August 21, the Times suggested Rosa "may be 'tipped off' not to criticize Don Sutton's fellow cadets lest she make him unpopular."

255 *Calling Roosevelt's actions a*: Newburgh Daily News (West Point, N.Y.), August 28, 1909; also citing the New York Sun.

255 *handwritten letters that survive*: File 20971, RG 80.

255 *One New York businessman*: William Bradford Jones to Hon. Jacob M. Dickinson, Secretary of War, September 5, 1909. The acting judge advocate general of the navy responded that no copies of the transcript had been published. File 20971, RG 80.

255 *the people are not satisfied*: William Bradford Jones to Hon. George L. Meyer, September 12, 1909, File 20971, RG 80. He sent a long editorial from the Jamestown Morning Post, August 19, 1909, describing the court's decision

as "so partisan as to be absurd." Moreover, the court had gone "out of its
way to wound the feelings of the distressed mother of the dead officer. . . .
Even Beekman Winthrop is not man
enough to cut the red tape and declare
this whitewashing report to be an insult to the good sense of the nation."
And the *Buffalo Express*, August 19,
1909, highlighted all the evidence indicating suicide had been unlikely and
emphasized how strange it was that
Edward Roelker could not be found.
The public, the paper observed, was
disappointed by the way the affair reflected on the Marine Corps.

256   *who called himself (or herself) "Justice"*: Written from New York on August 19,
1909, and received at the Navy Department the next day. File 20971, RG
80.

257   *"the outrageous decision"*: By mistake he addressed his letter, written on August
25, 1908, to the secretary of war. File
20971, RG 80. A note has been written on it stating "no answer."

257   Army and Navy Journal *editorial*: *Army and
Navy Journal*, September 18, 1909.
The comment was written in response to an editorial in the *Oregonian*
referring to the "overbearing aristocrats" in the army and navy. The *Army
and Navy Journal* incorrectly asserts
that no one in the Marine Corps
school mixed up in the Sutton case

had had any training at the Naval
Academy.

257   *A Naval Academy alumnus*: *Evening Star*
(Washington, D.C.), August 15, 1909.

257   *"in the interest of Mr. Harry M. Swartz"*:
Beekman Winthrop to Hon. Edwin S.
Stuart, July 2, 1909, File 26250, RG 80.

258   *Pennsylvania congressman Thomas S. Butler*:
Thos. S. Butler to Hon. Beekman
Winthrop, Wire, received August 4,
1909, File 26250, RG 80. Original
File number 13261-242 in the index
to RG 80.

258   *Swartz failed the Marine Corps exams*: Beekman Winthrop to Hon. John H.
Rothermel, August 12, 1909, who
had inquired about Swartz and asked
that the defect in one of his eyes be
waived. File 26250, RG 80.

258   *Butler thanked the secretary*: Thomas S. Butler to Hon. Beekman Winthrop, Au-
gust 16, 1909, File 26250, RG 80.

258   *had reason to be grateful to Swartz*: These letters, with the *Washington Post* com-
ment, indicate that the man endorsed
for promotion by Thomas Butler is the
same Harry Swartz. (At one point he
did spell his name Schwartz but
changed it by the time Rosa began
corresponding with him.) For more
on Butler's connection to the case, see
chapter 16. Swartz's personnel records
were ordered from the enlisted officers
files in St. Louis but as of May 30,
2007, not yet received.

CHAPTER 15: JIMMIE SUTTON'S BODY AND SOUL

259   *she wrote to the highest official*: Rosa B. Sutton to Cardinal Gibbons, August 21,
1909. The Archives of the Archdiocese of Baltimore are now at the Associated Archives at St. Mary's Seminary
and University, Baltimore, Md.

259   *"St Augustines Church"*: Saint Augustine
Catholic Church is Washington's old-
est African American church; until
1991 its pastors were white. www
.saintaugustine-dc.org.

259   *On his death in 1921*: *New York Times*,
March 25, 1921; *New York Herald*,
March 25, 1921; excerpts also cited
in John Tracy Ellis, *The Life of James
Cardinal Gibbons, Archbishop of Baltimore, 1834–1921*, 2 vols. (Milwaukee: Bruce Publishing, 1952), 630.
James Gibbons was born on July 23,
1834; he was ordained a bishop in
1868.

260   *"the most respected, and venerated"*: See www
.archbalt.org/our-history/ordinaries-
detail.cfm (accessed December 28,
2005).

260   *"the state of your churches"*: Charles R. Morris, *American Catholic: The Saints and Sinners Who Built America's Most Powerful
Church* (New York: Random House,
1997), 112. Morris is a bit harder on the
cardinal than his biographer (85). See
also Jay P. Dolan, *The American Catholic
Experience: A History from Colonial Times
to the Present* (Garden City, N.Y.: Doubleday & Co., 1987 [1985]), 332–33, on
his defense of workers' rights and the
Knights of Labor.

260   *"intense interest in people"*: He "never lost an
opportunity of putting before audiences
both at home and abroad the values he
attached to the American way of life."
Ellis, *The Life of James Cardinal Gibbons*,
1:5, 2:557–58, 636–39. Ellis believes
Gibbons was "probably the greatest single figure the Church in the United
States has produced." See his *American
Catholicism*, 2nd ed. (Chicago: University of Chicago Press, 1969 [1956]),106.

261   *"public face of the American Church"*: Morris,
American Catholic, 112.

261　"*less respect for religion*": *New York Times*, January 29, 1908. Later that year he would decry the deplorable increase in the divorce rate, "the result of a false, loose interpretation of the gospel." *New York Times*, November 29, 1908.

261　*Gibbons suggested his priests*: Ellis, *The Life of James Cardinal Gibbons*, 2:382.

261　*The* Washington Post *and the* Evening Star: *Washington Post*, August 25, 1909; *Evening Star* (Washington, D.C.), August 25, 1909: "The Cardinal is now in Portland, and it is understood that James M. Sutton, Lieutenant Sutton's father, laid the findings of the Annapolis court of inquiry before him there and that the Cardinal after studying them, raised the ban and directed the Church authorities in Washington to perform the necessary services." An excerpt from the "Episcopal Diary of James Cardinal Gibbons," from March 22–October 4, 1909, makes no mention of a trip outside of Maryland during the period between August 21 and September 14. But the records are sparse as to his specific whereabouts. He was sending and receiving letters from Baltimore. Letter from Simran K. Dhami, Assistant Archivist, Associated Archives, July 11, 2003.

261　*Gibbons' "favorite paper," the* Baltimore Sun: Ellis, *The Life of James Cardinal Gibbons*, 2:629; and "CARDINAL CONSIDERS THE CASE," *Baltimore Sun*, August 26, 1909. The Washington *Evening Star* interviewed the priest Rosa hoped would perform the burial rites for her son; Father Edward Griffith reportedly told the paper Cardinal Gibbons had the authority to direct a priest from Maryland or the District of Columbia to perform burial rites but not the power to consecrate ground in Virginia, "that prerogative belonging solely to the Bishop of Virginia." September 12, 1909.

261　*need to contact the bishop of Virginia*: *Evening Capital* (Annapolis, Md.), August 25, 1909: "Cardinal Gibbons [*sic*], it is said, considers that it has been established that Lieutenant Sutton did not take his own life, at least not with suicidal intent, and for this reason he accorded the desired permission."

262　"*Victory has come to Mrs. Sutton*": *Washington Post*, August 25, 1909.

262　"*The happiness which came suddenly*": *Washington Post*, August 25, 1909; see also *Baltimore Sun*, August 25, 1909; "TO CONSECRATE HIS GRAVE," *Evening Capital* (Annapolis, Md.), August 25, 1909; *Oregonian*, August 25, 1909.

262　*Davis had written the quartermaster*: Henry E. Davis to the Quartermaster General,

War Department, August 20, 1909: Davis asked that the response be addressed to Mrs. Sutton at the Burlington. File 20971, RG 80. A. E. Williams, captain and quartermaster, U.S. Army to Mrs. Rosa B. Sutton, August 23, 1909, File 240418, RG 92. E. H. Humphrey to Depot Quartermaster, August 23, 1909, File 20971, RG 80.

263　*But then the matter became more complicated*: E. H. Humphrey to Mrs. Rosa B. Sutton, August 25, 1909, File 240418, RG 92. See also the "Memorandum of the officer in charge of the Cemeterial Branch," Quartermaster General's Office, August 25, 1909. Between August 21 and September 10, Rosa's request generated close to thirty pieces of correspondence between officials at the Department of the Navy, and the War Department, including the men in charge of Arlington Cemetery. Copies of all the correspondence are in File 240418, RG 92.

263　*the constant scrutiny of the press*: *Evening Star* (Washington, D.C.), August 25, 1909; local newspapers kept in daily contact with Rosa and pestered officials at the War and Navy Departments and the cemetery, describing her indignation at the postponement. See *Washington Post*, August 26 and 27, 1909; *Baltimore Sun*, August 26 and August 27, 1909.

263　"*their own lives might be at stake*": Henry M. Morrow to the Secretary of War, August 28, 1909, File 240418, RG 92. It was Jacob Dickinson, the secretary of war, who suggests the marine officers be notified. Dickinson to Scofield, August 31, 1909, telegram, File 240418, RG 92. Beekman Winthrop, Acting Secretary of the Navy, to the Honorable Secretary of War, September 8, 1909, File 20971, RG 80.

263　"*one of the outstanding Surgeons*": "Raymond Spear," Biographical Sketch, United States Naval Historical Center.

263　*it is not considering desirable*: Acting Secretary of the Navy Beekman Winthrop to Surgeon Raymond Spear, September 8, 1909, File 20971, RG 80.

264　*Beekman Winthrop, signed off on a new date*: Robert Shaw Oliver to the Secretary of the Navy, and Beekman Winthrop to the Secretary of War, undated copies of letters, File 240418, RG 92.

264　"*one of the best-known surgeons*": *Baltimore Sun*, August 26, 1909.

264　*a man with strong military connections*: George Vaughan had been in charge of the U.S. Marine Hospital Service Exhibit for the Chicago World's Fair in 1893. During the Spanish-American War,

Major Vaughan was a brigade surgeon of the seventh U.S. Army Corps.

264 *Vaughan was assistant surgeon general:* "George Tully Vaughan," in *National Cyclopedia of American Biography*, vol. 38 (New York: J. T. White, 1953), 43–44; *Who's Who In America: 1908–1909* (Chicago: A. N. Marquis, 1945); Henry B. F. MacFarland, *American Biographical Directories: District of Columbia: Concise Biographies of Its Prominent and Representative Contemporary Citizens, and Valuable Statistical Data, 1908–1909* (Washington, D.C.: Potomac Press, 1908), 483; and George Tully Vaughan, "Last Will and Testament of George Tully Vaughan," May 3, 1948, District Court of the United States for the District of Columbia, Register of Wills, Superior Court of the District of Columbia. His well-known book was *The Principles and Practice of Surgery, Designed for Students and Practitioners* (Philadelphia: J. B. Lippincott, 1903).

264 *sent specific instructions:* Wiliam S. Cowles to Spear, File 20971, RG 80.

265 *He described the day's events in:* D. H. Rhodes to the Depot Quartermaster, September 14, 1909, File 240418, RG 92. All further references to Rhodes' report are from this letter.

265 *fifteen soldiers from Fort Myer:* Major Moses Gray Zalinski, Depot Quartermaster to the Quartermaster General of the Army, September 11, 1909, File 240418, RG 92.

266 *Rose Parker left for New York before:* *Washington Post*, August 27, 1909.

266 *"Mrs. Sutton was seen":* *Washington Post*, September 14, 1909. Newspapers across the country printed accounts of this dramatic afternoon. The *Washington Times* and the *Washington Post* were among those that must have had reporters on the scene.

266 *A* Washington Times *reporter:* *Washington Times*, September 14, 1909.

267 *"I want members of the press to notice":* *Washington Post*, September 14, 1909.

267 *carefully watched everything that happened:* "Surgeon Raymond Spear, U.S.N. Submits Report on the Observation of the Examination of the Body of the Late 2nd Lieut. Jas. N. Sutton, USMC" ("By direction of the Judge Advocate General, this is to be opened only by that officer"), September 16, 1909, File 20971, RG 80. No sketches or notebook accompany the report. Unless otherwise noted, the clinical details in the following paragraphs are taken from Spear's report.

267 *"the glass lid of the casket was removed":* *Washington Post*, September 14, 1909.

269 *"It is the mercy of God":* *New York Times*, September 14, 1909.

270 *Saint Augustine Roman Catholic:* No documents have been located to indicate why Rosa chose a pastor from this church. But the Church school "was staffed by the Oblate Sisters of Providence, the oldest religious order of Black women in the United States." It is possible that she felt a connection to the Church because of her childhood days among the Sisters of Charity of Providence. Also, "One of St. Augustine's neighbors was a large Catholic parish, St. Paul, whose original membership was primarily of Irish and German descent." The two parishes would merge in 1979; St. Augustine's is now at 15th and V Streets, NW. A photograph of the original church appears on the website along with its history. www.saintaugustine-dc.org (accessed January 17, 2007).

270 *"The brightest moment of the entire afternoon":* *Washington Times*, September 14, 1909. Although their details vary slightly, reporters from several papers, including the *New York Times*, were clearly moved by this scene.

270 *"God through Your mercy":* There is no record of the exact words spoken by Father Olds (in Latin), but an approximation of the scene can be constructed from newspaper accounts, and from Herbert Thurston, "The Ritual of Burial," in *The Catholic Encyclopedia*, vol. 3 (New York: Robert Appleton Company, 1908; online edition by Kevin Knight, 1999).

270 *"just as the evening gun at Fort Myer":* *New York Times*, September 14, 1909.

271 *"stepped waveringly up":* *Baltimore Sun*, September 14, 1909. Rosa and her attorney thanked Rhodes and the officers in the War Department for the "very satisfactory manner in which the whole proceeding had been conducted." Rhodes, in turn, asked that his staff be commended "for the successful accomplishment of this delicate and somewhat unusual and important undertaking." D. H. Rhodes to the Depot Quartermaster, September 14, 1909, File 240418, RG 92.

271 *"the surgeons were unable today to":* *Oregonian*, September 14, 1909. The *Oregonian* might well have had a reporter on the scene who saw the "ghastly bruises" that "showed Sutton had been severely pounded," mentioned in this article.

271 *"bore marks of having":* *Washington Post*, September 14, 1909.

271 *He argued the shot was fired:* *Washington Post*, September 14, 1909.

272   *Henry Davis gave at least part of it*: Davis was apparently satisfied with the report but lacked "his characteristic fire and denunciation" of the naval authorities in submitting it. *Baltimore Sun*, September 18, 1909.

272   *they regard it as sufficient proof*: *Baltimore Sun*, September 18, 1909.

272   *The printed excerpt from Dr. Vaughan's report*: *Baltimore Sun*, September 18, 1909. Excerpts of this report appeared in several papers including the *Evening Star* (Washington, D.C.) and the *Washington Times*.

274   *gun was indeed fired within six inches*: "When a bullet exits the barrel, it is accompanied by a 'flame' consisting of incandescent superheated gases and a 'ball of fire.' . . . The flame is of little significance except in contact and near contact wounds where it may scar the skin around the entrance wound." Vincent J. M. Di Maio, *Gunshot Wounds: Practical Aspects of Firearms, Ballistics, and Forensic Techniques* (Boca Raton, Fla.: CRC Press, 1999), 50. The newspaper accounts that came out immediately after the autopsy were inconsistent. I am grateful to Forensic Anthropologist Brad Adams and MD Medical Examiner Jonathan Eisenstat for looking at key passages in Spear's report and excerpts from the newspapers.

CHAPTER 16: POLITICS AND THE PARANORMAL

275   *"not a dead issue"*: "NOT A DEAD ISSUE," *Evening Capital* (Annapolis, Md.), October 13, 1909.

275   *James William Good*: "CONGRESS TO PROBE DEATH OF SUTTON," *Washington Times*, September 15, 1909. On Good, see the *Biographical Directory of the United States Congress, 1774–1989*, bicentennial edition (Washington, D.C.: Government Printing Office, 1989), 1072.

276   *"that the case be dropped right now"*: *Washington Times*, September 18, 1909.

276   *"officers implicated in the midnight campus fight"*: *Washington Times*, September 15, 1909. The case never made it into the Maryland courts a second time despite reports that Henry Davis hoped to "have a Federal jury investigate."

276   *William Wallace McCredie: Biographical Directory of the American Congress, 1774–1961* (Washington, D.C.: Government Printing Office, 1961), 1291. McCredie filled the vacancy caused by Francis W. Cushman's death. See also *Biographical Directory of the United States Congress*, 288n58. During the latter part of his life, McCredie would practice law in Portland.

276   *House Joint Resolution 186*: A copy of the McCredie Resolution is in File 19706, RG 127. United States Congress, 61st Congress, 2nd Session, House Joint Resolution 186, Authorizing an investigation into the facts and circumstances attending the death of Lieutenant James N. Sutton, at the United States Naval Academy, Annapolis, Maryland, on the thirteenth day of October, nineteen hundred and seven, copy in File 19706, United States Marine Corps General Correspondence File, 1904–1912, RG 127, NAB. A joint resolution can originate in either body of Congress and is treated much the same way as a bill, though it often addresses issues that are more limited in scope.

277   *His request was forwarded*: This correspondence is in File 20971, RG 80. See also "Digest of Evidence submitted before the Sutton Board of Inquest" [prepared by Henry Leonard], Submitted to the Chairman, Committee on Naval Affairs, House of Representatives, on May 27, 1910, File 20971, General Correspondence of the Office of the Secretary of the Navy, July 1897–August 1926, General Records of the Department of the Navy, 1798–1947, RG 80, NAB; "Digest of Evidence submitted" before the Sutton Board of Inquiry" [prepared by Henry Leonard], Submitted to the Chairman, Committee on Naval Affairs, House of Representatives, on May 27, 1910, File 20971, General Correspondence of the Office of the Secretary of the Navy, July 1897–August 1926, General Records of the Department of the Navy, 1798–1947, RG 80, NAB.

278   *The congressman's son was Smedley Butler*: In an odd twist of fate, Smedley Butler would lose out in his quest to become commandant, first to Wendell C. Neville, who had served on the Sutton court, and on the second occasion to then brigadier general Benjamin Fuller. J. Robert Moskin, *The U. S. Marine Corps Story*, 3rd rev. ed. (New York: Little, Brown, 1992), 208–9. Butler won two medals of honor but was so outspoken he had several detractors; some of them accused him of relying too much on his father's influence. Anne Cipriano Venzon, *General*

Smedley Darlington Butler: The Letters of a Leatherneck, 1898–1931 (New York: Praeger, 1992), 1–2. It is unfortunate that Thomas Butler's papers were all destroyed after his death (xi).

278 *a few congressmen requested information*: Among them were Oregon senator George Chamberlain. File 20971, RG 80.

279 *election figures for 1910*: *Congressional Quarterly's Guide to U. S. Elections*, 2nd ed. (Washington, D.C.: Congressional Quarterly, 1985).

279 *she rarely saw Jimmie's ghost*: Thacher, 623.

279 *were absorbed by Spiritualism*: An "estimated 10 million or so" became Spiritualists in the post–Civil War decade. (Rosa was born in 1860.) Barbara Goldsmith, *Other Powers: The Age of Suffrage, Spiritualism, and the Scandalous Victoria Woodhull* (New York: HarperCollins, 1999 [1998]), xi. In Victorian America "Spiritualism and the inception of women's rights were intertwined. At a time when women had no power to achieve equal rights, they relied on the 'other powers' provided by Spiritualism to sustain their efforts" (xiii).

279 *Public curiosity about the movement was intense*: R. Laurence Moore, *In Search of White Crows: Spiritualism, Parapsychology, and American Culture* (New York: Oxford University Press, 1977).

280 *sought new ways of coping*: Louis Menand, *The Metaphysical Club: A Story of Ideas in America* (New York: Farrar, Straus and Giroux, 2001), x.

280 *movement attracted serious attention*: Moore, *In Search of White Crows*, 43–44, 52–56. Both Christians and atheists could be Spiritualists, but they did insist on the "uniqueness of the individual soul before and after death" (52–53). Arthur S. Berger, "The Early History of the ASPR: Origins to 1907," *Journal of the American Society for Psychical Research* 79 (January 1985): 39–60.

280 *Census of Hallucinations*: G. N. M. Tyrrell, *Apparitions* (New York: Pantheon Books, 1953), 18. Chapter 1, 25–45, is a detailed analysis of the census.

280 *the wealth of stories and novels*: William Dean Howells and Henry Mills Alden, eds., *Shapes That Haunt the Dusk* (New York and London: Harper and Brothers, 1907), v–vi. Howard Kerr, John W. Crowley, and Charles L. Crow, eds., *The Haunted Dusk: American Supernatural Fiction, 1820–1920* (Athens: University of Georgia Press, 1983), 1–2, also makes reference to Howell. Among the well-known authors of supernatural fiction examined in this work are Edgar Allen Poe, Mark Twain, Henry James, Washington Irving, Nathaniel R. Hawthorne, Edward Bellamy, Ambrose Bierce, and Jack London.

281 *psychical researchers in the United States*: Moore, *In Search of White Crows*, 66, 134 (note), and chap. 5. Goldsmith, *Other Powers*, 34: "And it was to women that the appeal of Spiritualism was especially potent."

281 *"the universe has a spiritual dimension"*: Menand, *Metaphysical Club*, 90–91. James "was fascinated by mental states that suggest the existence of an extrasensory realm."

281 *"the first man to forward the cause"*: Moore, *In Search of White Crows*, 142.

281 *one of the most famous trance mediums*: Mrs. Lenore Piper has also been called "perhaps the most impressive mental medium in history." Seymour H. Mauskopf and Michael R. McVaugh, "Parapsychology and the American Psychologists: A Study of Scientific Ambivalence," in *The Philosophy of Parapsychology, Proceedings of an International Conference Held in Copenhagen, Denmark, August 25–27, 1976*, ed. Betty Shapin and Lisette Coly (New York: Parapsychology Foundation, 1977), 16.

281 *of her unusual ability*: Berger, "Early History of the ASPR," 46.

281 *"she has supernormal powers"*: Quoted in Moore, *In Search of White Crows*, 146.

281 *William James' "white crow"*: Moore, *In Search of White Crows*, 146, 148.

281 *"more life in our total soul"*: William James, *The Varieties of Religious Experience: A Study in Human Nature* (New York: Penguin, 1985; first published by Longmans, Green, 1902), introduction by Myron E. Marty, 511.

281 *"an abiding psychical entity"*: James, *Varieties*, 512.

282 *"a single fact that can be demonstrated"*: Moore, *In Search of White Crows*, 144.

282 *"utter inadequacy of current psychology"*: Quoted in Moore, *In Search of White Crows*, 153. See also Mauskopf and McVaugh, "Parapsychology and the American Psychologists," 218–19, on Hall's criticism of the methods used by psychical researchers. American psychologists framed elaborate arguments against psychical research in the 1880s and 1890s.

282 *number of academic psychologists*: Moore, *In Search of White Crows*, 155. See also Mauskopf and McVaugh, "Parapsychology and the American Psychologists": Psychologists were both critical of psychical research and curious about it. "They were willing to be

associated with psychical research societies and they took the research seriously enough to subject to it to elaborate rebuttal" (218). By 1917 "experimental psychical research had in fact found a precarious home in the psychology department at three major universities: Clark, Stanford, and Harvard" (220–21).

282   *Hyslop was born on a small Ohio farm*: For a discussion of Hyslop's life and work, see his typed autobiography at the ASPR, and Moore, *In Search of White Crows*, chap. 5: "Psychical Research as Psychology—from William James to James Hyslop," esp. 156–68. Rodger I. Anderson, "The Life and Work of James H. Hyslop," *Journal of the American Society for Psychical Research* 79 (April 1985): 167–204; Berger, "The Early History of the ASPR," 39–60; Arthur S. Berger, "Problems of the ASPR under J. H. Hyslop," *Journal of the American Society for Psychical Research* 79 (April 1985): 205–19. And see, most recently, Deborah Blum, *Ghost Hunters: William James and the Search for Scientific Proof of Life after Death* (New York: Penguin, 2006). Hyslop's huge file related to the Sutton case has been lost; however, other documents related to his life including his autobiography exist in the archives of the ASPR in New York City and at Columbia University.

283   *"extraordinary hits"*: Moore, *In Search of White Crows*, 157–58.

283   *fascinated by "exceptional occurrences"*: Anderson, "The Life and Work," 175.

284   *for health reasons*: James cited in Moore, *In Search of White Crows*, 159. A letter from Nicholas Murray Butler, Columbia University's president, written to Hyslop in 1914, makes the reason for his leaving clear. Berger, "Early History of the ASPR," 55, found the letter in the ASPR archives.

284   *A prodigious worker*: Anderson, "The Life and Work," 193–94.

284   *it struggled with a lack of funds*: Anderson, "The Life and Work," 177–78.

284   *"the best traditions of reflective and empirical science"*: Anderson, "The Life and Work," 186; see also Berger, "Early History of the ASPR," 216, and Moore, *In Search of White Crows*, 170. Berger takes issue with Moore's statement that, given his goals, "Hyslop accomplished relatively little as head of the ASPR." Anderson would as well (196–97).

284   *his high respect for Hyslop's work*: James, *Varieties*, 524. "Facts, I think, are yet lacking to prove 'spirit-return,' though I

have the highest respect for the patient labors of Messrs. Myers, Hodgson and Hyslop, and am somewhat impressed by their favorable conclusions."

284   *"is not the vanishingly small thing"*: Quoted in Anderson, "The Life and Work," 194.

285   *The only information he removed*: Hyslop in Thacher, 597–99.

285   *Oregon psychical researcher George Thacher*: Hyslop in Thacher, 600. Hyslop makes the point more than once in the article. Almost nothing is known about George Thacher except that Hyslop trusted him, and he had written at least one previous article for the *Journal of the American Society for Psychical Research*.

285   *"woman of unusual intelligence"*: Thacher, 601. The following discussion is based on George Thacher's report, 600–51.

286   *also obtained written descriptions*: Thacher, 602–7, and see chap. 1. He gives other examples as well.

286   *on the family's ambiguity*: Thacher, 617.

287   *"The family are Catholics"*: Thacher, 617.

287   *"the mental attitude of all"*: Thacher, 619.

287   *he secured a statement from Rosa*: "Mrs. Sutton's Statement," November 10, 1910, Thacher, 619–23.

287   *"he described some mediumistic séances"*: Thacher did not seem to realize that Jim Sutton was Presbyterian and not as concerned with Catholicism's stance on mediums. The conversation occurred on November 10, 1910.

287   *asked Thacher to draft a statement*: "Statement of James N. Sutton on Nov. 10, 1910, Concerning the Impressions of His Wife, Rosa B. Sutton, at the Time of the Death of Their Son Jimmie, at Annapolis, on October 13, 1907, Which Were Related to Him at the Time of Their Occurrence at 784 Hoyt St., Portland, Ore," Thacher, 624–26.

288   *"Mrs. Sutton saw their son"*: November 22, 1910, Thacher, 627.

288   *Thacher canvassed the Suttons' friends who*: These are Mrs. John Hincks and her three daughters Dorothy, May, and Chrissie; Elizabeth Gallagher; Mrs. Kathryn Kinsella and her daughter, Elizabeth; and Mrs. M. E. Vanatta. Thacher, 630–33.

288   *she could have been a medium herself*: Thacher, 602, and "Mrs. Sutton seems to have all around mediumistic capacity" (608).

288   *One of the "best incidents"*: This incident is described in Thacher, 608–10.

289   *The sitting occurred on November 13*: Thacher, 638–49.

290   *"he knew that Jimmie Sutton was murdered"*: Thacher, 645.

290   *Dr. Hyslop would follow up on*: Hyslop is also careful not to reveal the man's name: "The photograph which I have of this letter sustains Mr. Thacher's statement that the hand writing is not disguised." Thacher, 645–46.

290   *"Lieutenant Sutton received a scalp wound"*: Thacher, 638. The tracing and the account of footprints on Sutton's trousers are evidence that Thacher and Hyslop had available, apparently given to Thacher by the Sutton family.

291   *"Here is the material"*: Thacher, 637.

291   *Beekman Winthrop received two typed letters*: Hyslop's correspondence with Beekman Winthrop is in File 20971, RG 80. His comment states that there were no samples of the man's handwriting on record with the Navy Department, "except the man's signature of his name." "As this was not sufficient to determine the case," Hyslop wrote, "that source of evidence was abandoned. No one knew the man's address and so further inquiry was shut off and the circumstances made it doubtful whether we could secure the evidence if the address was accessible." Thacher, 646, footnote. This correspondence is not at the American Society for Psychical Research (ASPR).

292   *made several comments of his own*: The following discussion of Hyslop's analysis is based on the "Comments" by James H. Hyslop, in Thacher, 651–64.

294   *The* New York Times *took a special interest in the topic*: But the *Times* carefully

published the concerns of skeptics as well. For example, an editor wrote, "The hope of immortality is in us all, the survival of individuality after death a cherished belief, and unless we keep away from the adroit imposters who base their operations largely on this belief, and get their profits generally from ignorant and superstitious, the wisest among us is likely to be entrapped sooner or later." *New York Times*, February 1, 1908.

295   *"Here is an amazing case"*: This is a clear example of why officials at the Naval Academy bristled because the marines involved in the case had no official connection with it.

297   *he then regarded as "scientifically proved"*: However, he knew his opinion was "not upheld in scientific quarters." James H. Hyslop, *Contact with the Other World: The Latest Evidence as to Communication with the Dead* (New York: Century Co., 1919), 480.

297   *"the public will go straight"*: Hyslop, *Contact*, 481.

297   *"there is no proof"*: Hyslop, *Contact*, 483–84.

297   *Hyslop's biographer would observe*: Anderson, "The Life and Work," 197.

298   *"'To purify the Navy, Mamma'"*: Thacher, 64. This statement is clearly what Thacher might have called retrocognition—it appears to be, in fact, Rosa Sutton's justification to herself of the previous three years' work that she had done on Jimmie's behalf.

EPILOGUE

299   *an exercise in "active liberty"*: Stephen Breyer, *Active Liberty: Interpreting Our Democratic Constitution* (New York: Alfred A. Knopf, 2006), 3.

300   *"truly an agent of the popular will"*: Richard H. Kohn, ed., *The United States Military under the Constitution of the United States, 1789–1989* (New York: New York University Press, 1991), 1.

300   *"an integral part of the warrior ethic"*: *The Higher Standard: Assessing the United States Naval Academy.* Report of the Special Committee to the Board of Visitors, United States Naval Academy, June 1997, 6.

300   *According to a 1997 assessment*: Richard B. Cheney and Bill Taylor, *Professional Military Education: An Asset for Peace and Progress. A Report of the CSIS Study Group on Professional Military Education* (Washington, D.C.: Center

for Strategic & International Studies, 1997).

301   *op-ed piece by David Brooks*: "ALL POLITICS IS THYMOTIC," *New York Times*, March 19, 2006.

301   *"genuine evolutionary value"*: W. Brad Johnson and Gregory P. Harper, *Becoming a Leader the Annapolis Way: 12 Combat Lessons from the Navy's Leadership Laboratory* (New York: McGraw-Hill, 2005), 185.

302   *"Perceived outrage"*: Eugène R. Fidell, "The Culture of Change in Military Law," in *Evolving Military Justice*, ed. Eugene R. Fidell and Dwight H. Sullivan (Annapolis, Md.: Naval Institute Press, 2002), 165.

302   *"if it is to survive and thrive"*: John S. Cooke, "Manual for Courts-Martial 20X," in *Evolving Military Justice*, ed. Fidell and Sullivan, 174. See also

William T. Generous Jr., *Swords and Scales: The Development of the Uniform Code of Military Justice* (Port Washington, N.Y.: Kennikat Press, 1973).

302   "*left the service believing*": Cooke, "Manual for Courts-Martial 20X,"178.

302   *Once the armed forces were merged*: Jonathan Lurie, "Justice, Military: Uniform Code of Military Justice (1950– Present)," in *The Oxford Companion to American Military History*, ed. John Whiteclay Chambers II (Oxford: Oxford University Press, 1999), 355–56.

302   "*as both an instrument and a catalyst*": Cooke, "Manual for Courts-Martial 20X," 178, and the definitive works on this subject by Jonathan Lurie (see bibliography).

302   "*due process does indeed apply*": Jonathan Lurie, "The Role of the Federal Judiciary in the Governance of the American Military: The United States Supreme Court and 'Civil Rights and Supervision' over the Armed Forces," in *The United States Military under the Constitution of the United States, 1789–1989*, ed. Richard H. Kohn (New York: New York University Press, 1991), 417.

302   "'*the different character of the military community*'": Lurie, "The Role of the Federal Judiciary," 422.

302   "*military civilian free-speech dichotomy*": Cathy Packer, *Freedom of Expression in the American Military: A Communication Modeling Analysis* (New York: Praeger, 1989), 120–21, and chaps. 5 and 6.

303   "*truth is no defense*": See Packer, 120–21.

303   "*Life is no dress parade*": "Graduation Exercises. Class of Nineteen-thirteen. United States Military Academy, West Point, New York." Special Collections and Archives, USMA, West Point.

303   *every mother who had*: Sutton's violent death—and the navy's suicide verdict—put a glaring spotlight on an issue that remains a tragic one. In the decade after the Annapolis inquiry, more than three hundred men in the navy's files were listed as suicide victims. Like Sutton, over a third of these men died from bullet wounds. The navy has both a suicide-prevention hotline and a website. "Suicide has been the #2 or #3 leading cause of death among Sailors and Marines during the past decade." www.nehc.med.navy.mil/hp/suicide (accessed February 3, 2007).

304   *he died from friendly fire*: See www.pbs.org/now/transcript/246.11/17/06 (accessed February 3, 2007).

304   "*an accidental discharge*": See www.pbs.org/now/transcript/246.11/17/06 (accessed February 3, 2007).

304   "*fierce discontent*": "'So far as this movement of agitation throughout the country takes the form of a fierce discontent with evil, of a firm determination to punish the authors of evil, whether in industry or politics, the feeling is to be heartily welcomed as a sign of healthy life.'" April 14, 1906. Cited at the front of Michael McGerr's *A Fierce Discontent: The Rise and Fall of the Progressive Movement in America: 1870–1920* (New York: Free Press, 2003).

304   *today's discourse*: See www.sunshineweek.org (accessed February 3, 2007), now an annual national effort to promote the public's right to know and to an open government.

304   "*I should not have had to beg*": *NOW* Transcript, March 17, 2006. The army has begun to address these problems. For updates on these and related stories check the *NOW* page at www.pbs.org.

304   "*long, sometimes raw*": Monica Davey and Eric Schmitt, "2 YEARS AFTER SOLDIER'S DEATH, FAMILY'S BATTLE IS WITH ARMY," *New York Times*, March 21, 2006.

304   *They have made progress*: "Most of Karen's questions have been answered," and the army has "recently started requiring commanders in the field to 'review and certify the content of the casualty report' and have [sic] expanded casualty assistance for parents." *NOW* Transcript, March 21, 2006.

304   *a young Marine Corps officer*: Nathaniel Fick, *One Bullet Away: The Making of a Marine Officer* (Boston: Houghton Mifflin, 2005), 7.

305   "*Men love to believe*": Richard Rayner, "THE WARRIOR BESIEGED," *New York Times Magazine*, June 22, 1997 (cover story).

305   "*quasi imperial power*": Allan R. Millett, *Semper Fidelis: The History of the United States Marine Corps* (New York: Free Press, 1991), 147, and chap. 6, "To Sunny Tropic Scenes: 1899–1914."

305   *General Benjamin Fuller*: Benjamin Fuller, clearly affected by the Sutton case, would write how important "unity of administrative control" was to the Corps' efficiency. As commandant, Fuller hoped to be "regarded by all officers and enlisted men as their natural protector and friend." Benjamin H. Fuller, Major General Commandant, "The United States Marine Corps," *US Naval Institute Proceedings* 56, no. 10 (October 1930): 914.

305   "*I went to New York*": Lieutenant Adams' poignant five typed pages describing his various digestive problems, diets,

and discomforts is attached to his "Record of Proceedings of a Marine Examining Board Changed to a Marine Retiring Board Convened at Headquarters US Marine Corps, Washington, DC. In the Case of Major Robert E. Adams, U S Marine Corps, November 9, 1920," Adams, MEB File, RG 125.

306 *"exceptional ability and usefulness"*: According to Commodore C. M. Fahs, the President of the Court-Martial, "Report on the Fitness of Officers of the U.S. Marine Corps, for April 1, 1920 to September 30, 1920," Adams File, RG 125.

306 *Harold Utley served in Cuba*: As a major, Harold Utley's "writings eventually helped shaped the *Small Wars Manual* (1935), an official guide to pacification operations. Records related to this part of Utley's career can be found at the Library of the Marine Corps, Archives and Special Collections Branch, Quantico, Virginia. The records in Quantico do not refer to the Sutton case. Dr. Jim Ginther, e-mail to the author, December 19, 2005.

306 *the Eastern Area in Nicaragua*: An area he describes as ranging "from the Honduran border on the North to the Costa Rican border on the South, Caribbean Sea on the East, and as far West as my patrols could operate" (about 200 miles west to Poteca). See his testimony before the Examining Board, November 18, 1931, Utley, MEB File, RG 125.

306 *His official record*: The censure he received in August 1909 remained in his record; in June 1910 he was confined to his ship for ten days for neglect of duty ("careless in his preparation of the records of the summary court-martial"); his fitness report for November 1915 to March 1916 described him as indolent, "though in no other report is he so characterized." Major General Commandant Lagan to the Judge Advocate General, January 30, 1917; and "Report on the Fitness of Officers," Utley File, RG 125.

306 *his "moral fitness"*: Record of Proceedings of a Marine Examining Board Convened at Headquarters, U.S. Marine Corps, November 16, 1931, Utley, MEB File, RG 125.

306 *"had used a so-called electric chair"*: Marine-civilian relations and the treatment of prisoners in Nicaragua is worth further study.

306 *two months after Utley took command*: For Utley's response to the official Board of Investigation, see his testimony. As for the accusations against M. R. Carroll, Utley said the board found that he had "made preparations to apply Third degree methods." But "it appeared that actual force or ill-treatment was not applied to the prisoners, not actually applied." Testimony before the Examining Board, November 18, 1931, Day 2, page 9, Utley, MEB File, RG 125.

306 *ran into serious difficulties*: John Mackay, Manager of the Nicaraguan Division of the Standard Fruit Company and its subsidiary, the Bergmans Bluff Lumber Co.

306 *Utley's arrogant and self-absorbed behavior*: For this correspondence, which does give detailed accounts of Utley's reprehensible behavior, see the supporting documents included in the investigation cited above. Utley's defense of his behavior during one incident included the assertion that another officer had invited Utley's wife to go riding, while excluding Utley. Utley, MEB File, RG 125.

307 *"friction of Major Utley with the Manager"*: Testimony of Edwin McClellan before a Marine Corps Examining Board, November 30, 1931. These proceedings were an examination of Major Utley's moral fitness, and they took place when Benjamin Fuller was commandant. Utley, MEB File, RG 125. When he assumed the post, McClellan found there was no doubt "about the fact that liquor and a woman was very prominent in discussions," and "the woman in the case was publicly pointed out to me."

307 *"bring considerable discredit upon"*: The tendency to minimize offenses by men of high rank in situations where the victim is either a civilian or a person of lower rank is related to the "good soldier defense" clearly critiqued by Elizabeth L. Hillman, in "The 'Good Soldier' Defense: Character Evidence and Military Rank at Courts-Martial," in *Evolving Military Justice*, ed. Fidell and Sullivan, 63–80.

307 *"withdrawing approval of award"*: The letter is dated August 2, 1929. But Utley did receive a Medal of Merit and Citation awarded by the president of Nicaragua in September 1930.

307 *Harold Utley was reassigned to*: Officer Biography File for Harold Utley, Archives and Special Collections Branch, Library of the Marine Corps, Gray Research Center, Quantico, Virginia; also Harold Utley Alumni Jacket, USNA, Nimitz Library.

308 *"Roelker disappeared from the records"*: The details in the notation are incorrect.

File of Edward Porter Roelker, Class of 1906, Virginia Military Institute (VMI) Archives.

308   "*not long after his departure*": Mrs. Mildred R. Langenbeck to Joseph R. Anderson (VMI historiographer), August 9, 1922. His sister Marie had no information either in 1927. A memorandum, dated May 21, 1936, by a W. Couper states, "I recall that the newspapers of some 30 years ago carried a lot about a hazing investigation at Annapolis. The body of one of the victims was exhumed, as I recall it. 'Red' Roelker, as we called him, was involved, and he disappeared about that time. While at VMI . . . he was a cadet in my company ('B' Company)." Further efforts to find him in 1944 came to no avail—neither the Naval Academy nor VMI could solve this mystery. Edward Roelker file, VMI.

311   *the bullet was fired at close range*: most likely, according to MD Medical Examiner Jonathan Eisenstat, who reviewed the written material related to the Sutton autopsy. But without photographs or a fresh corpse it is impossible to draw definitive conclusions about the cause of Sutton's death. For example, no precautions were taken to protect the evidence on his hands, such as gunpowder residue or blood, which might have indicated that he fired the final shot (though he had fired four others).

312   *Sutton's modest grave*: At some point, the marker was changed to a less austere one, still without dates, but with bas-relief lettering and without the government's official number. On October 2, 1909, the *Army and Navy Journal* reported the following: "A number of friends of Mrs. James N Sutton . . . are arranging to raise a fund for the erection of a monument over the grave of Lieutenant Sutton at Arlington. It is the intention of the committee which has the matter in charge to make the move a general one throughout the country and allow all who sympathized with Mrs. Sutton in her fight to clear the name of her son to contribute any amount that they desire."

BIBLIOGRAPHY

GOVERNMENT DOCUMENTS

United States Marine Corps General Correspondence Files, 1904–1912, Record Group 127. National Archives Building (NAB), Washington, D.C.

Applicant for Commission Files:
Adams, Robert Emmet. File 14905.
Bevan, William Francis. File 14663.
Capron, Paul Allyn. File 16675.
Judson, Howard Campbell. File 17501.
Ludlow, Reginald Fairfax. File 17958.
McClellan, Edwin North. File 16965.
Osterman, Edward A. File 17434.
Potts, John. File 16754.
Roelker, Edward P. File 16334.
Sumner, Allen Melancthon. File 16240.
Sutton, James Nuttle, Jr. File 13977.
Utley, Harold Hickox. File 17545.
Willing, Edward Shippen. File 12946.

General Records of the Department of the Navy. 1798–1947. General Correspondence of the Office of the Secretary of the Navy, July 1897–August 1926, Record Group 80. In addition to extensive correspondence related to this case, the following key documents are in File 20971 in this record group.
———. "Compilation of the [Government] Arguments in the Sutton Case." Informal untitled document from Henry Leonard to Edward Campbell. Received August 20, 1909. File 20971, RG 80.
———. "Digest of Evidence submitted before the Sutton Board of Inquest" [prepared by Henry Leonard], Submitted to the Chairman, Committee on Naval Affairs, House of Representatives, on May 27, 1910. File 20971, General Correspondence of the Office of the Secretary of the Navy, July 1897–August 1926. General Records of the Department of the Navy, 1798–1947, RG 80. NAB.
———. "In the matter of the death of James N. Sutton, Late Second Lieutenant, United States Marine Corps, in the grounds of the Naval Academy, at Annapolis, Md., on the 13th of October, 1907. Notes on the Evidence before the Board of Inquest. E. W. Van Dyke, Attorney for Mrs. Rosa B. Sutton, the Mother of the deceased." General Correspondence of the Office of the Secretary of the Navy, July 1897–August, 1926. General Records of the Department of the Navy, 1798–1947, File 20971, RG 80. NAB.

Proceedings of Naval and Marine Examining Boards: Files of Frank C. Cook, Robert Emmet Adams, William Francis Bevan, Paul Allyn Capron, Howard Campbell Judson, Reginald Fairfax Ludlow, Edwin North McClellan, Edward A. Osterman, John Potts, Edward P. Roelker, Allen Melancthon Sumner, James Nuttle Sutton Jr., Harold Hickox Utley, and Edward Shippen Willing. Records of the Office of the Judge Advocate General (Navy), 1890–1941, RG 125. NAB.

Record of Proceedings of a Board of Inquest Convened at the U.S. Naval Hospital, U.S. Naval Academy, Annapolis, Md., October 13, 1907, in the Case of James N. Sutton, Second Lieutenant, United States Marine Corps, Found Dead in the Grounds of the Naval Academy, at Annapolis Maryland, on the 13th of October, 1907. General Correspondence of the Office of the Secretary of the Navy, July 1897–August 1926. General Records of the Department of the Navy, 1798–1947, File 20971, RG 80. NAB.

Record of Proceedings of a Board of Inquest Convened at the U.S. Naval Hospital, U.S. Naval Academy, Annapolis, Md., October 13, 1907, in the Case of Second Lieutenant James N. Sutton, U.S.M.C. File 19706, United States Marine Corps General Correspondence File, 1904–1912, Record Group 127. NAB.

Record of Proceedings of a Court of Inquiry in the Case of James N. Sutton. Parts I and II. Case Number 5140. Proceedings of Courts of Inquiry, Boards of Investigation, and Boards of Inquest, Records of the Office of the Judge Advocate General (Navy) 1890–1941, RG 125. NAB.

Record of Proceedings of a General Court-Martial in the Case of Edward P. Roelker. Case Number 16845. Proceedings of Courts of Inquiry, Boards of Investigation and Boards of Inquest, Records of the Office of the Judge Advocate General (Navy) 1890–1941, RG 125. NAB.

Records of the Bureau of Naval Personnel: 1798–1991. Record Group 24. NAB.

Records of the Office of the Judge Advocate General (Navy) 1890–1941. Record Group 125.

Records of the Office of the Quartermaster General, Document File 1800–1914. File 240418, Record Group 92. NAB. Extensive correspondence between the War Department and the Navy Department related to the exhumation of the body of James N. Sutton at Arlington Cemetery, August–September 1909.

"Regulations for the Government of Student Officers at Marine Barracks and School of Application, Annapolis, MD at time of death of Lt. Sutton, U.S.M.C." File 51158, RG 127. United States Marine Corps General Correspondence File, 1904–1912, RG 127. NAB.

Spear, Raymond. Surgeon, U.S.N. Submits report on the observation of the examination of the body of the late 2nd Lieut. Jas. N. Sutton, USMC. "By direction of the Judge Advocate General, this is to be opened only by that officer." September 16, 1909. General Correspondence of the Office of the Secretary of the Navy, July 1897–August, 1926. General Records of the Department of the Navy, 1798–1947, File 20971, RG 80. NAB.

United States Congress, 61st Congress, 2nd Session. House Joint Resolution 186, Authorizing an investigation into the facts and circumstances attending the death of Lieutenant James N. Sutton, at the United States Naval Academy, Annapolis, Maryland, on the thirteenth day of October, nineteen hundred and seven. Copy in File 19706, United States Marine Corps General Correspondence File, 1904–1912, RG 127. NAB.

United States Military Academy Library, West Point. Hazing Investigation Board, Proceedings, June 23, 1909. Records of Boards and Committees. Records of the U.S. Military Academy, Record Group 404. National Archives-Affiliated Archives: Record on Deposit at U.S. Military Academy Archives, West Point, N.Y. United States Naval Academy. Alumni Association, Inc. 1995. (List of 201 graduates in the Class of 1908; 82 Nongraduates including Meriwether, Chambers, Roelker, and Sutton.)

United States Naval Academy. Nimitz Library. *Register of Alumni*. Volume 1 (1845–1915).

United States Naval Academy. Nimitz Library. United States Navy Department. Annual Reports of the Navy Department for the Year 1905. Washington, D.C.: Government Printing Office, 1906. Annual Report of the Secretary of the Navy, Miscellaneous Reports, 1905. Report of the Bureau of Navigation, 1905.

United States Naval Academy. Public Works Office, Real Estate Records. No. 181 Halligan Hall. No. 106 Mahan Hall. Inventories by Sally K. Tompkins, June 1980.

United States Naval Academy. Records of the United States Naval Academy. National Archives—Affiliated Archives: Record Group 405. Records of the Office of the Superintendent, 1845–1950. All RG 405 records are in Nimitz Library.

———. Administrative Records, 1845–1930. Relating to Midshipmen and Cadets, 1846–1925. Academic Grades and Class Standing.

————. Administrative Records, 1845–1930. Relating to Midshipmen and Cadets, 1846–1925. Conduct Rolls of Edward P. Roelker 1904–1906; James N. Sutton 1904–1905; Harold H. Utley 1902–1906; and Benjamin H. Fuller 1885–1889.

————. Administrative Records, 1845–1930. Relating to Midshipmen and Cadets, 1846–1925. General Records. Midshipman Personnel Files of Henry L. Chambers; Edward P. Roelker; and James N. Sutton.

————. *Annual Register of the United States Naval Academy*, 1904–1905, 1907–1908. *Lucky Bag 1904, 1905, 1906, 1907, 1908.*

————. Correspondence, 1845–1950. General Correspondence, 1907–1927. File 526 Edward Roelker; File 525 James Sutton; File 524 Harold Utley; File 506 Gilbert Coleman.

————. Correspondence, 1845–1950. General Correspondence, 1907–1927. File 587 John Hoogewerff. (Copy of 1907 Inquest transcript attached to this file.)

United States Naval Academy. Records of the United States Naval Academy. RG 405. Records of Boards, 1836–1942. Board of Visitors Reports, 1904, 1905, 1906, 1907, 1908, 1909.

United States Naval Academy. Special Collections and Archives. Alumni Jacket, Harold Utley. Alumni Jacket, Benjamin Fuller.

United States Naval Academy. Special Collections and Archives. Vertical File (Reference File). Preparatory Schools, Annapolis, Md.

OTHER ARCHIVES AND LIBRARIES

American Society for Psychical Research, New York
The Cathedral Church of St. Paul's, Springfield, Ill.
Clark County Genealogical Society, Vancouver, Wash.
Eileen J. Garrett Library, Parapsychology Foundation, Greenport, N.Y.
Grace United Methodist Episcopal Church, Harrisburg, Pa.
Harry Ransom Humanities Research Center, University of Texas at Austin.
Historical Society of Washington, D.C.
Historic Annapolis Foundation, Annapolis, Md.
Knight Library, University of Oregon at Eugene
Library of Congress, Washington, D.C.
Maryland State Archives, Annapolis
Maryland State Law Library, Annapolis
Multnomah County Courthouse, Portland, Oreg.
Multnomah County Public Library, Portland, Oreg.
Multnomah County Records Office, Portland, Oreg.
New York Public Library, New York
Oregon Historical Society, Portland, Oreg.
Oregon State Archives, Salem, Oreg.
Seeley G. Mudd Manuscript Library, Princeton University, Princeton, N.J.
Sisters of Providence Archives, Seattle, Wash.
Special Collections and Archives, Wright State University, Dayton, Ohio
St. John's Episcopal Church, Washington, D.C. (Georgetown)
St. John's Northwestern Military Academy, Delafield, Wisc.
Sutton Family Papers, property of the author
United States Marine Corps Historical Center, Archives and Special Collections Branch, Gray Research Center, Quantico, Va.
United States Naval Historical Center, Operational Archives Branch, Washington Navy Yard, Washington, D.C.
University Archives and Records Center, University of Pennsylvania, Philadelphia
Virginia Military Institute Archives, Lexington, Va.

CEMETERY RECORDS

Arlington National Cemetery, Arlington, Va.
Riverview Cemetery, Portland, Oreg.

San Francisco National Cemetery, The Presidio, San Francisco, Calif.
St. James Cemetery, Vancouver, Wash.

BOOKS

Abbott, Carl. *Portland and the Lewis and Clark Exposition.* Rev. ed. Portland: Oregon Historical Society, 1996.

Ainsworth, Peter B. *Psychology, Law and Eyewitness Testimony.* Chichester, UK: John Wiley & Sons, 1998.

Andrews, Wayne. *Architecture, Ambition and Americans: A Social History of American Architecture.* London: Free Press of Glencoe, Collier-Macmillan Limited, 1964.

Angelo, Bonnie. *First Mothers: The Women Who Shaped the Presidents.* New York: HarperCollins Perennial, 2001.

Annapolis City Directory for 1910. Annapolis, Md.: Gould and Halleron, 1910.

Appleby, Joyce, Lynn Hunt, and Margaret Jacob. *Telling the Truth about History.* New York: W. W. Norton, 1994.

Ashley, Perry L., ed. *American Newspaper Journalists, 1873–1900.* Dictionary of Literary Biography, 23. Detroit: Gale Research Co., 1983.

———, ed. *American Newspaper Journalists, 1901–1925.* Dictionary of Literary Biography. Detroit: Gale Research Co., 1984.

Athearn, Robert B. *The Mythic West in Twentieth Century America.* Lawrence: University Press of Kansas, 1986.

Auerbach, Jerold. *Unequal Justice: Lawyers and Social Change in Modern America.* New York: Oxford University Press, 1976

Axinn, Sidney. *A Moral Military.* Philadelphia: Temple University Press, 1989.

Baker, Jean H. *Sisters: The Lives of America's Suffragists.* New York: Hill and Wang, 2005.

Barnett, Louise. *Ungentlemanly Acts: The Army's Notorious Incest Trial.* New York: Hill and Wang, 2000.

Barry, Colman James. *The Catholic Church and German Americans.* Washington, D.C.: Catholic University of America Press, 1953.

Bartlett, Merrill L., and Jack Sweetman. *The U.S. Marine Corps: An Illustrated History.* Annapolis, Md.: Naval Institute Press, 2001.

Baudot, Jules Léon. *The Roman Breviary: Its Sources and History. Translated from the French by a Priest of the Diocese of Westminster.* St. Louis, Mo.: B. Herder, 1909.

Bederman, Gail. *Manliness and Civilization: A Cultural History of Gender and Race in the United States, 1880–1917.* Chicago: University of Chicago Press, 1995.

Biographical Directory of the American Congress, 1774–1961. Washington, D.C.: Government Printing Office, 1961.

Biographical Directory of the United States Congress, 1774–1989. Bicentennial edition. Washington, D.C.: Government Printing Office, 1989.

Blair, George S. *American Legislatures: Structures and Process.* New York: Harper & Row, 1967.

Blum, Deborah. *Ghost Hunters: William James and the Search for Scientific Proof of Life after Death.* New York: Penguin, 2006.

Bok, Sissela. *Lying: Moral Choice in Public and Private Life.* New York: Vintage Books, 1999. First published in 1978.

———. *Secrets: On the Ethics of Concealment and Revelation.* New York: Vintage Books, 1989. First published by Pantheon Books in 1983.

The Book of Washington. Washington, D.C.: Washington Board of Trade, 1930.

Boyd, W. Andrew, ed., *Boyd's Directories of the District of Columbia.* Washington, D.C.: R. L. Polk & Co., 1902–1911.

Brandt, Patricia, and Lillian A. Pereyra. *Adapting in Eden: Oregon's Catholic Minority: 1838–1986.* Pullman: Washington State University Press, 2002.

Breyer, Stephen. *Active Liberty: Interpreting Our Democratic Constitution.* New York: Alfred A. Knopf, 2006.

Brooks, Van Wyck. *The Confident Years: 1885–1915.* New York: E. P. Dutton, 1952.

Broughton, Richard S. *Parapsychology: The Controversial Science.* New York: Ballantine Books, 1991.

Brown, Letitia W., and Elise M. Lewis. *Washington in the New Era, 1870–1970.* Washington, D.C.: Government Printing Office, 1972.

Burchard, John, and Albert Bush-Brown. *The Architecture of America: A Social and Cultural History.* Boston: Little, Brown, 1961.

Busey, Samuel C. *Pictures of the City of Washington in the Past.* Washington, D.C.: William Ballantyne and Sons, 1898.

Byrne, Edward M. *Military Law: A Handbook for the Navy and Marine Corps.* Annapolis, Md.: United States Naval Institute, 1970.

Caemmerer, Paul H. *Historic Washington, Capital of the Nation.* Washington, D.C.: Columbia Historical Society, 1948.

Cashman, Sean Dennis. *America in the Age of the Titans: The Progressive Era and World War I.* New York: New York University Press, 1988.

A Catechism of Christian Doctrine, No. 2. Prepared and enjoined by the Third Plenary Council of Baltimore, 1898. Seattle, Wash. (excerpt from the Sisters of Providence Archives).

Catechism of Christian Doctrine for Academies and High Schools, Intermediate No. III. Rev. M. Muller's (C.S.S.R.) Series. St. Louis, Mo.: Benziger Brothers, 1877.

Catholic Church Records of the Pacific Northwest. Vols. 1 and 2. Vancouver, Wash.: French Prairie Press, 1972.

Century Dictionary: An Encyclopedic Lexicon of the English Language. New York: Century Co., 1890.

Ceremonial for the Use of the Catholic Churches in the United States of America. Baltimore: Baltimore Publishing Company, 1890.

Chambers, John Whiteclay, II, ed. *The Oxford Companion to American Military History.* Oxford: Oxford University Press, 1999.

———. *The Tyranny of Change: America in the Progressive Era, 1890–1920.* 2000 ed. Reprint, New Brunswick, N.J.: Rutgers University Press, 2004. First published in 1992.

Cheney, Richard B., and Bill Taylor. *Professional Military Education: An Asset for Peace and Progress. A Report of the CSIS Study Group on Professional Military Education.* Washington, D.C.: Center for Strategic & International Studies, 1997.

Clark, George B. *Treading Softly: U.S. Marines in China, 1819–1949.* Westport, Conn.: Praeger, 2001.

Clark County Pioneers: A Centennial Salute. Vancouver, Wash.: Clark County Genealogical Society, 1989.

Clift, Eleanor. *Founding Sisters and the Nineteenth Amendment.* New York: John Wiley & Sons, 2003.

Coletta, Paolo Enrico. *American Naval History: A Guide.* 2nd ed. Lanham, Md.: Scarecrow Press, 2000.

———, ed. *American Secretaries of the Navy.* Annapolis, Md.: Naval Institute Press, 1980.

———. *A Bibliography of American Naval History.* Annapolis, Md.: Naval Institute Press, 1981.

———. *The Presidency of William Howard Taft.* Lawrence: University Press of Kansas, 1973.

Collins, Gail. *America's Women: 400 Years of Dolls, Drudges, Helpmates, and Heroines.* New York: HarperCollins, 2003.

Collins, Kathleen. *Washingtoniana Photographs: Collections in the Prints and Photographs Division of the Library of Congress.* Washington, D.C.: Library of Congress, 1989.

Columbia Historical Society. *Records of the Columbia Historical Society.* Washington, D.C.: Columbia Historical Society, 1902.

Congressional Quarterly's Guide to U.S. Elections. 2nd ed. Washington, D.C.: Congressional Quarterly, 1985.

Cook, Timothy E. *Governing with the News: The News Media as a Political Institution.* Chicago: University of Chicago Press, 1998.

Cott, Nancy F., ed. *No Small Courage: A History of Women in the United States.* New York: Oxford University Press, 2000.

Cott, Nancy F., and Elizabeth H. Pleck, eds. *A Heritage of her Own: Towards a New Social History of American Women.* New York: Simon & Schuster, 1979.

Covert, James T. *A Point of Pride: The University of Portland Story.* Portland, Oreg.: University of Portland Press, 1976.

Crichton, Judy. *America 1900.* New York: Henry Holt, 2000.

Croly, Herbert. *The Promise of American Life,* ed. Arthur M. Schlesinger Jr. Cambridge, Mass.: Belknap Press of Harvard University Press, 1965.

Cyclopædia of American Biography, Revision to 1914 Complete, ed. Hon. Charles Dick and James E. Homans. Vol. 1. New York: Press Association Compilers, 1915.

Davis, Elmer. *History of the New York Times, 1851–1921.* New York: New York Times, 1921.

Davis, Henry Edgar. *The Development of the District of Columbia.* Washington, D.C.: Government Printing Office, 1909.

Dawley, Alan. *Changing the World: American Progressives in War and Revolution.* Princeton, N.J.: Princeton University Press, 2003.

De Pauw, Gommar A. *Annotations and Translations of the Traditional Latin Roman Catholic Mass.* New York: Catholic Traditionalist Movement Publications, 1977.

Devine, Arthur. *The Ordinary of the Mass: Historically, Liturgically, and Exegetically Explained.* New York: Benziger Bros., 1906.

Dick, Charles, and James E. Homans, eds. *The Cyclopedia of American Biography.* New York: Press Association Compilers, 1915.

Dickerson, Vanessa D. *Victorian Ghosts in the Noontide: Women Writers and the Supernatural.* Columbia: University of Missouri, 1996.

Di Maio, Vincent J. M. *Gunshot Wounds: Practical Aspects of Firearms, Ballistics, and Forensic Techniques.* Boca Raton, Fla.: CRC Press, 1999.

Diner, Steven J. *A Very Different Age: Americans of the Progressive Era.* New York: Hill and Wang, 1998.

Dolan, Jay P. *The American Catholic Experience: A History from Colonial Times to the Present.* Garden City, N.Y.: Doubleday & Co., 1987 [1985].

————, ed. *The American Catholic Parish: A History from 1850 to the Present.* New York: Paulist Press, 1987.

————. *In Search of an American Catholicism: A History of Religion and Culture in Tension.* New York: Oxford University Press, 2002.

Drake, Emma F. Angell. *What a Woman of Forty-Five Ought to Know.* Philadelphia: Vir Publishing, 1902.

————. *What a Young Wife Ought to Know.* Philadelphia: Vir Publishing, 1908.

Drury, A. W. *History of the City of Dayton and Montgomery County, Ohio.* Vol. 1. Chicago: S. J. Clarke Publishing, 1909.

Dugan, Mary C. *Outline History of Annapolis and the Naval Academy.* Baltimore: B. G. Eichelberger, 1902.

Ebbert, Jean, and Marie-Beth Hall. *The First, the Few, the Forgotten: Navy and Marine Corps Women in World War I.* Annapolis, Md.: Naval Institute Press, 2002.

Ebbinghaus, Hermann. *Memory: A Contribution to Experimental Psychology.* psychclassics.yorku.ca/Ebbinghaus/index.htm.

Ellis, John Tracy. *American Catholicism.* 2nd ed. Chicago: University of Chicago Press, 1969 [1956].

————. *The Life of James Cardinal Gibbons, Archbishop of Baltimore, 1834–1921.* 2 vols. Milwaukee: Bruce Publishing, 1952.

Emery, Michael, and Edwin Emery. *The Press and America: An Interpretive History of the Mass Media.* 7th ed. Englewood Cliffs, N.J.: Prentice Hall, 1992.

Ettema, James S., and Theodore L. Glasser. *Custodians of Conscience: Investigative Journalism and Public Virtue.* New York: Columbia University Press, 1998.

Evelyn, Douglas E., and Paul Dickson. *On This Spot: Pinpointing the Past in Washington, D.C.* Washington, D.C.: Farragut, 1992.

Fick, Nathaniel. *One Bullet Away: The Making of a Marine Officer.* Boston: Houghton Mifflin, 2005.

Fidell, Eugene R., and Dwight H. Sullivan, eds. *Evolving Military Justice.* Annapolis, Md.: Naval Institute Press, 2002.

Fleming, Bruce. *Annapolis Autumn.* New York: New Press, 2005.

Fleming, Thomas J. *West Point: The Men and Times of the United States Military Academy.* New York: Morrow, 1969.

Ford, Charles V. *Lies! Lies!! Lies!!! The Psychology of Deceit.* Washington, D.C.: American Psychiatric Press, 1996.

Forms of Procedure for Courts and Boards in the Navy and Marine Corps. Published by Authority of the Secretary of the Navy. Washington, D.C.: Government Printing Office, 1910.

Fowler, Nathaniel C., Jr. *The Handbook of Journalism.* New York: Sully and Kleinteich, 1913.

Foy, Jessica H., and Thomas J. Schlereth, eds. *American Home Life, 1880–1930: A Social History of Spaces and Services.* Knoxville: University of Tennessee Press, 1997.

Frankfurt, Harry G. *The Importance of What We Care About.* New York: Cambridge University Press, 1988.

Freedman, Estelle B. *Maternal Justice: Miriam Van Waters and the Female Reform Tradition.* Chicago: University of Chicago Press, 1996.

Friedman, Lawrence M. *American Law: An Introduction.* New York: W. W. Norton, 1984.

————. *Law in America: A Short History.* New York: Modern Library, 2004. First Published in 2002.

Friedman, Lawrence M., and Harry N. Scheiber, eds. *American Law and the Constitutional Order: Historical Perspectives.* Cambridge, Mass.: Harvard University Press, 1988.

Friendly, Alfred, and Ronald L. Goldfarb. *Crime and Publicity: The Impact of News on the Administration of Justice.* New York: Twentieth Century Fund, 1967.

Froncek, Thomas, ed. *The City of Washington: An Illustrated History.* New York: Alfred A. Knopf, 1977.

Gaston, Joseph. *Portland Oregon: It's History and Builders.* Vol. 3. Portland, Oreg.: S. J. Clarke Publishing, 1911.

Gausted, Edwin S., and Leigh E. Schmidt. *The Religious History of America*. Rev. ed. San Francisco: Harper San Francisco, 2002.

Generous, William T., Jr. *Swords and Scales: The Development of the Uniform Code of Military Justice*. Port Washington, N.Y.: Kennikat Press, 1973.

The George Washington University Alumni Directory, 1824–1937. Washington, D.C.: George Washington University Press, 1938.

Gibbons, James Cardinal. *The Ambassador of Christ*. Baltimore: John Murphy Company, 1896.

———. *The Faith of Our Fathers: A Plain Exposition and Vindication of the Church Founded by Our Lord Jesus Christ*. Rockford, Ill.: Tan Books and Publishers, 1980. First published in 1876. 111th printing.

———. *A Retrospect of Fifty Years*. Baltimore: John Murphy Company, 1916.

Given, John L. *Making a Newspaper*. New York: Henry Holt, 1907.

Glasser, Theodore L., and Charles T. Salmon, eds. *Public Opinion and the Communication of Consent*. New York: Guilford Press, 1995.

Godson, Susan H. *Serving Proudly: A History of Women in the U.S. Navy*. Annapolis, Md.: Naval Institute Press, 2001.

Goldsmith, Barbara. *Other Powers: The Age of Suffrage, Spiritualism, and the Scandalous Victoria Woodhull*. New York: HarperCollins, 1999 [1998].

Goode, James M. *A Century of Washington's Distinguished Apartment Houses: Best Addresses*. Washington, D.C.: Smithsonian Institute Press, 1988.

Gould, Lewis L. *The Presidency of Theodore Roosevelt*. Lawrence: University Press of Kansas, 1991.

Graber, Doris A. *Mass Media and American Politics*. 4th ed. Washington, D.C.: Congressional Quarterly, 1993.

Griffith, Elisabeth. *In Her Own Right: The Life of Elizabeth Cady Stanton*. New York: Oxford University Press 1984.

Grunwald, Lisa, and Stephen J. Adler, eds. *Letters of the Century: America, 1900–1999*. New York: Dial Press, 1999.

Grutze, Albert L. *The Selection of Wills*. Portland, Oreg.: Title & Trust Company, 1925.

A Guide to Military Criminal Law. Annapolis, Md.: Naval Institute Press, 1999.

Guide to Research Collections of Former United States Senators: 1789–1995. Compiled by Karen Dawley Paul. Washington, D.C.: Government Printing Office, 1995.

Hall, Rinaldo M. *Oregon, Washington, Idaho and Their Resources*. Promotional booklet. Portland: Oregon Railway and Navigation Co. and Southern Pacific Co., 1905.

Higham, Robin, and Donald J. Mrozek, eds. *A Guide to the Sources of United States Military History*. Supplement I. North Haven, Conn.: Archon Books, 1981.

———, eds. *A Guide to the Sources of United States Military History*. Supplement IV. North Haven, Conn.: Archon Books, 1998.

The Higher Standard: Assessing the United States Naval Academy. Report of the Special Committee to the Board of Visitors, United States Naval Academy. June 1997.

Highsmith, Carol M., and Ted Landphair. *Union Station: A Decorative History of Washington's Grand Terminal*. Washington, D.C.: Chelsea Publishing, 1988.

Hinkley, Barbara. *The Seniority System in Congress*. Bloomington: Indiana University Press, 1971.

Howells, William Dean, and Henry Mills Alden, eds. *Shapes That Haunt the Dusk*. New York and London: Harper and Brothers, 1907.

Hungerford, Edward. *The Story of the Baltimore and Ohio Railroad, 1827–1927*. 2 vols. New York: G. P. Putnam, 1928.

Hyde, Grant Milnor. *Newspaper Reporting and Correspondence*. New York: D. Appleton, 1912.

Hyman, Ray. *The Elusive Quarry: A Scientific Appraisal of Psychical Research*. Buffalo, N.Y.: Prometheus, 1989.

Hyslop, James H. *Contact with the Other World: The Latest Evidence as to Communication with the Dead*. New York: Century Co., 1919.

James, William. *Pragmatism: A New Name for Some Old Ways of Thinking*. (The lectures were delivered in 1906 and 1907.) *William James' Writings, 1902–1910*, 559–71. New American Library edition. New York: Literary Classics of the United States, 1987. First published in 1909.

———. *The Varieties of Religious Experience: A Study in Human Nature*. New York: Penguin, 1985. First published by Longmans, Green in 1902.

Johnson, Allen, ed. *Dictionary of American Biography*. Vol. 1. New York: Charles Scribner's Sons, 1964.

Johnson, W. Brad, and Gregory P. Harper. *Becoming a Leader the Annapolis Way: 12 Combat Lessons from the Navy's Leadership Laboratory*. New York: McGraw-Hill, 2005.

Kaplan, Justin. *When the Astors Owned New York: Blue Bloods and Grand Hotels in a Gilded Age.* New York: Penguin, 2006.

Karston, Peter. *The Naval Aristocracy: The Golden Age of Annapolis and the Emergence of Modern American Navalism.* New York: Free Press, 1972.

Keefe, William J., and Morris S. Ogul. *The American Legislative Process: Congress and the States.* 8th ed. Englewood Cliffs, N.J.: Prentice Hall, 1993.

Kelly, Charles Suddarth. *Washington, D.C., Then and Now: 69 Sites Photographed in the Past and Present.* New York: Dover Publications, 1984.

Kerr, Howard, John W. Crowley, and Charles L. Crow, eds. *The Haunted Dusk: American Supernatural Fiction, 1820–1920.* Athens: University of Georgia Press, 1983.

Kinkead, Thomas L. *An Explanation of the Baltimore Catechism of Christian Doctrine.* New York: Benziger Brothers, 1891.

Kohn, Richard H., ed. *The United States Military under the Constitution of the United States, 1789–1989.* New York: New York University Press, 1991.

Kovach, Bill, and Tom Rosenstiel. *The Elements of Journalism: What Newspeople Should Know and the Public Should Expect.* New York: Three Rivers Press, 2001.

Kraditor, Aileen S. *The Ideas of the Woman Suffrage Movement: 1890–1920.* New York: W. W. Norton, 1981.

Kurtz, P., ed. *A Skeptic's Handbook of Parapsychology.* Buffalo, N.Y.: Prometheus, 1985.

Lang, Andrew. *Myth, Ritual and Religion.* 1906 reprint. New York: AMS Press, 1968.

Larsen, Lawrence H. *The Urban West at the End of the Frontier.* Lawrence: Regents Press of Kansas, 1978.

Lauchheimer, Charles H. *Forms of Procedure for General and Summary Courts-Martial, Courts of Inquiry, Investigations, Naval and Marine Examining and Retiring Boards, Etc., Etc.* 2nd ed. Washington, D.C.: Government Printing Office, 1902.

Lewty, Peter J. *To the Columbia Gateway: The Oregon Railway and the Northern Pacific, 1879–1884.* Pulman: Washington State University Press, 1987.

Lippmann, Walter. *Public Opinion.* New York: Free Press, 1997. First published in 1922.

Loftus, Elizabeth F. *Eyewitness Testimony.* Cambridge, Mass.: Harvard University Press, 1996.

Logan, Rayford Whittingham. *Howard University: The First Hundred Years, 1867–1967.* New York: New York University Press, 1969.

Lovell, John P. *Neither Athens nor Sparta? The American Service Academies in Transition.* Bloomington: Indiana University Press, 1979.

Lukas, J. Anthony. *Big Trouble: A Murder in a Small Western Town Sets off a Struggle for the Soul of America.* New York: Simon & Schuster, 1997.

Lurie, Jonathan. *Arming Military Justice: The Origins of the United States Court of Military Appeals, 1775–1950.* Princeton, N.J.: Princeton University Press, 1992.

———. *Law and the Nation, 1865–1912.* New York: Alfred A. Knopf, 1982.

———. *Military Justice in America: The U.S. Court of Appeals for the Armed Forces, 1775–1980.* Revised and abridged edition. Lawrence: University Press of Kansas, 2001.

———. *Pursuing Military Justice: The History of the United States Court of Appeals for the Armed Forces, 1951–1980.* Princeton, N.J.: Princeton University Press, 1998.

MacColl, E. Kimbark. *Merchants, Money and Power: The Portland Establishment 1843–1913.* Portland, Oreg.: Georgian Press, 1988.

———. *The Shaping of a City: Business and Politics in Portland, Oregon, 1885 to 1915.* Portland, Oreg.: Georgian Press, 1976.

MacFarland, Henry B. F. *American Biographical Directories: District of Columbia: Concise Biographies of Its Prominent and Representative Contemporary Citizens, and Valuable Statistical Data, 1908–1909.* Washington, D.C.: Potomac Press, 1908.

Maddux, Percy. *City on the Willamette.* Portland, Oreg.: Metropolitan Press, 1952.

Marshall, John R. *A History of the Vancouver Public Schools.* Vancouver, Wash.: Vancouver School District No. 37, 1975.

Marszalek, John. *Assault at West Point: The Court Martial of Johnson Whitaker.* (Reissue of *Court-Martial.*) New York: Charles Scribner's Sons, 1984.

Martin, Albro. *Enterprise Denied: Origins of the Decline of American Railroads, 1897–1917.* New York: Columbia University Press, 1971.

Mauskopf, Seymour H., and Michael R. McVaugh. *The Elusive Science: Origins of Experimental Psychical Research.* Baltimore: Johns Hopkins University Press, 1980.

McGerr, Michael. *A Fierce Discontent: The Rise and Fall of the Progressive Movement in America: 1870–1920.* New York: Free Press, 2003.

McGreevy, John T. *Catholicism and American Freedom.* New York: W. W. Norton, 2003.

Meany, Edmond S. *History of the State of Washington.* New York: Macmillan, 1909.

Meier, Gary, and Gloria Meier. *Oregon Outlaws: Tales of Old-Time Desperadoes.* Boise, Idaho: Tamarack Books, 1996.

Melton, Buckner F., Jr. *A Hanging Offense: The Strange Affair of the Warship Somers.* New York: Free Press, 2003.

Menand, Louis. *The Metaphysical Club: A Story of Ideas in America.* New York: Farrar, Straus and Giroux, 2001.

Merriken, John E. *Every Hour on the Hour: A Chronicle of the Washington Baltimore and Annapolis Electric Railroad.* Dallas: Leroy O. King Jr., 1993.

Michel, Sonya, and Robyn Muncy. *Engendering America: A Documentary History, 1865 to the Present.* Boston: McGraw-Hill College, 1999.

Miller, Marcia M., and Orlando Rideout V. *Architecture in Annapolis: A Field Guide.* 2nd ed. Crownesville: Maryland Historical Trust Press, 1998.

Millett, Allan R. *Semper Fidelis: The History of the United States Marine Corps.* New York: Free Press, 1991.

Moore, R. Laurence. *In Search of White Crows: Spiritualism, Parapsychology, and American Culture.* New York: Oxford University Press, 1977.

Morris, Charles R. *American Catholic: The Saints and Sinners Who Built America's Most Powerful Church.* New York: Random House, 1997.

Morris, Edmund. *Theodore Rex.* New York: Modern Library, 2002.

Moskin, J. Robert. *The U. S. Marine Corps Story.* 3rd rev. ed. New York: Little, Brown, 1992.

Mott, Frank Luther. *American Journalism: A History of Newspapers in the United States through 250 Years, 1690 to 1940.* New York: Macmillan, 1941.

———. *A History of American Magazines 1885–1905.* Vol. 4. Cambridge, Mass.: Harvard University Press, 1957.

Muncy, Robyn. *Creating a Female Dominion in American Reform: 1890–1935.* New York: Oxford University Press, 1991.

Northrup, Christiane. *The Wisdom of Menopause.* New York: Bantam, 2003.

Orsi, Robert A. *Between Heaven and Earth: The Religious Worlds People Make and the Scholars Who Study Them.* Princeton, N.J.: Princeton University Press, 2005.

Packer, Cathy. *Freedom of Expression in the American Military: A Communication Modeling Analysis.* New York: Praeger, 1989.

Parker, Alison M. *Purifying America: Women, Cultural Reform, and Pro-Censorship Activism, 1873–1933. Women in American History Series.* Champaign: University of Illinois Press, 1997.

Parker, Michael P. *President's Hill: Building an Annapolis Neighborhood: 1664–2005.* Annapolis, Md.: Annapolis Publishing Co., 2005.

Paullin, Charles Oscar. *Paullin's History of Naval Administration, 1775–1911.* Annapolis, Md.: Naval Institute Press, 1968.

Pittmon's Portland Official Guide with Maps of City. Portland, Oreg., 1915 (Oregon Historical Society [R 979.1105, P6898 Part1]).

Polk's Portland City Directory. Street and Additional Guide. No. 45. Portland, Oreg.: R. L. Polk & Co., 1907–1908.

Portland Block Book. Portland, Oreg.: Portland Block Book Company, 1907.

Portland City Directory, 1909. Portland, Oreg.: R. L. Polk & Co., 1909.

Portland City Directory, 1915. Portland, Oreg.: R. L. Polk & Co., 1915.

Pratt, Laurence. *I Remember Portland 1899–1915.* Portland, Oreg.: Binford & Mort, 1947.

Proctor, John Clagett, ed. *Washington Past and Present: A History.* Vol. 2. New York: Lewis Historical Publishing Company, 1930.

Reckner, James R. *Teddy Roosevelt's Great White Fleet.* Annapolis, Md.: Naval Institute Press, 1988.

Reynolds, Charles B. *The Standard Guide, Washington: A Handbook for Visitors.* Washington, D.C.: B. S. Reynolds Co., 1920.

Ricks, Thomas E. *Making the Corps.* New York: Charles Scribner's Sons, 1997.

Rogers, James Edward. *The American Newspaper.* Chicago: University of Chicago Press, 1909.

Roosevelt, Theodore. *The Works of Theodore Roosevelt: The Strenuous Life.* New York: P. F. Collier & Son, n.d.

———. *The Works of Theodore Roosevelt in 14 Volumes: Presidential Addresses and State Papers.* New York: P. F. Collier & Son, n.d.

Rosenberg, Charles E. *The Trial of the Assassin Guiteau: Psychiatry and Law in the Gilded Age.* Chicago: University of Chicago Press, 1968.

Safford, A. R. *Encyclopedia of Virginia and the District of Columbia of the Nineteenth Century: Eminent and Representative Men of Virginia and the District of Columbia of the Nineteenth Century.* Madison, Wisc.: Brant and Fuller, 1893.

Salisbury, William. *The Career of a Journalist.* New York: B. W. Dodge, 1908.

Sandel, Michael J. *Public Philosophy: Essays on Morality in Politics.* Cambridge, Mass.: Harvard University Press, 2005.

Schacter, Daniel L. *Searching for Memory: The Brain, the Mind and the Past.* New York: Basic Books, 1996.

———. *The Seven Sins of Memory (How the Mind Forgets and Remembers).* Boston: Houghton Mifflin, 2001.

Schlereth, Thomas J. *Victorian America: Transformations in Everyday Life: 1876–1915.* New York: Harper-Collins, 1992.

Schmidt, Hans. *Maverick Marine: General Smedley D. Butler and the Contradictions of American Military History.* Louisville: University Press of Kentucky, 1987.

Schneirov, Matthew. *The Dream of New Social Order: Popular Magazines in America: 1893–1914.* New York: Columbia University Press, 1994.

Schoenberg, Wilfred P. *A Pictorial History of the Catholic Church in the Pacific Northwest.* Portland, Oreg.: Knights of Columbus, 1996.

Schudson, Michael. *Discovering the News: A Social History of American Newspapers.* New York: Basic Books, 1978.

———. *The Good Citizen: A History of American Civic Life.* Cambridge, Mass.: Harvard University Press, 1998.

Schuon, Karl. *United States Marine Corps Biographical Dictionary.* New York: Franklin Watts, 1963.

Scott, Pamela, and Antoinette J. Lee. *Buildings of the District of Columbia.* New York: Oxford University Press, 1993.

Shanor, Charles A., and L. Lynn Hogue. *Military Law in a Nutshell.* 2nd ed. St. Paul, Minn.: West Publishing, 1996.

Sherrill, Robert. *Military Justice Is to Justice as Military Music Is to Music.* New York: Harper and Row, 1976.

Shulimson, Jack. *The Marines Corps' Search for a Mission: 1880–1898.* Lawrence: University Press of Kansas, 1993.

Siegel, Jay M. *Origins of the Navy Judge Advocate General Corps: A History of Legal Administration in the United States Navy, 1775–1967.* Washington D.C.: Government Printing Office, 1997.

Skocpol, Theda. *Protecting Soldiers and Mothers: The Political Origins of Social Policy in the United States.* Cambridge, Mass.: Harvard University Press, 1992.

Stevens, William Oliver. *Annapolis: Anne Arundel's Town.* New York: Dodd, Mead & Co., 1937.

———. *Unbidden Guests: A Book of Real Ghosts.* New York: Dodd, Mead & Co., 1946.

Stover, John F. *History of the Baltimore and Ohio Railroad.* West Lafayette, Ind.: Purdue University Press, 1987.

———. *The Life and Decline of the American Railroad.* New York: Oxford University Press, 1970.

Sullivan, Mark. *Our Times: America at the Birth of the Twentieth Century.* Abridged and edited with new material by Dan Rather. New York: Charles Scribner's Sons, 1996.

Sutherland, Daniel E. *The Expansion of Everyday Life: 1860–1876.* Fayetteville: University of Arkansas Press, 2000 [1989].

Sweetman, Jack. *American Naval History: An Illustrated Chronology of the United States Navy and Marine Corps, 1775–Present.* Annapolis, Md.: Naval Institute Press, 1984.

———. *The U.S. Naval Academy: An Illustrated History.* 2nd ed. Revised by Thomas J. Cutler. Annapolis, Md.: Naval Institute Press, 1995.

Townsend, Kim. *Manhood at Harvard: William James and Others.* New York: W. W. Norton, 1996.

Tyrrell, G. N. M. *Apparitions.* New York: Pantheon Books, 1953.

Ulmer, S. Sidney. *Military Justice and the Right to Counsel.* Lexington: University Press of Kentucky, 1970.

United States Congress, House Committee on Naval Affairs. *Hearing before a Subcommittee of the Committee on Naval Affairs of the House of Representatives at the United States Naval Academy, Annapolis, Maryland, on the Subject of Hazing at the Naval Academy,* February 15–24, 1906. Washington, D.C.: Government Printing Office, 1906.

———, House Committee on Naval Affairs, Legislative Calendar. *Sixty-First Congress, 1909–1911.*

———, House Select Committee. *Hazing at the Military Academy.* Washington, D.C.: Government Printing Office, 1901.

———, *Official Congressional Directory: For the Use of the United States Congress*, 61st Congress, 2nd Session, 3rd ed. Compiled by A. J. Halford. Washington, D.C.: Government Printing Office, 1910.

———, Senate Committee on Military Affairs. *Hearings before the Senate Committee on Military Affairs Relating to the Subject of Hazing at the United States Military Academy, March 4 and March 10, 1910*. Washington, D.C.: Government Printing Office, 1910.

United States Marine Corps. *Regulations Governing the Uniforms and Equipments of Officers and Enlisted Men of the United States Marine Corps*. Washington, D.C.: Government Printing Office, 1904.

———. *Regulations Governing the Uniforms and Equipments of Officers and Enlisted Men of the United States Marine Corps*. Washington, D.C.: Globe Printing Office, 1908.

United States Military Academy. *Annual Report of the Superintendent of the United States Military Academy*. Washington, D.C.: Government Printing Office, 1909, 1910, 1911, 1912, 1913.

———. *Ten Year Book: Class of Nineteen-Thirteen*. West Point: [The Class], 1923.

———. *Thirty-Five Year Book: Class of Nineteen-Thirteen*. West Point: [The Class], 1948.

———. *Twenty Year Book: Class of Nineteen-Thirteen*. West Point: [The Class], 1933.

Valle, James E. *Rocks and Shoals: Naval Discipline in the Age of Fighting Sail*. Annapolis, Md.: Naval Institute Press, 1980.

Vaughan, George Tully. *The Principles and Practice of Surgery, Designed for Students and Practitioners*. Philadelphia: J. B. Lippincott, 1903.

Venzon, Anne Cipriano. *General Smedley Darlington Butler: The Letters of a Leatherneck, 1898–1931*. New York: Praeger, 1992.

Wagenknecht, Edward. *American Profile: 1900–1909*. Amherst: University of Massachusetts Press, 1982.

Warren, Mary Elizabeth. *The Train's Done Been and Gone: Annapolis Portrait, 1859–1910*. Boston: David R. Godine in association with M. E. Warren, 1976.

West, Elliott. *Growing up with the Country: Childhood on the Far Western Frontier*. Albuquerque: University of New Mexico Press, 1991 (1989).

White, Richard. *"It's Your Misfortune and None of My Own": A New History of the American West*. Norman: University of Oklahoma Press, 1993 [1991].

Who's Who In America: 1908–1909. Chicago : A. N. Marquis, 1945.

Who's Who in the Nation's Capital. Washington, D.C.: Consolidated Publishing Company, published throughout the early twentieth century.

Who Was Who in America. Vol. 1, 1897–1942. Chicago: A. N. Marquis, 1942.

Wicker, Christine. *Lily Dale: The True Story of the Town That Talks to the Dead*. New York: HarperCollins, 2003.

Wiebe, Robert. *The Search for Order, 1877–1920*. New York: Hill and Wang, 1967.

———. *Self-rule: A Cultural History of American Democracy*. Chicago: University of Chicago Press, 1995.

Williams, Bernard. *Truth and Truthfulness: An Essay in Genealogy*. Princeton, N.J.: Princeton University Press, 2002.

Williams, Walter, and Frank L. Martin. *The Practice of Journalism: A Treatise on Newspaper Making*. Columbia, Mo.: Press of E. W. Stephens Publishing Co., 1911.

Winthrop, William. *Military Law and Precedents*. 2nd ed. Washington, D.C.: Government Printing Office, 1920. First Published in 1886.

Woloch, Nancy. *Women and the American Experience*. 3rd ed. New York: McGraw-Hill, 1999.

Wright, Sylvia Hart. *When Spirits Come Calling: The Open-Minded Skeptic's Guide to After-Death Contacts*. Nevada City, Calif.: Blue Dolphin Publishing, 2002.

Zelizer, Barbie. *Taking Journalism Seriously: News and the Academy*. Thousand Oaks, Calif.: Sage, 2004.

ARTICLES, CHAPTERS, AND PAMPHLETS

Alvarado, Carlos S. "The Concept of Survival of Bodily Death and the Development of Parapsychology." *Journal for the Society of Psychical Research* 67 (April 2003): 65–95.

Anderson, Rodger I. "The Life and Work of James H. Hyslop." *Journal of the American Society for Psychical Research* 79 (April 1985): 167–204.

Ansell, S. T. "Military Justice." *Cornell Law Quarterly* 5 (November 1919): 1–17.

Baker, Jean H. "Getting Right with Women's Suffrage." *The Journal of the Gilded Age and Progressive Era* 5, no. 1 (January 2006): 7–17.

Baker, Paula. "The Domestication of Politics: Women and American Political Society, 1780–1920." *American Historical Review* 89, no. 3 (June 1984): 620–47.

Berger, Arthur S. "The Early History of the ASPR: Origins to 1907." *Journal of the American Society for Psychical Research* 79 (January 1985): 39–60.

———. "Problems of the ASPR under J. H. Hyslop." *Journal of the American Society for Psychical Research* 79 (April 1985): 205–19.

Black, Charles N. "Portland Rose Carnival: The First Annual Rose Festival of Portland, Oregon." *Western Life* 1, no. 2 (August 1907): 89–91.

Bogert, George Gleason. "Courts-Martial: Criticisms and Proposed Reforms." *Cornell Law Quarterly* 5, no. 1 (November 1919): 18–47.

"Charles William Fulton." In *Biographical Directory of the United States Congress, 1774–1989*, 1034. Washington, D.C.: Government Printing Office, 1989.

Cheevers, James W. "United States Naval Academy: Part III, A Golden Age." *Shipmate Magazine* (July–August 1995): 35–40.

Cooke, John S. "Manual for Courts-Martial 20X." In *Evolving Military Justice*, ed. Eugene R. Fidell and Dwight H. Sullivan. Annapolis, Md.: Naval Institute Press, 2002.

Cox, Walter T., III. "The Army, the Courts and the Constitution: The Evolution of Military Justice." *Military Law Review* 118 (Fall 1987): 1–30.

Cronon, William. "The Competing Truths of History and Memory." Foreword to *Remembering Ahanagran: A History of Stories*, by Richard White. Seattle: University of Washington Press, 1998.

Davey, Monica, and Eric Schmitt. "2 Years after Soldier's Death, Family's Battle Is with the Army." *New York Times*, March 21, 2006.

Davis, Henry Edgar. "The Law Spirit: Its Source and Its Sway." In *Annual Address Delivered at the Tenth Annual Convention, Cape May, New Jersey, June 28, 1904*. Harrisburg: Pennsylvania Bar Association; Seeley G. Mudd Manuscript Library, Princeton University, N.J.

"Death of Arthur A. Birney." *Washington Law Reporter* 44 (September 8, 1916): 561.

"Death of Mr. Henry E. Davis." *Washington Law Reporter* 55 (April 1, 1927): 201.

Fawcett, Walldon. "Coal for the Battleship Cruise." *Western Life* 1, no. 6 (December 1907): 78.

Fidell, Eugène R. "The Culture of Change in Military Law." In *Evolving Military Justice*, ed. Eugene R. Fidell and Dwight H. Sullivan. Annapolis, Md.: Naval Institute Press, 2002.

Fuller, Benjamin H., Major General Commandant. "The United States Marine Corps." *US Naval Institute Proceedings* 56, no. 10 (October 1930): 913–16.

"George Tully Vaughan." In *National Cyclopedia of American Biography*. Vol. 38. New York: J. T. White, 1953.

Giltner, E. C. "Portland, Oregon." *Western Life* 1, no. 2 (August 1907): 84–86.

"Gossip of the Town." *Columbiad* 1, no. 5 (February 1903), University Park, Oreg.

"Graduation Exercises. Class of Nineteen-thirteen. United States Military Academy, West Point, New York." Pamphlet. Special Collections and Archives, USMA, West Point.

Hillman, Elizabeth L. "The 'Good Soldier' Defense: Character Evidence and Military Rank at Courts-Martial." In *Evolving Military Justice*, ed. Eugene R. Fidell and Dwight H. Sullivan. Annapolis, Md.: Naval Institute Press, 2002.

Lurie, Jonathan. "Andrew Jackson, Martial Law, Civilian Control of the Military, and American Politics: An Intriguing Amalgam." *Military Law Review* 126 (1989): 133–45.

———. "Justice, Military: Uniform Code of Military Justice (1950–Present)." In *The Oxford Companion to American Military History*, ed. John Whiteclay Chambers II. Oxford: Oxford University Press, 1999.

———. "The Role of the Federal Judiciary in the Governance of the American Military: The United States Supreme Court and 'Civil Rights and Supervision' over the Armed Forces." In *The United States Military under the Constitution of the United States, 1789–1989*, ed. Richard H. Kohn. New York: New York University Press, 1991.

Mackey, Thomas C. "The Judiciary and the Military." In *Encyclopedia of the American Military, Vol. 1*. New York: Charles Scribner's Sons, 1994.

———. "Military and Martial Law Issues." In *A Guide to the Sources of United States Military History*, ed. Robin Higham and Donald J. Mrozek. Supplement IV. North Haven, Conn.: Archon Books, 1998.

Mauskopf, Seymour H., and Michael R. McVaugh. "Parapsychology and the American Psychologists: A Study of Scientific Ambivalence." In *The Philosophy of Parapsychology, Proceedings of an International Conference Held in Copenhagen, Denmark, August 25–27, 1976*, ed. Betty Shapin and Lisette Coly. New York: Parapsychology Foundation, 1977.

McClay, Oelo. "My Trip to the Fair." *Oregon Historical Quarterly* 80, no. 1 (Spring 1979): 58–59.

Montez, Charlotte. "Ghostly Officer Called on Cadet." Unidentified clipping from a magazine article, October 31, 1975. U.S. Military Academy Archives.

Morgan, Edmund M. "The Background of the Uniform Code of Military Justice." *Military Law Review* 28 (1965): 17–35.

"Necrology of Sister Mary Dorothy [Catherine Burke], who died at Portland, Oregon, January 3, 1911." *The Little Journal of Providence* (April 1911): 291–93.

Nichols, D. B. "Military and Civil Legal Values: *Mens Rea*—A Case in Point." *Military Law Review* 28 (1965): 169–93.

Nieman, Donald G. "Military Law, Martial Law and Military Government." In *A Guide to the Sources of United States Military History*, ed. Robin Higham and Donald J. Mrozek. Supplement I. North Haven, Conn.: Archon Books, 1981.

Page, William Herbert. "Military Law: A Study in Comparative Law." *Harvard Law Review* 32 (1919): 349–73.

Pasley, Robert, Jr., and Felix Larkin. "The Navy Court Martial: Proposals for Its Reform." *Cornell Law Quarterly* 33 (1947): 195–234.

Quinn, Robert Emmet. "Courts-Martial Practice: A View from the Top." *Hastings Law Journal* 22 (January 1971): 201–12.

Rayner, Richard. "The Warrior Besieged." *New York Times Magazine*, June 22, 1997.

Regulations and Course of Instruction at the School of Application, United States Marine Corps, Annapolis, Md. Approved by the Brigadier General, Commandant, U.S.M.C, July 1, 1904. Washington, D.C.: Government Printing Office, 1905. (Found in RG 125.)

Schlup, Leonard. "Republican Insurgent: Jonathan Bourne and the Politics of Progressivism, 1908–1912." *Oregon Historical Quarterly* 87, no. 3 (Fall 1986): 229–44.

Sherman, Edward F. "The Military Courts and Servicemen's First Amendment Rights." *Hastings Law Journal* 22 (January 1971): 325–73.

Shulimson, Jack. "Daniel Pratt Mannix and the Establishment of the Marine Corps School of Application, 1889–1894." *Journal of Military History* 55, no. 4 (October 1991): 469–85.

———. "Military Professionalism: The Case of the US Marine Officer Corps, 1880–1898." *Journal of Military History* 60, no. 2 (April 1996): 231–42.

Thacher, George H. "The Case of Lieutenant James B. Sutton" [*sic*]. *Journal of the American Society for Psychical Research* 5, no. 11 (November 1911): 597–664. Introduction by James H. Hyslop, 597–600, and "Comments" by James H. Hyslop, 651–64.

Thurston, Herbert. "The Ritual of Burial." In *The Catholic Encyclopedia*. Vol. 3. New York: Robert Appleton Company, 1908 (online edition by Kevin Knight, 1999).

Wiegand, Wayne A. "The Lauchheimer Controversy: A Case of Group Political Pressure during the Taft Administration." *Military Affairs* 40, no. 2 (April 1976): 54–59.

UNPUBLISHED MATERIALS

Alvarez, Eugène. "The Cradle of the Corps: A History of the United States Marine Corps Recruit Depot, Parris Island, South Carolina, 1562–2002." Unpublished manuscript at the Parris Island Museum, Marine Corps Recruit Depot. Copy also at the Marine Corps Historical Center, Quantico, Va.

"Clark County Washington Marriages." Historical list compiled by the Clark County Genealogical Society, Vancouver, Washington.

Davis, Henry Edgar. "Address of Hon. Henry E. Davis before the Subcommittee of Law and Education of the Chamber of Commerce." Washington, D.C., June 17, 1909. Historical Society of Washington, D.C.

———. "Last Will and Testament." Records of the Superior Court of District of Columbia, Record Group 2, April 20, 1927 (probate date).

"Graduate List, the Couch School, June 1901." Records Management Department, Portland Public Schools, Vertical Files, Portland, Oreg. (James Sutton).

"Graduate List, Portland High School, February 1908." Records Management Department, Portland Public Schools, Vertical Files, Portland, Oreg. (John R. "Don" Sutton).

A List of Living Persons Who Are Connected with St. John's Church, Georgetown Parish, by Baptism, Confirmation, Communion, or Attendance, Giving Dates of Baptism and Confirmations, Present Addresses, and Other Information Beginning with the Year 1841; Arranged Alphabetically with Space after Each Letter for Additions. Presented by Edward F. Looker to the Rector and Vestry, November 5, 1888. Archives of St. John's Episcopal Church, Washington, D.C. (Georgetown).

Parker, Michael P. "Ghostlier Demarcations, Keener Sounds: The U.S. Navy and the Sutton Apparition Case." Paper presented at the Annual Meeting of the Popular Culture Association, San Diego, Calif., April 1, 1999.

Rosa B. Sutton vs. James N. Sutton. Complaint. Circuit Court of the State of Oregon for Multnomah County, February 19, 1915. Judgment No. 59952, Case No. E1400. Multnomah County Records Office, Portland, Oreg.

Rosa B. Sutton vs. James N. Sutton. Summons. Circuit Court of the State of Oregon for the County of Multnomah, filed August 19, 1914. Multnomah County Records Office, Portland, Oreg.

Strong, Barton D., Midshipman, USN. "A History of the Marine Barracks, Annapolis, Maryland." U.S. Naval Academy Course Paper. U.S. Naval Academy Archives. Special Collections, Vertical File, U.S. Marine Corps Barracks, Annapolis, Md., 1964.

Vaughan, George Tully. "Last Will and Testament of George Tully Vaughan." May 3, 1948. District Court of the United States for the District of Columbia, Register of Wills. Superior Court of the District of Columbia.

NEWSPAPERS

Advertiser (Annapolis, Md.)
Army and Navy Journal
Atlanta Constitution
Baltimore Sun
Boston Evening Transcript
Boston Globe
Boston Herald
Buffalo Express (New York)
Capital Journal
Chicago Daily News
Chicago Tribune
Christian Science Monitor
Cincinnati Enquirer
Daily Picayune (New Orleans)
Denver Post
Evening Capital (Annapolis, Md.)
Evening Journal (New York)
Evening Post (New York)
Evening Star or *Sunday Star* (Washington, D.C.)
Hartford Courant (Connecticut)
Illinois State Register

Jamestown Morning Post (New York)
Los Angeles Times
The Nation
Newburgh Daily News (West Point, N.Y.)
News of the Highlands (West Point, N.Y.)
New York American
New York Herald
New York Times
Oregon Daily Journal
Oregon Sunday Journal
Oregonian
Philadelphia Inquirer
Portland Evening Telegram
Portland News
San Francisco Chronicle
St. Louis Post-Dispatch
Sun (New York)
Wall Street Journal
Washington Post
Washington Times
World (New York)

ACKNOWLEDGMENTS

This book could not have been written without many good-natured and resourceful librarians and archivists. At the top of this list are the men and women who work in military records at the National Archives and Records Administration in Washington, D.C. The facilities for these records have been renovated since I began work in 1996 and are a pleasure to use. For their help with the many record groups that shed light on the Sutton case, I am indebted to former archivist Rebecca Livingston and to Charles Johnson, Trevor Plante, and Richard Peuser (who is now assistant branch chief at Archives II in College Park) for locating the Sutton transcript the first time.

Beverly Lyall in Special Collections and Archives, Nimitz Library, at the Naval Academy provided the photograph of the Richard Rummell sketch that became the cover illustration for this book; she also located numerous files for the men who attended the Naval Academy with Jim Sutton, as well as other documents related to the case. James A. Ginther at the Marine Corps Historical Center and Tom Sherlock, historian of Arlington National Cemetery, also helped, as did former assistant archivist Judith Sibley, USMA historian Dr. Stephen B. Grove, and Alan Aimone at West Point, who guided me to superb resources about Don Sutton's case in 1997. Terri Mitchell was at the Sisters of Providence Archives in Seattle when I sought information about Rosa's childhood and went to great lengths to locate records about the Brant children. The executive director of the American Society for Psychical Research, Patrice Keane, and archivist Colleen Phelan provided many valuable documents related to James Hyslop's life; Carlos Alvarado and Lisette Coly are owed thanks for their interest and advice while I used the Parapsychology Foundation Library. Lauren Gurgiolo at the Harry Ransom Humanities Research Center at the University of

Texas; Ruel J. Eskelsen at the Historical Society of Washington, D.C.; Christopher J. Kintzel at the Maryland State Archives; Alison M. Foley at the Associated Archives at St. Mary's Seminary & University in Baltimore; and Lucy Berkley and Mikki Tint at the Oregon Historical Society provided many of the images for the book.

The men and women who quietly devote so much of their lives to keeping the records of churches, schools, and smaller archives deserve enormous respect. Although I know most only by their voices and e-mails, their genuine interest cheered me on. Among them were Mary Grant at the archives of the archdiocese of St. Mary's Roman Catholic Cathedral in Portland, Oregon; Tara Kaeding at the Cathedral Church of Saint Paul in Springfield, Illinois; Lynette Ahlgren at St. John's Northwestern Military Academy in Delafield, Wisconsin; Pauline J. Jones, the former historian of St. Augustine's Church in Washington, D.C.; Jean Pugh, historian of Grace Methodist Episcopal Church in Harrisburg, Pennsylvania; and Irene Page, who spent days searching for Brant family records at the Clark County Genealogical Society.

I immersed myself in old newspapers and government documents for more than three years until I realized how little I knew about several fields that had a bearing on this complex story. Encouragement and suggestions from several professors who really are experts in the Progressive Era and military justice kept me going. These include John Whiteclay Chambers II, Jonathan Lurie, Thomas Mackey, Donald Mrozek, and, more recently, a Naval Academy English professor, Michael Parker, who is the only person I've ever met who had heard of this case before. I am grateful as well to Deborah Blum for her interest in the manuscript and her work on the search for scientific proof of life after death that preoccupied William James and James Hyslop, and to former Marine Corps captain and author Nathaniel Fick, whose recent experiences in the Corps—so well described in *One Bullet Away*—highlight the challenges in becoming a Marine officer today.

Before I left Washington in 1999, two outstanding graduate students who are now historians helped me track down material and photocopy hundreds of pages of government documents and old newspaper articles— Diana T. Reinhard and Brook Speer Orr. Liz Kimberlin typed nearly one hundred pages of academic endnotes in 2006; less than a year later Erika Hennings retyped a shortened version of these notes in the trade book style requested by the publisher.

I owe an inestimable debt to the perseverance of my agent (now writing his eleventh book), Ronald Goldfarb—my Henry Davis, his indispensable assistant, Charles Younger, and, of course, to the enthusiasm of my editor, Michael McGandy, who tactfully guided me toward a leaner text and many fewer notes; his editorial assistant, Asa Johnson, who never failed to answer dozens of questions with patience and thoroughness; and production editor Erin McGarvey, who worked through many weekends to keep this book on schedule.

The descendants of the two men who skillfully defended the Marines against the accusations of the Sutton family have been most gracious about my attempt to reconstruct this once-buried story: Henry Leonard's stepgranddaughter, Ellen MacVeagh Rublee, and Arthur Alexis Birney, a distinguished Washington attorney who shares his grandfather's name. My heartfelt thanks goes as well to the members of my book group and to longtime friends and an extended family of cousins for their encouragement over so many years: Jean and Christopher Angell, Dianne and John Avlon, Mary Carter Babcock, Jacqueline Bloom, Diana Brandenberg, Janna Smith Brown, Virginia Butters, Mary and Kenneth Edlow, Elspeth Furlaud, Lindsay Carter Gibson, Peter and Ainslie Grannis, Esther Hall, Gretchen Hall, Dina Harris, Kay and Wil Kohl, Betsy and Michael Kraft, Margo Langenberg, Margaret and Don Mahaney, Marcia and Herbert Marks, Leslie Vanderzee Marvin, Charles G. McIntosh, Tia McMillan, Carey Millard, the late Nancy Rademaker, Jane and John Seel, the late J. W. Smit, Isabel C. Stuebe, James R. Sutton, the late Mary Umbarger, Dave and Aurea Warren, Mary Bittner Wiseman, and our extraordinary aunt, Jean Maw Woodman. Over the past decade, Heloisa De Melo, Joan McElwee, Margarita Paez, Rosa Herrera, and David N. Ziska, P.T., have helped in so many ways to make my life or my computer arm run smoothly.

I am most thankful for two daughters, Elizabeth Cutler Maw and Carlyn Bailey Maw, whose character and accomplishments are an inspiration, and to my son-in-law, Gabriel Rogin, who accepts Liz's unusual greatgreat-grandmother with grace and good humor. Extra appreciation is owed Carlyn, who organized the art files and created the website for this book. Finally, I cannot omit Piper, Peanut, and now Rosie—always faithful.

INDEX